Relics and R

OXFORD JOURNALS
OXFORD UNIVERSITY PRESS

OXFORD
UNIVERSITY PRESS

1 Great Clarendon Street, Oxford OX2 6DP

Oxford University Press is a department of the University of Oxford.
It furthers the University's objective of excellence in research, scholarship,
and education by publishing worldwide in

Oxford New York

Athens Auckland Bangkok Bogotá Buenos Aires Cape Town
Chennai Dar es Salaam Delhi Florence Hong Kong Istanbul Karachi
Kolkata Kuala Lumpur Madrid Melbourne Mexico City Mumbai Nairobi
Paris São Paulo Shanghai Singapore Taipei Tokyo Toronto Warsaw

with associated companies in Berlin Ibadan

Oxford is a registered trade mark of Oxford University Press
in the UK and in certain other countries

Published in the United Kingdom
by Oxford University Press Inc., New York

A catalogue for this book is available from the British Library

Library of Congress Cataloguing in Publication
Data (data available)

ISBN 0-19-960058-8
ISBN 978-0-19-960058-8

Subscription information for Past & Present is available
from:jnls.cust.serv@oxfordjournals.org

Typeset by Glyph International, Bangalore, India
Printed by Bell and Bain Ltd, Glasgow, UK

Past and Present Supplements

Supplement 5, 2010

Relics and Remains
Edited by Alexandra Walsham

Relics and Remains

CONTENTS

List of Figures

Contributions and Communications (two copies), editorial correspondence, etc., should be addressed to The Editors, *Past and Present*, 175 Banbury Road, Oxford OX2 7AW, UK. Tel: +44 (0)1865 512318; Fax: +44 (0)1865 310080; E-mail: editors@pastandpresent. org.uk. Intending contributors should write for a copy of 'Notes for Contributors'.

© *World Copyright: The Past and Present Society, 2010.*

The Past and Present Society is a company limited by a guarantee registered in England under company number 2414260 and a registered charity under number 802281. Its registered office is at 9400 Garsington Road, Oxford.

Typeset by Glyph International, Bangalore, India, and printed by Bell and Bain Ltd, Glasgow, UK

Acknowledgements

This collection of essays arose out of a conference held at the University of Exeter in September 2008. I wish to thank all those who attended, chaired sessions, and delivered papers on that occasion, and am grateful to Claire Keyte, Jennifer Evans, and Sarah Scutts for their help with organizing this extremely stimulating event. Miri Rubin and Richard Clay were unable to contribute to the volume, but made a signal contribution to discussions that took place. I am very grateful to the Past and Present Society, the British Academy, and the University of Exeter for their financial support of the conference. Lyndal Roper offered wise advice and guidance as the volume began to take shape and the comments of the anonymous reviewers were of great assistance in revising individual chapters. David Davis provided invaluable aid in preparing the text for submission to the press. At Oxford University Press, I owe heartfelt thanks to Hilary Lamb and Clare Painter.

Alexandra Walsham

Fig. 1. The Vernicle of St Veronica, print made by Jakob Christoph le Blon, 1721. AN17568001 ©Trustees of the British Museum

Introduction: Relics and Remains

Alexandra Walsham

Depicted in this compelling early eighteenth-century print (Fig. 1), St Veronica's veil is among the most renowned examples of the cultural phenomenon that is the subject of this volume: a relic. According to the tradition that has crystallized around it over two millennia, the vernicle is the cloth with which a pious Jerusalem woman compassionately dried the face of the suffering Christ on the road to his crucifixion at Calvary, and upon which his visage was miraculously imprinted in photographic facsimile. Some versions of the welter of legend now surrounding it tell how this hallowed item was carried to Rome and presented to the Emperor Tiberius, whom it is said to have cured. Endorsed with indulgences and exposed for public veneration by the papacy, it was popularized in pen and paint by authors and artists in the later Middle Ages. Devotion to the relic survived the sack of Rome in 1527 and was reinvigorated in the period of the Counter-Reformation, when it circulated once more in multiple reproductions. Still preserved in St Peter's, displayed annually on Passion Sunday, and commemorated in the Stations of the Cross, the Vernicle attests to the deep yearning of generations of Christians for a visible and tangible remnant of the God who became man to redeem them from sin. Persisting uncertainties about its authenticity as an *acheiropoieton* (a likeness not made by human hand) have done more to titillate and invigorate than to undermine its cult. Along with the other holy images of Jesus with which it is linked, notably the famous Shroud of Turin, it bears witness to the capacity of religious faith to invest mundane objects with spiritual significance and numinous power. More broadly, it illuminates the process by which different societies and cultures interpret and shape the material world in accordance with their own convictions, values, preoccupations, and desires.[1]

This collection of essays considers the relic in a broad comparative and chronological perspective. It examines the ways in which human remains and physical things have become the focus of reverence, celebrity, curiosity, and conflict in a range of eras and cultures stretching from antiquity to the twenty-first century and from Europe to the Near East, Africa, Latin America, the Indian subcontinent and China. The contributors assess when and why bodies, personal belongings, and other objects come to be regarded as sacred by the adherents of different faiths, alongside the dynastic, ideological, and ethnic contests and rivalries they have served to precipitate in past and present societies. They explore the political, economic, and social dimensions of the identification, discovery, preservation, and fabrication of relics and remains and their meaning and function in the spheres of memory, history, and heritage.

Bringing together historians, anthropologists, archaeologists, and scholars of religion, this volume arises from a conference held at the University of Exeter in September 2008. Revised in the light of each other, the essays that comprise it should be regarded as the continuation rather than the end-point of the series of lively interdisciplinary conversations that took place on that occasion. Approaching the subject from various angles and

[1] See F. L. Cross and E. A. Livingstone (eds), *The Oxford Dictionary of the Christian Church* (Oxford, 1997 edn), 1688–9; *Acta Sanctorum,* Feb. I (1668), 449–57; Ewa Kuryluk, *Veronica and her Cloth: History, Symbolism, and Structure of a 'True' Image* (Cambridge, Mass. and Oxford, 1991); Ian Wilson, *Holy Faces, Sacred Places* (New York, 1991).

with diverse intellectual agendas in mind, they are designed to foster further research on this neglected but intriguing theme. In keeping with this spirit of enquiry, it would be inappropriate to insist upon a single or precise definition of the term 'relic'. Instead, what emerges as a keynote of the collection is the slippery, elastic, and expansive nature of this concept and category, and the nebulous boundaries that separate it from other classes of entity. How and where, when and why, these distinctions are drawn, moreover, is locally and culturally determined and historically contingent.

Definitions, concepts, and interpretative contexts

Nevertheless, it is necessary to make a preliminary attempt to identify some of the relic's properties and characteristics. At the most basic level, a relic is a material object that relates to a particular individual and/or to events and places with which that individual was associated. Typically, it is the body or fragment of the body of a deceased person, but it can also be connected to living people who have acquired fame, recognition, and a popular following. Alongside these corporeal relics (skulls, bones, blood, teeth, hair, fingernails, and assorted lumps of flesh) are non-corporeal items that were possessed by or came into direct contact with the individual in question. These may be articles of clothing (hats, girdles, capes, smocks, shoes, and sandals) or pieces of personal property (cups, spectacles, handkerchiefs, weapons, staves, and bells). They can be printed books, written texts, letters, and scraps of paper bearing an autograph signature or graphic inscription. Or they might be rocks or stones upon which the impression of a foot, hand or limb has been left as an enduring testimony of the presence of a departed saint, martyr, deity, or secular hero.

Durability and resistance to decay are frequently defining features of the relic: in medieval Europe the incorruptibility of a corpse was regarded as a certain sign of sanctity and a seal of divine approbation. However, relics can sometimes be perishable and even edible items, as in the case of the mangoes in Maoist China discussed by Adam Chau in his essay here. A further key element is transportability and mobility: relics are objects that carry meaning over space as well as allowing it to endure in time. Consequently they are usually items small in size and scale, though the example of the Holy House of Loreto, the home of the Virgin Mary, which reputedly flew from Jerusalem in the late thirteenth century and took refuge at successive sites in Dalmatia and Italy, is an intriguing exception to this general rule. It also highlights the intricate relationship that pertains between relics and the receptacles in which they are kept. Christian reliquaries and Buddhist stupas are not always easy to distinguish from the sacred remains they enclose, not least because of the capacity of the latter to infect things with which they exist in close proximity by a form of holy contagion or radioactivity.[2] When the relics in question have been lost, destroyed, or confiscated, the containers themselves have a tendency to become surrogate foci of devotion and reverence.

A relic is ontologically different from a representation or image: it is not a mere symbol or indicator of divine presence, it is an actual physical embodiment of it, each particle encapsulating the essence of the departed person, *pars pro toto*, in its entirety. In practice, however, the lines dividing them have often been equally permeable. In ancient Byzantium and modern Eastern Orthodox cultures, icons function in much the same way as relics, while within the western Christian tradition pictures and statues that bleed, sweat, or shed tears exemplify the ease with which images can make the transition from signifier to sacred object in their own right.[3] The ambiguities surrounding the status of Veronica's veil are no less revealing. And while uniqueness may be regarded as an essential attribute of this species of hallowed item, throughout history relics have been the subject of processes of forgery, fabrication, and reproduction that do not necessarily serve to demystify them in the eyes of believers. Medieval churchmen, for instance, reconciled the existence of multiple heads of John the Baptist and an improbably vast forest of splinters of the True Cross by means of an ingenious theory of self-generation that took inspiration from the gospel story of the handful of loaves and fishes that miraculously fed the five thousand.[4] Reproductive technologies such as printing and photography undoubtedly diminish the aura surrounding such objects and the familiarity they create can breed contempt, but the modern distinction between original and copy is arguably anachronistic in reference to earlier centuries 'before the era of art'.[5] In this

---

[2] On reliquaries, see Caroline Walker Bynum and Paula Gerson, 'Body-Part Reliquaries and Body Parts in the Middle Ages', *Gesta*, 36 (1997), 3–7, and other essays in this special issue.

[3] See John Wortley, 'Icons and Relics: A Comparison', repr. in his *Studies on the Cult of Relics in Byzantium up to 1204* (Aldershot, 2004); John Dillenberger, *Images and Relics: Theological Perspectives and Visual Images in Sixteenth-Century Europe* (New York and Oxford, 1999), esp. 5–15. For essays on this interface, see Sally J. Cornelison and Scott B. Montgomery (eds), *Images, Relics, and Devotional Practices in Medieval and Renaissance Italy* (Tempe, Ariz., 2006).

[4] See Nicholas Vincent, *King Henry VIII and the Westminster Blood Relic* (Cambridge, 2001), 63; R. N. Swanson, *Religion and Devotion in Europe, c.1215-c.1515* (Cambridge, 1995), 159.

[5] As argued by Walter Benjamin in his famous essay of 1936, *The Work of Art in the Age of Mechanical Reproduction*, trans. J. A. Underwood (Harmondsworth, 2008 edn). See also

sense, it is unhelpful to situate relics and replicas, sacred objects and imitative artefacts, in sharp opposition. The interface between them is both unstable and frequently breached.

Relics may also be defined as material manifestations of the act of remembrance. They sublimate, crystallize, and perpetuate memory in the guise of physical remains, linking the past and present in a concrete and palpable way. In the words of Annabel Wharton, they are 'remnant[s] of a history that is threatened by forgetting': they 'postpone oblivion' and evoke 'an absent whole'.[6] A kind of umbilical cord that connects the living and the celebrated dead, they carry messages from beyond the grave and provide a mnemonic ligature to a world that has been lost. Vestiges, fossils, and (literally in Latin) 'leftovers' of individuals, traditions, and cultures that are in danger of disintegration and extinction, relics cannot always be neatly distinguished from souvenirs, mementos, and antiquities. Like them, they serve as reminders and memorials and create senses of belonging and identity. Some societies, in fact, collapse them together completely, and use the words more or less interchangeably. The shifting and porous membrane between relics and these cognate concepts further complicates the task of pinpointing their meaning and writing their history.

Relics do, however, have one compelling feature that marks them out from other kinds of material object, and that is their capacity to operate as a locus and conduit of power. This power can take various forms. It can be supernatural, salvific, apotropaic, and magical: religious relics within the Christian, Buddhist, and Islamic systems are often conceived of as 'a potentially wonder-working bridge between the mundane and the divine', physical and metaphysical realms.[7] They channel redemptive and intercessory forces and are vehicles of grace, blessing, and *baraka* in the guise of miracles of healing or inner enlightenment. They operate as 'spiritual electrodes' that transmit waves of sacred energy into the sphere of the terrestrial and temporal. Technically, theologians may insist that they do this though the intervention of a transcendent deity, but in the minds of the faithful the holy is often believed to be immanent in them.[8] Unlike sacramentals or amulets, they are not invested with divine power through human rituals of liturgical

---

Hans Belting, *Likeness and Presence: A History of the Image before the Era of Art*, trans. E. Jephcott (Chicago and London, 1994).

[6] Annabel Jane Wharton, *Selling Jerusalem: Relics, Replicas, Theme Parks* (Chicago and London, 2006), 9–10; also quoted by Julia Smith, 75 below.

[7] Vincent, *Holy Blood*, 135.

[8] See A.T. Lucas, 'The Social Role of Reliquaries in Ancient Ireland', *Journal of the Royal Society of Antiquaries of Ireland*, 116 (1986), 5–37, at 9. For a useful discussion of some of

consecration or spells: rather their capacity to tap and focus it is inherent in them. Once again, though, these distinctions sometimes break down in practice, nowhere more so than in the case of the transubstantiated host of the Eucharist, which came to be regarded in the medieval period as a special type of relic itself.[9] Where some see the possession of supernatural virtue as a *sine qua non*,[10] others are inclined to adopt a wider definition that recognizes the capacity of relics to contain and unleash charismatic power in a broader, Weberian sense: to arouse awe and enthusiasm, to foster emotion and loyalty, and to galvanize people to take dynamic action to transform their everyday lives. More inclusively still, though perhaps at the risk of diluting some of its distinctiveness, one might classify the relic as an object that has an autonomous ability to prompt an intense human response.

This brings us to the important point that material remains have no intrinsic status as relics. The former become the latter as a consequence of the beliefs and practices that accumulate around them. They are the products and confections of the cultures that engender and reverence them. The making of them is both a social and a cognitive process. Outside the cultural matrix and environment within which they were created, they are inert and lifeless objects devoid of significance and worth. As Patrick Geary has remarked, 'the bare relic—a bone or a bit of dust—carries no fixed code or sign of its meaning': divorced from a specific milieu it is unintelligible and incomprehensible.[11] What one society or religious tradition designates and venerates as a relic is liable to be dismissed by another as distasteful and dirty bodily waste or the useless detritus of daily existence. Alternatively, it may carry a range of other connotations dependent on the perspective of the viewer: as John Strong shows in his essay, the tooth captured and destroyed by the Portuguese viceroy in Goa in 1561 as a devilish idol and crafty ivory fake was polyvalent: interpreted by Buddhists as a remnant of the founder of their religion and by Muslims as a vestige of Adam, according to the local Tamil people it was the molar of a divine monkey-king. The symbolic and semiotic value of such objects is a reflection of the subjectivity of the society that honours and prizes them. The manner in which relics are discovered, identified, preserved, displayed, and used by particular communities is thus

---

the complexities, see Karmen MacKendrick, *Fragmentation and Memory: Meditations on Christian Doctrine* (New York, 2008), ch. 5.

[9] See G. J. Snoeck, *Medieval Piety from Relics to the Eucharist: A Process of Mutual Interaction* (Leiden, 1995).

[10] As reflected here in Alan Knight's essay, esp. 250–55 below.

[11] Patrick J. Geary, *Furta Sacra: Thefts of Relics in the Central Middle Ages* (Princeton, NJ, 1990 edn; first pub. 1978), 5.

singularly revealing about the attitudes and assumptions that structure their outlook. 'Relichood', as Paul Gillingham comments below, 'lies in the eye of the beholder'.[12]

For all their potential to illuminate large questions of this kind, relics have, until recently, failed to attract much in the way of serious and sophisticated scholarly attention.[13] Earlier work on this subject was generally written from within the confines of individual religious traditions: an extension of Catholic hagiographical tradition, it often consisted of a celebratory description and antiquarian inventory of holy items, with sometimes little in the way of critical analysis.[14] Scholars of a Protestant disposition, by contrast, treated relics as an embarrassing manifestation of irrationality and superstition, an unedifying reflection of the conjunction between blind faith and amazing credulity, fervour, and greed, that blighted pre-modern civilization. Echoing vehement critics of relics from Guibert of Nogent and Desiderius Erasmus to Jean Calvin and Voltaire, the self-congratulatory tone they adopted betrayed the conviction that the cult of relics (as of saints in general) was primarily a phenomenon of the illiterate masses.[15] Mixing humour with a lingering strain of bigotry, it relegated Christian relics to the margins of academic history. Somewhere between these two poles lies a host of popular accounts of relics and related mysteries like miracles, visions, weeping icons, and stigmata, in which sensationalism and scepticism coexist in an uneasy mixture.[16] Interestingly, a similar set of influences has distorted the study of their

[12] See 206, below.

[13] Art historians are an exception, but they have largely been preoccupied by the aesthetic qualities of the receptacles in which relics have been preserved. For pioneering work, see Stephan Beissel, *Die Verehrung der Heilegen und ihrer Reliquien in Deutschland im Mittelalter* (Freiburg, 1890); Joseph Braun, *Die Reliquiare des christlichen Kultes und ihre Entwicklung* (Freiburg, 1940); Marie-Madeleine Guthier, *Highways of the Faith: Relics and Reliquaries from Jerusalem to Compostela* (Secaucus, NJ, 1983); and the recent exhibition catalogue compiled by Henk van Os, *The Way to Heaven: Relic Veneration in the Middle Ages* (Amsterdam, 2001). For notable foreign language studies, see N. Hermann-Mascard, *Les Reliques des saints: formation coutumière d'un droit* (Paris, 1975); A. Angenendt, *Heilige und Reliquien: die Geschichte ihres Kultes vom frühen Christentum bis zur Gegenwart* (Munich, 1994).

[14] E.g. Bede Camm, *Forgotten Shrines: An Account of Some Old Catholic Halls and Families in England and of Relics and Memorials of the English Martyrs* (London, 1910).

[15] For this tendency, see Wilfrid Bonser, 'The Cult of Relics in the Middle Ages', *Folklore,* 73 (1962), 234–56; Patrice Boussel, *Des reliques et de leur bon usage* (Paris, 1971).

[16] See, e.g., Joe Nickell, *Looking for a Miracle: Weeping Icons, Relics, Stigmata, Visions and Healing Cures* (Buffalo, NY, 1993); *The Jesus Relics: From the Holy Grail to the Turin Shroud* (Stroud, 2008).

Buddhist counterparts. The historiography of this subject has likewise been afflicted by a tendency to regard them as evidence of a 'primitive' or archaic mentality at odds with the true philosophical spirit of this religion, as a concession to the devotional needs of an ignorant plebeian majority. Evident in the writings of Asian apologists as well as western scholars, the Protestant and indeed orientalist bias of much Buddhology has likewise served to inhibit the emergence of new approaches and insights.[17] These instincts and prejudices have arguably lingered even longer in the field of Islamic studies, where they have conspired with the relative paucity of Muslim relics to minimize investigation of this category of religious object for much of the twentieth century.[18]

The renewal of interest in relics that has emerged within the last thirty years and is now on the cusp of reaching maturity may be attributed in large part to the cross-fertilization of theology and ecclesiastical history with the disciplines of religious sociology and cultural anthropology. Medievalists have been at the forefront of these trends, the readiest to embrace these methodological tools and use them to cast fresh light on one of the most conspicuous features of the religious culture of that era. But scholars of other periods and faith traditions have begun to follow the lead of pioneers like Patrick Geary and Peter Brown and subject relics to deeper and more detailed scrutiny.[19]

Several other intellectual and theoretical developments that have served to raise the visibility of relics and to inspire this *Past and Present* Supplement

---

[17] See the incisive discussions by Gregory Schopen, 'Archaeology and Protestant Presuppositions in the Study of Indian Buddhism', in *Bones, Stones, and Buddhist Monks: Collected Papers on the Archaeology, Epigraphy, and Texts of Monastic Buddhism in India* (Honolulu, 1997); Robert H. Scharf, 'On the Allure of Buddhist Relics', *Representations*, 66 (1999), 75–99; John S. Strong, *Relics of the Buddha* (Princeton, NJ and Oxford, 2004), 2–5.

[18] See 97, below.

[19] Geary, *Furta Sacra*; idem, 'Sacred Commodities: The Circulation of Medieval Relics', in his *Living with the Dead in the Middle Ages* (Ithaca and London, 1994); Peter Brown, *The Cult of Saints: Its Rise and Function in Latin Christianity* (Chicago and London, 1981), ch. 5. We also look forward to Benedicta Ward, *Relics and the Medieval Mind* (Oxford, forthcoming 2010). The study of relics in the post-Reformation period remains comparatively underdeveloped. For Buddhism, see the items cited in n. 17; Kevin M. Trainor, 'When is Theft not a Theft? Relic Theft and the Cult of the Buddha's Relics in Sri Lanka', *Numen*, 39 (1992), 1–26; Dan Martin, 'Pearls from Bones: Relics, Chortens, Tertons and the Signs of Saintly Death in Tibet', *Numen*, 41 (1994), 273–324; Brian D. Ruppert, *Jewels in the Ashes: Buddha Relics and Power in Early Medieval Japan* (Cambridge, Mass. and London, 2000). For Islam, see esp. Brannon Wheeler, *Mecca and Eden: Ritual, Relics and Territory in Islam* (Chicago and London, 2006).

may be identified. One of these is a burgeoning awareness of the capacity of material culture of all kinds to enhance our knowledge of the societies that manufacture and modify it in its various guises. Historians have been much slower than practitioners of object-based disciplines like archaeology, art history, and museum studies to recognize the benefits of tracing the 'cultural biographies' and 'social lives' of physical things. But there are now plentiful signs that they are starting to exploit objects as a source for understanding the beliefs and motivations of the men and women who imbued them with form and meaning. They are becoming increasingly adept at unlocking the logic and grammar of the human and social relationships that such items express and mediate, and which, moreover, they create as active agents. The study of relics is but one of several subsets of a branch of anthropological and historical enquiry that is seeking new points of entry and 'routes to past experience'.[20]

A second and closely related frame of reference is the growing industry that is the history of the human body. Predicated on the productive idea that the body is not just a biological entity but also a carefully crafted artefact, a large corpus of literature dedicated to exploring the conjunctions between corporeality and cultural identity has developed. While the focus of many of these endeavours has been gender and sexuality, other dimensions of this nexus have not been entirely neglected. Caroline Walker Bynum's remarkable explorations of the body as a locus for the sacred and as an integral element of notions of personhood have greatly illuminated medieval attitudes towards human remains and their fragmentation.[21] Historians and

---

[20] For some key contributions, see Arjun Appadurai, *The Social Life of Things: Commodities in Cultural Perspective* (1986); Steven Lubar and W. David Kingery (eds), *History from Things: Essays on Material Culture* (Washington and London, 1993); Victor Buchli (ed.), *The Material Culture Reader* (Oxford and New York, 2002); Karen Harvey (ed.), *History and Material Culture: A Student's Guide to Approaching Alternative Sources* (London and New York, 2009), quotation at 7; David Morgan (ed.), *Religion and Material Culture: The Matter of Belief* (London and New York, 2009), as well as articles in the *Journal of Material Culture* and *Journal of Material Religion*.

[21] Caroline Walker Bynum, *Fragmentation and Redemption: Essays on Gender and the Human Body in Medieval Religion* (New York, 1992); *Resurrection of the Body in Western Christianity, 200–1336* (New York, 1995); 'Why all the Fuss about the Body? A Medievalist's Perspective', *Critical Inquiry*, 22 (1995), 1–33. For other recent work in this field, see, e.g., Michel Feher et al. (eds), *Fragments for a History of the Human Body*, 3 vols (New York, 1989); Florike Egmond and Robert Zwijnenberg (eds), *Bodily Extremities: Preoccupations with the Human Body in Early Modern European Culture* (Aldershot, 2002); Christopher E. Forth and Ivan Crozier (eds), *Body Parts: Critical Explorations in Corporeality* (Oxford and Lexington, 2005).

archaeologists of death have also taught us to read bodies as products of the myriad practices in which they are enveloped. Approaching mortuary customs like burial, cremation, and mummification as strategies for perpetuating the physical presence of the dead in the world of the living, they have explored what the treatment and disposal of corpses reveals about how particular communities conceptualize the connection between the invisible soul and carnal flesh, and between earthly existence and the realm of the afterlife. They have shown that the propensity of different cultures to revere relics is related in direct but complex ways to these assumptions. Transformed by the funerary rituals carried out by mourners, cadavers and skeletons supply striking insight into how the body functions as a metaphor and synecdoche of the central values of a given society.[22]

A further strand of scholarly activity that provides a context for this collection of essays is the current surge of work in the field of memory studies. Investigation of the processes by which we remember and forget the pasts we have inherited has naturally directed attention towards the manner in which material objects act as mnemonic triggers and pegs. Readily assimilated into Pierre Nora's model of *lieux de mémoire,* relics and human remains are concrete sites and entities around which people weave legends and invent traditions that supply them with a sense of legitimacy, authority, and longevity. They are instruments and vehicles of the creation and circulation of what James Fentress and Chris Wickham have called social memory.[23] Precipitants of division and conflict as well as agents of consensus and unity, they play a key part in forging the competing notions of history and identity that have been the focus of much recent analysis by students of the wars, revolutions and atrocities of the twentieth century, as well as of medieval and early modern moments of disjuncture, violence, reformation, and rupture.[24]

---

[22] See, e.g., Mike Parker Pearson, *The Archaeology of Death and Burial* (Stroud, 2003 edn; first pub. 1999), esp. ch. 3; Elizabeth Hallam and Jenny Hockey, *Death, Memory and Material Culture* (Oxford and New York, 2001), ch. 6 and *passim;* Howard Williams, *Death and Memory in Early Medieval Britain* (Cambridge, 2006), ch. 3.

[23] See Pierre Nora (ed.), *Les Lieux de mémoire* (Paris, 1984–92) and 'Between Memory and History: Les Lieux de Mémoire', *Representations,* 26 (1989), 7–24; David Lowenthal, *The Past is a Foreign Country* (Cambridge, 1985), esp. 238–59; James Fentress and Chris Wickham, *Social Memory* (Oxford, 1992).

[24] The literature is vast, but for some examples, see Patrick J. Geary, *Phantoms of Remembrance: Memory and Oblivion at the End of the First Millennium* (Princeton, NJ, 1994); Nicholas J. Saunders (ed.), *Matters of Conflict: Material Culture, Memory and the First World War* (London, 2004); Jan Werner Muller, *Memory and Power in Post-War Europe: Studies in the Presence of the Past* (Cambridge, 2002).

Building on the fruits of these converging strands of research and drawing out key themes from the fourteen essays that follow, the remainder of this introduction is organized under three umbrella headings. The first is the link between relics and religion; the second is the politics of human remains and sacred objects; and the third the various social and cultural practices associated with their acquisition, accumulation, curation, and display.

Relics, remains, and religious cultures

Many contributions to this Supplement use relics to explore the nature and texture of the religious cultures and environments from which they emerge. They investigate the ways in which some belief systems encourage the veneration of human and material remains, while others inhibit, if not fiercely prohibit it.[25] Robert Morkot's essay unravels the apparent paradox at the heart of ancient Egyptian religion: despite its profound preoccupation with preserving the bodies of dead kings in mummified form, it did not regard either their whole or parts as sacred objects. A mere vessel for the soul, the corpse had to be kept intact so that the spiritual elements of the shadow, *ka*, and *ba* could be reunited with it in the afterlife. The dismemberment that underpins the cult of relics in some other faith traditions was utterly inimical to the Egyptians, whose insistence on completeness even compelled them to add prosthetic limbs to bodies from which the originals were missing. Robin Osborne tackles a similar problem in the context of ancient Greece, exploring the obstacles that stood in the path of a full flowering of hallowed remnants of its multiple anthropomorphic deities. His argument turns on the insight that the Greeks believed that their gods were too hot and hazardous to handle: the dangers thought to be associated with divine epiphany explain the displacement of these tendencies onto mythological and ancestral heroes like Herakles and Agamemnon, whose bones and weapons were employed as potent talismans and thaumaturgic resources.

The complexity with which Hellenic culture negotiated the intersections between supernatural power and the material world finds many parallels when we turn to other world religions. In Islam, as Josef Meri shows, an emphasis upon the impurity of human remains and the sanctity and inviolability of the body has restrained but not wholly precluded reverence of physical vestiges of the Prophet Mohammed and other holy personages in the Near East and North Africa, which function both as memory objects and as touchstones of divine blessing or *baraka*.

[25] For a useful brief overview of relics in relation to the various religious traditions, see John S. Strong, 'Relics', in Mircea Eliade (ed.), *The Encyclopedia of Religion*, 16 vols (New York, 1987), 274–82.

In Judaism, similar concerns about the pollution associated with decaying corpses have combined with a deep-seated Hebraic fear of idolatry to repress the idea of the immanence of the divine and to all but prevent the adoration of corporeal remains. Nevertheless, liturgical texts such as the Torah and Talmud scrolls are regarded as in some sense sacred, less because of their materiality as artefacts than because of their content as scripture. In her essay, Zoë Waxman considers how these attitudes should frame our interpretation both of the items belonging to the victims of the Holocaust displayed at museums like Auschwitz-Birkenau and of the historical narratives that those annihilated in the gas chambers left behind to document their experiences. The doctrine of reincarnation and the notion of the transience of temporal things that lies at the heart of Hinduism has likewise militated against relic veneration, together with the convention of totally obliterating the bodies of the deceased by burning them on ceremonial pyres.[26]

Buddhism, by contrast, has been much more conducive to the development of forms of relic culture and behaviour. While it shares with many other religious traditions an emphasis on the impurity and impermanence of human remains and aspires to a transcendence that renders the material world an irrelevance, these views have not proved incompatible with an enduring fascination with the remnants of the Buddha after he passed away into the freedom of final nirvana. Divided into eight equal shares and preserved in a series of stupas, according to legend, his ashes were distributed throughout the Indian subcontinent and revered by his followers, along with his hair, teeth, written verses (*dharma*), and footprints. Instantiations of the absence of an enlightened being, they are mementos of his liberation from the cycle of rebirth. But they are also objects in which he is thought by those who venerate them to retain some kind of physical presence and essence and which have the potential to provide karmic benefits.[27]

The emergence of relic veneration within Christianity is a no less puzzling, ambivalent, and internally contradictory phenomenon. The instinct to collect bones and other material traces of the Roman martyrs was at odds with inherited taboos about corporeal remains as sources of contamination. The tendency to fragment these skeletons and disperse them to the faithful in other locations that was firmly entrenched by the fourth century is ostensibly hard to reconcile with the idea of the resurrection of the body to rejoin the soul on the day of judgement that lies at the heart of Christian dogma.

---

[26] Strong, 'Relics', 276.
[27] See Scharf, 'On the Allure of Buddhist Relics'; Strong, *Relics of the Buddha*; Martin, 'Pearls from Bones'; Ruppert, *Jewel in the Ashes*, ch.1.

Reverence for holy relics is also somewhat difficult to square with the practice of subjecting the corpses of those beyond the spiritual pale—heretics, suicides, and criminals—to the humiliation of dismemberment and mutilation. Fraught with controversy and inconsistency, the evolution of relic piety in Europe continued to be accompanied by the articulation of clerical anxiety and criticism, not least about its capacity to spill over into superstition and to attract abuse and fraudulent practices.[28] But it somehow overcame these challenges and flourished in the central and later Middle Ages.[29] Nor did the precept that Christ and Mary had been assumed bodily into heaven restrict the contemporary appetite for sacred objects connected with them. Secondary relics of the Virgin and the Passion—maternal milk, the crown of thorns, splinters of the Cross, and drops of the Saviour's blood—proliferated. On the eve of the Reformation, the insatiable hunger of the laity for these tangible manifestations of the holy fostered the formation of massive collections: Frederick the Wise of Saxony had accumulated nearly 19,000 such items by 1520.[30] Domesticated, appropriated, and manipulated by the pious, they epitomized the intimate intersection between religion and magic that provoked the fury of Protestants and their heretical precursors.[31] The Catholic Church reacted to the claims of scandalous fakes that formed one main prong of the reformers' attack with a period of prudence and humanist caution, before vigorously reasserting the validity of devotion to sacred relics. Reflective of the dynamic interplay between local and universal,

---

[28] See esp. Bynum, 'Material Continuity, Personal Survival and the Resurrection of the Body: A Scholastic Discussion in its Medieval and Modern Contexts', in her *Fragmentation and Redemption*, 239–97; *Resurrection of the Body*; MacKendrick, *Fragmentation and Memory*, ch. 5. For traditions of scepticism, see Vincent, *Holy Blood*, esp. chs 5–6. Classic critiques of relic abuse include Guibert of Nogent's *De sanctis et eorum pignoribus* and Geoffrey Chaucer's 'Pardoner's Tale'.

[29] In addition to the work of Geary and Snoeck, *Medieval Piety from Relics to the Eucharist*, see David Rollason, *Saints and Relics in Anglo-Saxon England* (Oxford, 1989); Barbara Abou-El-Haj, *The Medieval Cult of Saints: Formations and Transformations* (Cambridge, 1994), esp. 138–46.

[30] See Ulinka Rublack's essay, 145–7 below.

[31] For illuminating explorations of late medieval relic devotion, see Jacqueline Marie Musacchio, 'Lambs, Coral, Teeth and the Intimate Intersection of Religion and Magic in Renaissance Tuscany', in Cornelison and Montgomery (eds), *Images, Relics and Devotional Practices*, 139–56; Sheila Sweetinburgh, 'The Archangel Gabriel's Stone and Other Relics: William Haute's Search for Salvation in Fifteenth-Century Kent', *Archaeologia Cantiana*, 126 (2006), 311–30.

Fig. 2. The translation of the relics of St Anthony of Padua, etching of *c.*1691 after Bartholommeo Montagna. British Museum AN781667001. ©Trustees of the British Museum

elite and popular religion in the era of the Counter-Reformation, they became a vibrant hallmark of baroque piety in regions that remained loyal or were reclaimed to the faith of Rome, as Howard Louthan shows here in relation to Bohemia. They were a point of contact between traditional and Tridentine piety (Fig. 2).[32]

The polemical and iconoclastic assaults that were launched against relics in the early and mid-sixteenth century are emblematic of the paradigm shift in understanding of the sacred that was implicit in the theology of Zwingli and Calvin. As I argue in my own essay in this volume, the Reformation involved a redefinition of the relic as a symbolic memento rather than a miraculous divine entity. Its violent reaction against medieval Catholic materialism should not, however, be equated with a repudiation of religious objects per

---

[32] On relics in the Counter-Reformation, see Trevor Johnson, 'Holy Fabrications: The Catacomb Saints and the Counter-Reformation in Bavaria', *Journal of Ecclesiastical History,* 47 (1996), 274–97; Simon Ditchfield, 'Martyrs on the Move: Relics as Vindicators of Local Diversity in the Tridentine Church', in Diana Wood (ed.), *Martyrs and Martyrologies,* Studies in Church History 30 (Oxford, 1993), 283–94. See also Alexandra Walsham, 'Miracles and the Counter-Reformation Mission to England', *Historical Journal, 46* (2003), 779–815.

se, or indeed of respect for the bodily remains of those who had suffered or died for their faith. Instead, we need to pay attention to the ways in which Protestantism engendered its own forms of material culture and how these were implicated in the making of a distinctive confessional identity and of reformed memory.[33] Moreover, as Ulinka Rublack suggests in her piece on 'grapho-relics', the signatures and inscriptions of Martin Luther and other reformers collected and treasured by their contemporaries are evidence less of the anti-sensual and logocentric character of Lutheranism than of the ways in which it engendered its own strategies for assuring the literate faithful of 'attainable grace'. Themselves the subject of forms of cultic reverence, the autographs she assesses are indicative of the subtle mental and cultural transpositions precipitated by the advent of Protestantism that the late Bob Scribner has inspired us to investigate.[34] Along with the bloodied handkerchiefs and discarded shirts gathered up by the disciples of English evangelicals burnt at the stake in the reign of Mary I, they raise important questions about the process and effects of religious change in the sixteenth and seventeenth centuries. Rather than leap to the conclusion that such practices are deviations from orthodoxy that bear witness to subconscious popular resistance to the Reformation and attest to the strength of stubborn Catholic survivalism, we need to interpret them as authentically Protestant phenomena. This is not to rule out the possibility of syncretism completely: some individuals did, no doubt, treat these objects as if they had inherent magical power. The subliminal influence exercised by older structures of belief and practice in shaping reformed culture is a force to be reckoned with.

The resilience of older religious archetypes and dispositions and their capacity to reassert themselves in apparently hostile ideological climates has also been a theme of some recent work on relic-like behaviour in various modern societies. Forms of remembering the revered dead tend to follow 'inherited scripts' deeply rooted in the soil of the Christian tradition even

---

[33] See also Lyndal Roper's forthcoming essay on 'Luther Relics'.

[34] See esp. Robert W. Scribner, 'The Reformation, Popular Magic, and the "Disenchantment of the World" ', *Journal of Interdisciplinary History*, 23 (1993), 475–94; Robert W. Scribner, 'Reformation and Desacralisation: From Sacramental World to Moralised Universe', in R. Po-Chia Hsia and R. W. Scribner (eds), *Problems in the Historical Anthropology of Early Modern Europe*, Wolfenbütteler Forschungen 78 (Wiesbaden, 1997), 75–92; Robert W. Scribner, 'The Impact of the Reformation on Everyday Life', in *Mensch und Objekt im Mittelalter und in der frühen Neuzeit*, Österreichische Akademie der Wissenshaften, Philosphisch-Historische Klasse Sitzungsberichte 568 (Vienna, 1990), 315–43.

where the latter has been repudiated as the opium of the people.[35] Nina Tumarkin's study of the cult of the embalmed body of Lenin points to its underpinnings in Russian Orthodoxy and in a recent article Steve Smith has highlighted how by the 1920s primary elements of Marxism fused with elements that were alien to it, such as veneration of relics. Ironically, in the initial phases of the Revolution, the Bolsheviks had engaged in a systematic but only partially successful campaign to disabuse the laity of this brand of what they regarded as gross credulity. It is not necessary to see Bolshevism as a form of 'secular religion' to recognize the deep resonances that the preservation of Lenin's corpse in its Moscow mausoleum, and the visits made to it by those who mourned his death, had with the mental world which his movement sought to debunk and obliterate. Reconfigured and re-articulated in new idioms, ingrained instincts lingered.[36]

In his essay Adam Chau similarly identifies traditional rituals of Buddhist relic worship as one of the wider contexts within which the extraordinary story of Mao's travelling mangoes should be interpreted. Alan Knight, meanwhile, firmly resists any suggestion that there is any kind of kinship between the Mexican general Santa Anna's several legs and the religious relics with which this Catholic country and continent was and still is awash. He detects evidence of alliance and plagiarism but not hybridization and vigorously rejects the idea that this episode reveals the cannibalization of religion by modern nationalism. We should not, he concludes, confuse metaphor with description. The loose language used by historians, like that employed within the sources upon which they rely, can be deceptive. For Knight, the saga of Santa Anna's various limbs is less revealing about how religious beliefs, structures, and practices persist at the level of what Pierre Bourdieu called *habitus* than about the political culture of nineteenth- and twentieth-century Latin America.[37]

The politics of human remains and sacred objects

The second thread that links many of the essays in this collection is the manner in which relics and remains operate as instruments of legitimation, as vectors and embodiments of authority, and as foci for political protest and

---

[35] See the comments of Lyman L. Johnson, 'Why Dead Bodies Talk: An Introduction', in *Body Politics: Death, Dismemberment and Memory in Latin America* (Albuquerque, N.Mex., 2004), 8, 16–17.

[36] Nina Tumarkin, *Lenin Lives! The Lenin Cult in Soviet Russia* (Cambridge, Mass. and London, 1997 edn), ch. 1; S. A. Smith, 'Bones of Contention: Bolsheviks and the Struggle against Relics 1918–1930', *Past and Present*, 204 (2009), 155–94, esp. 188–94.

[37] Pierre Bourdieu, *The Logic of Practice*, trans. Richard Nice (Cambridge, 1992), 53.

ethnic rivalry. The capacity of the relic to act as a form of symbolic capital has already been widely recognized. The circulation, transfer, presentation, and purchase of hallowed body parts and other objects within early and medieval Christian culture is, in the words of Peter Brown, 'a faithful "trace element" ' that enables the historian 'to take an X-ray photograph of the intricate systems of patronage, alliance and gift-giving that linked the lay and clerical elites of East and West in the late Roman Empire'.[38] Their distribution was an act of imperial favour and integrally related to the subordination of the Latin West to Byzantium. The beginning of the translation of the relics of the early Christian martyrs from the catacombs is also closely associated with the expression of the papacy's monarchical pretensions and the assertion of Rome's autonomy and sovereignty in relation to Constantinople.[39] In northern Europe, as Julia Smith demonstrates in her contribution, Carolingian, Ottonian, and West Saxon kings were likewise alert to the value of aggregating and dispensing this special type of royal treasure for bolstering insecure dynasties and consolidating claims to territory and hegemony between the eighth and tenth centuries. Offering a sacral 'plus factor' in times of conflict as well as stability, they allowed rulers to demonstrate a magnanimity that bound the privileged recipients of their gifts tightly to them. Possession and control of the sacred also strengthened the credentials of monastic houses, diocesan prelates, and regional churches: their acquisition—whether by purchase or by the 'ritual kidnapping' of theft—supplied protection and bestowed a sense of heavenly sanction.[40]

The use of relics as a form of political discourse continued in the era of the Counter-Reformation. The collection that Philip II of Spain assembled in the Escorial from the four corners of Europe has recently been presented as a mechanism for the sacralization of the Habsburg monarchy—as 'an active instrument of a broader rhetoric of power' and as one strand of an elaborate programme of propaganda for his regime and for the triumph of Catholicism over its Protestant enemies and the Muslim infidel.[41] The fresh wave of relic 'discoveries', such as the bodies of the Christian martyrs allegedly uncovered

---

[38] Brown, *Cult of Saints*, 89–90.

[39] Holger A. Klein, 'Eastern Objects and Western Desires: Relics and Reliquaries between Byzantium and the West', *Dumbarton Oaks Papers*, 58 (2004), 283–314. I have also benefited from reading unpublished work by Irina Oryshkevich on this subject.

[40] Geary, *Furta Sacra*. See also Amy Remensnyder, 'Legendary Treasure at Conques: Reliquaries and Imaginative Memory', *Speculum*, 71 (1996), 884–906; Thomas Head, 'Art and Artifice in Ottonian Trier', *Gesta*, 36 (1997), 65–82.

[41] Guy Lazure, 'Possessing the Sacred: Monarchy and Identity in Philip II's Relic Collection at the Escorial', *Renaissance Quarterly*, 60 (2007), 58–93, quotation at 62.

Fig. 3. The discovery of the relics of the saints on the Sacromonte, Granada, 1588–95. Spanish engraving by Francisco Heylan (*c.*1620–50). AN695090001. ©Trustees of the British Museum

at Sacromonte in Granada between 1588 and 1595 (Fig. 3),[42] gave expression to an attempt to harness the 'useable past' that finds striking echoes in Howard Louthan's exploration of the role of holy remains of the saints in the process of re-converting Bohemia after the Battle of White Mountain in 1620. Here too Catholic elites deliberately sought to revive the memory of the Czech nation's pre-Hussite heritage and to repair a major rupture in its history by means of a species of ecclesiastical antiquarianism. The recovery and translation of relics was central to the resurgence of the Church of Rome in Italy and the Holy Roman Empire in the seventeenth and eighteenth centuries, as well as to its mission to evangelize the New World. Bavaria was one beneficiary of the new trade in relics initiated by the excavation of the Catacombs of Priscilla in 1578: the Wittelsbach dynasty imported thousands of bones from Italy as part of a strategy to re-sanctify a land that had

---

[42] David Coleman, *Creating Christian Granada: Society and Religious Culture in an Old-World Frontier City, 1492–1600* (Ithaca, 2003), 188–201; Katie Harris, 'Forging History: The *Plomos* of the Sacromonte of Granada in Francisco Bermúdez de Pedraza's *Historia Eclesiástica*', *Sixteenth Century Journal*, 30 (1999), 945–66.

temporarily been stained with heresy. This was inextricably linked with an aggressive project of confessional state-building.[43]

Relics have also functioned as political devices in a range of other cultures. As Josef Meri reveals, Muslim rulers and caliphs yoked themselves to the prophet Mohammed through ownership of his staff and mantle, by employing these objects in investiture ceremonies, and by carrying them into battle as powerful totems. These portable artefacts provided a tangible link between states and the origins of Islamic civilization, as well as evidence of the Fāṭimid dynasty's descent from the hallowed founder of the faith.[44] In early medieval Japan Buddhist relics were likewise instruments of political power brokerage and charisma exploited by imperial families and shogunates.[45] Their continuing ability to act as a palladium is demonstrated by the epilogue to John Strong's essay in this volume: the legitimacy of British colonial rule of Sri Lanka after 1815 in the eyes of its inhabitants was apparently sealed by its custodianship of the Buddha's tooth—possession of which was an ancient prerogative and attribute of kingship. And as recently as 1994, the state of Myanma transformed the tour of a similar Chinese relic into a piece of ritual theatre to validate the rule of the Burmese military.[46]

Nor have bodies and body parts been absent from politics elsewhere in the modern world. In Latin America the remains of dead leaders and popular heroes have frequently been a means of underpinning the authority of that continent's precarious regimes and governments, as well as a rallying point for protest against and resistance to them. They have been conductors of patriotic feeling and mechanisms for mobilizing memory in the service of a range of agendas. Their post-mortem careers illustrate the vagaries of power in this region. The posthumous peregrinations of Evita Perón in Italy, Spain, and Argentina, for instance, underline the contentiousness of the political legacy left by the presidency of her husband. Initially buried anonymously to hinder veneration, the body of Che Guevara, Castro's chief lieutenant in the Cuban Revolution executed in Bolivia in 1967, was later resurrected and

---

[43] In addition to his essay here, see Howard Louthan, *Converting Bohemia: Force and Persuasion in the Catholic Reformation* (Cambridge, 2009), chs 4, 9; Luke Clossey, *Salvation and Globalization in the Early Jesuit Missions* (Cambridge, 2008), 220–3; Johnson, 'Holy Fabrications'; Trevor Johnson, *Magistrates, Madonnas and Miracles: The Counter Reformation in the Upper Palatinate* (Aldershot, 2009), 253–6. See also Paul Gillingham's essay below, 205–12.

[44] See also Wheeler, *Mecca and Eden,* esp. 87–98.

[45] Ruppert, *Jewel in the Ashes,* ch. 6.

[46] Juliane Schober, 'Buddhist Just Rule and Burmese National Culture: State Patronage of the Chinese Tooth Relic in Myanma', *History of Religions,* 36 (1997), 218–43.

revered as that of a martyr to his anti-imperialist and anti-capitalist ideals. The recovery (or forgery) of the bones of the last Aztec emperor Cuauhtémoc, put to death by the Spanish conquistador Hérnan Cortés in 1524, in the closing years of the nineteenth century can similarly be seen an index of the emergence of Mexican nationalism: his symbolic reclamation by later generations reflects the harnessing of archaeology as a political tool, not merely by elites but also by what Paul Gillingham calls 'grassroots instrumentalists'.[47] The manipulation of corpses and other material objects as nationalist symbols is, as he argues once again here, 'a cross class activity' in which peasants, politicians, and bureaucrats 'co-author' a mythical narrative about the material remains they have excavated and/or invented.

Twentieth-century Europe has also been the scene of various brands of 'body politics'. The exhumation of corpses of priests, nuns, and saints in Civil War Spain was a graphic symbol of the rabid anti-clericalism that infused this revolutionary movement and a dramatization of the country's liberation from bondage to its religious past. These episodes are reminiscent of the frenzied desecration of the graves and skeletons of the Valois and Bourbon kings at the height of the French Revolution and the vicious treatment of the English regicides after Charles II's restoration in 1660.[48] The expulsion of Stalin's body from Lenin's mausoleum in Moscow in 1961 was a measure of shifting attitudes towards his dictatorship within the political establishment, while the tangled web of myth, hope, and dream that has been woven around the bodies of the last tsar, Nicholas II, and his family since their shooting in Ekaterinberg in 1918 is symptomatic of the undercurrents of ideological tension and conflict that persist within Russian society. Disinterred from their obscure grave in 1991, controversies between communists, monarchists, and the leaders of the Orthodox Church ensured that seven years transpired before the remains of the Romanovs were solemnly reburied in their crypt in

---

[47] See Donna J. Guy, 'Life and the Commodification of Death in Argentina: Juan and Eva Perón'; Paul J. Dosal, 'San Ernesto de la Higuera: The Resurrection of Che Guevara'; Lyman B. Johnson, 'Digging up Cuauhtémoc', all in *Body Politics*, as well as other essays in this volume. Paul Gillingham, 'The Emperor of Ixcateopán: Fraud, Nationalism and Memory in Modern Mexico', *Journal of Latin American Studies*, 37 (2005), 1–24; Paul Gillingham, *Cuauhtémoc's Bones: Forging National Identity in Modern Mexico* (forthcoming).

[48] Bruce Lincoln, 'Revolutionary Exhumations in Spain, July 1936', *Comparative Studies in Society and History*, 27 (1985), 241–60. For the French Revolutionary disinterments, see E. A. R. Brown, 'Burying and Unburying the Kings of France', in R. C. Trexler (ed.), *Persons in Groups* (Binghampton, NY, 1985), 241–66. For the exhumation of Cromwell and other regicides, see below, 139.

St Petersburg.[49] In Ireland, debates about the repatriation of the body of Roger Casement, hanged by the British government in 1916 for traitorously conspiring with Germany to arm Irish separatists and buried in the grounds of Pentonville Prison in London, shed significant light on the politics of rebellion and partition, Anglo-Irish relations, and evolving attitudes towards the homosexuality of this controversial figure.[50]

In the context of Eastern Europe, Katherine Verdery has done much to delineate the meanings of what she describes as 'postsocialist necrophilia'. Here too dead bodies have become the focus of efforts to 'reorder meaningful worlds' and re-evaluate national pasts in the wake of the collapse of communism. Verdery considers the restless bones of prominent and famous figures such as the eighteenth-century Romanian bishop Inochenie Micu and the Hungarian prime minister Imre Nagy, whose remains were dug up and reburied in Budapest in 1989, but she is also concerned with the anonymous dead—with the victims of war and judicial massacre dumped in the unmarked mass graves that litter the landscape of these troubled countries.[51] James Mark's contribution to this volume extends our understanding of the construction of anti-communist memory and identity in Lithuania and Romania, and the formative part played by forensic archaeology in this process. He shows how unnamed bodies have assisted in the forging of narratives about Soviet genocide and communist terror, but also how the bones uncovered have the capacity to tell alternative stories. Mingled with those of Holocaust martyrs and ethnic minorities, they have had to be carefully 'repackaged' in the museums that now memorialize them 'to exclude inconvenient truths'. Even as this introduction was being written in April 2010, the deaths of the Polish president and his entourage en route to Russia to commemorate the victims of the Katyn massacre of 1943 provided a further example of how human bodies have political afterlives. The tragedy has been an unexpected fillip to reconciliation: the sight of Vladimir Putin paying respect to Lech Kaczyński's coffin has done as much to heal rifts and encourage a new juncture in relations between the two nations as the service of remembrance held at the cemetery of the Polish soldiers killed by the Soviets.

---

[49] Wendy Slater, *Tsar Nicholas II: Relics, Remains and the Romanovs* (London and New York, 2007).

[50] Kevin Grant, 'Bones of Contention: The Repatriation of the Remains of Roger Casement', *Journal of British Studies*, 41 (2002), 329–53.

[51] Katherine Verdery, *The Political Lives of Dead Bodies: Reburial and Postsocialist Change* (New York, 1999), quotation at 35.

Africa has also had its fair share of 'eloquent corpses', as Daniel Branch demonstrates in his essay on the hunt for the remains of the Mau Mau leader Dedan Kimathi. The elusiveness of the bones of the Kikuyu hero has not proved a bar to his transformation into an emblem of the complexities of politics in post-colonial Kenya. Interest in recovering Kimathi's bones is in fact a relatively recent phenomenon, partly the product of the spread of Christianity and associated funeral practices, and partly a reflection of the unsteady progress of democratization and nation-building. The other side of the process of rewriting African history is exemplified by the demand of some pressure groups in Zimbabwe that the remains of Cecil Rhodes be disinterred from their resting place on a hill in the Matopos National Park held sacred by the local people as the 'home of the spirits', which is perceived to have been desecrated by his burial there in 1902. The ongoing dispute about this issue is a measure of the difficulties of managing the country's heritage in the aftermath of colonial occupation.[52]

Regrettably, it has not been possible to include anything in this volume about one other critical dimension of the modern politics of human remains: the struggles for cultural and political recognition that surround calls for the repatriation of the skeletons of the indigenous peoples of North America, Australia, and New Zealand collected by nineteenth- and early twentieth-century settlers and scientists and preserved in local, national, and foreign museums. There is now a considerable literature on this subject, and the legislation and voluntary codes of ethics that have been enacted and adopted within the last twenty years. As many commentators have stressed, native American, aboriginal, and Maori claims to the bones of their tribal ancestors must be interpreted as acts of political self-assertion and empowerment. Originally acquired under conditions of racial subordination, their recovery and reburial is one aspect of a demand for recognition, autonomy, and equality. Such attempts to insist upon the rights of the dead are inseparably linked with efforts to defend those of the living. They are also a reaction against cultural and scientific practices that have been perceived as the handmaiden of western colonialism.[53]

---

[52] Svinurayi Joseph Muringaniza, 'Heritage that Hurts: The Case of the Grave of Cecil John Rhodes in the Matapos National Park, Zimbabwe', in Cressida Fforde, Jane Hubert, and Paul Turnbull (eds), *The Dead and their Possessions: Repatriation in Principle, Policy and Practice* (New York and London, 2002), 317–25.

[53] The literature is extensive. See, among others, S. Powell, C. E. Garza and A. Hendricks, 'Ethics and Ownership of the Past: The Reburial and Repatriation Controversy', *Archaeological Method and Theory*, 5 (1993), 1–42; Andrew Gulliford, 'Bones of Contention: The Repatriation of Native American Human Remains', *The Public*

Relics and remains: consumption, collection and display

The third and final theme that surfaces at various points in the essays in this volume is an interest in relics and remains as objects of consumption, accumulation, and display. If corporeal vestiges and material artefacts function as forms of religious and political capital, they are also frequently items that have other types of economic and cultural value. Throughout history and across the globe they have been the subject of commerce—of trade, purchase, sale, and exchange. To use the phrase coined by Patrick Geary, they have been 'sacred commodities': forms of treasure looted and confiscated as the spoils of war, precious articles pawned to provide ransoms and to raise funds for cash-strapped regimes, coveted objects given graciously to allies and friends or cunningly stolen from their owners to enhance the prestige of the burglars.[54] Enclosed in gold and silver reliquaries studded with gems, they carry a monetary price as well as a freight of spiritual meaning. While a certain unease and hesitancy has always accompanied it, all cultures display evidence of the 'commoditization of the holy'.[55] A further consequence of this process is the promotion of forgery and fabrication. Paul Gillingham's essay places this form of entrepreneurial activity under the spotlight in the context of Latin America, demonstrating how lucrative the production of fake relics and pre-hispanic antiquities has been since the sixteenth century, not merely to the wealthy and their middlemen, but also to individuals lower down the social scale. The same was true of early modern England, where humble people as well as gentleman scholars were equal partners in the

---

Historian, 18 (1996), 119–43; Pearson, *Archaeology of Death and Burial*, ch. 8; Fforde, Hubert, and Turnbull (eds), *The Dead and their Possessions;* Jerry O'Sullivan, 'Ethics and the Archaeology of Human Remains', *Journal of Irish Archaeology*, 10 (2001), 121–51. Howard Morphy of the Australian National University had hoped to present a paper to the *Past and Present* conference, on skeletal remains as a focus of memory in Yolngu society, but was unfortunately prevented from attending.

[54] Geary, 'Sacred Commodities'. See also Klein, 'Eastern Objects and Western Desires'; Paul Hetherington, 'A Purchase of Byzantine Relics and Reliquaries in Fourteenth-Century Venice', in his *Enamels, Crowns, Relics and Icons: Studies on Luxury Arts in Byzantium* (Aldershot and Burlington, Vt., 2008), 1–38. On theft of Buddhist relics, see Trainor, 'When is a Theft not a Theft?'; Ruppert, *Jewel in the Ashes*, ch. 5.

[55] Klein, 'Eastern Objects and Western Desires', 314. More broadly, see Igor Kopytoff, 'The Cultural Biography of Things: Commoditzation as Process', in Appadurai (ed.), *The Social Life of Things*, 64–91.

'archaeological economy' of coins, pots, urns, fossils, and bones that emerged in this era.[56]

To the multivalency of relics and remains as sources of sacred power, political charisma, and fiscal profit, we must add their status as items of intellectual and antiquarian fascination. All of these elements have served to encourage their collection and presentation for the benefit of a range of spectators—in the reliquaries and shrines of the Middle Ages, the *wunderkammer* and cabinets of curiosities of the sixteenth and seventeenth centuries, and in modern museums and galleries. It is often impossible to disentangle the mixture of motives that has inspired their collectors and the sensual, aesthetic, religious, and scientific elements of visitor experience. But it may be argued that certain historical moments and movements have adjusted the relationship between these and precipitated shifts in the ways that such objects are comprehended by those who touch and view them. One such crossroads may be the Reformation, as Daniel Woolf has suggested, and as I echo and qualify in my own essay below.[57] Protestantism's horror of relic idolatry had the side-effect of assisting the migration of items formerly venerated as hallowed traces into a different realm of apprehension: it transformed them from things valued because they were able to transcend time to things valued because they were bounded by it.

It would be wrong to imply that the relic was inexorably disenchanted by its translation into the environment of the museum. Responses to human remains and revered artefacts have always involved a compound of emotion, wonder, curiosity, and devotion. This reflected the eclecticism of those who collected them: medieval repositories of relics contained more than a few oddities that we might classify as anatomical and biological specimens, apocryphal artefacts, and esoterica rather than relics, while fragments of the True Cross and the physical belongings of saints and biblical figures also retained a presence in early modern *wunderkammer*. Neither the rise of scientific empiricism and forensic medicine nor the birth of the museum can be seen as inexorable agents of secularization.[58] Sanctity was authenticated by

[56] Daniel Woolf, *The Social Circulation of the Past: English Historical Culture 1500–1730* (Oxford, 2003), ch. 7.

[57] Ibid., 191–7.

[58] Some important contributions include Paula Findlen, *Possessing Nature: Museums, Collecting, and Scientific Culture in Early Modern Italy* (Berkeley, 1994); Katie Whitaker, 'The Culture of Curiosity', in N. Jardine, J. A. Secord, and E. C. Spary (eds), *Cultures of Natural History* (Cambridge, 1996), 75–90; Lorraine Daston and Katharine Park, *Wonders and the Order of Nature, 1150–1750* (New York, 2001); R. J. W. Evans and Alexander Marr (eds), *Curiosity and Wonder from the Renaissance to the Enlightenment*

autopsy as early as the thirteenth century: bodies were scrutinized for physical signs of incorruptibility and organs discovered to contain miraculous objects or supernatural properties were removed by doctors for display in churches.[59] Designed to demonstrate the superiority of science over religion, Bolshevik exposures of the bones of Russian saints during the Revolution were conducted in a distinctly clinical spirit, but sometimes had the unexpected effect of reinforcing rather undermining the piety of those who witnessed such spectacles, particularly when the bodies were revealed to have resisted putrefaction. The relocation of these relics to provincial museums could serve to prolong rather than pre-empt the 'superstition' it was intended to dispel.[60] The sentiments provoked by visiting the memorial parks that are the subject of James Mark's paper are perhaps not so far removed from those of pilgrims to medieval shrines as might initially be thought.

The tourist gaze is not necessarily devoid of religious feeling. As current research on visitor interaction with religious objects on display in public museums looks set to reveal, the subjectivities and sensibilities that shape perception and engagement with them in these settings are not purely secular. Encounters with the holy in these institutional settings can inspire contemplation and a sense of divine presence no less than when they take place in explicitly ecclesiastical milieux.[61] Curatorial decisions about what should be kept in museums and what returned to monasteries and cathedrals do not necessarily determine the ways in which these sets of objects are understood by observers. Attitudes towards the cloth fragments said to have enclosed relics of the reed and garment of Christ still held in the collections of the British Museum, together with their vellum *tituli,* may not be so different from those evoked by the splinters of bone for which they served as wrappers and identifiers, which were sent back to Basle after the opening of the head

---

(Aldershot, 2006); Paul Grinke, *From Wunderkammer to Museum* (London, 2006 rev. edn).

[59] Nancy G. Siraisi, 'Signs and Evidence: Autopsy and Sanctity in Late-Sixteenth-Century Italy', in her *Medicine and the Italian Universities 1250–1600* (Leiden, 2001), 356–80; Katharine Park, 'Relics of a Fertile Heart: The "Autopsy" of Clare of Montefalco', in Anne L. McClanan and Karen Rosoff Encarnacion (eds), *The Material Culture of Sex, Procreation, and Marriage in Premodern Europe* (Basingstoke, 2002), 115–33.

[60] Smith, 'Bones of Contention', quotation at 174.

[61] 'Seeing the Sacred in the Museum' is the subject of a research project for which Professor Gordon Lynch of Birkbeck College is currently seeking funding. See also John Kieschnick, 'Material Culture', in John Corrigan (ed.), *The Oxford Handbook of Religion and Emotion* (Oxford, 2008), 223–37.

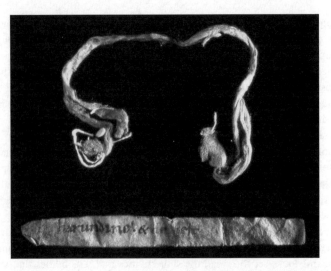

Fig. 4. Fragment of cloth that enclosed the relics of the Reed and Garment of Christ found in the head reliquary of St Eustace, *c.*1210. British Museum AN451288001. British Museum. ©Trustees of the British Museum

reliquary of St Eustace in 1850 (Fig. 4). Devout Catholics might consider them as secondary, contact relics scarcely less sacred than the items whose aura they have absorbed.

Moreover, the ways in which modern visitors to museums respond to material artefacts and human remains are not always compatible with the theological tenets of the cultures from which they emerge. Robert Morkot points out that the ways in which mummies are displayed and in which people view them are far more closely related to veneration of relics in the Christian tradition than to ancient Egyptian beliefs and rituals. As Zoë Waxman comments, if the piles of shoes, suitcases, toiletries, spectacles, and other personal effects of Holocaust victims at Auschwitz are regarded by some as hallowed remnants of martyrs, this is quite at odds with Jewish precepts.

More generally, it is necessary to underline the ambiguities that surround the retention of bodies and bones in museums, and their presentation to the public at large. Here we might include bog bodies like the Lindow Man and the casts and skeletons of the Pompeiian victims of the eruption of Mount Vesuvius in AD79.[62] Are these legitimate objects of scientific scrutiny and

---

[62] Estelle Lazer, *Resurrecting Pompeii* (London and New York, 2009).

antiquarian curiosity, or is our interest in them disrespectful, ghoulish, and voyeuristic? These issues have been most explicitly addressed and articulated in relation to indigenous remains. Archaeologists and museum curators have struggled to steer a course between defending the integrity of their research and acknowledging the dignity of the deceased as human beings rather than historic and anthropological artefacts. One of the difficulties here has been the fact that the origins of many ethnographic collections lie in the racist colonial past. Their initial assembly was predicated on assumptions about the Neanderthal character and backwardness of disappearing races, and on the belief that they ought to be preserved for the edification of posterity. Gathered by phrenologists and advocates of the theory of Darwinian evolution, their skulls and skeletons were thought to provide vital clues about the link between apes and modern humans. Hence the determination of Victorian scholars and anatomists to secure the corpses of the last Tasmanians of unmixed aboriginal descent, William Lanney and Truganini, for dissection. The latter foresaw that she would be transformed into a specimen and sought to prevent it by requesting that a friend ensure that her remains were cremated and the ashes scattered. But other interests prevailed and her bones were displayed in Hobart until 1947; not until 1976 were her last wishes honoured.[63] The relationship between native peoples and museum professionals is not, however, always one of confrontation. Some communities have reached a 'quiet truce' or modus vivendi with scientists and found ways of reconciling the needs of researchers with due sensitivity to their dead forebears.[64]

This introduction has endeavoured to sketch a series of frameworks within which the essays that follow may be read. The contributors to this Supplement have not been obliged to adhere to a prescriptive brief and consequently their texts pull in several different directions and tackle the subject from contrasting perspectives. Nevertheless, it is hoped that their juxtaposition in this volume will set an agenda for future research in this area and provoke fresh

---

[63] See Cressida Fforde, 'Collection, Repatriation and Identity', in Fforde, Hubert, and Turnbull (eds), *The Dead and their Possessions*, 25–46; Christine Quigley, *Skulls and Skeletons: Human Bone Collections and Accumulations* (Jefferson, NC, and London, 2001). On Truganini, see Pearson, *Archaeology of Death and Burial*, 176–7; Helen McDonald, *Human Remains: Episodes in Human Dissection* (Melbourne, 2005), ch. 4.

[64] Gulliford, 'Bones of Contention', 142 and passim; Lissant Bolton, 'The Object in View: Aborigines, Melanesians and Museums', in Laura Peers and Alison K. Brown (eds), *Museums and Source Communities: A Reader* (London and New York, 2003), 42–54.

thinking about the relationships between absence and presence, remember-ing and forgetting, material culture and the spiritual realm, and between relics and remains. This is a collection that may well raise more questions than it answers. If it opens up the subject to debate and stimulates discussion about broad processes of social, cultural, intellectual, and political change, then it will have achieved the aims and objectives that lie behind all *Past and Present*'s endeavours.

Divine of Body: The Remains of Egyptian Kings—Preservation, Reverence, and Memory in a World without Relics

Robert Morkot

The Egyptians' preservation of the body is well known, as is their practice of mummifying animals and birds. Yet this care of the bodies of the dead does not appear to be related in any way to cults of relics of the dead. Throughout Egyptian history there is no clear evidence that body parts of earlier kings were displayed and worshipped, or that there was any tradition of souvenirs of relatives or notable individuals in the form of hair, clothing, or personal items. But Egypt did respond very directly to the divine world, and to its past and to past rulers and individuals, and whilst the vehicles used (mainly statues) are not what we would consider to be relics, they did serve some of the same functions.

The issue of relics has not been widely discussed within Egyptology. Some late nineteenth- and early twentieth-century writers did describe certain objects of cult as 'relics', but others criticized this as being too reminiscent of Roman Catholicism. When used, the term was most frequently applied in relation to the dismembered god Osiris whose body parts were revered in different sanctuaries throughout Egypt. The lack of discussion reflects the nature of the surviving Egyptian evidence, both archaeological and textual, that emphasizes the act of offering rather than the role of contemplation in human interaction with the divine world.

Mummies and preserving the body

To us, and indeed to their contemporaries in western Asia, Greece, and Rome, the Egyptians seem to have been more obsessed with the preservation of the body than any other society. Indeed, for many contemporary societies, just as for us, it was the way in which the Egyptians preserved their dead that singled them out as different. The Egyptian preservation of the body presents us with a wide range of issues; it enables us to know a considerable amount about the Egyptians' diet, nutrition, disease, and physical appearance; and it highlights our own attitudes both towards them and towards human remains.[1]

Egyptian mummies have been familiar in western Europe for centuries. In the sixteenth century *mumiya* was imported for medicinal purposes, being ground into powder and added to other ingredients, such as rhubarb. By the eighteenth century a more antiquarian interest saw human and animal mummies enter the emerging museum collections, and the 'mummy pits' at Saqqara, near Cairo were increasingly visited by European travellers to the city.[2] The mummy returning to life became a motif of early nineteenth-century literature. In some instances, through their revelations, the revivified dead could be used as a means of criticizing aspects of modern society, whereas other authors exploited them for more light-hearted romantic tales;[3] the threatening aspects—the mummy with a curse, or used for vengeance—are later introductions.[4] This more sinister theme has constantly metamorphosed with new genres to become a classic of film and television, itself fuelling both interest in mummies and Egypt, and emphasizing mummies as one of the powerful icons of ancient Egyptian culture.[5]

By the nineteenth century, a mummy had become a fashionable tourist acquisition, although not without problems in transportation, and on return to Britain it was quite normal to hold a mummy-unwrapping party for friends. Fortunately these days have passed, and non-invasive techniques are now used to learn about the diseases and diets of the ancient Egyptians. The large number of mummies acquired by nineteenth-century tourists has ensured that almost every provincial collection has one or two to display. Public fascination with mummies places them as part of our culture, and they serve an educational purpose: indeed they are perhaps one reason why Egypt forms part of the National Curriculum.

---

[1] There are many books on mummification: one of the most recent and authoritative is John H. Taylor, *Death and the Afterlife in Ancient Egypt* (London, 2001).

[2] Brian A. Curran, 'The Renaissance Afterlife of Ancient Egypt (1400–1650)', in Peter Ucko and Timothy Champion (eds), *The Wisdom of Egypt: Changing Visions through the Ages* (London 2003), 101–31, at 126–7 for mummies from Sakkara being taken to Rome in the early 17th century; David Boyd Haycock, 'Ancient Egypt in 17th and 18th Century England', in Ucko and Champion (eds), *The Wisdom of Egypt*, 133–60, 149, 152, and 150 (fig. 6:2 for 18th-century British acquisitions).

[3] Carter Lupton, '"Mummymania" for the masses—is Egyptology cursed by the mummy's curse?' in Sally MacDonald and Michael Rice (eds), *Consuming Ancient Egypt* (London, 2003), 23–46, at 24.

[4] Lupton '"Mummymania"' points out the varying literary uses of the mummy and that it was not until 1869 that the curse motif first appears.

[5] Lupton, '"Mummymania"', 31–46.

With many museums updating their perennially popular Egyptian galleries, mummified bodies and the way in which they are displayed has become an issue within museology. This debate is not new: Lupton points out that H. Rider Haggard, himself an enthusiast for Egypt, and author of mummy stories, argued in the *Daily Mail* in 1904 against the display of mummies.[6] The current debate in Britain owes much to a travelling exhibition of material from the Petrie Museum (UCL) in which the case containing the mummy was completely covered, requiring the viewer to make the decision to look at the mummy.[7] The debate around display reflects our attitudes to the dead—whether complete bodies or body parts—and is also influenced by the antiquity of the bodies and the cultures from which they come. The most recent episode in this controversy, stimulated by Karen Exell's decision to cover three partially unwrapped mummies at Manchester Museum, highlights the public's desires and expectations. Exell covered the bodies of the mummies, leaving heads and feet exposed, a practice employed with the royal mummies in the Egyptian Museum, Cairo, in order to show respect. The action provoked a large number of responses on the Museum's weblog and in the local media. Some of these responses were, inevitably, 'outraged' and questioned the reasons for covering the bodies at all. The subsequent public consultation in relation to development of the museum's galleries revealed the wide range of attitudes. There were distinct views on the presentation of recent and long-dead human remains, degrees of exposure of the body, and offering visitors the choice to view the mummies, or not. The discussion around ethics, which pointed out that the ancient Egyptians themselves would not have wanted to be on public display, failed to convince: display was considered acceptable if respect was shown. It is clear from the debate that the antiquity, and also the 'alien' nature of the individuals played a part: the bodies were not of people that had any direct relationship to the viewers, and this dissociation was important in their attitudes. Altogether, it could be said that the ways in which modern museums display, and visitors view, Egyptian mummies is far more closely related to the reverence and veneration of relics in the western tradition than it is to ancient Egyptian practices.[8]

[6] Lupton, ' "Mummymania" ', 30.

[7] Dominic Montserrat, *Ancient Egypt: Digging for Dreams* (Glasgow, 2000), 25–6.

[8] Karen Exell and C. Lord, *Egypt and Archaeology Gallery Redevelopment at the Manchester Museum Consultation Report* (Manchester, 2008); Simon Stephens, 'New Perspectives', *Museums Journal* (August 2008), 22–7, at 27. The discussion and weblogs are archived on the Manchester Museum website: http://egyptmanchester.wordpress.

Display and reverence for bodies and body parts is central to the issue of relics. Egyptian attitudes were strangely different: despite the insistence on preservation, and the elaborate lengths gone through to achieve it, there seems to be nothing that in any way corresponds to or parallels the reverence for human relics that is given to Christian saints and martyrs, but also to other figures with religious and political 'cults' as discussed elsewhere in this volume. This is perhaps the more striking in that western attitudes to Egyptian culture—and particularly religion—have emphasized the material and denied the philosophical aspects. We might, therefore, expect the Egyptians, as 'materialists', to reverence physical remains.

There is much in western culture that has roots in Egypt—usually filtered through a Roman and early Christian prism—but reverence of relics does not appear to be one of those transmissions. Relics and their display may be, or become, a feature of Late Antiquity: it may require a religion such as Christianity which had a period of suppression with the consequent martyr-ing of individuals to stimulate the collection and reverencing of body parts. It also requires specific attitudes towards the body and the soul and their place in any afterlife. There is no clear evidence, textual or visual, from pharaonic Egypt for relics and their cults: the display of Alexander's body (which had an important role in Ptolemaic legitimacy) is the first possible example that comes to mind. This immediately emphasizes a key problem with the study of 'ancient Egypt': we are dealing with over 3,000 years of written sources, and a 2,000-year unwritten prelude to that. Inevitably Egyptian civilization saw enormous changes during that period. The timescale also introduces numer-ous problems in the survival of evidence from particular periods and phases, and a rationalizing process both by us in interpreting the scattered evidence, and by the Egyptians themselves.

Within the context of Egyptian religious belief, it is perfectly logical that human relics did not become the focus of reverence and worship. Certainly the Egyptian dead were revered, and their tombs became places of pilgrimage for many reasons, but there are no temples, or shrines to the little toe, or the elbow, of Ramesses II: that was because Ramesses II wanted to be, and remain, complete. The dismemberment implied by relics was anathema to the Egyptians.

?com/2008/07/29/covering-the-mummies-summary-of-discussion-and-museum-response/. The issue has been addressed again in the recently revamped Liverpool Museum, see Simon Stephens, 'Ancient Egypt, World Museum Liverpool', *Museums Journal* (May 2009), 48–9.

Body and soul

The reasons for a lack of veneration of relics in Egypt are linked to religious ideas of completeness, and the view that the body was a receptacle for the soul, and needed to be kept intact. The ancient Egyptian was remarkably complex, made up of many separate elements: the body, the heart, the shadow, the *ka*, the *ba*, the *akh*, and the name.

The body (in life, *iru*) and the corpse (*khet*) were the containers for the various spirits and other elements that are the essence of a person. Egypt's deserts were ideal burial places, desiccating the body, and mummification was a response to this natural preservation. The process is well known and has been a subject of fascination for non-Egyptians since ancient times, Herodotus writing the first detailed account.[9] The mummified body was designated *sah* when the appropriate rites had been performed over it. The mummy was also described as *tut*, which also has the meaning 'image' and was used of statues, and occasionally in names (as in Tut-ankh-Amun—'Living Image of Amun').

The body is itself made up of separate elements: this is evident from funerary texts in which the body parts are associated with different deities. Early burial practices involved dismembering and reconstituting the body.[10] In the morning ritual of the temples, the gods are invoked as if made up of separate elements: 'take to yourself your head, bind to yourself your eyes'. In both cases there is an analogy with the dismembered god Osiris. Completeness of the body for the afterlife became essential and for this reason the incomplete could have prosthetic limbs added.[11]

Even though the body was meticulously preserved, it was to act as a vessel for those other, more important spiritual elements: the Egyptians did not believe in any form of bodily resurrection, the afterlife was a spiritual place. The heart was regarded as the seat of reason, and the 'weighing of the heart' in the presence of Osiris in the Judgement hall was the final act in the journey of the deceased through the underworld. To enjoy the afterlife the heart had to balance the feather of *maet* (truth, divine order) otherwise the deceased was consumed by the ferocious beast Ammut, part crocodile, part hippopotamus,

[9] The literature on mummification is vast. The most comprehensive and authoritative modern general study is Taylor, *Death and the Afterlife*. He discusses the importance of the narratives of Herodotus and Diodorus Siculus on pp. 50–1.

[10] Taylor, *Death and the Afterlife*, 48–9.

[11] Taylor, *Death and the Afterlife*, 57–8 (figs. 27, 87).

part leopard, that signified non-existence. The heart was mummified separately and returned to the body.[12]

The other elements of a person were spiritual, not physical. The shadow (*šwt—shōōt*) as an inseparable element of a person is found in many cultures and particularly so in parts of Africa. In European tradition, *lack* of a shadow is highly significant, and indicative of some non-human status such as that of Dracula, or the princess in Richard Strauss and Hugo von Hofmannsthal's opera *Die Frau Ohne Schatten*. In Egypt, the shadow, represented by the semi-circular fan, is also an indicator of divine presence. This is particularly so in relation to kings, and the semi-circular fan held over the king is found on the earliest royal monuments showing that the shade or spirit of the god has descended onto the king. The semi-circular fan is found later held over statues and other images which the divine presence can occupy.

The *ka*, often called the 'double', was manufactured by the god Khnum on the potter's wheel along with the body: it might be associated with the placenta.[13] The *ka* accompanied and protected the individual during life, to be reunited at death. The royal *ka* was an especially powerful spirit, and considered to be the force that descended upon the physical, living ruler at a particular moment during coronation. The royal *ka* was the ongoing divine kingship with which the physical person of the king was temporarily united: as such, there are parallels with the medieval concept of kingship and the king's two bodies.[14]

The *ba*, by contrast, was a spirit released at death taking the form of a human-headed bird.[15] The *ba* left the body to receive the food and drink offerings presented to it in the tomb chapel. It could also leave the tomb to enjoy the light of day and visit the deceased's favourite places, returning to the body at night. The *akh*, most difficult to interpret, was perhaps the transfigured total of aspects of the deceased.

The name (*ren*) identified a person—and a statue, sculpted or painted image, or mummified body. The name is essential as an indicator for the *ba*. The *ba* could then descend into the image to partake of the offerings, whether actual, or in sculpted and painted tomb scenes. The mummy too

---

[12] Taylor, *Death and the Afterlife*, 18, 36 (fig.17), 37–8 (Spell 30B of the *Book of the Dead*), 205–6 (heart-scarab).

[13] Taylor, *Death and the Afterlife*, 18–20.

[14] Lanny Bell, 'Luxor Temple and the Cult of the Royal Ka', *Journal of Near Eastern Studies*, 44 (1985), 251–94. Lanny Bell, 'Aspects of the Cult of the Deified Tutankhamun', in *Mélanges Mokhtar* I. (Cairo, Institut française d'Archéologie orientale du Caire. BdE XCVII/1, 1985), 31–59.

[15] Taylor, *Death and the Afterlife*, 20–3.

needed to be identified with the name so that the *ba* could return to it. All of these elements made up a person—and a king (or god) had more elements: kings had five names, and several *bas*.

Mummification was only the start of body preservation. In ideal, and elaborate, cases, a mask protected the head. This would be gilded, or of beaten gold. It was protective, but the gold also signified divinity, being the flesh of the gods. In death one became a god, an Osiris. Other protection came in the form of amulets, some protecting individual elements, such as the heart scarab. The body was placed inside coffins, again gilded (or painted yellow), often three in number, and then inside sarcophagi and tombs. Of course, these all concealed the body: and their purpose was the protection and preservation of the body as a place for the soul—the *ba*—to rest in and to return to.

This was the purpose of the preservation of the body: and if the body was destroyed the Egyptians had substitute bodies for the continuance of the soul. The statue (*tut*) was a key element of a tomb chapel, and it did not matter if it was produced in a workshop and did not have individualized features, as long as it had the name for identification. This was also the case with depictions on tomb walls: the name was the essential identifier.

It is this focus on the preservation of the body as a necessary vessel for the spiritual elements that distinguishes the Egyptians from later cultures. Although the Egyptians made provision for the destruction of the body through multiple images in two and three dimensions, bodily preservation was the ideal. In this sense, then, the Egyptians might be deemed to be 'materialist': for other cultures destruction of the body, either purposeful (for example, through cremation) or accidental, was not necessarily an impediment to the continued existence of the soul in some form of afterlife.

Therefore, to kill the dead, the Egyptians needed to destroy the body—the mummy—so that the soul had no place to rest in. Equally important was to cut out the eyes, noses and mouths of their images so that they could not see, breathe or eat: and most importantly, to cut out their names, so that their souls could not find the images through which to partake of offerings.

The Egyptians became obsessive mummifiers, and during the 'Late Period' (664–332 BC) almost any type of animal or bird could be mummified. Animals were mummified from early in Egyptian history. Some had religious importance, such as the Apis bull, revered at Memphis. Others, such as cats and monkeys, were pets. The Late Period saw a proliferation of animal cults associated with numerous deities: the ibis and baboon with Thoth; cats with Bastet; falcons with Horus; snakes with Atum. It was possible to buy a mummified animal and offer it for burial at a large number of religious sites throughout the country. The most extensive were the underground galleries at Saqqara (the 'mummy pits' of early travellers), stacked with tens of thousands of mummified cats, ibises, hawks, baboons, and monkeys. But again, these mummies were not displayed; they formed part of a religious act, presented by the pious as part of a reciprocal exchange with a god. This frequently involved overnight residence in part of the temple complex and interpretation of dreams. Modern investigation of numerous animal mummies has shown that they may not be complete: some are bundles of bones from several different individuals (but the same creature).[16]

This attitude to the body and the souls prevented the development of a cult of relics. There are no known instances of veneration of body parts in temples or places of private worship. Nor is there any evidence for the public reverence of the entire body—this was buried within the tomb. Tombs of certain revered individuals did, however, become cult places.

Unsurprisingly, given the nature of the language and our understanding of its nuances, there appear to be no words in Egyptian that correspond directly (or only) to 'relic', 'heirloom',[17] 'souvenir', or 'memento'. Modern Egyptological literature scarcely addresses the issue of relics, and that which does focuses on the myth of Osiris.[18]

The legend of the dismembered god Osiris is a striking exception to the general rule of completeness. The legend of Osiris's murder and dismemberment is well known, and has been extensively discussed in western literature. In Renaissance times the legend served as an imperfect prefiguring of the death and resurrection of Christ, and as such was exploited by Alexander VI Borgia and used in the decorative scheme of his throne-room in the Vatican.[19] By the Late Period (664–332 BC) there were temples that were identified as the finding- and burial-places of the various parts of the god. Some Egyptologists have referred to these body-parts as relics, but there is no clear evidence that they were revered as 'relics' in our sense.[20] There are

---

[16] On animal mummies and cults generally, see Taylor, *Death and the Afterlife*, 244–63 with references.

[17] David G. Jeffreys, 'All in the Family? Heirlooms in Ancient Egypt', in John Tait (ed.), *'Never Had the Like Occurred': Egypt's View of its Past* (London, 2003), 197–211, at 197.

[18] Horst Beinlich, *Die 'Osirisreliquien'. Zum Motiv der Korperzergliederung in der altägyptischen Religion* (Wiesbaden, 1984) (*Ägyptologische Abhandlung*, 42). The entry, also by Beinlich, in the most extensive encyclopaedia of Egyptology: Wolfgang Helck and Eberhard Otto (eds), *Lexicon der Ägyptologie* (Wiesbaden, 1972–1992), refers only to Osiris.

[19] One of the most notable discussions is in Sir George Frazer, *The Golden Bough*. On Osiris in the Renaissance see conveniently, and succinctly, Curran, 'The Renaissance Afterlife', 111–14.

[20] Beinlich, *Die 'Osirisreliquien'*, 17–42, esp. 41–2.

variant versions of the Osiris myth, and most emphasize the reconstitution of the body.

One of the most important sources of evidence for the places associated with the different parts of Osiris's body are the texts in the Ptolemaic period temple of Edfu, constructed in the second and first centuries BC. Eve Reymond proposed that in some of the texts, the Egyptian word *ikhet* should be rendered 'relic' because of the context.[21] The word is actually used quite frequently in a range of texts, but clearly with vastly different meanings and nuances, and although the *ikhet* appear to be the most sacred of objects, as Reymond observes, their nature 'is never explicitly stated'.[22]

At Edfu, one chamber is designated the 'House of the Leg', associating the temple with that element of the god. The texts state that some of the *ikhet*-'relics' were kept in a casket in the crypt.[23] Reymond suggests that the temple's rites saw the removal of the casket with the 'relics' from the temple crypt and their processional journey to the necropolis mounds to the west of the temple where they were joined by the statue of the god Osiris. Here, various ceremonies would have re-enacted the events of the primeval age of the gods.[24] Even so, there is nothing in the Edfu texts that indicates that the 'relics' were visible or displayed (at least to the mass of people). That perhaps does not matter: it may have been generally known that the rites involved the veneration of primeval 'relics' even if these were not seen and their precise nature not known. The fact that these things were ancient and holy may have sufficed for observers at second remove from the actual rites. The nature of the *ikhet*-'relics' is not made specific in any of the Edfu texts: but this conforms to the Egyptian concept of restricted knowledge.

There are many problems surrounding the Edfu texts. Firstly, they were carved on the temple walls in the second to first centuries BC, probably from versions of much older texts, and there must be issues around transmission and interpretation. Secondly, the language of the Edfu texts is extremely

---

[21] Eve A. E. Reymond, 'The God's *iḫt*-relics', *Journal of Egyptian Archaeology*, 53 (1967), 103-6. Eve A. E. Reymond, *The Mythical Origin of the Egyptian Temple* (Manchester, 1969), 14, n.4.

[22] Reymond, *Mythical Origin*, 153–4; for a list of occurrences with this usage see, 16 n.4, 347. The sacred nature and importance of these *iḫt*-'substances' is detailed in the discussion, 288-90. Elsewhere, in a different context, she translates the term *ikhet* as 'offerings'. In other places (ibid., 14 n.4; cf. 27, n.7) the meaning is totally obscure and in many cases it is rendered simply as 'thing'.

[23] Reymond, 'The God's *iḫt*-relics', 104. In support of the interpretation Reymond cites the Morning Hymn of the temple which refers to 'the god's image hidden in thy casket, the *ikhet* ("relic") of thy Father which thou didst find in the domain, awaketh in peace'.

[24] Reymond, 'The God's *iḫt*-relics', 106.

difficult, and the Egyptian tendency for religious texts to be oblique inevitably makes our understanding and interpretation doubly difficult: the original authors knew exactly what they meant, but this may not even have been clear to the Ptolemaic priesthood.

The dismemberment of Osiris's body seems to be a comparatively late introduction to the myth, which may explain why it is contrary to other ideas of completeness, but one essential element of the Osiris myth is the act of collecting the parts by Isis and Nephthys, and the reconstitution of the body by Anubis. The main focus for the god's worship was the burial place of his reconstituted and mummified body at Abydos. Completeness was the desired result: to be reborn, one needed to be complete.

If the textual evidence for 'relics' is uncertain, similarly, from archaeological contexts, certain evidence of 'heirlooms' is equally difficult to identify. David Jeffreys cast the net very widely, but ultimately unsatisfactorily, to identify archaeological survivals that could be described in any sense as 'heirlooms'.[25] Frequently, artefacts that are deemed to be 'old' (or 'too old') when found within archaeological contexts are described as 'heirloom' although there may be several other more valid explanations.[26]

One of the few archaeological contexts that certainly contained objects that could be considered by us to be 'heirlooms' is the tomb of Tutankhamun (reigned c.1336–1327 BC), but even here, amongst the thousands of artefacts, there were remarkably few that could be, even loosely, described as 'heirlooms': Reeves lists a total of 31.[27] All of these 'heirlooms' carried the names of earlier rulers or members of Tutankhamun's family. However, as Reeves comments, some of the objects were clearly being re-used as elements of the funerary equipment. A number of non-funerary artefacts carrying the names of members of his family were included within the burial but were shown no particular reverence and may simply have passed into his possession on the deaths of their owners.

The most notable 'heirloom' found in Tutankhamun's tomb was the lock of hair that belonged to Queen Tiye, who was probably Tutankhamun's grandmother. This clearly had been preserved in an unusual fashion: the hair was plaited and placed within a small mummiform box (l.13.2 cm) which carried inscriptions with the queen's name and titles; this box had

[25] Jeffreys, 'All in the Family?'

[26] Peter J. James, I. J. Thorpe, Nikos Kokkinos, Robert G. Morkot, and John A. Frankish, *Centuries of Darkness* (London, 1991), 45–6, 80–1, 251–3.

[27] Jeffreys, 'All in the Family?', 208–210; Nicholas Reeves, *The Complete Tutankhamun* (London, 1990), 168–9 with list. Reeves gives a considered assessment of these artefacts as 'heirlooms', regarding the lock of Tiye's hair as the only really significant one.

been wrapped in linen and covered with unguents, then placed in a small undecorated mummiform coffin. The small coffin had been placed inside two further mummiform coffins: the inner of these was gilded and carried a line of text naming Tutankhamun; the outer one was partially gilded with the king's name. These outer coffins were much larger than required and clearly made for some other purpose. The lock of hair was certainly carefully preserved, but begs the question whether it was specifically prepared within the coffins for Tutankhamun's burial. The unguent-soaked wrappings would not have allowed the hair itself to be removed from its container for contemplation or reverence. This preserved lock of Tiye's hair raises questions about the survival of such items. This is a unique survival, but such 'mementos' were probably more numerous. Most importantly, what was its function? Did it serve as a relic that was venerated within the palace? If so, what was the context and how was it used?

Tombs, tomb robbery, and restoration

The tomb and its associated chapel became the focus of rituals at the time of burial, and for some time afterwards. In the case of kings, provision of the cults lasted for some considerable time, even if there were changes and modifications as time passed. For private individuals it is more difficult to know how long the offerings continued to be made. Only one royal burial place seems to have become the focus of major religious activity: the tomb of Djer (reigned c.2980 BC), a king of the First Dynasty, at Abydos, which became identified with the burial place of the god Osiris. Other burial places were restored—for example the pyramids of Menkaure (r. c.2532–2503 BC), and Unas (r. c.2350 BC) both by prince Khaemwaset (fl.1250–1220 BC), son of Ramesses II. The burial of Menkaure was again restored, and the king himself received a new coffin around 600 BC nearly 2000 years after the original burial.[28]

Tombs of private individuals who were highly revered for reasons that usually remain unknown to us, also became the focus of cults: notable are the tomb of Isi at Edfu and Heqaib at Aswan. Heqaib is a particularly unusual case since, not only did his tomb become a focus of cult, but a chapel was constructed in the town nearby.[29] The most significant individual to be elevated to divine status was Imhotep, the Vizier of the pharaoh Netjerkhet ('Djoser' r. c.2680). He was revered as a sage by the Middle Kingdom, and later as a god. In the Late Period (664–332 BC) his burial place became a focus

---

[28] For the coffin of Menkaure see Taylor, *Death and the Afterlife*, 181.

[29] Labib Habachi, *Elephantine IV: The Sanctuary of Heqaib* (Mainz, 1985).

of pilgrimage, and was associated with the galleries of mummified falcons, ibises and its healing sanctuary.[30]

Early in the New Kingdom (c.1550–1070 BC) royal burial practices changed from the form that had been usual since the Old Kingdom (2868–2125 BC): the kings were now buried in deep rock-cut tombs in the 'Valley of the Kings' rather than in pyramids, and the temples which had been attached to the pyramid now became a separate temple complex far from the burial place. This affected the continuation of offerings and cults in a number of ways. Each pharaoh of the New Kingdom began the construction of his tomb and temple shortly after his accession. It was endowed with land to provide for the temple workers and the cult. Of course, within Egypt land was finite, and on a change of reign, there generally seems to have been a re-allocation of much of the temple's land to that of the new ruler. The cult images of kings may have remained in their temples, but there are indications that temples were eventually closed down, and the cults and their images transferred to the newer temples. This is particularly clear with Ramesses II: when Ramesses III (c.1184–1153 BC) had his own temple constructed it included a sanctuary and suite of cult rooms for the image of Ramesses II that was then transferred from that king's temple. There is documentary evidence that cult statues of earlier rulers and their consorts still possessed land and received their due offerings, long after their deaths, and the abandonment of their temples.[31] That temples did cease to function is demonstrated by the case of Amenhotep III (r. 1390–1352 BC), whose temple was used as a quarry for statues and other building material by Merneptah (r. 1213–1203 BC) and Ramesses III, even though documents confirm the continuation of the cult.[32]

Of course, both royal and private tombs were opened and robbed, and, in the process, the bodies might be damaged or destroyed.[33] A series of papyri from the later 20th Dynasty (c.1130–1070 BC) records investigations into robberies of royal tombs. In one case, in year 16 of Ramesses IX, it is explicitly

---

[30] Dietrich Wildung, *Egyptian Saints. Deification in Pharaonic Egypt* (New York, 1977) also discusses Amenhotep son of Hapu, an official of the reign of Amenhotep III (r. 1390–1352 BC), who received worship in the Theban region.

[31] Robert G. Morkot, '*Neb-Maet-Re*-United-with-Ptah', *Journal of Near Eastern Studies*, 49 (1990), 323–37, discusses these temples, their statues, and cults and their continuance, with specific reference to the temple of Amenhotep III at Memphis. The cult of Menkaure was practised in the much altered pyramid temple in the late 6th Dynasty, some 300 years after the king's death.

[32] Morkot, '*Neb-Maet-Re*-United-with-Ptah', 336, n.94.

[33] For a convenient, and very clear, summary of the issues see Nicholas Reeves, *The Complete Valley of the Kings* (London, 1996), 190–2.

stated that the burial of Sobekemsaf II (*c.*1600 BC), of the 17th Dynasty, and his wife Nubkhaas was entered and the bodies looted of their masks and gold jewellery. This robbery took place some 500 years after the burial, and the papyrus implies that it had remained unviolated until that time. The prime motivation of tomb robbery was to acquire any valuables: gold and other precious metals, linen, and ointments or unguents. With the exception of the precious metals and stones, most of the valuables were perishable. In consequence, many burials were robbed very soon after the interment. In the burial of Yuya, in the Valley of the Kings, the portable precious metal was stolen, along with the perfumes and unguents, and the non-funerary linen.[34]

When burials were robbed and mummies partially unwrapped, removal of parts of the body does not appear to have been part of the culture—either as souvenir, or relic. Here, we are at the mercy of what the Egyptians themselves wrote (and our understanding of that), but we also have large numbers of bodies surviving, including many royal bodies.

The most significant group of royal bodies enhancing our understanding of Egyptian attitudes is that of the kings of the New Kingdom (*c.*1550–1070 BC). Following a period of tomb robberies around 1100 BC, the bodies of the kings were removed from their tombs by priests, rewrapped and buried in two large caches, where they lay undisturbed until the late nineteenth century. The first cache, known as the 'Royal Cache' (or 'TT 320'), was made in a tomb on the west bank of Thebes in the bay of the cliffs known as Deir el-Bahri. The tomb was discovered in the 1870s by a local family who removed papyri and other artefacts over a number of years, selling them on the antiquities market.[35] The official clearance of the tomb by Heinrich Brugsch took place in 1881 and recovered the mummies of nine (perhaps ten) kings, including some of the most significant rulers of the New Kingdom such as Ramesses II and Ramesses III. There were another nine identified members of the 18th Dynasty royal family and seven unidentified mummies, along with many members of the family of the High Priests of Amun of the 21st Dynasty.[36] A second cache was discovered in the tomb of Amenhotep II in the Valley of the Kings by Victor Loret in 1898. Amenhotep II himself was in his original sarcophagus, but in a replacement coffin, and with bouquets laid at his head and feet. In a side chamber were coffins containing the mummies of eight

---

[34] Reeves, *Complete Valley*, 177.

[35] TT (Theban Tomb) 320: Andrzej Niwiński, 'The Bab El-Gusus Tomb and the Royal Cache in Deir El-Bahri', *Journal of Egyptian Archaeology*, 70 (1984), 73–81. Andrzej Niwiński, *21st Dynasty Coffins from Thebes* (Mainz, 1988); Reeves, *Complete Valley*, 194–207.

[36] A convenient list in Reeves, *Complete Valley*, 196, with account and discussion, 194–7.

pharaohs. Elsewhere in the tomb were another six royal bodies, including princes, possibly two queens, and the pharaoh Sethnakht.[37]

The bodies of the kings found in the Deir el-Bahri tomb had been carefully rewrapped and placed in coffins which, in most cases, were not originally their own. The bodies, the linen used for rewrapping, and the coffins had been carefully labelled with the name of the deceased and information on the date of the rewrapping. These 'dockets' are remarkably informative about the care taken and the length of time that it took. It becomes clear that the bodies had been collected together following inspections of the tombs, and then stored somewhere where they were rewrapped—probably using all of the rites that had accompanied the original mummification process—and only then reburied. The rewrapping was carried out under the authority of the High Priests of Amun, Pinudjem I, and Pinudjem II, both members of the new ruling 21st Dynasty and also distantly related to the preceding 20th Dynasty. The reburials of some of the kings are specifically dated to the burial of Pinudjem II himself: dockets and wall texts state that the mummies of Ramesses I, Sety I, and Ramesses II were removed from the tomb of Sety I three days before the re-burial, and that they were buried on the same day as Pinudjem II. The texts imply that the body of Amenhotep I was already in the Deir el-Bahri tomb, and Pinudjem II's wife, Nesikhons, had been buried there several years before.[38]

Brugsch removed the mummies and coffins from TT 320 hastily (in two days) because he feared there would be attempts to steal the coffins, mummies, and other objects. As a result there has been controversy over the original positioning of bodies within the tomb, and the length of time over which they were interred. The tomb itself was entered by a shaft over 10 metres deep. This opened onto a corridor which turned at a right angle and running for a further 21 metres led to a chamber from which a further corridor of 30 metres in length ended in a second chamber some 7 metres long. The inner chamber contained the burial of Pinudjem II and his family.

It is clear from the brief reports of Brugsch that the first chamber and parts of the corridor were filled with coffins, and some of the largest coffins were over 3 metres long. Some commentators have argued that coffins may have been moved by the Abd er Rassoul family that discovered the tomb and removed (mainly small) objects for a period of about ten years prior to official intervention. However, the clear problems implicit in moving large wooden

---

[37] Reeves, *Complete Valley*, 198–9.

[38] Jaroslav Černý, 'Studies in the Chronology of the Twenty-first Dynasty', *Journal of Egyptian Archaeology*, 32 (1946), 24–30, at 30.

coffins around in the confined space would suggest that the majority of the coffins and mummies were in their original positions, with perhaps only those that were most accessible being moved closer to the entrance. In any case, the family claimed to have visited the tomb only three times: small objects such as shabti figures, papyri, boxes, were easier to remove and far easier to sell. Although Brugsch's records are not detailed enough to allow a full reconstruction of the layout of the mummies, it is probably safe to assume that most were in, or very close to, the place they had been left in the 21st Dynasty.

The coffins and mummy wrappings carry ink texts that give information on the reburial process which are of enormous historical significance. Some of these texts state that the reburial was made on the day of the burial of Pinudjem II himself. If Pinudjem was buried in the inner chamber of TT 320, the implication is that the other coffins followed him into the tomb having been rewrapped and then held elsewhere. In such august company, Pinudjem no doubt guaranteed himself an excellent entry in the underworld. The rewrapping of some of the bodies took place in the temple complex at Medinet Habu. A docket on the mummy of Ramesses IX explicitly states this, and some royal funerary artefacts were also excavated there. A small tomb in the Valley of the Kings (numbered KV 49) was used in the process, perhaps as a store for linen, brought from the temple for rewrapping the bodies. There is also evidence from the tomb of Ramesses XI that some related activities were carried out there.

This apparent care of the royal dead is not perhaps all it seems, and it is certain that the rewrapping followed the removal of all gold and valuables, the gold covering from the coffins being stripped off too. Some of the jewellery (and perhaps the gold masks) was recycled in the burials of the 21st Dynasty kings at Tanis. At the end of the 20th Dynasty, Egypt was in economic crisis, and rather a lot of the state wealth was in royal tombs. There is, as Nicholas Reeves has argued, considerable evidence for the state-controlled gathering of wealth from the crisis years of the reign of Ramesses XI.[39] The royal burials in the Valley of the Kings and the Valley of the Queens, and then the elite necropoleis, were systematically looted. The gathering, rewrapping, and eventual reburial of the royal bodies took place over an extended period. Beginning in the reign of Ramesses XI, this activity continued in the pontificate of Pinudjem I, which followed. The final reburial of the bodies following the death of Pinudjem II took place in year 10 of the pharaoh Siamun.

---

[39] Summarized in Reeves, *Complete Valley*, 204–5, 207.

Following the conventional chronology for the 21st Dynasty, the process took place over a period of one hundred years.[40]

Some of the jewellery and other precious metals reclaimed from the burials found its way into the tombs of the new ruling dynasty at Tanis. Some other, purely funerary, objects were recycled. Notable amongst these is a *shabti* figure of Ramesses II.[41] This particular statue was converted into a figure of the god Osiris, again for funerary use. However, as Reeves notes, in its reused state, the original ownership was obscured.[42] So, even if, as a royal object, the statue did possess extra potency, this was not obviously, or visibly, exploited in its new form. The object hardly seems, therefore, to fall into the category of a relic. Indeed, although the royal tombs had been pillaged—often on more than one occasion—and subjected to this state looting, they still contained numerous small funerary objects, such as *shabtis*, when they became the subject of European interest in the nineteenth century. Had such objects been deemed valuable in religious terms by the Egyptians of the late New Kingdom, or succeeding periods (and the tombs did contain burials down to the Roman period) they would surely have been removed.

The stripping of the wealth reveals a pragmatic attitude to the burial equipment, but also that what was really important was the preservation of the body—and naming it. Many of the bodies were in coffins that had belonged to other kings, or non-royals, and the mummies themselves carried large ink texts to identify them. The fact that the bodies were carefully rewrapped and reburied shows that the idea of completeness was respected and that there was no concept of removing a part of a king as a relic or a souvenir. It is surely significant that this process did not stimulate cults of relics, and that the bodies were reburied in particularly remote and inaccessible tombs where they did lie undisturbed for a further three thousand years.

Body and statue: receptacles of divine spirit

Ultimately the body was the receptacle for the soul and not reverenced because of itself. The body and the statue performed basically the same function, but within different contexts: the body, preserved within its wrappings and coffin deep within the tomb; the statue in the chapel above to receive the

---

[40] Approxmiately 1070 BC (a text of Ramesses XI) to 969/8 BC estimated as year 10 Siamun. A radically shorter chronology for the dynasty proposed by e.g. James et al., *Centuries of Darkness*, would reduce this to a period of about fifty years.

[41] The *shabti* was a particular type of small funerary statue used by all classes of society, that carried prayers and when called on would perform agricultural labour on behalf of the deceased in the afterlife.

[42] Reeves, *Complete Valley*, 206.

offerings for the continuance of the *ka* which moved from the body to the statue.

Statues of gods and kings similarly served as the temporary home of the *ka*. This is emphasized during the daily rituals: at a specific point within the ceremonies the divine spirit entered the statue. This took place during the incense rite, when the statue was circled by the censing priest. In Egyptian the word 'incense' is *se-netjer* from the causative verb, 'to make godlike' or 'cause to be a god'.

Furthermore, the statue of a king could become the temporary residence of the *ka* of a god. In the so-called 'Ritual of Amenhotep I', the statue of the King Amenhotep I is the focus of the action up to the incense rite, after which point, the god Amun dominates. The incense rite forms the key point in the liturgy: it is at this moment that the *ka* of Amun descends into the statue of Amenhotep I.[43]

In the city of Thebes, Amenhotep I (r. 1525–1504 BC) was one of Egypt's most potent dead kings and was worshipped for the remainder of the New Kingdom.[44] A number of scenes on stelae and in tombs show the statue of the king carried in procession, during which it gave oracles. The statue is sometimes shown with a small image of the god Amun hovering over it, and with the open fan indicating a divine presence: it is clear that the statue of the king has become the vehicle for the *ka* of the god.

It is not, therefore, surprising that living kings could also merge with gods. The divine status of the pharaoh has been extensively discussed and the idea that the pharaoh had the *potential* for becoming a god, rather than being a living god, appeared to satisfy western sensibilities. Recently, a more nuanced approach to divine kingship has developed.[45] Bell drew attention to the similarity to the medieval European concept of the 'king's two bodies', and the position of the pharaoh as the human occupant of a divine office, with divine power descending at the moment of anointing during the coronation rites.

---

[43] Alan H. Gardiner, *Hieratic Papyri in the British Museum. Third Series. Chester Beatty Gift. Vol I: Text* (London, 1935), 79–106 (Papyrus BM 10689); Harold H. Nelson, 'Amun of United with Eternity', *Journal of Near Eastern Studies*, 1 (1942), 127–55. Harold H. Nelson, 'Certain Reliefs at Karnak and Medinet Habu and the Ritual of Amenophis I', *Journal of Near Eastern Studies*, 8 (1949), 201–32.

[44] Jaroslav Černý, 'Le culte d'Amenophis Ier chez les ouvriers de la nécropole thébaine', *Bulletin de l'Institut française d'Archéologie orientale du Caire*, 27 (1927), 159–203.

[45] Wildung, *Egyptian Saints*, 3, states that the living king was *never* a god, and that he only became divine after death. There is a large literature on royal divinity see Bell, 'Luxor Temple' and 'Aspects of the Cult'; David O'Connor and David P. Silverman, *Ancient Egyptian Kingship* (Leiden, 1995) (*Probleme der Ägyptologie*, 9).

Bell detailed the ways in which the king was able to merge with the essence of divine kingship, the royal *ka*. As in medieval kingship, the divine office was conceived as an ongoing powerful force and each ruler was the temporary human holder, but (at times) endowed with divine powers.[46] In Egypt, this was made visible in many ways, such as by use of the 'throne name' rather than the personal name for the cult statues of dead kings.

The living pharaoh could thus function in the same way as a statue, and at certain times (presumably through ritual) could become the vessel for the spirit of a god. This brings us to a central issue of Egyptian religion: the revealed and the concealed.

Although, in the New Kingdom (evidence is less clear for the Old and Middle Kingdoms) statues of gods were carried in public processional rites from one temple to another; and although these rites were times when the gods delivered oracles, the statues themselves usually remained hidden. When carried in procession, the statue of the god was placed inside the shrine of a portable barque, the shrine itself veiled. The focus of 'popular' and intermediary cult therefore became visible images. One of the most notable in the city of Thebes was the *šfyt* (*shefyt*) of Amun which was the ram's head with broad collar ('aegis') that was found on the prow and stern of the sacred barque of the god, and on the main doors of the god's temple 'Ipet-Sut' (Karnak). Similar images served for other deities. Foremost of the visible divine images was the Pharaoh, in statue and in living form.

If religious relics serve as a source of contemplation and a way to communicate with the divine, the evidence from ancient Egypt seems to offer no direct parallels. The evidence is strongly negative that human remains (or remains of gods) served as relics, and the ideas and rites relating to death explain the reasons for this. Although there is less evidence, there seems to be no cult of objects associated with significant individuals, or attributed to gods. The only pre-Christian Egyptian parallel to the cult of relics appears to be the statue.

Statues of kings and revered individuals and high officials were set up at the entrance to temples. They could act as intermediaries between individual petitioners and the divine world, in exchange for offerings; sometimes all that was required was an offering of pure water. Probably the most sacred royal statues were those which had served as cult images and which remained in temples, being brought out at festivals (as in the processions of royal statues paraded at the Festival of the god Min).

Although the evidence is very sparse, it is clear that 'ancient' divine statues were kept within temples. One such was a statue of the goddess Hathor,

---

[46] Bell, 'Luxor Temple', and 'Aspects of the Cult'.

preserved in the temple constructed in the later Ptolemaic and early Roman periods (first century BC- first century AD) at Dendera. This statue depicted the goddess squatting, in the act of giving birth, and was housed in a chamber behind the sanctuary, at a point where the 'ordinary people' could communicate directly from outside the temple with the deity inside. We are also told that an ancient statue of the 6th Dynasty pharaoh Pepy was revered in the temple. How far either of these images might have been thought of as 'relics' is impossible to say; but clearly their antiquity associated them with the earlier history of the temple.

The ancient Egyptians' relationship with the numinous employed a range of intermediaries. In some cases those were mummified animals and birds; but the mummies were used as part of a rite, not as objects of devotion and contemplation. Numerous other types of object could be offered, many perishable (flowers, food): it was the ritual act that was significant. The nature of temple rites and public access to them also affected the development of contemplative foci. The preservation of a body intact was fundamental to the Egyptians' idea of the afterlife: so human remains and relics appear to have had no part in Egyptian religion that is in any way comparable to later western traditions and other means were found for invoking the past and relating to the divine world. Egypt was a world filled with remains, but apparently without relics.

Relics and Remains in an Ancient Greek World full of Anthropomorphic Gods

Robin Osborne

Sacred relics are the guarantee that the supernatural powers are available to humans. In religions where God is thought of as being in significant respects what man is not (omniscient, omnipotent, immortal, ineffable, and incorporeal), God's interest and involvement in the world is demonstrated by the existence of material objects charged with supernatural power by their association with individuals closer to the divine than ordinary men. But in ancient Greece the gods were, although immortal and very powerful, in almost all other significant ways just like men; in particular they had bodies. The gods intervened on earth in their own interests and might give material objects to mortals to use. In this chapter I look at the statues and gifts that came to be associated with gods, and at remains of the heroes who were thought to be unusually close to the gods, and ask how the associations came about. The images of the gods, the remains of heroic mortals who enjoyed particularly intimate relations with the gods, and objects associated with gods and heroes, were, I argue, important in this world both in life and in discourse; but what men could show to other men by the way they treated these objects was very much more important than what they could show about the gods.

Bones

In the aftermath of the Persian War and as part of their campaign to clear both Persians and all other potentially hostile parties out of the Aegean, the Athenians captured the Aegean island of Skyros.[1] The commander of the expedition, the famous general Kimon, proceeded to discover there bones which he claimed answered the command of an oracle that the Athenians should recover the remains of Theseus, who was the mythical king of Athens who had rid the country of monsters, killed the minotaur (so putting an end to annual sacrifice of young Athenians in service to the Cretan king Minos),

---

[1] Thucydides 1.98.

and brought together the separate villages of Attica into a single state.[2] What Kimon is reported to have found, at a site indicated by an eagle tearing up the ground, was 'a coffin of a large body, a bronze spear lying by its side, and a sword'.[3] The shrine in which the remains were re-deposited in the centre of Athens, a place where no ordinary bones were allowed to be buried, was decorated with murals and these, according to second-century AD traveller Pausanias in the first book of his *Guide to Greece*, showed Athenians fighting Amazons and a battle of Centaurs and Lapiths.[4] Pausanias makes Theseus explicitly an actor in the latter battle, and we should presume him to have been visibly active in the former also. The hero whose bones the Athenians now possessed was thus reanimated in adventures and among creatures of the mythical past. In recovering Theseus' bones the Athenians signalled their claim to a mythological inheritance; along with the bones they were recovering Theseus' mission. Not only Skyros' Dolopian pirates needed to look out.

Fifty years later, in the winter of 426/5 BC, the Athenians, in response to an oracular command, dug up all those buried on the Cycladic island of Delos and re-deposited their bones and grave goods on the neighbouring island of Rheneia.[5] It is hard to believe that the oracular command to do this was spontaneous, and the fourth-century historian Ephoros apparently suggested that the action was taken in response to the plague.[6] That these actions clearly commanded intense interest in Athens is apparent from the coverage given to them by Thucydides. Thucydides has occasion to refer to them at the very beginning of his history, when reconstructing the past history of the Greek world. As proof that the Aegean islands were settled by Carians or Phoenicians, who were addicted to piracy, he cites the fact that, when the graves were excavated on Delos, more than half of them turned out to be

---

[2] Plutarch, *Theseus* 36, *Kimon* 8. See further F. Pfister, *Der Reliquienkult im Altertum*, 2 vols (Giessen, 1909, 1912), 198–204. This and other ancient accounts of finding extraordinary bones are discussed in A. Mayor, *The First Fossil Hunters: Paleontology in Greek and Roman Times* (Princeton, 2000) ch. 3 and J. Boardman, *The Archaeology of Nostalgia: How the Greeks Re-created Their Mythical Past* (London, 2002), ch. 2.

[3] Plutarch, *Theseus* 36.2. If we take the presence of spear and sword seriously then these bones must have been human, and are unlikely to have been notably large.

[4] Pausanias 1.17.2–3. The appearance of the murals is discussed by J. Barron 'New Light on Old Walls', *Journal of Hellenic Studies*, 92 (1972), 20–45.

[5] Thucydides 3.104; 5.1. For the deposit on Rheneia, excavated in 1898 see K. A. Rhomaios *Arkhaiologikon Deltion* (1929), 181–223 and R. M. Cook 'Thucydides as Archaeologist', *Annual of the British School at Athens*, 50 (1955), 266–70 at 267–9.

[6] Diodoros 12.58.6, following Ephoros.

graves of Carians, identified by the arms buried with them and the mode of burial.[7]

It cannot have been rare in the ancient Greek world to come across human bones.[8] Earlier burials can often be shown to have been disturbed by later ones, and in some circumstances earlier burials might be deliberately removed. We do not know how widely shared was Thucydides' view of the identity of the majority of these Delian burials—we cannot rule out the possibility that he was himself closely involved with the operation and derives his knowledge from that.[9] But even if it was only those responsible for the digging who observed how these remains differed from what could be expected from current burial practices, it remains true that the differences noted were explained without reference to a heroic past. Distinctive though these burials were, their distinctiveness did not demand that they be identified with individuals of legend or individuals demanding cult. Delos too had abundant mythical associations, including with Theseus, but no reference is made to any of those in association with these excavations.[10]

What was it that meant that digging up the grave of one large man buried with arms on Skyros led to the remains being identified with a hero and made the basis of a hero shrine in Athens, while the discovery of a large number of men buried with arms on Delos led only to them and their grave goods being re-deposited in a single pit?[11] Size itself is not enough: Pausanias is at one point insistent that large bones may nevertheless be human, although size might lead to association with the Giants whose battles against the Olympian gods were a favourite subject of archaic and classical temple sculpture.[12] Rather than size, the issue here is partly number, and partly political

---

[7] Thucydides 1.8.

[8] Cf. e.g. C. M. Antonaccio, *An Archaeology of Ancestors: Tomb Cult and Hero Cult in Early Greece* (Lanham, 1995), 117: 'The Iron Age users of the West Cemetery seem to have had an easy familiarity with earlier graves'.

[9] S. Hornblower, *Thucydides* (London, 1987), 184, suggests that Thucydides might himself have been in command of the operation. The interest generated in Athens by the purification of Delos and the re-invention of the Delia festival is suggested by the attention to Delian cult in Euripides: see G. W. Bond, *Euripides* Heracles *with an Introduction and* Commentary (Oxford, 1981), 241, on *Herakles*, 678.

[10] The Athenians annually sent a delegation to Delos in celebration of Theseus' slaying of the minotaur which delivered the Athenians from the obligation to send seven youths and seven maidens as sacrificial victims to Crete each year.

[11] Albeit treated with a good deal more respect in 426 than in 1898 when the excavation of the pit resulted in the broken pottery among the grave goods being mended, but the bones thrown into the sea.

[12] Pausanias 3.22.9, 8.32.5.

convenience. The heroic world was a world of individuals and individualized powers. But there were possible collective heroes—take the 'Seven against Thebes', whose tombs were identified and perhaps given cult at Eleusis, or the Argives who fought and died in or during their return from the Trojan War, whose cenotaph Pausanias saw at Argos.[13] Attributing heroic status to the discovery of Theseus' bones was politically convenient, both for the Athenians generally and for Kimon himself.[14] Attributing heroic status to bones which the Athenians wish to see as polluting, would be politically very inconvenient.

So was it politics, at a personal, community, or inter-community level that determined whether or not remains became relics, acquired cultic importance? The stories of the Athenian excavation of the graves on Delos and of Kimon's excavation of a grave on Skyros share, with each other and with many other stories of the digging up of bones, the motif of oracular instruction. In both these stories and in most other cases we find a pattern: the digging follows the oracle. But there are variants on this pattern, including stories with no oracle involved at all or with the finding of bones occasioning the oracular consultation. By considering these alternative stories we can clarify what is happening in the more common story pattern.

Pausanias rarely tells stories of recent history, but he relates in book eight, in a digression designed to demonstrate once and for all that the Giants did not have serpents instead of feet, how a Roman emperor (unnamed) wanted to make the river Orontes navigable up to Antioch, and to do so diverted the river into an alternative channel. In the dried up river bed a coffin appeared containing a body sixteen feet long. The Syrians consulted the oracle at Klaros about this and were told that the man was Orontes, the homonym of the river.[15]

Not only is this a rather different sort of story, the story of a discovery by men who are not looking, rather than of discovery by those instructed to look; it is also a story told with no mention of cult. We simply hear no more once the body has been identified. This despite the fact that we might expect the homonym of a river not only to be a god but to be a god demanding of worship! Whatever the interest of the Syrians who consulted about these remains, Pausanias is not interested in what the oracle instructed about

---

[13] Seven: Plutarch *Theseus* 29.5, Pausanias 1.39.2; on the archaeological identification of these graves see Antonaccio, *Archaeology of Ancestors*, 112–17; Argives: Pausanias 2.20.6.

[14] Cf. S. Mills, *Theseus, Tragedy, and the Athenian Empire* (Oxford, 1997), 36: 'it is not possible to draw too clear a line between [Kimon's] private interests and the enthusiasms of the Athenian people'.

[15] Pausanias 8.29.3–4.

their fate. For him they establish something about Giants, and offer support for a view about the origins of life; they remain 'exotica', 'mirabilia', not relics.

We find a similar lack of interest in any cultic associations in Pausanias' story of how Homer's heroes were revealed to be as as big as Homer says they were when the sea washed away the grave-mound and allowed easy entrance to the tomb of Telamonian Aias. The body, Pausanias reports, was said to have kneecaps the size of the discus for the boys' pentathlon.[16] Once more here Pausanias is concerned neither with the fate of the body, nor with whether or not there was or should be cult. These stories of recent history show that Pausanias does indeed think large bodies found in his own day are something interesting, as Thucydides finds the burials of the 'Carians' interesting, but not something of religious significance.

By contrast to these two examples, the pattern that we have seen in the case of the bones of Theseus is repeated in a whole group of stories about the archaic and classical past told in Pausanias. We find it in the stories of the bones of Orestes son of Agamemnon (told briefly by Pausanias, but already in Herodotos), the bones of Aristomenes of Messene, the bones of Hippodameia bride of Pelops, the bones of Teisamenos the seer, and the bones of Arkas eponym of Arkadia. In all these cases the heroic status of the remains is both predetermined and also confirmed by their physical properties.[17] Those who look for the bones know already what they are looking for, and, crucially, that what they are looking for is going to be decisively powerful for them. The peculiar features of the remains that they find then confirm that they have indeed found what they are looking for.

Once more it is cases where there is some variation on the story that show up the power of its plot. Three cases deserve discussion: Linos, Hesiod, and Pelops.[18] In the case of Apollo's musical son Linos, no oracle is involved. Instead it is as a result of a dream that Philip of Macedon takes away the bones after winning the battle of Khaironeia—and after another dream that he restores them. The dream here fulfils the role of the oracle, but dreams have none of the external authority of oracles, and that Philip sees more to

---

[16] Pausanias 1.35.3.

[17] Orestes: Pausanias 3.3.5, 3.11.10, 8.54.4 (his finger, which he is supposed to have bitten off in his madness, was separately commemorated with a stone finger monument, Pausanias 8.34.2), Herodotos 1.66–8; Aristomenes: Pausanias 4.32.3 (with Pfister, *Reliquienkult*, 206–7); Hippodameia: Pausanias 6.20.7; Teisamenos: Pausanias 7.1.3; Arkas: Pausanias 8.8.3–4, 8.36.8 (with Pfister, *Reliquienkult*, 204–6).

[18] Linos, 9.29.8; Hesiod 9.38.3; Pelops: Pausanias 5.13.4–6, 6.22.1: see further Pfister, *Reliquienkult*, 230–33 on Hesiod.

be gained by returning the bones than by retaining them suggests he understood well the conventions. In the case of the poet Hesiod, there is an oracle but the bones are distinguished not by their physical properties but because indicated by a pre-selected bird. Not only might we think that Hesiod had a different stature to the heroes about whom he himself wrote; this story expects him to have a different stature. But his presence is none the less powerful for all that. Finally in the case of the bones of Pelops we have both the standard motif of extra large bones, and the motif of an oracle, but the oracular motif is doubled. We have both Demarmenos, a fisherman, like the Syrians who discovered Orontes, going to the oracle to discover what he has found, and simultaneously we have the Eleans looking for a cure for their woes. The oracle, displaying, we might think, no little opportunism, declares Demarmenos' bone to match the Elean need.

What was wrong with Aias? Why did he not receive cult? The problem is not anything to do with the bones themselves, it is that no one has had to ask an oracle about them. Those who are not actively seeking supernatural power do not find it, however literally super-natural what they find is. It takes predetermination to turn remains into relics.

The shield of Herakles and other heroic paraphernalia

In 99 BC the people of Lindos on Rhodes decided to carry out a research project and to publish the results. The temple of Athena at Lindos had, they noted, 'been adorned with many beautiful objects from the earliest times because of the visible presence (*epiphaneia*) of the goddess', but both the objects themselves and their dedicatory inscriptions had been lost through time. They therefore appointed two men to search the various literary works which had discussed Lindos, its history and its temple, and to make and inscribe on stone a list of the dedications mentioned in those works.[19]

A modern scholar who undertook such a search of surviving literature would come up with just one item. Diodoros records a striking bronze cauldron dedicated as a votive offering to Lindian Athena by Cadmus, inscribed in Phoenician letters.[20] But the surviving inscription records that Tharsagoras and Timakhidas managed a very much larger haul: they were able to list

---

[19] The resulting inscription, known as the 'Lindian Chronicle' was discovered by Danish excavators in the early twentieth century. The definitive edition is C. Blinkenberg, *Lindos. Fouilles de 'acropole 1902–1914. II. Inscriptions*, 2 vols (Berlin and Copenhagen 1941), no. 2 (I:148–99); there is a recent text translation and commentary in C. Higbie, *The Lindian Chronicle and the Greek Creation of their Past* (Oxford, 2003).

[20] Diodoros 5.58.3.

thirty-one dedications from before the time of the Persian War and a further twenty-one between then and the end of the third century BC.

The first dedication they recorded was by the eponymous Lindos of a libation bowl (phiale) 'which no one was able to discover what it is made from, on which had been inscribed: "Lindos to Athena Polias and Zeus Polieus"'.[21] There follow dedications made by the Telchines, Kadmos (as in Diodoros), Minos, and then Herakles. What Herakles dedicated was 'two wicker shields, one sheathed in leather, the other in bronze'. Of these the leather one had been inscribed, 'Herakles, from the Meropes, the shield of Eurypylos'. On the one of bronze, 'The shield of Laomedon, Herakles from the Teucrians, to Athena Polias and Zeus Polieus'.[22] Eight separate literary sources are cited for this dedication. Herakles' adventures on Kos had been described in the fifth-century BC by Pherekydes, and his encounter with Laomedon, king of Troy, who tried to cheat him out of the reward he had promised if Herakles rid his city of a monster, was already alluded to in the *Iliad*.[23] The dedication links Lindos in to two separate episodes in the life of the great hero, episodes which brought him as close to Rhodes as he is ever known to have been, and made the Lindians heroic by association.

Just as the first dedications recorded gave no indication of the occasion of their dedication, so several that follow are similarly unrevealing about how the particular heroic or historic figure came to made a dedication at this sanctuary, but others offer anything from minor hints ('Telephos to Athena, a supplicatory gift, as Lycian Apollo said') to pretty well full stories ('The men making an expedition with Tlapolemos against Ilion, nine shields, nine daggers, nine leather caps, nine pairs of greaves. It had been inscribed on the shields, "the men making an expedition with Tlapolemos against Ilion to Athena the Lindian, spoils [of those] from Troy"').[24] Readers of these dedicatory inscriptions can find a place for the act of dedication in their knowledge of the hero or historical figure's activities.

In the best circumstances the dedication itself evokes some central episode in the dedicator's life. Herakles' encounters with Eurypylos and Laomedon may be overshadowed by his canonical labours, but when Menelaos dedicates a leather cap, inscribed 'the cap of Alexander' (where Alexander is the alternative name of Paris) the reader is thrown directly into the one episode upon which Menelaos' fame rests—his being cuckolded and its

---

[21] Lindos Chronicle B2–4, (tr. Higbie).

[22] Ibid. B 23–8. Dedications of the arms of various heroes are mentioned in literary texts, and collected, along with other heroic paraphernalia, by Pfister, *Reliquienkult*, 331–9.

[23] Pherekydes *FGH* 3 F78; *Iliad* 5.638–42, 20.144–7.

[24] Lindos Chronicle B48–53, 54–9 (tr. Higbie).

consequences.[25] Plausibility, charm, an implied narrative, and a certain wry humour come when the next dedication recorded is by Helen, and of a pair of bracelets.[26]

It is impossible to tell from the inscription at what point these doubly virtual relics turn into virtual relics, or even real relics. There is no reason at all to think that the Hellenistic kings whose offerings are recorded in the latter part of the Chronicle did not make those offerings at this sanctuary. Take the final dedication recorded, of arms dedicated by Philip V of Macedon following victory over the Dardanians and Maidoi. Philip V is known to have made dedications both at Delos and at the sanctuary of Zeus at Panamara, and there are no grounds for doubting that this dedication, for which the public records of the Lindians are cited as a source, was really made.[27] But at some point we move from dedications that are still visible, to dedications made by the individuals identified in the circumstances declared but no longer visible, to items no longer visible but that had once become identified with heroic or historical figures although they were not, and in some cases cannot have been, in fact dedicated by those figures on the occasion alleged.

No doubt many of the writers cited by the Lindian Chronicle as sources for particular items got their information from other of the sources it cites (three sources are consistently cited for the same items and in the same order), and not from autopsy in the sanctuary, but there is no single source from which the whole list can have derived.[28] We cannot here be dealing with the creation of a virtual catalogue by a single imaginative writer, whose work has then been latched onto by others. Rather we must be dealing with a tradition at the temple which led to the identification of certain dedications with certain mythical and historical dedicators, and, it appears, to the appending of appropriate dedicatory inscriptions to those items.

Although the Lindian Chronicle is our best evidence for the identification of dedications as relics of either a mythical or a historical past, the practice was widely spread. Herodotos already in the fifth century attests to tripods in the sanctuary of Ismenean Apollo at Thebes which claimed to have been dedicated by Amphitryon, the human father of Herakles, in celebration of his victory over the Teleboae.[29] Pausanias too, more than half a millennium later, came across dedications that claimed to have been made by heroic figures.

[25] Ibid. B62–3.

[26] Ibid. B70–1.

[27] Ibid. B127–31.

[28] See Higbie 188–203. The most frequently cited source, Xenagoras, is cited nineteen times in all, out of the 52 dedications.

[29] Herodotos 5.59; cf. Pausanias 9.10.4.

The dedications by heroic figures recorded by Pausanias include some objects which claimed to have been made by the gods. Of these he is confident about the historicity of only one. This is the sceptre of Agamemnon, which he found being worshipped as a god at Chaironeia in Boiotia.[30] Pausanias gives the pedigree of this sceptre, made by Hephaistos for Zeus who passed it on to Hermes and Hermes to Pelops who gave it to Atreus, from whom, via Thyestes, it came to Agamemnon. He holds that it was Agamemnon's daughter Elektra who brought it to Chaironeia. Pausanias denies, by contrast, on the grounds that bronze-working was a much later invention, that the bronze at Patara in Lykia can have been made by Hephaistos and dedicated by Telephos, and that the necklace at the sanctuary of Adonis and Aphrodite at Amathous in Cyprus was once Eriphyle's and dedicated by Harmonia; and is doubtful about the chest of Eurypylos at Patrai, supposed to be the work of Hephaistos, on the grounds that it is never shown.[31]

Like the Lindian Chronicle, Pausanias is aware that heroic figures belong farther back in time than historical figures, but he otherwise is happy to believe that they inhabited the world in just the way historical figures had done. Not only do they have tombs which can be visited, as Pausanias evidently visited them, and bones which can be viewed, at least if you make enough nuisance of yourself, but objects which they used, even objects which they received from the gods, can in principle still be viewed.[32] The objects used and dedicated by heroes are indistinguishable in kind from the objects used and dedicated by historical figures.[33] The dedicatory inscriptions written upon those objects obey the general conventions of dedicatory inscriptions on other objects.[34]

It is striking, therefore, that the sceptre of Agamemnon and the chest of Eurypylos are treated differently. Neither of these comes into the class of objects commonly dedicated, for all that there are other famous chests (cf. the chest of Kypselos from Olympia) and we know archaeologically of

---

[30] Pausanias 9.40.6–41.2

[31] Curiously there is no trace of this scepticism when the story of the chest is told in the book on Achaia at 7.19.6–10.

[32] Visiting tombs: Pausanias 2.22.2–4; bones to be seen: Pausanias 1.28.7.

[33] 'The objects dedicated run the gamut of what seems to have been customarily given to the gods.' Higbie, *Lindian Chronicle*, 171.

[34] 'the inscriptions quoted by the compilers in the Chronicle would have been plausible to them . . . The inscriptions do not fit particularly neatly into the typologies developed by Raubitschek for the votives from the Athenian acropolis or by Lazzarini in her study of votives, but neither do they vary greatly'. Higbie, *Lindian Chronicle*, 177.

some dedicated sceptres.[35] But it is how they are treated that really marks them out. Agamemnon's sceptre is, Pausanias insists, worshipped as a god. It is not, in fact, in a sanctuary at all, but is kept in the priest's house and receives daily sacrifices in the form of an offering table 'full of every kind of meat and sweet-cake'. Frazer collects all sorts of parallels for the worship of a sceptre or spear worldwide ('The Gonds in India . . . In Samoa . . . In the Arorae or Hurd islands . . . In Aneitum, New Hebrides . . . In ancient Mexico'), and finds parallels also in the claim made by ancient scholia that Kaineus forced people to treat his spear as a god, but this does not alter the fact that the treatment of Agememnon's sceptre at Khaironeia was exceptional.[36] So too the treatment of the chest of Eurypylos. Pausanias knows more than one story about who Eurypylos was and where the chest came from, but those stories concur that the chest functioned as a sort of miniature temple, containing an image of Dionysos that was the work of Hephaistos, that Eurypylos having looked upon this image went mad and was told by the Delphic oracle that he would be healed if he set down the chest where he found people making a strange sacrifice. He came across the people of Patras about to sacrifice a youth and a maiden and sorted out both his madness and the local anomaly. Pausanias then goes on to relate that the god in the chest is named Aisumnetes (= 'arbiter'), and has nine men and nine women specially appointed as his overseers, and that the chest is put outside the temple by the priest on just one occasion during the year. All of this is thoroughly obscure to us, but more than enough to indicate that this is not an ordinary votive object. Objects made by the gods evidently need to be handled with especial care.

Present gods

So far we have been exploring an ancient Greek world full of the remains of a heroic past, in which it was a familiar task set by the Delphic oracle to uncover the remains of that past, and in particular the bones of the heroes. The heroes inhabited a world which was continuous with that of the Greeks themselves, worshipping at the same sanctuaries and making dedications in the same ways, but a world which was also somehow distinct. The heroes themselves were not only better but literally bigger, and they enjoyed closer relations with the gods, receiving material objects from and made by the gods. Gods nevertheless still made their presence directly manifest to the Greeks of the classical period. The Lindian Chronicle concludes with a record not of dedications but

---

[35] Chest of Kypselos: Pausanias 5.17.5–19.10.

[36] J. G. Frazer, *Pausanias's* Description of Greece *translated with a commentary*, 6 vols (London, 1898), 5. 211 (on Pausanias 9.40.11).

of epiphanies, telling of three occasions, the first during the Persian wars, the second perhaps in the fourth century, and the third in 305–4 BC, when Athena had decisively appeared either to the magistrates of Lindos or to her own priest and had given instructions. But material gifts no longer passed from the gods to men on earth.

Greek gods were just like men. Notoriously so, even as far as the Greeks themselves were concerned. They were like men in their appearance, and they were like men in their behaviour. Greek thinkers worried about this. In the fifth century Xenophanes drew attention to the relativism and to the immorality involved; in the fourth century Plato wanted to censor stories in which the gods were presented as behaving badly, or even being swayed by emotion.

One of the most immediate ways in which gods were like humans was that they looked like humans. They were described in human terms in the epic poetry which classical Greeks came to think had given the Greeks an account of how the gods came to be and had defined what the gods were called, what their reputations and means were, and their forms.[37] And they were also present in human shape in temples and sanctuaries. And present in a strong sense. For Greek usage as regularly talked of 'Zeus' being in the temple as they did of 'a statue of Zeus' being in the temple.[38]

A vivid example of this is provided by Pausanias at Olympia. When he describes the temple he first of all describes how, if you ascend into the galleries, you can view the statue; but then, when he turns to the statue itself, he says 'The god is sitting on a throne; he is made of gold and ivory', and continues to describe 'the god' in similar terms.[39] When he describes the dedications in the sanctuary, he starts by singling out the statues of Zeus, beginning with the 'Zanes', the images of Zeus erected as fines for bad behaviour in the Olympic games. He then goes on to other images of Zeus, and once more moves between referring to them as *agalmata* (literally 'things of delight', but which came to mean statues, in particular statues of gods) and simply referring to them as 'Zeus'. 'As you go on Zeus is turned towards the rising sun . . . the Phliasians dedicated Zeus and the daughters of Asopos and Asopos himself; the images are arranged in this way . . . Individual men of Leontinoi erected Zeus not at state expense . . . As you pass by the entrance to

---

[37] Herodotos 2.53.2.

[38] R. L Gordon, 'The Real and the Imaginary: Production and Religion in the Graeco-Roman World', *Art History*, 2 (1979), 5–34 at 9–10. My debt to this classic paper is extensive.

[39] Pausanias 5.10.10–11.1.

the Bouleuterion Zeus stands without an inscription, and again as you turn north there is an *agalma* of Zeus . . . In front of this Zeus is a bronze tablet' and so on.[40]

This usage not only treated statues of gods (*agalmata*) as gods, it treated gods as like men. For the same slippage between reference to statues as 'statue of X' and as 'X' (where X is the name of the man represented) is found in precisely Pausanias' text. 'Ikkos [= Ikkos the man] son of Nikolaidas from Taras gained the Olympic crown in the pentathlon and is said to have been afterwards the best trainer of those of his time. After Ikkos [= statue of Ikkos] stands Pantarkes [= statue of Pantarkes] of Elis, the beloved of Pheidias, who won the boys wrestling. After Pantarkes [= statue of Pantarkes] is the chariot [= statue of the chariot] of Kleosthenes of Epidamnos'.[41]

Not making a distinction between statue and god or statue and man was not simply a trivial matter of verbal convenience, but involved, or at least could involve, a strong sense of identification. This is brought out strongly by a story told by Pausanias about one particularly famous Olympic victor, Theagenes, whose statue at Olympia Pausanias introduces as 'the Thasian Theagenes son of Timosthenes', as if it were the man himself.[42] In this story Theagenes' statue on Thasos is treated as if it were Theagenes himself, being whipped by his enemy and then punished for homicide after it kills the man whipping it by falling upon him. What is more, because that punishment causes Theagenes to be forgotten, and treated like an exile, Thasos suffers, and can only thrive again once the statue is recovered.[43] In a trope that exactly parallels those stories in which oracles command the recovery of bones, here the oracle commands the recovery of the statue. The statue is Theagenes' bones, and it becomes the site of cult. Once it is recovered it is treated no longer as a man but as an object with supernatural powers: sacrifices are

---

[40] Ibid. 5.22.5–23.4.

[41] Ibid. 6.10.5–6.

[42] Ibid. 6.11; the story is also told by Dio Chrysostom 31.95–99 and Eusebios *Praep. Evang.* 5.34 (and cf. Souda s.v. Nikon). For the motif of the statue that punishes see also Aristotle *Poetics* 1460b. Theagenes' story is discussed in S. C. Jones, 'Statues that Kill and the Gods who Love them', in K. J. Hartswick and M. C. Sturgeon (eds), *Stephanos: Studies in Honor of Brunilde Sismondo Ridgway* (Philadelphia, 1998), 139–43.

[43] For the motif of the statue regarded as responsible for causing death compare Pausanias 5.27.10, where the statue in question is the statue of an ox, the Eleans propose to remove it from the sanctuary, and the Delphic oracle says it should remain but be purified as for involuntary homicide.

offered to it as to a god, and just as the powers of a god proliferate so other images of Theagenes are found to have healing powers.[44]

What the story of Theagenes reveals, however, is that just as it requires the act of an oracle to turn bones into bones of a hero, so it requires the pronouncement of an oracle to recognise the power of this statue.[45] The Thasians considered Theagenes' own theft of the statue of a god to be a feat of strength that did not have to be treated as an act of sacrilege, though they do insist on the statue's return. The Thasians also expected that they can remove the statue of Theagenes with impunity. In this case, however, their failure to return the statue proves problematic and they are compelled to recognize the special status of the statue, and thereby the special status of the man, or rather the hero. When the Thasians fail to insist on the statue's return, the gods insist on it. Pausanias highlights Theagenes' ambition to win races in the homeland of Achilles, whom he refers to as 'the fastest runner of those who are called heroes'. The fate of his statue reveals that Theagenes had indeed become a hero. This is a man whose status had to reflect, or be reflected in, divine parentage.

All this helps us to understand why the relics and remains variously celebrated and made objects of cult in the Greek world included only with some difficulty objects made by gods, and included no divine relics or remains. To understand further how the inscrutable power of the gods was at issue here it is useful to look at stories of divine epiphany.

That none of the colossal bones was identified as 'the finger of Zeus', in the way that such bones have been identified as the finger of the Buddha, is not in itself surprising:[46] though we might wonder about the gods of earlier ages of Hesiod's *Theogony*, the Olympian gods had bodies intact. Much more striking, at first sight, is the absence of objects associated with divine epiphanies

---

[44] Those powers are also mentioned by Lucian 52 *Deorum Concilia* 12, where the statue of another remarkable athlete, Polydamas (on whom see Pausanias 6.5) is also said to have healing powers.

[45] A variety of other stories could be told to illustrate the same point. Pliny *Natural History* 36.9–10 (trans. Eichholz) reveals this for statues of the gods: Dipoenus and Scyllis 'made their way to Sicyon, which was for long the motherland of all such industries. The men of Sicyon had given them a contract in the name of the state for making statues of gods; but before these were finished the artists complained that they had been wronged and went away to Aetolia. Sicyon was instantly stricken with famine, barrenness and fearful affliction. When the people begged the oracle for relief, Apollo of Delphi replied that relief would come "if Dipoenus and Scyllis completed the images of the gods". This they were prevailed upon to do thanks to the payment of high fees and high compliments. The statues, incidentally, were those of Apollo, Diana, Hercules and Minerva, the last of which was later struck by lightning'.

[46] For the Buddha's finger cf. http://news.bbc.co.uk/1/hi/world/asia-pacific/1879607.stm

and other divine interventions on earth. Divine epiphanies in the classical period tend to conform to a single model, in which a god stands over a human while the human sleeps. This is true both of the epiphanies related at the end of the Lindian Chronicle and of the epiphanies recorded in the Epidaurian records of Asklepios' healing activities.[47] The material results of these epiphanies are the events that follow or the bodies that are healed. But the epiphanies described in, for example, Homeric epic or the *Homeric Hymns*, involve the gods materializing—whether to take pleasure in mortals, as Aphrodite takes her pleasure of Anchises (and so becomes the mother of Aineias), or to inflict punishment, as Dionysos punishes the sailors who failed to recognize him.[48] Just as Menelaos could be imagined to have taken and dedicated the leather cap of Paris, so we might expect these materializations of the gods to leave disposable body-parts or associated objects to be dedicated. After all, Christ's bodily resurrection and ascension did not prevent objects associated with him—his shroud, his tears, his blood, his foreskin—becoming relics.

But these Greek stories of divine epiphany have another side to them. The appearance of the gods is dangerous. Teiresias is blinded at the sight of Athena, Aktaion torn apart by his own dogs at the sight of Artemis, Anchises threatened with a terrible fate if he ever admits to having had sex with Aphrodite, the sailors turned into dolphins for seeing and failing to recognize Dionysos. Seeing a god's body, a god's real body, has devastating effects. In a story preserved only in Antoninus Liberalis (who cites Boios' *Birth of the Birds* (*Ornithogonia*) as his source) looking upon the swaddling clothes of Zeus causes Laios, Keleus, Kerberos and Aigolios to burst out of their bronze armour and have Zeus turn them into the four varieties of birds named after them, whose appearance, Liberalis claims, is a particularly good sign 'because they saw the blood of Zeus'.[49] Even seeing the body of a statue of one god made by another god drives you mad, as in the case of Eurypylos looking upon the image of Dionysos made by Hephaistos. The message in all these stories is that direct access to the divine is afforded by gods on their own conditions: humans cannot acquire, even accidentally, a true vision of the divine and survive to employ that knowledge.

If we did have an object cast off by a god, it would be too dangerous to handle, would attest too graphically that the god had a body—could move,

---

[47] Lindos Chronicle D14, 68–9, 98–9; P. J. Rhodes and R. Osborne (eds), *Greek Historical Inscriptions 404–323 B.C.* (Oxford, 2003), no. 102.

[48] Homeric Hymns 5, 7. On Homeric epiphanies, and the way in which they fall into no single pattern, see A. D. Stevens, 'Telling Presences: Narrating Divine Epiphany in Homer and Beyond' (University of Cambridge, Ph.D thesis, 2002).

[49] Antoninus Liberalis, *Metamorphoseon Synagoge*, 19.

grip, wear clothes—that had been there. We see this in the closest we come to such objects—the sceptre made by Hephaistos and eventually inherited by Agamemnon and the chest made by Hephaistos and eventually inherited by Eurypylos. These objects are distanced from the gods by the length of their genealogies: the sceptre 'that Homer says Hephaistos made for Zeus, and Zeus gave Hermes; Hermes gave it to Pelops who left it to Atreus; and Atreus left it to Thyestes from whom Agamemnon got it'; the chest comes to Eurypylos having been a gift from Zeus to Dardanos and is then brought from Troy by Eurypylos. Nevertheless, neither sceptre nor chest functions as the objects dedicated by figures from mythology function. Rather they function precisely as do the bones to which men in need of aid are directed by an oracle, and as Theagenes' statue functions once it too has been identified by the oracle as a source of power.

The power and authority of relics and remains

Two important conclusions are to be drawn from this discussion about the presence of the gods in the Greek world. First, gods' presence is both vital and fearful; problematic if encountered unprepared, it needs to be controlled. Second, different representations of the gods render them variously present. If Pheidias' statue at Olympia *is* Zeus and if the various statues erected by athletes and others in the sanctuary are also Zeus, nevertheless to see Pheidias' statue is to have an experience of seeing Zeus that is quite different from seeing Zeus in those other statues, and neither of them can be like seeing Zeus himself. The relationship between image and god depends in part on the impact which the image makes: it was the effect which Pheidias' statue made that set it apart.[50] But it depends also on what the gods declare about it. Theagenes' statue was empowered by the oracular declaration that to rescue it was crucial to Thasos flourishing again.

Representations of the gods not only make the gods differently present, but achieve that presence by different means. The ancient accounts of Pheidias' Zeus at Olympia are obsessed with its appearance and with its size—indeed Pausanias does not give the measurements he has been told because 'they fall a long way short of the impression this statue has created in those who see it'.[51] But it is its effects that reveal the statue of Theagenes to embody the power of a

---

[50] The best evidence for this effect is Dio Chysostom 12, *Olympian Oration*, 50–2.

[51] Pausanias 5.11.9. Strabo mentions that the measurements were given by Kallimakhos in one of his *Iambi*; for a reconstruction of Kallimakhos' *Iambus* 6 see A. Kerkhecker, *Callimachus' Book of* Iambi (Oxford, 1999), 147–81. Note: 'The playful identification of god and statue lies at the heart of *Iambus* VI' (150). Kerkhecker 179 makes the case for Kallimakhos' poem being itself about the impossibility of description of such a

hero. And Pausanias has no sooner appealed to the impression that Zeus makes upon those who view him than he invokes a story of Zeus himself expressly showing that he was pleased with it.[52] It is attractive to read into this story the very way in which the creation of the colossal gold and ivory cult statue in the fifth century attempted to compel such recognition from the gods. If Zeus *had* to thunder at Pheidias' statue then those who could afford gold and ivory, and the skills of a master sculptor, could compel divine presence and take divine authority into their own hands. By contrast, the bones uncovered by Kimon, by Likhas the Spartan, and by the Euboian fisherman Demarmenos, like Theagenes' statue, required recognition by the gods through the oracular pronouncements to acquire supernatural powers.

It is conventional to deny that there was any parallel in the ancient Greek world to the Christian Church: 'There is no church, no organized body persisting through time comprising those with dogmatic authority, able to *define* divinity and rule on what is correct or incorrect in religious belief . . . Greek religion remains fundamentally improvisatory.'[53] Cults were not connected one to another in any way. There were no seminaries for priests, and the rules that applied in one sanctuary were irrelevant in another. The body of myth linked the deities in a network, but that network could always be added to.[54] What a cult could get away with depended only on what it could persuade others about, and the recognition of others' festivals was more a matter of political expediency than shared belief.

What this discussion of relics and remains suggests, however, is that such a view of the ancient Greek world seriously underestimates the importance, and use, of a central religious authority. Individuals, groups and cities could not simply by their own declaration turn the bones they found, or the statue they made, into a source of power. Certainly, they could have a statue of Zeus made and it became Zeus. They could, and from the archaeological

---

statue: 'Callimachus takes a convention, pushes it to its limits, argues its consequences, and exposes its latent absurdities'.

[52] Pausanias 5.11.9.

[53] J. Gould, 'On Making Sense of Greek Religion', in P. Easterling and J. V. Muir (eds), *Greek Religion and Society* (Cambridge, 1985), 1–33, at 7 [repr. in J. Gould, *Myth, Ritual, Memory and Exchange* (Oxford, 2001), 203–34 at 209–10]. This links with two broader claims scholars make: that Greek religion was embedded and that we should not talk of Greek religion but of Greek religions. For the former see J. Bremmer *Greek Religion* (Oxford, 1999), 2–4; for the latter see S. Price, *Religions of the Ancient Greeks* (Cambridge, 1999). For a critique of which embeddedness see B. Nongbri, 'Dislodging "Embedded" Religion: A Brief Note on a Scholarly Trope', *Numen*, 55 (2008), 440–60.

[54] See R. Buxton, *The Complete World of Greek Mythology* (London, 2004).

finds evidently did, dedicate fossil bones as evidence of some vaster beings who needed to be offered recognition.[55] Individuals and groups no doubt experienced the gods in a wide variety of ways, as Homeric epiphany already insists.[56] But for the images or the remains to acquire power demanded that that power be recognized or affirmed from outside. Pausanias dismisses all but one of the objects sanctuaries claimed to have been made by the gods. With luck, or acute hearing, Zeus' thunder might occur at the opportune moment, but in almost all the stories the form that divine approbation or confirmation takes is a Delphic oracle, which either retrospectively recognized an image or object to have already exercised power or prospectively promised that such an image or object would bring power. In ascribing power to images and to things, the oracle no doubt responded to leading questions, but not all such questions had to be answered in the affirmative.[57]

We may or may not have relics surviving in the archaeological record; no real sceptre or chest has ever been identified as made by Hephaistos, no bones as those of Theseus. We simply do not know what associations the massive bones dedicated in the sanctuary of Hera at Samos acquired.[58] But what we *can* discover is the discourse of relics. That discourse reveals that in the Greek world the negotiation of the intersection of the supernatural world with the material world was every bit as complex as it would be in Christian tradition. That intersection was explored through the material remains of heroes, the objects associated with heroes and gods, and the embodiment of gods in images, both concrete and epiphanic. Images, objects, and bones were all potential sources of a supernatural power which there was a desire both to access and to control. Access and control alike were necessary because the power was real: what the gods did mattered. But for that very reason control was of greater importance than power. However much claims about relics may seem to serve primarily political ends, the Delphic oracle acquired so overwhelming a monopoly on the authorization of relics and remains because when it came to relations with divine power no one was prepared to risk getting it wrong.

---

[55] On actual bone dedications see Mayor, *First Fossil-Hunters*, 180–91.

[56] Stevens, 'Telling Presences', is fundamental here.

[57] For recent debate about the Delphic oracle and its role, see H. Bowden, *Classical Athens and the Delphic Oracle: Divination and Democracy* (Cambridge, 2005), 154–7; R. Osborne, *Greece in the Making 1200–479 BC*, 2nd edn (London, 2009), 332–4.

[58] H. Kyrieleis 'Offerings of the "common man" in the Heraion of Samos', in R. Hägg, N. Marinatos, and G. Nordquist (eds), *Early Greek Cult Practice* (Stockholm, 1988), 215–21, at 220–1.

Rulers and Relics c.750-c.950: Treasure on Earth, Treasure in Heaven*

Julia M. H. Smith

'Long ago', it was said, 'most trustworthy men' told the story of a visit to Exeter by King Æthelstan (924–939). While he was there, 'he began to ponder and think about how it might be best for him to use his royal treasures for the glory for God, and for himself, and for the eternal benefit of his people'. The 'good king' received a divine command *þæt he mid þam gewytendlicum madmum, þa unateoridenlican madmas begitan sceolde*—that he should use his 'transitory treasures' to obtain 'everlasting ones'. So he sent trusted and discerning men abroad, who travelled as far and as wide as they could, using the king's riches to secure 'the most precious treasures which could ever be purchased on this earth, which was the greatest of relic collections'. The tale went on to explain how, in generosity to the city where the divine inspiration came to him, Æthelstan subsequently endowed the church he had built there with one third of his relic collection.[1]

Æthelstan did indeed visit Exeter on several occasions, though in its written form, the narrative survives from more than a century after the purported events.[2] It prefaces a list of the 138 relics of Christ and his saints which the

* I am grateful to participants at the conference at which this volume originated for helpful suggestions which did much to improve the first version of this paper. I would also like to thank audiences in Princeton and Chicago for their responses to intermediate versions. Special thanks go to Simon MacLean and Peter Brown for generous help and detailed comments on the draft.

[1] Preamble to the Old English version of the Exeter relic list, ed. Max Förster in *Zur Geschichte des Reliquienkultus in Altengland*, Sitzungsberichte der Bayerischen Akademie der Wissenschaften, Philosophisch-historische Abteilung, Jahrgang 1943 Heft 8 (Munich, 1943), 63–8. Patrick W. Conner, *Anglo-Saxon Exeter: A Tenth-century Cultural History* (Woodbridge, 1993), 176–87, also provides an edition with translation. William of Malmesbury preserves a variant version of the story, *Gesta regum anglorum*, II.140, ed. and trans. R. A. B. Mynors, R. M. Thomson, and M. Winterbottom, 2 vols (Oxford, 1998–9), I.228.

[2] N. R. Ker, *Catalogue of Manuscripts Containing Anglo-Saxon* (Oxford, 1957), nos. 291 and 351. Recorded visits of Æthelstan and his retinue to Exeter occurred at Easter 928, at

impoverished church of Exeter claimed already to possess when promoted to episcopal status in 1050, and serves as its origin legend. Its blunt prose neatly encapsulates the main themes to be explored here: the eagerness of rulers to amass relics and their impulse to distribute them in pious generosity; the role of relics in mediating distinct value systems; and the added value provided by the stories which adhered to these relics in later times. The question of whether Æthelstan might actually have donated relics to Exeter will be addressed towards the end of the discussion.[3]

In his avidity to accumulate relics, Æthelstan conformed to a model of piety already many centuries old. The role of relics in Christianity had twin roots in the material memorialization of martyrs and in pilgrim mementoes fetched back from the Holy Land. Whereas the latter confirmed the earthly reality of Christ's life and the story of his redemptive death, the former offered tangible pledges of the eternal reality that awaited believers. Moreover, in Late Antiquity, there had gradually emerged the normative medieval theology of relics—that of *pars pro toto*: a tiny fraction of a fragmented body was as holy and as potent as the complete, undivided body. This was combined with an affirmation that saints remained whole and entire in their corporeal identities, however fragmented their physical remains might become. Also, by a process of 'holy contagion', the sanctity of saints' bodies could be transferred to associated objects—items of clothing, dust from the grave, and the like. All this was becoming common practice by the end of the fourth century, and collections of tangible tokens of saintly identity survive from *c*.600 onwards. By the eighth century, relic collections consisted of dozens of tiny fragments which encapsulated Christian history from the time of Moses to the present, linking each locality into the universal narrative. By the ninth century, they might number over one hundred items, and by the end of the Middle Ages could total many thousands, as the impulse to collect escalated still further.[4]

'midwinter' (Christmas? Epiphany?) in *c*.929, and on 9 November 932. Anglo-Saxon Charters: The Electronic Sawyer, http://www.trin.cam.ac.uk/sdk13/chartwww/eSawyer .99/S%20386-458.html [accessed 11 Dec. 2009], S399, S400, S418a; Felix Liebermann, *Die Gesetze der Angelsachsen*, 3 vols (Halle, 1903–16), I.166 for the issuing of Æthelstan's fifth lawcode *æt Eaxanceastre to middanwintre*, with a date of *c*.929 proposed at III.108. For the suggestion that a deliberate decision to collect relics was made in 928–930, see Michael Wood, ' "Stand strong against the monsters": Kingship and Learning in the Empire of King Æthelstan', in Patrick Wormald and Janet L. Nelson (eds), *Lay Intellectuals in the Carolingian World* (Cambridge, 2007), 192–217, at 202.

[3] Below, 90–1.

[4] The best account of the early history of relic cults remains H. Leclercq, 'Reliques et reliquaires', in. Fernand Cabrol and Henri Leclercq (eds), *Dictionnaire d'archéologie*

Neither metonymy nor synechdoche captures their full significance, however. A relic, as Annabel Wharton has remarked, 'is the remnant of a history that is threatened by forgetting'. She continues: 'It records duration and postpones oblivion. It offers reassurance that the past retains its authority. It collapses time. A relic is a sign of previous power, real or imagined. It promises to put that power back to work. A relic is a fragment that evokes a lost fullness. It is a part that allows the embrace of an absent whole. It is the living piece of a dead object [or person]. It is an intensely material sign entangled in a spiritual significance.'[5] Although that spiritual significance was fixed and unambiguous, this essay argues that it might combine with political and historical meanings which shifted with time and circumstance. In effect, a relic was a materialization of complex abstractions, an inert fragment equally suggestive of cosmological entirety and historical circumstance.

More than that, a relic was a small object fashioned from common substances such as dust, oil, stone, cloth, or bone, a tiny thing which bore negligible or no economic value in its own right.[6] With the exception of one particular item to be discussed below which, by any standard of assessment, was an object of inherent material value, almost all medieval relics acquired 'costliness' through the casings in which they were presented: precious silk wrappings and embroidered purses, reliquaries of ivory, gold, crystal, and gemstones, skilfully fashioned by the best craftsmen of the day. These wrappings and containers could be changed or discarded at will; small reliquaries could be places inside larger, more ornate ones.[7] Wrapped or unwrapped,

---

chrétienne et de liturgie (1948), XIV. ii. cols. 2294–2359. See also Joseph Braun, *Die Reliquiare des christlichen Kultes und ihre Entwicklung* (Freiburg, 1940); Arnold Angenendt, *Heilige und Reliquien: die Geschichte ihres Kultes vom frühen Christentum bis zur Gegenwart* (Munich, 1994); Anton Legner, *Reliquien in Kunst und Kult: zwischen Antike und Aufklärung* (Darmstadt, 1995).

[5] Annabel Wharton, *Selling Jerusalem: Relics, Replicas, Theme Parks* (Chicago, 2006), 9–10. As the following pages will make clear, I cannot fully agree with the final two sentences of her definition, that 'A relic avoids intrinsically valuable materials. It works in part through the uniqueness of its survival'.

[6] For a discussion of relics within frameworks of economic exchange, see Patrick Geary, 'Sacred Commodities: The Circulation of Medieval Relics', in Arjun Appadurai (ed.), *The Social Life of Things: Commodities in Cultural Perspective* (Cambridge, 1986), 169–91, with the comments of Appadurai, in ibid. 23–4.

[7] Exemplified by the early medieval relics enclosed within many small containers inside the reliquary-altar of the Sancta Sanctorum in the Lateran Palace: see Bruno Galland, *Les Authentiques de reliques du Sancta Sanctorum*, Studi e Testi, 421 (Vatican City, 2004), 27–31.

relics were also placed inside altars where, concealed within the stonework, they remained an invisible presence. Even when relics were enshrined within a reliquary, only on very rare occasions prior to *c*.1200 could they be seen directly by the viewer, who saw generally only the valuable trappings, not the modest objects themselves.[8] If relics' spiritual meaning was mediated by the containers which enclosed them, their concealment transformed them into objects of great material worth, rendering the valueless invaluable.

In essence, then, Christian relics were paltry remains endowed with an abundance of values and meanings. Relics, I contend, stood at the intersection of several different medieval discourses of value—material, spiritual, political, historical—but not all these need be active simultaneously. As will be seen, they fluctuated between one discourse and another, for a change of ownership superimposed a new story and a revised value on older ones; new shrines concealed older wrappings; and earlier significances lapsed into oblivion. Only the underlying premise that these earthly tokens were pledges of eternal life remained unaffected.

This paper proposes that relics which passed through royal hands evinced an unusual, indeed exceptional, ability to transform one kind of value into another.[9] According to the anonymous eleventh-century author, Æthelstan had turned 'transitory treasure' into 'everlasting treasure' by acquiring relics; in effect, he converted economic capital into symbolic capital.[10] In view of the various possible components of that symbolic value, royal possession greatly enhanced the potential for a political or commemorative 'charge' to overlay relics' inherent spiritual value; it also increased the likelihood that these mean fragments might be enclosed in new, sumptuous wrappings and display containers. An 'inter-convertability' of valencies thus marked relics as a special type of royal treasure.

From the middle of the fourth century onwards, Christian emperors are known to have associated themselves with the cults of Christ and his martyrs, above all by gathering their relics together in Constantinople. In the early medieval Christian West, by contrast, references to royal interest in relics are

---

[8] Braun, *Reliquiare*, 100, notes the rarity of crystal reliquaries prior to the thirteenth century. Cf. Christof L. Diedrichs, *Vom Glauben zum Sehen. Die Sichtbarkeit der Reliquie im Reliquiar. Ein Beitrag zur Geschichte des Sehens* (Berlin, 2001).

[9] This approach adapts ideas from Arjun Appadurai, 'Introduction: Commodities and the Politics of Value' in Arjun Appadurai (ed.), *The Social Life of Things*, 3–63; David Graeber, *Toward an Anthropological Theory of Value: The False Coin of our Own Dreams* (New York, 2001).

[10] Cf. Pierre Bourdieu, *Outline of a Theory of Practice*, trans. Richard Nice (Cambridge, 1977).

inadequate to build a coherent picture prior to *c.*750. Although the evidence for the following two centuries remains fragmentary and frequently oblique, there is nevertheless a sufficient, if gradual, increase in both type and quantity for some clear trends to be discerned. In confining itself to the centuries from *c.*750 to *c.*950, this paper stops on the cusp of the sharp upturn both in the textual documentation of relic cults which marks the high Middle Ages, and in the survival of reliquaries themselves.[11]

The deficiencies in evidence are offset by the political coherence of the period under review. It was characterized by political systems which were simultaneously immensely powerful and potentially fragile, for although this was an age of dynastic monarchy, there were no agreed rules of succession: royal power was usually contested between the males of a ruling family but, in exceptional circumstances, outsiders might challenge for the throne. It also witnessed the spread of potent forms of Christian sacralization which strengthened kings' position with the sanction of ritual anointing, yet could not eliminate the insecurity of a disputed succession or failed blood line.[12] It remains to be seen how relics of Christ and his saints could offer a sacral 'plus factor' both in times of acknowledged hegemony and during dynastic conflict. It will emerge that their ability to function as political capital depended on place, time and context, but that they could easily lose that value as circumstances changed. The ease with which relics could transform one type of capital into another depended on the convergence of sacred material with contingent situation.

Let us consider that conjunction in the context of the life-cycle of the Carolingian dynasty, from insecure origins, through the peak of empire, to challenge, decline, and failure. In 751, Pippin the Short had dislodged the Merovingian dynasty that had ruled Frankish Gaul since the end of the fifth century, but his audacious coup was not the effortless, inevitable démarche which Charlemagne's biographer Einhard would have us believe. Rather, his

---

[11] Overviews: Martin Heinzelmann, *Translationsberichte und andere Quellen des Reliquienkultes*, Typologie des sources du moyen âge occidental, 33 (Turnhout, 1979); Percy Ernst Schramm and Florentine Mütherich, *Denkmale der deutschen Könige und Kaiser, 1: Ein Beitrag zur Herrschergeschichte von Karl dem Grossen bis Friedrich II. 768–1250*, 2nd edn (Munich, 1981); Matthias Hardt, *Gold und Herrschaft. Die Schätze europäischer Könige und Fürsten im ersten Jahrtausend*, Europa im Mittelalter, 9 (Berlin, 2004); Edina Bozóky, *La Politique des reliques de Constantin à Saint Louis: protection collective et légitimation du pouvoir* (Paris, 2006).

[12] Surveyed by Janet L. Nelson, 'Kingship and Royal Government', in Rosamond McKitterick (ed.), *The New Cambridge Medieval History, II: c.700–c.900* (Cambridge, 1995), 383–430; and Julia M. H. Smith, *Europe after Rome: A New Cultural History 500–1000* (Oxford, 2005), 239–52.

reign was dominated by the hard work of countering opposition from aristocratic rivals, neighbouring princes and, notably, from within his own family.[13] In effect, Pippin had to build both a kingdom and a dynasty. To this end, it is well known that he took the novel step of invoking the sacrality of ecclesiastical anointing for himself, his wife Bertrada and his two young sons Charles (the future Charlemagne) and Carloman.[14] His reliance on saints' relics as a supplementary means of divine support deserves comparable attention, for the sacralization of his lineage was not achieved by anointing alone.

In the early years of his reign he tightly bound Bertrada, Charles, and Carloman to carefully chosen saints of the distant Frankish past: Denis and Martin—with both of whom his Merovingian predecessors had been closely associated—and also Germanus of Paris.[15] As mayors of the palace, Pippin's ancestors had already managed to wrest from the Merovingians guardianship of the *cappa*, the cloak of St Martin of Tours, a relic so symbolic that it gave its name to the clergy who cared for it—and thence to the sacral centre of the palace, the chapel.[16] Alongside Martin, the support of the Gallic martyr Denis mattered equally: in 754, Pippin selected his grave as the site at which Stephen II would sacralize his lineage by anointing the new king, his wife, and young sons.[17] A year or so later, in 755 or thereabouts, he and his sons personally

---

[13] Matthias Becher and Jörg Jarnut (eds), *Der Dynastiewechsel von 751: Vorgeschichte, Legitimationsstrategie und Erinnerung* (Münster, 2004).

[14] That Pippin III and his family were consecrated by Pope Stephen II in 754 is universally accepted; whether he was anointed by Frankish bishops immediately upon seizing power in 751 is contested. Rosamond McKitterick, *History and Memory in the Carolingian World* (Cambridge, 2004), 133–55; cf. Janet L. Nelson, 'Charlemagne the Man', in Joanna Story (ed.), *Charlemagne: Empire and Society* (Manchester, 2005), 22–37, esp. 24–5; repr. in Janet L. Nelson, *Courts, Elites and Gendered Power in the Early Middle Ages: Charlemagne and Others* (Aldershot, 2007), ch. XVI.

[15] Cf. Olivier Guillot, 'Les saints des peuples et des nations dans l'Occident des VIe-Xe siècles', in *Santi e demoni nell'alto medioevo occidentale*, 2 vols (Spoleto, 1989) (Settimane di studio dell'Centro italiano di studi sull'alto medioevo, 36), I.205–51, esp. 223–9, 232–45. Major contrasts between later Merovingian and Carolingian interactions between kings and cults are identified by Paul Fouracre, 'The Origins of the Carolingian Attempt to Regulate the Cult of Saints', in James Howard-Johnston and Paul Antony Hayward (eds), *The Cult of Saints in Late Antiquity and the Middle Ages: Essays on the Contribution of Peter Brown* (Oxford, 1999), 143–65.

[16] Josef Fleckenstein, *Die Hofkapelle der deutschen Könige*, 2 vols, MGH Schriften XVI (Stuttgart, 1959–66), I.11–15.

[17] *Le Liber Pontificalis: texte, introduction et commentaire*, ed. Louis Duchesne, 3 vols (Paris, 1955–57), I.448.

supervised the translation and elevation of the remains of St Germanus at his resting place at Saint-Germain-des-Prés, notable as the occasion on which the young lad Charles lost his first milk tooth when he jumped into the open grave.[18] A retrospective and self-serving narrative composed during the reign of Charlemagne has the relics of all three saints, Denis, Germanus, and Martin fulfil another vital role in further strengthening the fragile new dynasty in 757.[19] It was alleged that Pippin's nephew and arch-rival, Tassilo duke of Bavaria, had sworn an oath of loyalty on these holy remains to the new Carolingian king and his sons in that year, an oath whose repudiation in 763 led, finally, to Tassilo's deposition and imprisonment in 788. However specious the narrative may be, the writer's choice of relics at this juncture cannot have been haphazard: the very least we can say is that, from the perspective of Charlemagne's propagandists, these three saints were assigned an iconic status in aiding the new king and his sons at a crucial moment in consolidating their lineage.

A few years later, in 762, Pippin returned north after an overwhelming victory over the Aquitanians, and celebrated his newly secured power by joining Bertrada in refounding her family monastery at Prüm, in the Ardennes, and together they issued a grandiose diploma.[20] Its vital clues to the key role of Bertrada and the female line in dynastic formation, its adumbration of a cogent new vision of Christian rulership and its contribution to shaping family memory via post-mortem liturgical commemoration have attracted much comment, but not its significance in reinforcing the bonds between Pippin's preferred saints and his family.[21] Now Prüm was dedicated

---

[18] *Translatio Sancti Germani*, chs 2–6, MGH SS XV, I.5–8. Both boys were explicitly present but Bertrada's whereabouts is unknown; perhaps the boys frisked around in her absence. The reliability of this account is assessed by Nelson, 'Charlemagne the Man', 24–8.

[19] *Annales regni francorum*, a. 757, ed. Friedrich Kurze, MGH SSRM, 6, 14–16. On the *ex post facto* narrative of Tassilo's treachery, see Matthias Becher, *Eid und Herrschaft: Untersuchungen zum Herrscherethos Karls des Grossen* (Sigmaringen, 1993); also Stuart Airlie, 'Narratives of Triumph and Rituals of Submission: Charlemagne's Mastering of Bavaria', *Transactions of the Royal Historical Society*, 6th ser, 9 (1999), 93–119.

[20] MGH Diplomata Karolinorum I, no. 16, 21–5, interpreted as a victory offering by Karl Hauck, 'Von einer spätantiken Randkultur zum karolingischen Europa', *Frühmittelalterliche Studien*, 1 (1967), 3–93, at 89.

[21] Of the extensive literature on this diploma, see Herbert Zielinski, 'Die Kloster- und Kirchengründungen der Karolinger', in Irene Crusius (ed.), *Beiträge zu Geschichte der mittelalterlichen Germania Sacra* (Göttingen, 1989), 95–134, esp. 99, 102–9; Janet L. Nelson, 'Bertrada', in *Der Dynastiewechsel*, 93–108 (repr. in her *Courts, Elites and Gendered Power*, ch. IX); Brigitte Merta, 'Politische Theorie in den Königsurkunden Pippins I.', *Mitteilungen der Österreichischen Instituts für Geschichtsforschung*, 100

to Christ the Saviour, *Sanctus Salvator*, and to his mother Mary, so it was fitting that among Pippin's rich gifts to the house were the Sandals of Christ, together with unspecified relics of the Virgin. By including Germanus, Denis, and Martin among the selected saints with whose relics Pippin and Bertrada endowed Prüm, the royal couple consolidated the importance of their favoured patrons as guarantors of future dynastic power as well as the intercessors for the souls of its deceased members.[22] Gifts of relics were reciprocated by prayer for ruler, family and realm: they were the tangible tokens of invisible bonds between the earthly and the heavenly king. Saints' relics, then, were as central to Pippin's dynasty-building as was anointing. Both contributed to setting his lineage apart from relatives and rivals—and established a precedent to which subsequent generations responded.

Pippin, it seems, by no means gave all his relics to Prüm, for, on the testimony of Angilbert of Saint-Riquier (d. 814), Charlemagne inherited a royal assemblage of holy remains.[23] He certainly supplemented it, however. In building an empire that was effectively coterminous with Roman Christianity on mainland Europe, and engaging in diplomatic negotiations as far afield as Constantinople, Baghdad, and Jerusalem, Charlemagne was the nodal point in a vast network of political communication: diplomatic gifts and courtiers' contacts throughout and far beyond his realms swelled whatever relic collection he had inherited, although details of its contents and manner of safe-keeping elude us.[24] Perhaps, like King Alfred of Wessex (871–99), Charlemagne kept part or all of his holy treasure hoard with him wherever he went, sacralizing his presence, whether in stone palace or military tent.[25]

(1992), 117–31; W. E. Wagner, 'Zum Abtswahlprivileg König Pippins für das Kloster Prüm von 762', *Deutsches Archiv für die Erforschung des Mittelalters*, 57 (2001), 149–56.

[22] MGH Diplomata Karolinorum I, no. 16, 22, lines 33–40. On the liturgical significance of this passage, see Giselbert Knopp, '*Sanctorum nomina seriatim*. Die Anfänge der Allerheiligenlitanei und ihre Verbindung mit den "laudes regiae"', *Römische Quartalschrift*, 65 (1970), 185–231, at 209–10.

[23] *De ecclesia Centulensi libellus*, ch. 2, MGH SS XV, I.176.

[24] For specific examples of diplomatic gifts, see below, 82–3. The reconstitution of the collection proposed by Heinrich Schiffers, *Der Reliquienschatz Karls des Grossen und die Anfänge der Aachenfahrt* (Aachen, 1951) is over-enthusiastic and implausible.

[25] *Asser's Life of King Alfred*, ch. 104, ed. W. H. Stevenson (Oxford, 1904), 90. Alfred's chaplains burned specially designed candles *per viginti quattuor horas die nocteque sine defectu coram sanctis multorum electorum Dei reliquiis quae semper eum ubique comitabantur*. See also Fleckenstein, *Die Hofkapelle*, I.14–18. Ludwig Falkenstein argued

Three-quarters of a century later, his grandson Charles the Bald (840–877) believed that Charlemagne had maintained his relics safely in the palatine chapel at Aachen, and that the collection was 'massive'.[26] But he was looking back to the heyday of empire from a changed world. In the closing decades of the ninth century, rivalry between Charlemagne's grandsons and great-grandsons for the imperial title and for control of Aachen crystallized deeper struggles for supporters, resources, and legitimacy: amidst such an intense competition for power, prestigious relics—especially those associated with Charlemagne—became tinged with associative significance. In founding his own imperial chapel at Compiègne in 877, Charles the Bald made his emulation of Aachen explicit, and in endowing it with the relics of Cornelius referenced a martyr enshrined in the imperial model monastery of Inden, near Aachen.[27] A few years later, in 881, when the monks of nearby Stavelot-Malmédy had managed to rescue Aachen's relics as Viking raiders descended on the imperial chapel, Charles the Fat (880–87) rewarded the monks generously for having forwarded the *pignora sanctorum* to him in Alemannia.[28] These rescued treasures may have been among the relics which he subsequently placed in a 'shrine of solid gold made in the shape of a chapel, royally studded with gems and filled with the greatest relics, the like of which we had never seen'.[29] Simon MacLean has proposed that this reliquary was intended as 'a miniature substitute Aachen, quite literally Carolingian legitimacy in a box': container and contents together strengthened Charles the Fat's association with the great-grandfather whose name he bore and whose empire he strove to reconstitute.[30] By the late ninth century, these relics had become so redolent of empire and, specifically, of Charlemagne, that their move effected a *translatio imperii*. Portability, sacrality, and legitimacy mutually reinforced each other.

---

vigorously that Charlemagne's relic collection was not, in his lifetime, kept at Aachen: *Karl der Grosse und die Entstehung des Aachener Marienstiftes* (Paderborn, 1981), 90–4.

[26] *Congerie quamplurima reliquiarum eundem locum sacrasse . . . dinoscitur.* Georges Tessier, *Recueil des actes de Charles II le Chauve*, 3 vols (Paris, 1943–55), no. 425, II.451.

[27] Janet L. Nelson, *Charles the Bald* (London, 1992), 235, 247; Falkenstein, *Karl der Grosse*, 34 n8; Matthew Zimmern, 'Hagiography and the Cult of Saints in the Diocese of Liège, *c.*700–980', unpublished PhD thesis, (University of St Andrews, 2007), 97–8 on the relics of St Cornelius.

[28] Zimmern, 'Hagiography', 196–8; Simon MacLean, *Kingship and Politics in the Late Ninth Century: Charles the Fat and the End of the Carolingian Empire* (Cambridge, 2003), 156–8.

[29] Ekkehard, *Casus Sancti Galli* ch. 10, ed. Hans Haefele in *Sankt Galler Klostergeschichten* (Darmstadt, 1980), 34.

[30] MacLean, *Kingship and Politics*, 157.

In the tenth century, with the political symbolism of relics now well established, another king-turned-emperor emulated the link between relics and empire with skill and determination. Otto I (936–73) pushed much further a strategy of relic accumulation begun by his father, the Saxon Henry I (918–36), and seized every possible opportunity to amass his own collection. As his political reach grew beyond that of his father, so he exploited familial and diplomatic links as much as military success to create an assemblage which epitomized his hegemony on both sides of the Alps and across the Rhine. His demands for relics could not be ignored by churches in northeastern France, Lotharingia, Burgundy and later Italy; the chief beneficiary was his personal dynastic foundation established in 937 at Magdeburg, which he elevated into an archiepiscopal see in 968.[31] As at Pippin III's Prüm, familial commemoration and privileged saintly remains buttressed an insecure dynasty, and the redistribution of some of these relics around other imperial churches helped sustain an empire of saintly alliance and prayer. But above all, Otto's determined extortion of relics showed up his devotion to the saints for what it was: the aggressive creation of empire by the accumulation of symbolic capital.[32]

The relics which rulers exchanged as diplomatic gifts were unlikely to have been exclusively the unprepossessing fragments of cloth, bone, dust, and soil wrapped in linen or silk which undoubtedly comprised a significant proportion of any royal collection. In addition, we should pay attention to prestige items—grand visual statements of ostentatious wealth and piety. Moreover, such objects had a pedigree of ownership which added another layer of historical value to their possession, just as the names of prior heroes (real or legendary) added extra value to aristocratic weapons.[33] When given as gifts, relics of this sort enhanced the status of donor and recipient alike, and caught the attention of chroniclers and annalists in a way which handfuls of dust and shards of bone never could. Examples in this category include the relics of the

---

[31] Gottfried Wentz and Berent Schwineköper, *Das Erzbistum Magdeburg.* I pt i, *Das Domstift St. Moritz in Magdeburg* (Berlin, 1972), 82–96, 216–18.

[32] As argued by Jörg Oberste, 'Heilige und ihre Reliquien in der politischen Kultur der früheren Ottonenzeit', *Frühmittelalterliche Studien*, 37 (2003), 73–98.

[33] For a superb example of a relic whose value was enhanced by its pedigree of ownership, see Karl Leyser, 'Frederick Barbarossa, Henry II and the hand of St James', *English Historical Review*, 90 (1975), 481–506; cf. Régine Le Jan, 'Frankish Giving of Arms and Rituals of Power: Continuity and Change in the Carolingian Period', in Frans Theuws and Janet L. Nelson (eds), *Rituals of Power from Late Antiquity to the Early Middle Ages* (Leiden, 2000), 281–309, at 286; Heinrich Härke, 'The Circulation of Weapons in Anglo-Saxon Society', in ibid., 377–99, at 383–6.

Holy Sepulchre which the Patriarch of Jerusalem sent to Charlemagne in 799; the 'crystal of amazing size in a setting of gold and precious gems with a large piece of the True Cross [inside it]' which the Byzantine emperor Basil I sent to Louis the German in 872; and the gold and jewelled chapel-shaped reliquary which had belonged to Charles the Fat before passing to King Arnulf, who then gave it to the monastery of Sankt Gallen at the very end of the ninth century.[34] These were objects where precious materials and superb crafts-manship transformed fragments of bone, stone, or wood into works of art of great rarity and wonder.

The True Cross was believed to have been discovered by Helena, mother of the first Christian Roman emperor, Constantine, and sent to him as a symbol of his authority.[35] For this reason, relics of the True Cross had a dual religious and historical potency which set them in a class apart, as signifiers of imperial and regal legitimacy as well as of redemption. Claims to possess particles of its wood occur from the later fourth century onwards, but from the sixth century, their circulation in the West commonly began as gifts from popes or Byzantine emperors.[36] In Carolingian ownership, however, they quickly came to the fore as markers of dynastic succession. Indeed, the more the succession to the throne became contested, the more these relics conferred legitimacy. Louis the Pious seems to have given each of his heirs a piece of the True Cross encased in a grand liturgical cross whose function as regalia as much as relic Louis the German certainly exploited to the full.[37] In his turn, Louis the German's heir Charles the Fat evidently accumulated several such fragments; when faced with the prospect of a coup led by his nephew Arnulf of Carinthia in November 887, he sent the latter 'the wood of the holy cross on which he [Arnulf] had earlier sworn that he would keep his faith' with a plea 'not to act in such a ferocious and barbarian manner' against his uncle. On seeing the Cross, Arnulf wept—but refused to be deflected.[38] When the political stakes were so high, as they were that autumn, all legitimacy and authority came to reside in that tiny piece of wood.

---

[34] *Annales regni francorum*, a.799, ed. Kurze, 108; *Annales Fuldenses*, a.872, ed. Friedrich Kurze, MGH SSRG, 7, 75; Ekkehard of Sankt-Gallen, as note 29 above.

[35] Jan Willem Drijvers, *Helena Augusta: The Mother of Constantine the Great and the Legend of her Finding of the True Cross* (Leiden, 1992).

[36] Anatole Frolow, *La Relique de la Vraie Croix: recherches sur le développement d'un culte* (Paris, 1961).

[37] As argued by Eric Goldberg, ' "More devoted to battle than the splendor of banquets": Frontier Kingship, Martial Ritual, and Early Knighthood at the Court of Louis the German', *Viator*, 30 (1999), 41–78, at 61–2.

[38] *Annales Fuldenses*, a. 887, 106, with the comments of Goldberg, op. cit., 72–3.

Fragments of the True Cross sometimes occurred in conjunction with another group of relics which blurred, indeed collapsed, any distinction between religious and political symbolism which sceptics might be tempted to draw. These were trophy objects imbued with a sacred past that presented them as relics of key actors in Christian history. One such was the crown of gold and gems 'which had formerly belonged to the Emperor Constantine', brought from Rome to Rheims in 816 by Pope Stephen IV; another was the 'sword of St Peter' which Charles the Bald sent from his deathbed in 877 to his heir Louis the Stammerer as a token of the transfer of regality.[39] The lance which 'they claim . . . belonged to Constantine the Great, son of St Helena, the discoverer of the life-giving cross' was the most famous of all these. The Burgundian king Rudolf II had acquired it in Italy, but Henry I, that 'lover of all things religious', seized it in 926. The centre of its blade had been excised, and in its place were mounted 'crosses made from the nails driven through the hands and feet of our Lord and Redeemer Jesus Christ'.[40] There is a consensus that this description refers to the so-called Holy Lance still extant in Vienna. This is, in fact, a well-known type of eighth-century lance blade, which may well originally have been a mount for a pennant, and which shows no sign of use in battle. Furthermore, the piece of iron mounted inside the blade is utterly unlike a nail and instead resembles a shield grip.[41] Like any Carolingian iron weapon, it was a costly example of the smith's craft, but it was unique in the way its origin legend and pedigree of ownership imbued it with superabundant layers of meaning.

Rulers amassed relics not only to harness their sacred energy for personal advantage and manifest piety, but also to be liberal in their gift-giving. Recipients occasionally identified relics by donor or origin: Sens cathedral, for example, possessed relics of St Peter which were labelled as coming *de palatio*, and at some point acquired a bundle of relics of Christ and many

---

[39] Ermoldus Nigellus, *In honorem Hludovici*, lines 1076–7, ed. Edmond Faral in *Poème sur Louis le Pieux* (Paris, 1932), 84; *Annales de Saint-Bertin*, a. 877, eds. Félix Grat, Jeanne Vielliard and Suzanne Clémencet (Paris, 1964), 218–19.

[40] Liudprand, *Antapodosis*, IV.25, ed. Joseph Becker in *Die Werke Liudprands von Cremona*, MGH SSRG 41, 118–19. English translation by Paolo Squatriti, *The Complete Works of Liudprand of Cremona* (Washington DC, 2007), 158.

[41] Liudprand, ibid., for a description of how it looked in the early tenth century; for its later refashionings and for a detailed scientific analysis, see Erik Szameit, 'Die Heilige Lanze der Wiener Schatzkammer. Bemerkungen zu Form und Verwendung von Flügellanzen aus dem Blickwinkel der Archäologie und der Waffenkunde', in Franz Kirchweger (ed.), *Die Heilige Lanze im Wien. Insignie—Reliquie—"Schicksalspeer"* (Vienna, 2005), 145–67. Franz Kirchweger, 'Die Forschung zur Heilige Lanze', in ibid., 11–21, reviews the vast and contentious scholarly literature concerning this relic.

saints whose origin was betrayed by the royal seal listed amongst its contents.[42] Such scraps of information are rare, however, and the little we know about Charlemagne's relic collection derives from the testimony of Angilbert, courtier, networker, builder, bureaucrat, and live-in lover of the emperor's daughter Bertha. In inventorying the relics which he lodged in his abbey at Saint-Riquier (173 named, plus uncounted unidentifiable ones), Angilbert claimed that he had exploited the emperor's web of diplomatic contacts to build his own collection, but that its single greatest source was Charlemagne himself, who, he insisted, had allowed his son-in-law to take a 'piece' of every relic in the *sacrum palatium*, the 'sacred palace'.[43] As with Pippin III's donations to Prüm, the transfer of relics to Saint-Riquier bound family, courtiers, and monasteries into both political alliance and, in retrospect, commemorative association.

Gifts such as these epitomized Carolingian court culture.[44] On the one hand, the conflation of religious and secular authority lent a sacral quality to the palace, while its political centrality ensured its status as a privileged site of memory at the heart of a network of royal residences. On the other hand, that idealized authority was made real by the palace's ability to suck in career officials and grandees, authoritative texts and precious books, resources and gifts of all forms, and then, by arterial circulation, to redistribute them around the empire. This ebb and flow was the lifeblood of the Carolingian empire: relics also pulsed around its circuits, enhancing the sacred aura of the palace, binding privileged recipients to their ruler, and strengthening the dynastic associations of familial monasteries.

The nature of these bonds might change over time, for each gift had its own after-life. Prüm, the frequent beneficiary of imperial grants of land and judicial privilege over many generations, received from Lothar I in 852 a donation

---

[42] Maurice Prou and E. Chartraire, 'Authentiques de reliques conservées au trésor de la cathédrale de Sens', *Mémoires de la Société Nationale des Antiquaires de France*, 59 (1900), 129–72; nos. 10, 112 at 143, 158; and plates X, XII.

[43] *De ecclesia Centulensi libellus*, ch. 2, MGH SS XV, I.176. On the notion of the 'sacred palace', see Mayke de Jong, '*Sacrum palatium et ecclesia*: l'autorité religieuse royale sous les Carolingiens (790–840)', *Annales HSS*, 58 (2003), 1243–69; Josiane Barbier, 'Le Sacré dans le palais franc', in Michel Kaplan (ed.), *Le Sacré et son inscription dans l'espace à Byzance et en Occident*, Byzantina Sorboniensia, 18 (Paris, 2001), 27–41.

[44] De Jong, '*Sacrum palatium et ecclesia*'; Stuart Airlie, 'The Palace of Memory: The Carolingian Court as Political Centre', in Sarah Rees Jones, Richard Marks, and A. J. Minnis (eds), *Courts and Regions in Medieval Europe* (York, 2000), 1–20; Florin Curta, 'Merovingian and Carolingian Gift Giving', *Speculum*, 81 (2006), 671–99, esp. 687–90; Donald A. Bullough, 'Charlemagne's Court Library Revisited', *Early Medieval Europe*, 12 (2003), 339–63.

of sumptuous altar vessels and relics which he recorded in an exceptional charter.[45] When the recently crowned Emperor Henry II commissioned an inventory of the monastery's treasures in 1003, the monks commenced the list by reminding him of his predecessors' generosity.[46] Saint-Riquier, by contrast, preserved Angilbert's inventory but elaborated a contradictory legendary origin story, in which Louis the Pious (814–40) became the proximate donor of some of Saint-Riquier's relics, and Constantinople their point of origin.[47] At Sens, a modest list of relics deposited at the dependent church of Melun 'in the ninth year of the imperium of the Lord Charles and the thirteenth year of the episcopate of Magnus' (i.e. 809) became the basis for a formal statement in 1192 that 'the largest [number] and greatest part'— *plurimam et maximam partem*—of the cathedral's huge relic collection had been Charlemagne's gift to Magnus.[48] In such ways, fact became legend, and relics its stimulus. It is symptomatic that we know far more about Charlemagne's legendary reputation as a donor of fabulous relics than about his actual gifts.[49] Stories of regal generosity accreted round relics, whether to spur later kings to match their predecessors' gifts, to reassure later generations of monks about their community's illustrious past, or to enhance the renown of their church.

Relics could also help to anchor political identities, especially those of new, insecure rulers.[50] In 888, lack of adult, legitimate male heirs triggered a protracted but terminal dynastic crisis in the Carolingian empire. In several regions, ambitious non-royals seized power and, in so doing, confronted a deficit of legitimacy at least as great as Pippin III over a century earlier. In

---

[45] MGH Diplomata Karolinorum, III, no. 122, 179–81.

[46] Aloys Finken, 'Das Prümer Schatzverzeichnis von 1003', in Reiner Nolden (ed.), *Lothar I. Kaiser und Mönch in Prüm. Zum 1150. Jahr seines Todes* (Prüm, 2005), 161–70.

[47] At the end of the eleventh century, Hariulf incorporated Angilbert's *libellus* verbatim into his house history and also told the story about Louis the Pious: Hariulf, *Chronique de l'abbaye de Saint-Riquier*, II.8–10, III.5, ed. Ferdinand Lot (Paris, 1894), 57–69, 100.

[48] Prou and Chartraire, 'Authentiques', quotations from 139–40 (procès-verbal of 1192), 161–2 no. 133 (inventory of 809). See also plate IX.

[49] Amy Remensnyder, *Remembering Kings Past: Monastic Foundation Legends in Southern France* (Ithaca, 1995), 150–211; Anne Latowsky, 'Charlemagne as Pilgrim? Requests for Relics in the *Descriptio qualiter* and the *Voyage of Charlemagne*', in Matthew Gabriele and Jace Stuckey (eds), *The Legend of Charlemagne in the Middle Ages* (New York, 2008), 153–67.

[50] Gabriele Signori, 'Patriotische Heilige? Begriffe, Probleme und Traditionen', in Dieter Bauer, Klaus Herbers, and Gabriele Signori (eds), *Patriotische Heilige: Beiträge zur Konstruktion religiöser und politischer Identitäten in der Vormoderne*, (Stuttgart, 2007), 11–31 concentrates on the high and late Middle Ages.

Upper Burgundy (the area between the Jura and Alps), Rudolf I had himself crowned king in the ancient, prestigious monastery church of Saint-Maurice d'Agaune. The martyred leader of the Theban legion, Maurice had been the focus of a widespread cult in the early Middle Ages, but only now emerged as the symbol of Burgundian identity. In the tenth century, when Otto I set covetous eyes on this upland kingdom which impeded his access to Italy, he dedicated his new foundation at Magdeburg to St Maurice, and although, at its foundation in 937, he only possessed relics of the saint's adjutant, Innocent, by 961 he had managed to donate significant relics of the legionary commander himself.[51] The 'holy lance' which Henry I had extorted from Rudolf II came to play a key role too. At the turn of the millennium, while Otto's heirs equated the relic that was now in their possession with St Maurice's military lance and brandished it as a token of German imperial legitimacy and military might, Rudolf's successors simultaneously claimed Maurice's lance as the regnal symbol of their own Burgundian kingdom.[52] In other words, relics of St Maurice became emblematic of Burgundian royal legitimacy—and Ottonian determination to take over the kingdom of Upper Burgundy was manifested in an aggressive effort to hijack the cult. On inspection, the dissemination of the trophy relics of a famous saint turns out to be a political discourse displaced into the realm of cult.

In the fraught politics of the post-888 world, relics functioned time and again in this way, acting as talismanic tokens of legitimacy and territorial claims, in northern France and the Rhineland above all.[53] Some saints' bodies had been prised from their original tombs and shrines for hurried removal to safekeeping as Viking raids on the Carolingian western seaboard escalated in the late ninth century: this simply exacerbated the massive redistribution of relics which accompanied the long, slow collapse of Carolingian power between the crisis of 888 and the death of the last Carolingian king in 987.[54] In the early tenth century, whole bodies, body parts and tiny fragments

---

[51] Wentz and Schweinköper, *Erzbistum Magdeburg*, 216–18; Oberste, 'Heilige und ihre Reliquien', 88.

[52] Maurice Zufferey, 'Der Mauritiuskult in Früh- und Hochmittelalter', *Historisches Jahrbuch*, 106 (1986), 23–58.

[53] Details in Oberste, 'Heilige und ihre Reliquien'.

[54] N. Huyghebaert, *Une Translation de reliques à Gand en 944* (Brussels, 1978); Hubert Guillotel, 'L'Exode du clergé breton devant les invasions scandinaves', *Mélanges de la Société d'Histoire et d'Archéologie de Bretagne*, 59 (1982), 269–315; Felice Lifshitz, 'The Migration of Neustrian Relics in the Viking Age: The Myth of Voluntary Exodus, the Reality of Coercion and Theft', *Early Medieval Europe*, 4 (1995), 175–92; Hedwig Röckelein, 'Just de *Beauvais* alias Justin d'Auxerre: l'art de dédoubler un saint', in

of local saints and martyrs found their way in unprecedented quantities to different homes; bodies which had hitherto remained intact dis-articulated into multiple fractions in multiple homes; competing claims spawned a flurry of hagiographical activity. A clear political dynamic can be detected: successful dynasts accumulated relics for their family foundations, but churches in regions where political cohesion was contested—or failing altogether—lost them. The skilfulness of Henry I and Otto I has already been noted; further west, the counts of Flanders Baldwin II (879–918) and Arnulf I (918–964) were both adroit at employing relics as a means of enhancing and legitimating princely power.[55]

So too were their Anglo-Saxon relatives-in-law, Edward the Elder (901–924) and his sister Æthelflæd, Lady of the Mercians (d. 918), both of whom relocated selected relics in strategic burhs in a manner that evinces close parallels with—and presumably knowledge of—Flemish practice.[56] Their activities laid the groundwork for those of Æthelstan, son and successor to the former on the West Saxon throne, but raised by his aunt in the relic-aware environment of her Mercian court.[57] Moreover, Æthelstan was heir, as the Saxon Otto I was, to the Carolingian ideology of empire. The architect of a new style of imperial Anglo-Saxon monarchy, he extended his lordship far further throughout the British Isles than any previous ruler. Moreover, he exercised this hegemony on an international stage, as his interventions in Brittany, Ponthieu, and Flanders make clear.[58] In addition, via his many

Martin Heinzelmann (ed.), *Livrets, collections et textes. Etudes sur la tradition hagiographique latine*, Beihefte der Francia, 63 (Sigmaringen, 2006), 323–60.

[55] Edina Bozóky, 'La Politique des reliques des premiers comtes de Flandre (fin du IXe siècle-fin du XIe siècle)', in Edina Bozóky and Anne-Marie Helvétius (eds) *Les Reliques: objets, cultes, symboles. Actes du colloque internationale de l'Université du Littoral-Côte d'Opale (Boulogne-sur-Mer) 4–6 Septembre 1997* (Turnhout, 1999), 271–92; Brigitte Meijns, 'The Policy on Relic-Translations of Baldwin II of Flanders (879-d. 918), Edward of Wessex (899-d. 924), and Æthelflæd of Mercia (d. 924): A Key to Anglo-Flemish Relations?', in Conrad Leyser, David Rollason, and Hannah Williams (eds), *England and the Continent in the Tenth Century* (Turnhout, forthcoming). I am very grateful to Dr Meijns for allowing me to read her paper in advance of publication.

[56] For details, see Meijns, 'The Policy on Relic-Translations'.

[57] Cf. the accounts of Æthelstan's relics offered by J. Armitage Robinson, *The Times of Saint Dunstan* (Oxford, 1923), 71–80; Laura Hibbard Loomis, 'The Holy Relics of Charlemagne and King Athelstan: The Lances of Longinus and St Maurice', *Speculum*, 25 (1950), 437–56.

[58] Wood, ' "Stand strong against the monsters" '; Michael Wood, 'The Making of King Æthelstan's Empire: An English Charlemagne?', in Patrick Wormald, Donald Bullough, and Roger Collins (eds), *Ideal and Reality in Frankish and Anglo-Saxon Society: Studies*

half-sisters, Æthelstan found himself bound in a web of continental marriage alliances.[59] These spread his reputation and, through the indirect contacts they afforded, ensured that he was remembered in the prayers of several prestigious religious houses.[60] Paradoxically perhaps, he both exploited the political instability in north and northwestern France to extend his influence and took steps to help perpetuate the legitimate Carolingian dynasty. The political advantage he gained from engagement with continental affairs can best be estimated by the inflow of relics to his court, and the evidence deserves reassessment in this perspective.

Whether by inheritance or as a result of his own acquisitiveness prior to his accession, Æthelstan came to the throne with a notable relic collection.[61] Early in his reign, at least one Breton religious community forced by the Vikings into exile in northern France implored his help and accompanied their plea with a gift of relics;[62] it is highly plausible that similar circumstances

---

presented to J. M. Wallace-Hadrill (Oxford, 1983), 250–72; David N. Dumville, *Wessex and England from Alfred to Edgar* (Woodbridge, 1992), 141–71; supplemented by Simon MacLean, 'Making a Difference in Tenth-Century Politics: King Athelstan's Sisters and Frankish Queenship', in Paul Fouracre and David Ganz (eds), *Frankland: The Franks and the World of the Early Middle Ages. Essays in Honour of Dame Jinty Nelson* (Manchester, 2008), 167–90, at 175–8 for intervention in Flanders and Ponthieu; Julia M. H. Smith, *Province and Empire: Brittany and the Carolingians* (Cambridge, 1992), 196–7, for intervention in Brittany; Charles Insley, 'Athelstan, Charters and the English in Cornwall', in Marie-Therese Flanagan and Judith A. Green (eds), *Charters and Charter Scholarship in Britain and Ireland* (London, 2005), 15–31, for intervention in Cornwall.

[59] MacLean, 'Making a Difference'; Wolfgang Georgi, 'Bischof Koenwald von Worcester und die Heirat Ottos I. mit Egitha im Jahre 929', *Historisches Jahrbuch*, 115 (1995), 1–40; Karl Leyser, 'The Ottonians and Wessex', in Timothy Reuter (ed.), *Communications and Power in Medieval Europe: the Carolingian and Ottonian Centuries* (London, 1994), 73–104.

[60] Georgi, 'Bischof Koenwald', 31–2 for commemoration of Æthelstan in the confraternity books of Sankt Gallen and Reichenau; *Cartulaire général de Paris, I: 528–1180*, ed. Robert de Lasteyrie (Paris, 1887), 53 for commemoration at Saint-Germain-des-Prés.

[61] It is invoked in a manumission made immediately after his accession: Simon Keynes, 'King Athelstan's Books', in Michael Lapidge and Helmut Gneuss, (eds), *Learning and Literature in Anglo-Saxon England: Studies Presented to Peter Clemoes on the occasion of his sixty-fifth birthday* (Cambridge, 1985), 143–201, at 185–9, with translation in Dorothy Whitelock (ed.), *English Historical Documents I, c.500–1042*, 2nd edn (London, 1979), 607, no. 140.

[62] Letter of Radbod of Dol to Æthelstan, preserved by William of Malmesbury, *Gesta pontificum anglorum* V.249, ed. and trans. M. Winterbottom and R. M. Thomson,

explain the notable influx of Breton relics, hagiographical texts and liturgical manuscripts into early tenth-century England, although in no other case can the precise political circumstances be recovered.[63] It is also an attractive hypothesis that his wide-ranging continental contacts, above all his network of sisters, may have funnelled relics to his court.

Beyond that, Æthelstan's politics of relic accumulation emerges indirectly, from his reputation in the eleventh and twelfth centuries. In Flanders, he was remembered as having been in competition with Count Arnulf for relics from Boulogne, whereas in England, many churches recalled his generosity.[64] Exeter's eleventh-century collection included a large number of relics which derived from churches in regions deeply affected by his politics of overlordship—the Continental littoral of Flanders, Picardy, Normandy, Brittany, plus also Cornwall—the collection which, the eleventh-century Exeter Anonymous averred, resulted from the king's generosity.[65] This story of a royal pedigree is fully concordant with a view of Æthelstan behaving just as his brother-in-law Otto I was doing—or as Charlemagne had done—and accumulating sacred tokens of political superiority. The analogy has an additional dimension, however, for Exeter claimed no monopoly on the generosity of a king whose fame as a donor of relics was widely attested in the twelfth century.[66] Late though these traditions are, they suggest a ruler who

2 vols (Oxford, 2007), I.596–9, II.297–8. For the hypothesis that Radbod wrote from Paris in 926, see Hubert Guillotel, 'L'Éxode du clergé breton', 297.

[63] David N. Dumville, *Liturgy and the Ecclesiastical History of Late Anglo-Saxon England* (Woodbridge, 1992), 112–16. Veneration of specific Breton saints can now be easily tracked via Rebecca Rushforth, *Saints in English Kalendars before A.D. 1100*, Henry Bradshaw Society, 157 (London, 2008).

[64] *Vita Bertulfi*, ch. 24, MGH SS XV, II.635. Huyghebaert, *Une Translation de reliques à Gand*, lxxiii, demonstrates this was written at Ghent, 1073x88; Huyghebaert discusses subsequent, derivative versions of the story in 'Le "Sermo de adventu SS. Gudwali et Bertulfi": edition et étude critique', *Sacris Erudiri*, 24 (1980), 87–113.

[65] Above, 73. See Förster, *Zur Geschichte*, 59–62 for the geographical origins of the Exeter relics.

[66] William of Malmesbury, *Gesta pontificum anglorum*, II.85 (Milton Abbas), II.93 (Muchelney), V.246–8 (Malmesbury), ed. Winterbottom and Thomson, 292–3, 312–13, 592–7; William of Malmesbury, *De antiquitate Glastonie ecclesie*, ch. 54, in John Scott (ed.), *The Early History of Glastonbury* (Woodbridge, 1981), 114; *The Liber Vitae of the New Minster and Hyde Abbey Winchester (British Library Stowe 499)*, ed. Simon Keynes, Early English Manuscripts in Facsimile, 26 (Copenhagen, 1996), 106 and fol. 58v; Richard of Devizes (?), *Annales monasterii de Wintonia*, a.924, ed. H. R. Luard in *Annales Monastici*, Rolls Series 36 pt ii (London, 1865), 10; for Abingdon, see n.69 below.

built political allegiances by distributing holy remains to favoured ancient communities and whose endowment of new religious houses as centres of dynastic prayer was confirmed by the relics they received. In all likelihood, relics circulated into and out of Æthelstan's court, consolidating religious, familial, and political alliances abroad and at home. Viewed in this context, Exeter's claim to hold 'one third'—in other words, a significant portion—of the king's collection suggests that this city was to Æthelstan what Magdeburg was to Otto I: a well-defended frontier city which doubled as a centre of sacral hegemony and was bound to other churches by the dissemination of gifts of relics.

In 926, the West Saxon king agreed to the marriage of his half-sister Eadhild to the leading West Frankish magnate, Hugh the Great, duke of Francia (d. 956).[67] Writing in the 1120–30s, William of Malmesbury supplied an account of the gifts 'on a truly munificent scale' presented by the Frankish envoys at Abingdon: unheard-of perfumes, jewellery, emeralds, an antique carved onyx vase, caparisoned horses, a gold, jewelled crown—and relics. William specified these as the sword of Constantine the Great 'on which was to be read the name of the ancient owner in letters of gold', and which had a nail of the crucifixion attached to the hilt in a gold mounting; the invincible lance of Charlemagne which was said to be the lance with which Christ had been pierced as he hung on the cross; the banner of St Maurice, which Charlemagne had carried into battle; a piece of the True Cross, displayed in crystal; and a tiny piece of the crown of thorns, similarly displayed.[68] Although the boundary between factual reportage and William's lively imagination remains open to debate, this story must be taken seriously, both for what it reveals about the politics of relics, and for what it suggests about the stories that subsequently attached themselves to holy objects.

As Karl Leyser pointed out, luxury gifts of this sort were typical of ninth- and tenth-century diplomatic exchange, whose standard was set by the dazzling offerings brought by Byzantine envoys to the West.[69] We can hardly doubt that Hugh did indeed send rich gifts, and, although somewhat different in its details, Abingdon tradition confirms that prestige relics

---

[67] Flodoard, *Annales* a. 926, ed. P. Lauer (Paris, 1905), 36.

[68] *Gesta regum anglorum* II.135, ed. Mynors, Thomson, and Winterbottom, I.218–21, II.123–5.

[69] Karl Leyser 'The Tenth Century in Byzantine–Western Relations', in his *Medieval Germany and its Neighbours, 950–1250* (London, 1982), 103–37. See now also Peter Schreiner, 'Diplomatische Geschenke zwischen Byzanz und dem Westen ca. 800–1200: Eine Analyse der Texte mit Quellenanhang', *Dumbarton Oaks Papers*, 58 (2004), 251–82.

were among them.[70] One notable aspect of William's report is its overlay of typically twelfth-century legendary associations with Charlemagne, but once that has been stripped away, there remains a list of objects which would have been readily available in early tenth-century royal or ecclesiastical treasuries. Collections of gemstones and antique carved onyx vases, similar to that described here, still survive with their Carolingian mountings in the treasuries of Saint-Denis and Saint-Maurice d'Agaune; written texts remind us that these examples were once not as rare as they now are.[71] Moreover, almost all these objects can be closely paralleled in the diplomatic gift-giving of late Carolingian and early Ottonian rulers, and the selection must have been deliberate.[72]

Hugh the Great had sent his envoys to Æthelstan at an uncertain moment in West Frankish affairs. Three years earlier, the Carolingian king Charles the Straightforward (898–923) had been deposed and imprisoned by his own magnates as he struggled unsuccessfully to cling on to the final remnants of his authority in northern France. He languished under arrest until he died in 929, his infant son Louis in exile overseas, and his kingdom under the rule of non-Carolingian claimants, first Robert (922–3) and then Ralph of Burgundy (923–936)—the father and brother-in-law of Hugh the Great.

---

[70] This house reported in the mid-twelfth century that the gifts included fine horses; silken cloths; Constantine's sword with the tip of one of the nails from the crucifixion in its hilt; the tip of another such nail; and fragments of the Cross and the crown of thorns. See *De abbatibus Abbendoniae*, ed. Joseph Stevenson in *Chronicon monasterii de Abingdon*, 2 vols, Rolls Series 2 (London, 1858), II.276–7. For the view that this was probably compiled 1130–58, see John Hudson (ed.), *Historia ecclesie Abbendonensis. The History of the Church of Abingdon*, 2 vols (Oxford, 2002–7), I.lvi–lvii, II.xxi–xxiii. By the thirteenth century, Abingdon had adjusted the list to include the banner of St Maurice and a finger of St Denis but had deleted the sword of Constantine: see the revised ('B') text of the *Historia ecclesie Abbendonensis*, ed. Hudson, 282–3 (I.xl).

[71] For extant examples, see *Le Trésor de Saint-Denis: Musée du Louvre, Paris, 12 mars- 17 juin 1991* [exh. cat.] (Paris, 1991); Pierre Bouffard, *Saint-Maurice d'Agaune: Trésor de l'abbaye* (Geneva, 1974). Textual references are assembled by Emile Lesne, *Histoire de la propriété ecclésiastique en France III: L'inventaire de la propriété. Eglises et trésors des églises* (Lille, 1936), 177–9, 227–32, 238–40; and Schramm and Mütherich, *Denkmale*, 53–9, 68–70.

[72] The crown of thorns is a probable exception. Reichenau claimed to have acquired one of its thorns in 923, but the story dates from the early eleventh century, when references to this particular dominical relic begin to proliferate in the Latin West. Walter Berschin and Theodor Klüppel, *Die Reichenauer Heiligblut-Reliquie*, 2nd edn (Stuttgart, 1999), 34.

When the political symbolism of Hugh's gifts to Æthelstan is taken into consideration, it becomes clear that they did far more than seal his marriage to an Anglo-Saxon princess. The events of ten years later suggest that the very continuation and legitimacy of the Carolingian dynasty itself was at stake. When King Ralph died in 936, Louis was of age: Hugh the Great sent a delegation which fetched him back and duly crowned him king.[73] In the intervening years, the child had been growing up at the court of his uncle, Æthelstan, where his mother Eadgifu, another of Æthelstan's half-sisters, had taken the toddler for safety in 923. In 936, Æthelstan aided the now adult Carolingian prince in his recovery of the West Frankish throne. Rather than assuming, as hitherto, that the coronation of Louis 'd'Outremer' resolved months of undocumented magnate factionalism between Hugh the Great and his rivals and detractors,[74] it makes more sense to see the gifts given in 926 as pledges of a carefully constructed pre-agreed succession pact in which Æthelstan represented his young nephew's interests, and which was sealed by Duke Hugh's marriage to Eadhild, the boy's aunt.

This would not have been the first time that an anticipatory succession agreement had been reached, for there were at least two precedents for ensuring that a Carolingian acceded to the throne upon the death of a non-Carolingian usurper. In 879, the usurpation of Boso of Provence had prompted the four Carolingian cousins who were then ruling to reach just such a pact in an effort to guarantee the long-term future of their dynasty.[75] Then, in 897, the childless usurper Odo (888–898) recognized the rights of his Carolingian opponent Charles the Straightforward by giving him part of the realm and, it seems, acknowledging him as heir to the whole kingdom.[76] In 926, such a pact would have enabled Hugh to reassure his peers that he was a

[73] Flodoard, *Annales*, a. 936, ed. Lauer, 63.

[74] Cf. Jan Dhondt, *Etudes sur la naissance des principautés territoriales en France (IX-Xe siècle)*, (Bruges, 1948), 66; Karl-Ferdinand Werner, 'Westfranken-Frankreich unter den Spätkarolingern und frühen Kapetingern (888–1060)', in *Handbuch der europäischen Geschichte, I: Europa im Wandel der Antike zum Mittelalter*, ed. Theodor Schieffer (Stuttgart, 1976), 745–6; Bernd Schneidmüller, *Karolingische Tradition und frühes französisches Königtum: Untersuchungen zur Herrschaftslegitimation der westfränkisch-französischen Monarchie im 10. Jahrhundert*, Frankfurter Historische Abhandlungen, 22 (Wiesbaden, 1979), 147–9.

[75] Simon MacLean, 'The Carolingian Response to the Revolt of Boso, 879–887', *Early Medieval Europe*, 10 (2001), 21–48.

[76] *Annales Vedastini*, a. 897, ed. B. de Simson, *Annales Xantenses et Vedastini*, MGH SSRM, 12, 79; Werner, 'Westfranken-Frankreich', 738.

kingmaker, not a potential usurper; above all, it would have brought relief from the vicious magnate in-fighting which had dominated much of Charles the Straightforward's reign. So in 936, Hugh sent for his wife's nephew not because he failed to muster enough support for a coup, but because ten years previously he had solemnly bound himself to this course of action.[77]

In 926, the broker whose proactive efforts secured the deal was almost certainly not Æthelstan but Eadgifu, West Saxon by birth and only Carolingian by marriage.[78] The specific connotations of the relics presented to Æthelstan allow us to deduce that she had arranged a coalition which, in addition to the bridegroom Hugh the Great, doubtless included the childless West Frankish King Ralph, the Saxon Henry I, and Arnulf of Flanders (whose brother led the delegation to England), with other possible members such as Rudolf II of Upper Burgundy. She had also persuaded them to recognise the rights of the Carolingian Louis whenever the West Frankish throne would fall vacant. In this reading, the marriage and its accompanying exchange of gifts constitute the historically visible tip of a much more complex negotiation. In effect, Æthelstan received carefully selected tokens of regality as the most potent possible pledge of his nephew's royal rights. When William of Malmesbury's narrative of prestigious gift-giving is pared back, it reveals yet another occasion on which iconic relics marked political actions. Relics in settings of rare beauty thus functioned as a form of political discourse, fusing their inherent sacrality and historical symbolism with great material value to guarantee the best of all possible futures, the succession of an able, adult heir of the ancestral line.

Their value as political capital was fleeting, however. In the mid-eleventh century, Exeter claimed that, among the relics with which Æthelstan had endowed it, was a relic *Of þam spere, þe ures Drihtenes halige syd wæs mid geopenod on þære rode*, a relic of 'the spear with which our Lord's holy side was opened on the Cross' which, in a Latin version of this list, was accompanied by a 'sword'.[79] In the twelfth century, Malmesbury possessed many gifts reputedly bestowed upon it by the king, which included 'a fragment of the

---

[77] MacLean, 'Making a Difference', 174, for a thumbnail sketch of Louis d'Outremer's reign, with full bibliography.

[78] This develops the discussion of Eadgifu's significance presented by MacLean, 'Making a Difference'.

[79] Förster, *Zur Geschichte*, 69, 81 on relic no. 6. Exeter's relics of Maurice and his companion Candidus might also have derived from the gifts of 926. Ibid., 73, 75, 84, for relics nos. 37, 38 and 69.

Lord's cross which [Æthelstan] had been sent by Hugh king [sic] of the Franks'.[80] For its part, by the thirteenth century, Abingdon claimed all of Hugh's gifts, where they were known to have been given in conjunction with Eadhild's marriage. Æthelstan, it was said, had given them 'concealed with all honour in a silver reliquary' to this 'most sacred house' where they still acted as a conduit for divine clemency and aid.[81]

Although we lack information about where any of these gifts were stored or when they were put on show, it is reasonable to suppose that, as in later centuries, they would have been displayed upon the altar on feast days and, above all, on royal visits. As such, they would have enhanced liturgical splendour, reminded monks of their obligations to pray for deceased benefactors and urged living rulers to make equally generous donations. Later centuries thus supplied revised values and meanings, for these relics' original significance had been altered by the passage of time. Yet their scintillating presence remained, and called for comment in chronicles, stories, legends. As historians, we may interpret these stories as a legacy of Æthelstan's generosity in distributing the gifts he received from Hugh the Great, or as part of the growth of legends around his reputation, or even as a reflection of the gradual twelfth-century recovery of knowledge of the Anglo-Saxon past. But at Exeter, Malmesbury, and Abingdon in the decades after the Norman Conquest, they testified to the antiquity of each foundation and its close relation with one of the most powerful and famous of Anglo-Saxon monarchs. That they also hinted at competitive relic collecting and ecclesiastical status emulation suggests that post-Conquest chroniclers were quick to exploit the value of relics as convincing bearers of new political truths.[82]

At one level, the authenticity that they conveyed in the eleventh and twelfth centuries was quite different from their tenth-century significance as tokens of political alliance and pledges of oath-taking. But at an enduring level, these relics were eternal treasures that transcended the earthly treasures within which they were encased, and we should not lose sight of the contents, whether sword, lance and banner, pinches of dust, or splinters of wood and bone. Certainly, only kings could afford the materials and craftsmanship to transform these objects into things of rare beauty and great value, but in so doing, they supplemented, rather than displaced, the relics' religious value.

---

[80] William of Malmesbury, *Gesta pontificum anglorum*, V. 246.2, ed. Winterbottom and Thomson, 592–3. William elsewhere reports that the fragment of the crown of thorns was also given to Malmesbury: *Gesta regum anglorum* II.135, ed. Mynors, Thomson, and Winterbottom, I.220–21, II.125.

[81] *Historia ecclesie Abbendonensis*, ed. Hudson, I.282–3.

[82] Cf. ibid., I.clxxiii–iv.

As these objects passed in and out of the treasuries of early medieval rulers, then, they gave added lustre to recipient and donor alike. At the same time, they might acquire new and precious mountings, gain a precise but evanescent political symbolism, or substitute a new pedigree for an old one. In the early Middle Ages, only kings could fully exploit the multiplicity of meaning, value, and purpose of these highly portable fragments of sacrality.

Relics of Piety and Power in Medieval Islam[*]

Josef W. Meri

The study of the veneration of relics in medieval Islam is only now emerging as a sub-field of study after investigations by European Orientalists during the first half of the twentieth century.[1] The scarcity of sources, particularly in the Islamic context, seemingly relegates the Islamic experience to a secondary status vis-à-vis the medieval European Christian experience despite the ubiquity of relics and ritual practices associated with them in the devotional life of the Muslims and Christians of the Near East and North Africa.[2] Furthermore, in the study of the cult of relics a misperception persists that the Islamic experience is marginal, because of the perceived absence of relics in Islam. Commenting on what he considers to be the 'relative paucity' of relics in Islam Lionel Rothkrug observes that it 'may be partly attributed to the fact that Islamic religious experience largely came out of conflict with other monotheistic religions'.[3]

[*] This paper would not have been possible without the generous support of the *Past and Present* conference organizer Alexandra Walsham which enabled me to deliver a talk at the University of Exeter, UK upon which it is based. My sincerest thanks and appreciation for her encouragement and most helpful suggestions. I would also like to express my appreciation to Annabel Keeler and Robert Kitchen for their invaluable comments and also to the anonymous *Past and Present* reviewers who realized the value of polishing up the first draft of the article.

[1] See e.g., Ignaz Goldziher, 'The Cult of Saints in Islam', *Muslim World*, 1 (1911), 302–12 and the Oxford orientalist D. S. Margoliouth, 'The Relics of the Prophet Mohammed', *Muslim World*, 27 (1937), 20–7. More recently, see Brannon Wheeler's *Mecca and Eden: Ritual, Relics and Territory in Islam* (Chicago, 2006) which explores man's fall from Eden and how relics are a reminder of that against the backdrop of the establishment of the Islamic state and its geographical focus of Mecca.

[2] The argument for the greater significance of relics to the practice of Catholic Christianity and Buddhism than to other religious traditions is made by J. S. Strong, 'Relics', in Lindsay Jones (ed.), *Encyclopedia of Religion*, 2nd edn (Detroit, 2005), 7686–92.

[3] Lionel Rothkrug, *Death, Trust, and Society: Mapping Religion and Culture* (Berkeley, 2006), 113.

By placing undue emphasis on undefined conflicts between Islam, Judaism, and Christianity Rothkrug minimalizes the historical reality of relics in Islam. In Rothkrug's analysis religious experience is a product of conflict rather than a phenomenon to be studied in and of itself. A more precise explanation as to why a cult of bodily relics did not develop in Islam may be found in its emphasis on the inviolability of human remains and the sanctity of the human body. Muslims regard human remains as impure and touching them generally necessitates undertaking major ablutions (*ghusl*). However, the bodies of the special dead deserve particular attention. The *ḥadīth* traditions of the Prophet Muḥammad mention that the bodies of the prophets are incorruptible:

> The Prophet, may peace be upon him, said: 'Verily your best day is Friday, so invoke blessings upon me in abundance on this day, for your invocation is shown to me'. [The people] said to him, 'O Messenger of God! How can our invocations be shown to you after your bones have turned to dust?' He replied: 'Verily God has forbidden the earth from consuming the bodies of the Messengers (i.e. prophets to whom a scripture was revealed)'.[4]

Similarly, the bodies of some martyrs and righteous individuals are uncorrupted through the grace of God[5] as in the example of two Companions of the Prophet Muḥammad who had died forty-six years prior to their reburial:

> ʿAmr ibn al-Jamūḥ al-Anṣārī and ʿAbdullāh ibn ʿUmar al-Anṣārī, both of the tribe of Banū Salama, had their grave uncovered by a flood. . . . They were in the same grave, having been among those martyred at Uḥud. They were dug up so that they might be moved. They were found unchanged. It was as if they had died only the day before. One of them had been wounded, and he had put his hand over his wound and had been buried like that. His hand was pulled away from his wound and released, and it returned to where it had

---

[4] See e.g., Aḥmad ibn Ḥanbal, *Musnad, awwal* Musnad al-Madanīyīn, ḥadīth Aws ibn Abī Aws al-Thaqafī wa huwa Aws ibn Ḥudhayfa, no. 15575; Abū Dāwūd, *Sunan*, Kitāb al-Witr, Bāb fil-istighfār, no. 1533. See also with variations Abū Dāwūd, *Sunan*, Kitāb al-Ṣalāt, Bāb faḍl yawm al-jumuʿa wa laylat al-jumuʿa, no. 1049.

[5] See e.g., Ibn Ḥajar al-ʿAsqalānī, *Fatḥ al-Bārī bi-Sharḥ Ṣaḥīḥ al-Bukhārī*, Bāb hal yukhraj al-mayyit min al-qabr wal-laḥd li-ʿilla, no. 1287: http://islamweb.net/newlibrary/display_book.php?bk_no=52&ID=873&idfrom=2484&idto=2489&bookid=52&startno=2.

been. It was forty-six years between Uḥud and the day they were dug up.[6]

The veneration of the Companions of the Prophet and other holy persons and making *ziyāra* to their tombs and shrines became normative practice throughout the Islamic world.[7] However, belief in the inviolability of human remains and the sanctity of the body did not preclude the emergence among Muslims of a variety of forms of 'corporeal' and 'non-corporeal' relics belonging to or coming into contact with a holy person which demonstrate reverence for the holy dead and honouring their memory. The twelfth century marked an historic turning point for the proliferation of relics in Islam and western Christianity. In the latter the fragmentation of the bodies of saints became the norm.[8] This is in marked contrast with the Islamic world where the Crusades and the Islamic Counter-Crusade under Nūr al-Dīn ibn Zangi (r. 541/1146–569/1174) and his successor Ṣalāḥ al-Dīn (Saladin) (r. 569/ 1174–589/1193) along with the revival of Islamic learning under them and their successors spurred a growth in the veneration of saints, including the foundation of shrines and the veneration of relics in Greater Syria, Iraq and elsewhere. What is the nature of relics in Islam? What role did relics play in the devotional life of Muslims?

In Islam as in Christianity relics embody religious experience. That is the deep spiritual connection the believer has with the Creator and more immediately with the holy person to whom the relics once belonged. Relics are also receptacles for individual and collective memory. Muslim devotees yearned to preserve the memory of holy persons in objects which symbolized a tangible link between them and the holy person. Through the mere act of remembrance of holy persons and their miracles and memorializing the past, memory becomes lived and shared experience. The use of relics by medieval Muslims focused memories on sacred objects, thus giving them profound meaning and creating the context for their veneration. Relics are enablers of historical memory.[9]

---

[6] Mālik, *al-Muwaṭṭa'*, Kitāb al-jihād, Bāb al-dafn fī qabr wāḥid min ḍarūrat inqādh Abī Bakr ʿuddāt rasūl Allāh, no. 1010. Trans. Aisha Bewley (modified), 21.21 (no. 50): http://www.sunnipath.com/Library/Hadith/H0001P0021.aspx.

[7] See J. W. Meri, *Cult of Saints among Muslims and Jews in Medieval Syria* (Oxford, 2002).

[8] See e.g., Caroline Bynum, *Resurrection of the Body in Western Christianity, 200–1336* (New York, 1995), ch. 5. I am grateful to Professor Bynum for sharing her various works with me.

[9] About memory and saint cults see e.g., Peter Brown, *Cult of Saints: Its Rise and Function in Christianity* (Chicago, 1980), 4 and throughout.

A brief comparison of the salient features of the Christian and Islamic experiences of relic veneration is in order. First, Christian relics are often classified as corporeal or non-corporeal or as primary or secondary.[10] The latter designations as applied to the Islamic context are both imprecise and reductionist in nature. Notwithstanding, devotional objects or relics (Arab. *āthār*) (lit. traces or remnants) were a fundamental aspect of Muslim and Christian daily life throughout the Islamic lands of the Near East and North Africa during the Middle Ages.[11] Secondly, relics were never accorded any official status in Muslim canonical prayer as in Christian liturgy nor were altars erected around them nor were there priests to translate the efficaciousness of those relics to devotees. However, as will be shown later this did not preclude the emergence in the Islamic context of a class of individual scholars and theologians who were the keepers and transmitters of the traditions of the Prophet Muḥammad and who were responsible for protecting relics by controlling access to them, displaying them at times of crisis, and in certain instances permitting their replication. Thirdly, in the Christian context, it was necessary for churches or monasteries to possess the tangible relics of saints in a reliquary or altar. Moreover, the *praesentia* or the physical manifestation of the holy person at the relic was a tangible aspect of the Christian veneration of saints.[12] The physical presence and display of the relic as well as contact with it were necessary in the Islamic context. Finally, the competition for corporeal relics was an essential characteristic of the medieval European and Byzantine Christian experience as churches and monasteries vied to possess the relics of saints which were at least in Byzantium essential to the consecration of churches. Similarly, in the Islamic context competition for relics emerged in the context of dynastic legitimacy and learning.

Although human remains were not venerated in the same manner as in Christianity, one finds among Sunni and Shi'i Muslims the veneration of the

---

[10] See e.g., Phyllis Jestice's distinction between first, second, and third class relics and her view that second class relics are venerated in Islam, 'Veneration of Holy People', in Phyllis G. Jestice (ed.), *Holy People of the World*, 3 vols (Santa Barbara, 2004), 887. This is mentioned in an earlier work: Heinrich Fichtenau, *Living in the Tenth Century: Mentalities and Social Orders*, trans. Patrick J. Geary (Chicago, 1991), 324. A useful comparison with European and Roman perceptions of ordinary human remains and those of saints can be found in Patrick Geary, *Living with the Dead in the Middle Ages* (Ithaca, 1994), 200–8.

[11] I have made the same argument elsewhere in the case of the veneration of holy persons and places in Islam and Judaism, see Meri, *Cult of Saints*.

[12] Brown, *Cult of Saints*, 89.

head of the Prophet Muḥammad's grandson Ḥusayn b. ʿAlī at Cairo.[13] The Ismaili Shiʿi Fāṭimid dynasty (r. 909–1171) which ruled Egypt and Greater Syria evacuated the head to the Palace of the Fāṭimid Caliphs in Cairo from Ascalon with the utmost reverence during a crusader siege of the city in 549/1154.[14] Apart from the head of Ḥusayn and the pre-Islamic veneration of the head of St John the Baptist (Yaḥyā b. Zakarīyā) in Damascus, the head cult did not take hold in Islam to be certain. In contrast with the experiences of the eastern rite churches of the Islamic world, medieval Europe and Buddhism, no evidence exists to suggest that physical contact with these sacred human remains with the notable exceptions of the hairs and nail parings of the Prophet Muḥammad, played any part in Muslim devotion. The divine blessings (*baraka*) of the nail parings and hairs above all of the Prophet's relics are mentioned in the canonical *ḥadīth* literature.[15] It is thus not surprising that the person of the Prophet was the embodiment par excellence of *baraka* (often translated as divine blessings or divine grace), since he was the recipient of a divine revelation from God. Yet, exceptionally through the veneration of the head of the Prophet's grandson Ḥusayn in Cairo the Fāṭimids sought primarily to derive *baraka* for themselves and for the deceased Fāṭimid caliphs buried in its vicinity. Ḥusayn was martyred in the year 61/680. His head was decapitated from his body by his killer. While the body was buried at Karbalāʾ in Iraq, the head was taken to Syria, then later to Ascalon in Palestine, and eventually to Cairo and became the locus of veneration at multiple shrines throughout the region.[16] The Fāṭimids restricted access to the relic of Ḥusayn which came to figure prominently in ceremonies on holy days where his shrine was designated a station in their elaborate ceremonial processions.[17] Today the head, by some accounts, remains housed in the Masjid of Ḥusayn at Cairo where it remains a popular object of veneration among Egyptians and Shiʿite visitors from India, Pakistan, and Iran.

The experience of medieval Muslims, Christians, and Jews is largely one of cross-fertilization of similar yet unique devotional practices enriched by a

---

[13] The veneration of Ḥusayn existed in Cairo as well as at shrines throughout the Islamic world, including at Karbalāʾ, Iraq where it is believed his body is buried. Cf. Meri, *Cult of Saints*, 191–5.

[14] Meri, *Cult of Saints*, 192–4.

[15] The *ḥadīth* are the sayings, deeds and silent affirmations of the Prophet and the second most important source for Muslims after the Qurʾan.

[16] Concerning the accounts of Ḥusayn's head and his shrines, Meri, *Cult of Saints*, 191–5.

[17] See Sanders, *Ritual, Politics, and the City in Fatimid Cairo* (Albany: State University of New York Press, 1994), 19, 131–2.

shared belief in the efficacy of holy places and persons. Muslims like the Christian communities of the Islamic world venerated sacred objects as did to a lesser extent Jews.[18] In Egypt, Historic Syria, and Iraq holy men and ascetics renowned for their extraordinary abilities and attributes roamed the land from late antiquity. Irruptions of the sacred manifested themselves in the landscape of Historic Syria and the Mediterranean, in persons, and in objects. In Eliadan terms, each of these elements represents a hierophany recognizable to Jews, Christians, and Muslims, sometimes to two or all three faiths.[19]

Throughout the medieval Islamic world from Andalusia, North Africa, and Sub-Saharan Africa to Historic Syria, Iraq, Persia, and India the common veneration of the 'traces' (i.e. footprints and handprints) of the prophets and other holy persons became widespread, a case in point being the cults of the prophets Elijah (the Islamic prophet al-Khaḍir) and Moses and the veneration of rocks, grottoes, chairs, and sacred footprints associated with them.[20] Moreover, talismanic objects were an essential feature of medieval Islamic villages, towns, and cities and many sites containing portable objects and talismanic designs associated with holy persons, including prophets, saints, and holy men existed at places of worship, city gates, near sacred trees and springs.[21] Teaching colleges for the religious sciences (*madrasas*) and mosques became repositories for sacred objects. Spiritual cross-fertilization born out of religious experience, though not necessarily of the physical manifestations of the sacred, occurred precisely because of Muslims, Jews, and Christians' shared reverence for the sacred. This discussion will illustrate the varieties of relics Muslims venerated and the rituals associated with them, and in so doing demonstrate that relics were exemplars of piety and power. Relics became emblems of power in an increasing struggle against secular rulers or in dynastic rivalry. Yet, it will be shown that relics represented the power of the religious scholars or *'ulamā'*. Relics were used to

---

[18] An example of this veneration includes sacred places associated with the Islamic prophet al-Khaḍir who is identified with the Prophet Elijah. In the Jewish context, this included Torah scrolls. See Meri, *Cult of Saints*, ch. 4.

[19] For a discussion of 'irruption', see M. Eliade, *The Sacred and the Profane: the Nature of Religion* (New York, 1959), 97. For 'hierophany', see M. Eliade and L. E. Sullivan, 'Hierophany', in Jones (ed.), *Encyclopedia of Religion*, 6:3970–74. For a discussion of sacred landscape see Meri, *Cult of Saints*, ch. 1.

[20] See J. W. Meri, 'Re-appropriating Sacred Space: Medieval Jews and Muslims Seeking Elijah and al-Khaḍir', *Medieval Encounters: Jewish, Christian and Muslim Culture in Confluence and Dialogue*, 5 (1999), 237–64.

[21] See Meri, *Cult of Saints,* chs. 2 and 3.

establish authority and boundaries between dynasties, rulers, and the common people.[22] It will also explore the ritual uses of relics by devotees and examine how they were employed. Relics came to be employed in the context of learning as well as at times of disaster and in the struggle of the people against oppression.

In medieval Islam relics served four functions which were not mutually exclusive:

1. Relics represented metonymies[23] of holy persons who were endowed with *baraka* (divine blessings)[24] (e.g. the relics of the Prophet Muḥammad were buried with the deceased and meant to facilitate access to paradise);[25]

2. delimited sacred space: a relic's presence in holy places, such as mosques and shrines and in secular buildings, such as palaces and teaching colleges, endowed these places with *baraka* and thus afforded them a measure of protection from thieves and invaders;

3. symbolized the learning and piety of individuals and institutions; and

4. legitimated the rule of a ruler or dynasty through a physical link to the Prophet Muḥammad and additionally, in the case of the Fāṭimid dynasty of Egypt, to the Prophet's Family. Through their association with men of exemplary piety and learning (no historical record of venerated objects belonging to holy women exists), such objects came to be endowed with *baraka*.

Early examples of the use of relics

In Islam the exemplar par excellence of sanctity is the Prophet Muḥammad whom Muslims seek to emulate in their daily lives. Muslims memorialize,

---

[22] See Caroline Bynum and Paula Gerson, 'Body-Part Reliquaries and Body Parts in the Middle Ages', *Gesta*, 36 (1997), 4.

[23] In a fundamental sense, a relic is a metonymy for the person of a prophet, saint, or other holy person.

[24] For a discussion of *baraka*, see Meri, *Cult of Saints*, index 'baraka'; J. W. Meri, 'Aspects of Baraka (Blessings) and Ritual Devotion among Medieval Muslims and Jews', *Medieval Encounters: Jewish, Christian and Muslim Culture in Confluence and Dialogue*, 5 (1999), 46–69.

[25] The basic underlying idea is not entirely different from the idea of 'metonymic contact points'. According to Elizabeth Edwards who comments on the shoes of Nazi concentration camp victims, 'Approaching relics as metonymic contact points allows for the multiple histories and contexts signified by the shoes to come to light'. E. Edwards, C. Gosden, and R. Phillips (eds), *Sensible Objects: Colonialism, Museums and Material Culture* (Basingstoke, 2006), 262.

praise, and honour the person of the Prophet in prayer, poetry, and architec-ture.[26] Objects associated with him were imbued with and came to embody the sacrality of his person. However, unlike other prophets and holy persons, Muḥammad became the object of veneration precisely because his teachings, sayings and silent affirmations were meticulously preserved by his Companions and transmitted to subsequent generations, who preserved and employed his relics seeking to derive blessings (*baraka*) from them even after his death.

One of the earliest known examples of individuals deriving *baraka* from relics is of the Umayyad caliph Muʿāwiya (r. 41/661–60/680) who acquired the Prophet's nail parings:

> The Prophet once clothed me with a shirt, which I put away, and one day when he pared his nails I took the parings and placed them in a bottle. When I die, clothe me in that shirt, and chop up and pulverize the parings; sprinkle them over my eyes and into my mouth, on the chance that God may have mercy on me through their *baraka*.[27]

In the *ḥadīth* traditions, one finds that the Companions and Family of the Prophet collected his sweat and water from prayer ablution. They also regu-larly sought to possess his hair which would be dipped in water to facilitate a cure for the evil eye or some other disease.

> It is related that Ibn Sīrīn said: 'I said to ʿĀbida [as-Salmānī], "I have some of the hair of the Prophet, may peace be upon him, which I got from Anas or Anas's family".' He replied, 'If I had a single one of those hairs, it would be dearer to me than this world and every-thing in it'.[28]

Thumāma related that Anas said, 'Umm Sulaym[29] used to spread a leather mat for the Prophet, peace be upon him, and he would have a midday nap on that mat at her home'. He said, 'When he slept, [Umm Sulaym] would collect

---

[26] In this regard, cf. Anne-Marie Schimmel, *And Muhammad is His Messenger* (Chapel Hill, 1985).

[27] D. S. Margoliouth, 'The Relics of the Prophet Mohammed', *Moslem World*, 27 (1937), 20–7. Translation is Margoliouth's. There is a similar account concerning the pious caliph ʿUmar b. ʿAbd al-ʿAzīz.

[28] Bukhārī, *Ṣaḥīḥ*, ch. 4, no. 168.

[29] Mother of the Prophet's servant Mālik.

some of his sweat and hair and put it in a bottle and added it to perfume (*sukk*).'[30] [Thumāma] said, 'When Anas ibn Malik was dying, he told me to put some of that perfume in his embalming scent (*ḥanūṭ*),[31] and that was done.'[32]

> Isrā'īl related that ʿUthmān b. ʿAbdullāh b. Mawhab said, 'My people sent me with a cup of water to Umm Salama—Isrā'īl put three fingers together indicating the size—for the container in which was one of the hairs of the Prophet, may God bless him and grant him peace. When someone was afflicted by the Evil Eye or some other affliction, he would send a vessel [containing water] to [Umm Salama].[33] I looked in the bell-like vessel and saw some red hairs'.[34]

In a commentary on the tradition further details are given:

> If any person suffered from the evil eye or some other disease, he would send a vessel containing water to Umm Salama and she would dip the Prophet's hair into it and would return the vessel to its owner, and he would either drink the water or would wash himself with it seeking a cure [from God] through it and he would derive its *baraka*.[35]

These *ḥadīth* and others provided theological justification for the Muslim veneration of the relics of the Prophet and other holy persons. In another *ḥadīth* commentary, one finds that it is 'permissible to employ the relics (*āthār*) of the righteous (*ṣāliḥīn*) and their garments (*malābis*) in order to derive *baraka* and good fortune (*taymmun*)'.[36] This holds true for dead and living persons. While the curative properties of relics are widely attested to, none of these relics came to be associated with learning as the Prophet's sandal did.

---

[30] A type of perfume which often includes musk as a component.
[31] The mixed scent used for preparing corpses for burial.
[32] Bukhārī, *Ṣaḥīḥ*, ch. 82, no. 5925.
[33] Meaning that Umm Salama would dip the Prophet's hair into it and it would be drunk.
[34] Bukhārī, *Ṣaḥīḥ*, ch. 80, no. 5557.
[35] Ibn Ḥajar al-ʿAsqalānī, *Fatḥ al-Bārī bi-Sharḥ Ṣaḥīḥ al-Bukhārī*, ed. ʿAbd al-ʿAzīz b. ʿAbd Allāh b. Bāz et al., 3rd edn (Beirut, 1996), 10:353.
[36] Ibn Ḥajar al-ʿAsqalānī, *Fatḥ al-Bārī bi-Sharḥ Ṣaḥīḥ al-Bukhārī*, ed. M. al-Khaṭīb (Cairo, 1986), 341 (no. 5540): http://www.islamweb.net/newlibrary/display_book.php?flag=1&bk_no=52&ID=10742.

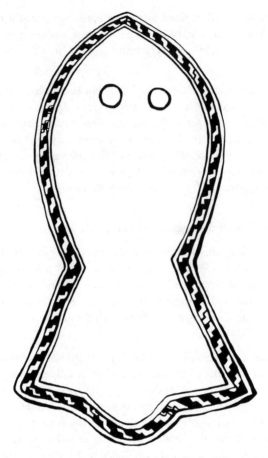

Fig. 1. The sandal of the Prophet Muḥammad, housed at the Ashrafīya teaching college in Damascus. Illustration produced by Josef W. Meri

The Sandal (na'l) of the Prophet

One of the best-documented relics of the Prophet is his sandal (Fig. 1). Today a single specimen of the sandal exists in the Topkapı Museum in Istanbul, though purported specimens can be found on the Indian subcontinent. It was believed that the Prophet had touched the Throne of God with his sandals while on his famous Night Journey and Ascension to Heaven.[37]

---

[37] Schimmel, *And Muḥammad is His Messenger*, 40; al-Maqqarī, *Fatḥ al-Mutaʿ āl fī Madḥ al-Niʿāl*, ed. Aḥmad Farīd al-Mizyadī (Beirut, 2006), 240, where al-Maqqarī writing in the 17th century discounts this belief.

One of the earliest references to the sandal outside of the *ḥadīth* traditions is a particularly revealing episode which exemplifies the fear that rulers had of the common people. One of the ʿAbbāsid Caliph al-Mahdī's (r. 158/775–169/785) subjects presented him with a purported sandal of the Prophet which he promptly kissed and placed over his eyes. If the sceptical caliph were to reject the sandal as being of dubious origin, he feared that word of this would spread among the common people. The caliph reasoned that the people would support the weak over the strong even if the weak were wrong. Consequently, al-Mahdī paid the person who sought his audience a handsome sum for the purported relic. Al-Mahdī remarked to his companions: '[With the 10,000 dirhams], we bought his tongue, accepted his gift, and [pretended] to give credibility to what he said. In our opinion this serves our ends better and is preferable'.[38]

The most famous accounts concerning the sandal are from the reign of the Ayyūbid ruler of Damascus al-Malik al-Ashraf Mūsā (r. 626/1229–635/1237) who built a college for the teaching of the *ḥadīth* traditions of the Prophet named after him next to the Citadel of Damascus, perhaps in order to be in close proximity to the relic and derive *baraka* from it.[39] The sandal which al-Ashraf acquired from an itinerant Damascene *ḥadīth* scholar who displayed the relic to rulers who would seek its blessings (*yatabarrakūna bihi*) in return for gifts,[40] initially became al-Ashraf's personal possession from which he sought *baraka* for himself and those pious individuals close to him. The historian al-Yūnīnī (d. 726/1326) reports that

> [Al-Malik al-Ashraf] desired to send it to my father so that he might make *ziyāra*[41] to it and obtain *baraka* from it. Then he said, 'We have missed the Shaykh. It is befitting that we travel to him. We shall inform him to visit (*yazūr*) this noble relic (*athar sharīf*) and behold it.' He sent him [word of that]. My grandmother who was then still alive said to my father, 'I have longed to visit this holy relic, visit it in my stead'. When he travelled to Damascus and visited the holy relic, he informed al-Malik al-Ashraf what his mother had said. Al-Ashraf

---

[38] Al-Khaṭīb al-Baghdādī, *Taʾrīkh Baghdād*, Alwaraq.net edn, 397.

[39] See Meri, *Cult of Saints*, 109–11. Eerik Dickinson in a study of *ḥadīth* literature highlights the role of the sandal as a symbol of learning, 'Ibn al-Ṣalāḥ al-Shahrazūrī and the Isnād', *Journal of the American Oriental Society*, 122 (2002), 481–505.

[40] See al-Maqqarī, *Fatḥ al-Mutaʿāl*, 279.

[41] *Ziyāra* (lit. a visit, visiting) is a pious visitation or pilgrimage to a sacred object or more generally, to the tomb or shrine of a saint or holy person. See Meri, *Cult of Saints*, ch. 3.

prepared [to send] the holy relic to Ba'labakk [especially for her].
She made a visit to it and fulfilled her desire from that.[42]

The sandal became a semi-public relic after al-Malik al-Ashraf built for it a special receptacle and appointed for it a salaried custodian.[43] The Damascene ruler's desire to build a college for teaching the prophetic traditions and deposition of the sandal there were an affirmation of his continuing support for the 'ulamā' or religious scholars. Moreover, the sandal was part of the Ayyūbid ruler's broader plan to repair and patronize the holy places of the city. Indeed, the sandal came to represent his authority and rule as a righteous ruler and defender of Sunni orthodoxy. This is in marked contrast to the role of the 'ulamā' who were not only keepers of religious knowledge but in actual fact the true custodians of relics such as the sandal.

When Muslims living in the far reaches of the Islamic world, such as in North Africa and Andalusia were unable to visit the sandal, a tradition was established, perhaps from the twelfth century, of pious travellers to Damascus making 'exact' paper patterns of the original, or of reliable patterns and bringing them back home where they were revered. This is attested to by the Damascene ḥadīth scholar Abū'l-Yumn 'Abd al-Ṣamad b. 'Abd al-Wahhāb Ibn 'Asākir (d. 686/1287),[44] the author of Juz' Timthāl Na'l al-Nabī, the earliest extant work dedicated to the sandal, and by al-Maqqarī (d. 1631/1040) author of Fatḥ al-Muta'āl fī Madḥ al-Ní āl.[45] These scholars equally composed verses for honouring these copies.[46]

These patterns or replicas were known to be in the possession of the famous Qur'ān memorizer and traditionist Abū Ṭāhir Aḥmad b. Muḥammad al-Silafī (d. 576/1180) in Alexandria, al-Amīn Hibat Allāh b. Aḥmad b. Muḥammad al-Akfānī (d. 524/1129) in Damascus,[47] and Aḥmad b. Muḥammad b. Yūsuf b. Mas'ada al-Fazārī (d. c. 6th/12th c.) in Isfahan. These learned men were responsible for transmitting and propagating the teaching of the ḥadīth traditions of the Prophet Muḥammad. That several replicas of the sandals are attested to in the twelfth century indicates that they had assumed an important place in the revival of the religious sciences, a process which began during the eleventh century under the Seljuk Turkish dynasty accompanied by the building of teaching colleges for the religious

[42] Quoted in Meri, Cult of Saints, 109.

[43] Ibid. This is attested to in late medieval sources, namely al-Maqqarī and Ibn al-Ḥawrānī.

[44] He was buried in Medina in the Baqī' cemetery near the Prophet's mosque.

[45] See e.g., al-Maqqarī, Fatḥ.

[46] Al-Maqqarī, Fatḥ al-Muta'āl, 289.

[47] Teacher of Ibn 'Asākir's ancestor, 'Alī b. al-Ḥasan (d. 571/1176), the famous historian and author of Ta'rīkh Madīnat Dimashq (History of Damascus).

sciences. These policies of strengthening Sunni Islam continued under the ruler of Aleppo Nūr al-Dīn and his successor Saladin.

A common practice associated with the study of the *ḥadīth* traditions of the Prophet is the use of the sandals in facilitating cures. For instance, surrogate sandals were placed over the eyes of the blind in order to cure blindness.[48] The *ʿulamāʾ* who were custodians of the sandals vouchsafed that they would not be destroyed by controlling access to them. Unlike the Qurʾanic codex of ʿUthmān which was made accessible to the common people, the Prophet's sandal symbolized the authority of the *ʿulamāʾ* and that of the *ḥadīth* scholars in particular as keepers of the traditions of the Prophet.

Ibn ʿAsākir mentions the account of the miraculous healing qualities of the sandal which is narrated by 'the righteous and God-fearing shaykh' Abū Jaʿfar Aḥmad b. ʿAbd al-Majīd:

> I cut the pattern [of this sandal] for one of my students. [He came to me one day] and said: 'Yesterday I saw a wonder from the *baraka* of this sandal. My wife was suffering from a pain which almost took her life. I placed the [image of the] sandal on the spot of her pain and said: O God, show me the blessing (*baraka*) of the owner of this sandal. God cured her instantly.'[49]

The divine blessings (*baraka*) of the sandal which derived from the person of the Prophet were transmitted to surrogate images by scholars and theologians. In another account, the narrator relates that the sandal was 'tried-and-proven' and that Muslims who sought blessings through it would also be given 'protection from the oppression of the oppressor and the victory of the enemy. It is also a talisman against every rebellious satan and the envy of the envier. Should the pregnant woman hold it while in labour, she would deliver safely by the power and strength of God'.[50]

The North African scholar and preacher Ibn Rushayd al-Fihrī (d. 721/ 1321) sought the holy sandal which was accessible to the public on Mondays and Thursdays, both voluntary days of fasting in Islam. Al-Yūnīnī (d. 726/1326) mentions Monday and Thursday afternoons.[51]

---

[48] See Schimmel, *And Muḥammad is His Messenger*, 40. Such hand-drawn images were common, particularly in pre-16th century North African works.

[49] Ibn ʿAsākir, *Juzʾ Timthāl Naʿl al-Nabī*, ed. Ḥusayn Shukrī (Medina, n/d), 25. (Reissued with corrections and additions by Dār al-Kutub al-ʿIlmīya, 2010). My thanks to Ḥusayn Shukrī for making his work available to me. The passage is also quoted in al-Qasṭallānī, *al-Mawāhib al-Ladunnīya*, 2:467.

[50] Ibn ʿAsākir, *Juzʾ*, 25.

[51] Al-Yunini, *Dhayl Mirʾāt al-Zamān*, 2:46.

Ibn Rushayd observed that people would seek blessings (*baraka*) through kissing the sandal (*lathmihā*). According to him: 'whoever kisses it, his mouth would [taste] its sweet fragrance.'[52]

Ibn Rushayd observed that the sandal was encased in a box visible through an opening cut in the shape of the sandal.[53] The face of the box was constructed from an ebony slab atop an ebony box fastened together with silver nails. The sandal was accessed through an opening in the box. This was a necessary precaution in order to prevent its destruction or perhaps to preserve what was left of it. The teaching professor of the college asked its salaried custodian to make it accessible to Ibn Rushayd who commented upon beholding it: 'I was able to kiss it, seek blessings from it, and trace it and make this copy which you [dear reader] see in velum and which is made from the direct copy.'[54] (Fig. 1)

A contemporary of Ibn Rushayd the Mālikī jurisprudent Abū Ḥafṣ al-Fākihānī (d. 734/1334) visited the sandal seeking its *baraka*. The *ḥadīth* scholar Jamāl al-Dīn Ibn Ḥadīda al-Anṣārī narrates from a ṣūfī disciple of al-Fākihānī's:

> I was with him. When he saw the most honoured sandal, he bared his head (*ḥaṣara 'an ra'sihi*) and began to kiss it (*yuqabbiluhu*) and rub (*yamragh*) his face in it. His tears flowed. Then he recited:
>
> 'If it were said to Laylā's Madman:[55] Is it Laylā and her relation
>   you wish, or the world and all that it contains?
> He would reply: Dust from the dirt of her sandals
>   is dearer to my soul and more healing of its ills!'[56]

The renowned Cairene theologian al-Qasṭallānī (d. 923/1517) mentions the following tradition in which the miraculous qualities of the sandal are enumerated:

> Abū Isḥāq [al-Zuhrī] said: al-Qāsim b. Muḥammad, [son of the first caliph Abū Bakr] said: Of the proven blessing of the similitude

---

[52] Al-Maqqarī, *Fatḥ al-Mutaʿāl*, 278. The MSS of Ibn ʿAsākir's work reveals where it has been worn from kissing the image of the sandal. The image is reproduced herein (Fig. 1).

[53] Years earlier Ibn Rushayd's teacher visited the sandal which at the time was not encased in an ebony box, al-Maqqarī, *Fatḥ al-Mutaʿāl*, 277.

[54] Al-Maqqarī, *Fatḥ al-Mutaʿāl*, 277–8.

[55] Ar. Majnūn Laylā—a seventh-century story based on the true account of Qays, a Bedouin poet and shepherd, who falls in love with Laylā and is refused her hand in marriage by her father, whereupon he goes mad.

[56] Ibn Farḥūn, *Al-Dībāj al-Mudhahhab fī Maʿrifat Aʿyān ʿUlamāʾ al-Madhhab*, Alwaraq.net edn, 108.

of the Prophet's sandal is that whoever has it in his possession for seeking blessings (*tabarruk*), it will safeguard him from the sedition of rebels and the mastery of enemies, and will be a barrier against every recreant devil and the evil eye of the envious (*ʿayn kull ḥāsid*). If the pregnant woman holds it in her right hand at the time of labour, her delivery will be facilitated by God's strength and His might.[57]

In as much as the sandal symbolized the revivification of religious scholarship in Damascus, so too it came to symbolize the fight against injustice and oppression. According to al-Yūnīnī, the sandal was visited in the late afternoon on Monday and Thursday.[58] Al-Maqqarī mentions that 'the people of Damascus used to seek intercession [from God] by means of the prophetic sandal when problems befell them and they witnessed its *baraka*'.[59] In the year 711/1312, the Mamlūk governor of Syria ordered a conscription of 1,500 cavalrymen. The people of Damascus protested. The preacher of the Umayyad Mosque Jalāl al-Qazwīnī took the ʿUthmānī codex of the Qurʾān and the sandal of the Prophet and marched with them accompanied by religious scholars and the common people. The governor and his deputies struck the people and threw down the Qurʾān and the sandal. The people invoked imprecations against the governor who imprisoned the preacher. After learning of this disgraceful display and his governor's desecration of the sacred objects, the Mamluk Sulṭān al-Nāṣir Muḥammad b. Qalāwūn (r. 693/1293–694/1294, 698/1299–708/1309, 708/1309–741/1341) had his governor shackled and imprisoned.[60]

The right and left sandals were housed in two teaching colleges in Damascus until Tamerlane's siege of the city in 803/1401.[61] Al-Nuʿaymī mentions a second sandal in the Damāghīya teaching college which was endowed for the Shāfiʿī and Ḥanafī schools of Islamic jurisprudence in the year 638/1240 by the wife of a friend of the Ayyūbid ruler of Damascus al-Malik al-ʿĀdil (r. 592/1196–615/1218). The teaching colleges did not compete with each other to acquire relics. Nevertheless possessing the relic conferred *baraka* but also prestige to the teaching college or mosque that housed it, thus attracting pupils and scholars from faraway lands. The chronicles are vague about the sandals' fate except that it is commonly believed that when

---

[57] Al-Qasṭallānī, *Al-Mawāhib*, 2:467.

[58] Quoted in Meri, *Cult of Saints*, 110.

[59] Al-Maqqarī, *Fatḥ*, 282.

[60] Ibid., 282–3.

[61] Al-Nuʿaymī, *al-Dāris fī Tārīkh al-Madāris*, 2:227.

the Mongol ruler Timur (Tamerlane) besieged Damascus in 803/1401 he carried away the right and left sandals.[62]

Teaching colleges and mosques were associated with other relics of the Prophet, most notably the Prophet's hairs and impressions of footprints in rock. During the 9th/15th century the pious itinerant scholar Muḥammad b. al-Zamān (d. 897/1492) met up during his peregrinations with a holy man who gave him a strand of hair purportedly belonging to the Prophet, an impression of the Prophet's footprint in rock, and a letter in the handwriting of Shuraḥbīl b. Ḥasana, one of the scribes of inspiration who wrote down the Qur'an after its revelation to the Prophet.[63] These relics were stored in a teaching college which Ibn al-Zamān founded in Cairo.[64]

The Mamlūk amir Sayf al-Dīn Manjak al-Yūsufī who was renowned for his pious endowments during the 8th/14th century and who built a teaching college[65] also possessed a strand of hair of the Prophet until his death. However, there is no evidence that he bequeathed the strand of hair to the teaching college. By contrast, the example of Ibn al-Zamān clearly suggests that other relics were often associated with teaching colleges and mosques and that they served as symbols of learning bestowing perpetual blessings upon Muslim visitors as well as students and professors.

The staff and mantle of the Prophet

The staff (qaḍīb) of the Prophet and his mantle (burda) represented first and foremost the power and authority of the ʿAbbāsid caliphs which derived from the personhood of the Prophet, though notably the ʿAbbāsid caliphs, like their Fāṭimid counterparts, claimed the title of 'vicegerent of God (khalīfat Allāh) on Earth',[66] not vicegerent of the Prophet. Mantles have always been

---

[62] Al-Nuʿaymī, *Al-Dāris fī Tārīkh al-Madāris*, 2:227.

[63] Al-Sakhāwī, *Al-Ḍawʾ al-Lāmiʿ*, 8:260–62.

[64] Similar examples of the hairs of the Prophet employed in the founding of mosques abound in the pre-modern and modern contexts. See Aḥmad Taymūr, *Al-Āthār al-Nabawīya*, 82–96.

[65] Al-Nuʿaymī, *Al-Dāris fī Tārīkh al-Madāris*, 1:461–2.

[66] For a discussion of this term see most notably P. Crone and M. Hinds, *God's Caliph: Religious Authority in the First Centuries of Islam* (Cambridge, 1986), ch. 2. This is similar to the notion of the Divine Right of Kings in the European context or the Shah-en-Shah of Sassanian Iran, the latter of which was a conscious model for the ʿAbbāsid rulers. See also the earlier work of E. H. Palmer, *Harun Alraschid: Caliph of Bagdad* (London and Belfast, 1881), 37–8.

symbols of kings and rulers from Sassanian Persia to the Byzantine Empire. In the Biblical context the mantle of the Prophet Elijah which he passed on to the Prophet Elisha represented his person.[67] Similarly, the mantle of the Prophet Muḥammad represents his person. Moreover, the *burda* was regarded by the ʿAbbāsid caliphs as a symbol of the Prophet's protection which conferred upon them his *baraka*.[68] The eleventh-century Iraqi jurist and *ḥadīth* scholar al-Māwardī (d. 450/1058) specifically mentions that both objects became synonymous with the caliphate (*min shiʿār al-khilāfa*),[69] though he does not include the ring mentioned by the historian al-Ṭabari that was present at the death of the Caliph Hārūn al-Rashīd[70] (r. 170/786–193/809) and also at the investiture of the Caliph al-Mustaʿīn (r. 248/862–252/866).[71] A contemporary of al-Māwardī, the Būyid chancery official and historian Hilāl b. al-Muḥassin al-Ṣābiʾ (d. 448/1056) produced a work on the rules and regulations of the ʿAbbāsid court. Therein he mentions that the caliph

> wears a black *ruṣāfiyyah*[72] on his head, and adorns himself with the sword of the Prophet, may God bless him. . .and in front of him he has the Qurʾān of ʿUthmān, may the mercy of God be upon him, which in those days used to be kept in the closets. On his shoulders

---

[67] 2 Kings 2:13–15.

[68] Like their rivals the ʿAbbāsid dynasty, the Fāṭimid dynasty claimed the caliphate. Among their most prized treasures was the sword of the Prophet which he gave to his cousin and son-in-law ʿAlī b. Abī Ṭālib. However, the sword was never regarded as a symbol of ʿAbbāsid rule, though it could be interpreted as such. The earliest mention of the sword in connection with the ʿAbbāsids is in 145/762 during the reign of Al-Manṣūr who was facing an ʿAlid rebellion by Muḥammad b. ʿAbd Allāh al-Nafs al-Zakīya (d. 145/762). See e.g., Al-Rashīd b. al-Zubayr, *Kitāb al-Hadāyā wal-Tuḥaf*, ed. Muḥammad Ḥamīd Allāh (Kuwait, 1959), 231. The sword is described in much detail in Qāḍī al-Nuʿmān, *al-Majālis wal-Musāyarāt*, ed. Al-Ḥabīb al-Faqī, Ibrāhīm Shabbūḥ, and Muḥammad al-Yaʿlāwī (Tunis, 1978; Beirut: Dār al-Muntaẓar, 1996), 114. An important study of the Fāṭimid acquisition of Dhūʾl-Fiqār and its ceremonial function at the Fāṭimid court is Paul Walker, 'Purloined Symbols of the Past: The Theft of Souvenirs and Sacred Relics in the Rivalry between the Abbasids and Fatimids', in F. Daftary and J. W. Meri (eds), *Culture and Memory in Medieval Islam* (London, 2003), 364–87. Also see Anne-Marie Schimmel (trans.), 'Dhūʾl-Fiqār', from Nasir Khusraw, *Make a Shield from Wisdom*, 59.

[69] Al-Māwardī, *al-Aḥkām al-Sulṭānīya wal-Wilāyāt al-Dīnīya*, Alwaraq.net edn, 103.

[70] Al-Ṭabari, *Taʾrīkh*, Alwaraq.net edn, Year 193 H., 2062.

[71] Al-Ṭabari, *Taʾrīkh*, Alwaraq.net edn, Year 248 H., 2345.

[72] A turban. Black was the royal colour of the ʿAbbāsid dynasty.

he wears the [mantle] of the Prophet, may God bless him; and in his hand he holds the Prophet's staff.[73]

The 'Abbāsids had claimed legitimacy to rule through the Prophet's paternal uncle 'Abbās. The famous mantle (*burda*) of the Prophet is fairly well documented in historical accounts.[74] Like the *khirqa* or Sufi robe passed from master to disciple, the *burda* was a source of *baraka* for its possessor. Similarly, certain robes were believed to be those of Muḥammad.[75] The *burda* was worn by the 'Abbāsid caliphs in succession and apparently was destroyed along with the staff upon the Mongol siege of Baghdad and the murder of the last 'Abbāsid caliph al-Mustaʿṣim in 656/1258. According to one account the Mongol ruler Hülegü, who was most probably a Buddhist, destroyed both these relics by burning them. A somewhat apocryphal story is recounted of the Mongols claiming that they had burned the relics in order to cleanse them of their impure association with the caliph.[76]

Two mantles are attested to in the historical sources. The first was given by the Prophet in the year 9/630 to the Christian inhabitants of Byzantine Ayla (modern-day 'Aqaba in Jordan) as a way of granting them protection. It was taken from them by the governor of the last Umayyad caliph Marwān II (r. 125/744–132/749) and given to his overlord. After the caliph's death it was stolen and later sold to the first 'Abbāsid caliph Abū'l-'Abbās al-Saffāḥ (r. 132/750–136/754) for 300 dinars.[77] Al-Māwardī mentions another tradition which states that the mantle is the one which the Prophet gave to his Companion Kaʿb b. Zubayr from whom the Umayyad Caliph Muʿāwiya purchased it. He states that 'this is the one which the caliphs wear'.[78]

[73] Hilāl al-Ṣābi', *Rusūm Dār al-Khilāfa*, ed. Mīkhā'īl 'Āwwād (Beirut, 1986), 90–1; trans. by Elie A. Salem as *The Rules and Regulations of the 'Abbāsid Court* (Beirut, 1977), 73 (modified).

[74] In the year 9 H. upon becoming a *Muslim* Kaʿb b. Zubayr was given a cloak by the Prophet which the Umayyad caliph Muʿāwiya purchased for 20,000 dirhams from Kaʿb's children. This cloak remained with the 'Abbāsid caliphs. Ibn al-Athīr, *Ta'rīkh*, Alwaraq.net edn, 340. See also al-Māwardī, *al-Aḥkām al-Sulṭānīya wal-Wilāyāt al-Dīnīya*, Alwaraq.net edn, 103 where the sum paid is not mentioned.

[75] Jamal J. Elias, 'The Sufi Robe (Khirqa) as a Vehicle of Spiritual Authority', in Stewart Gordon (ed.), *Robes and Honor: the Medieval World of Investiture* (New York, 2001), 275–89. My thanks to Jamal Elias for sending me an offprint of his work.

[76] Abū'l-Fidā', *al-Mukhtaṣar fī Tārīkh al-Bashar*, Alwaraq.net edn, Year 535 H., 320; D.S. Margoliouth, 'The Relics of the Prophet Mohammed', *Moslem World*, 27 (1937), 24.

[77] See al-Māwardī, *al-Aḥkām al-Sulṭānīya wal-Wilāyāt al-Dīnīya*, Alwaraq.net edn, 103.

[78] Ibid.

Upon the death of Hārūn al-Rashīd, his eunuch collected the *burda*, along with the seal and the staff.[79] These were transmitted to Hārūn's son al-Amīn. In 195/810 a civil war broke out which led to the deposition and murder of the caliph al-Amīn and the ascendancy of his brother al-Maʾmūn. Al-Amīn's severed head along with the *burda*, staff, and ring were brought to al-Maʾmūn.

The mantle not only served a ceremonial function, but also a talismanic one as well. The ninth and tenth centuries witnessed the waning of caliphal political authority and were characterized by great political turmoil and instability in the Abbāsid domains. In the year 211/826, shortly before being deposed by his cousin al-Muʿtazz, an embattled ʿAbbāsid Caliph al-Mustaʿīn (r. 248/862–252/866), appeared before the people of Baghdad donning the mantle of the Prophet with staff in hand. He invoked caliphal authority to assure his followers that his vizier Ibn Ṭāhir was loyal. However, al-Muʿtazz, who demanded his surrender also required al-Mustaʿīn to surrender the mantle, staff, and signet ring of the Prophet and sign an agreement that he was relinquishing the Prophet's heritage (*turāth al-nabī*) to its rightful heir. He was betrayed by al-Muʿtazz who had initially promised him safe passage to Mecca but who later had him summarily executed.[80]

During the tenth century, the caliph equipped himself with the mantle and armour in battle in the year 320/932 when the politically impotent caliph al-Muqtadir (295/908–320/932) was forced to wage war on his enemies.[81] According to the *ḥadīth* scholar and historian al-Dhahabī, al-Muqtadir was killed by a Berber soldier, his body stripped naked and the relics taken.[82] Much later, the caliph al-Mustarshid (r. 513/1118–529/1135) in 527/1132 personally rallied his troops dressed in military regalia and the *burda* at the head of 2,000 cavalry and successfully routed his enemies.[83] A tragic fate befell al-Mustarshid who attempted boldly to shake off the yoke of his Seljuk overlords in a battle in which he was taken prisoner. While in custody, he was murdered. Upon al-Mustarshid's death the Seljuk ruler Sanjar (c. 490/1097–552/1157) apparently returned the Prophet's mantle and staff to the former's successor al-Muqtafī. The ʿAbbāsids were not the first to employ the relics of

[79] Ṭabarī, *Taʾrīkh*, Alwaraq.net edn, Year 193 H., 2062; *The History of al-Ṭabarī* (The War between Brothers), trans. M. Fishbein (Albany, 1992), 11, 195, 196, 199.

[80] Al-Ṭabarī, *Taʾrīkh*, Alwaraq.net edn, Year 211 H., 2345.

[81] Miskawayh, *Kitāb Tajārib al-Umam*, ed. H. F. Amedroz, 4 vols (Cairo, 1914–16), 1:235–7.

[82] Al-Dhahabī, *Taʾrīkh*, Alwaraq.net edn, Year 320 H., 2372.

[83] Ibn al-Jawzī, *al-Muntaẓam*, Alwaraq.net edn, Year 527 H., 2118.

the Prophet in battle. The prophetic Companion Khālid b. al-Walīd (d. 21/642) wore a tall hat containing hairs of the Prophet during the conquest of Syria.

> It was said of Khālid b. al-Walīd, who was buried in Ḥimṣ, that 'He conquered Damascus [wearing] a [tall hat] containing hairs of the Messenger of God . . . seeking victory through them and their blessing (*baraka*)'.[84]

The Qur'anic codex of ʿUthmān[85]

The Qur'anic codex of the third rightly-guided caliph ʿUthmān ibn ʿAffān (r. 23/643–35/655) was itself a sacred object which conferred legitimacy on rulers in the Islamic East and West. The Caliph ʿUthmān was murdered while copying the Qur'an. It is believed that drops of his blood were to be found on pages of the Qur'an. Four copies of the ʿUthmānic codex had been made each of which was dispatched to a different part of the Islamic world—one remained in the Ḥijāz (Mecca and/or Medina), another was sent to Damascus, and two copies to Iraq (Baṣra and Kūfa). Perhaps, the best documented codex was the one kept in the Umayyad Mosque in Damascus. The people of Damascus were given access to the codex after the noon prayer and debtors were made to swear on it. It assumed a public role as did the sandal of the Prophet, particularly in processions at times of crises or impending invasions of the city.

Devotees also derived *baraka* from relics without coming into physical contact with them. In the case of the ʿUthmānic codex, the historian Sibṭ Ibn al-Jawzī (d. 654/1256) mentions that devotees derived *baraka* through beholding it.[86] Yet, its efficacy was fully realized when it was touched, held, or taken out in procession.

In addition to the previously mentioned example of the people of Damascus confronting an unjust governor with the codex and the sandal of the Prophet, one incident in particular illustrates the invocation of relics at times of crisis. The codex was taken into public view during a procession meant to avert a Crusader invasion of Damascus in 543/1148. The historian Ibn al-Jawzī (d. 597/1200) reports:

> The whole land was weeping and wailing and spreading ashes on themselves for days. The ʿUthmānī codex was brought out into the

[84] See Meri, *Cult of Saints*, 108.

[85] Meri, *Cult of Saints*, 114–16.

[86] Sibṭ b. al-Jawzī, *Mir'āt al-Zamān fī Ta'rīkh al-Aʿyān* (Hyderabad, 1951–2), 8:2.

courtyard of the Congregational Mosque and men, women and children congregated around it, baring their heads and supplicated. God responded to them.[87]

Apart from the fact that scriptures and other sacred objects were never hidden as were relics of saints in Europe, one may afford a comparison with the example of the relics of St Martin of Tours in 903 which illustrates a fundamental principle in common with Islam about how sacred objects empower the populace and theologians to overcome the enemy, in this case the Vikings.[88]

In the Islamic West, the codex figured in the processions of the Almohad dynasty of the Maghrib. As Amira Bennison concludes, the Almohad dynasty's acquisition of an ʿUthmānī codex during the twelfth century was a 'symbolic and divinely ordained confirmation of the caliph's legitimacy.'[89]

Conclusion

Relics in medieval Islam emerge as receptacles for *baraka*, sacred symbols for the legitimation of rule and for the *ʿulamā*'s guardianship of the prophetic traditions and the transmission of the knowledge embodied therein. The ʿUthmānī codex in the Ummayad Mosque and the sandal of the Prophet in the Ashrafīya teaching college assumed a fundamental public role in the spiritual life of Damascenes. The people of Damascus as well as visitors from all over the Islamic world continued to believe in the efficacy of these sacred objects through which they derived *baraka*. Upon obtaining the sandals and other relics of the Prophet, teaching colleges came to be possessed with *baraka*, thus becoming loci for pious visitations and those seeking knowledge of the prophetic traditions. The sandal as metonymy for the Prophet and the Qur'an as the Word of God were routinely invoked in order to combat the abuse of power by rulers and those who would swear false oaths.

By contrast, the head of Ḥusayn along with other relics served as legitimators of the Fāṭimid dynasty. However, the Fāṭimids strictly controlled access to these relics. Perhaps, with no other dynasty than the ʿAbbāsids did several of the relics of the Prophet assume a role in the conferment of power, i.e. the physical transference of the symbolic power and authority of the Prophet to

---

[87] Meri, *Cult of Saints*, 115.

[88] Sharon Farmer, *Communities of Saint Martin: Legend and Ritual in Medieval Tours* (Ithaca, 1991), 32–3.

[89] Amira K. Bennison, 'The Almohads and the Qurʾān of ʿUthmān: The Legacy of the Umayyads of Cordoba in the Twelfth Century Maghrib', *Al-Masāq* 19 (2007), 151. I am grateful to Dr. Bennison for an offprint of her article.

the ʿAbbāsid caliphs as heirs to the legacy of the Prophet through his paternal uncle ʿAbbās. The ʿAbbāsids employed the mantle (*burda*), staff (*qaḍīb*), and ring (*khātim*) of the Prophet Muḥammad in their investiture ceremonies, during the conferment of honours to rulers, in public displays, and in battle, thus emphasizing the power and legitimacy of the ʿAbbāsid dynasty as sole heirs to the legacy of the Prophet despite the existence at various points in the caliphate's history of the rival Fāṭimid and Córdoban caliphates. However, the Shiʿi Buyids and their successors the Sunni Seljuk dynasty, the actual rulers over the ʿAbbāsid dominion, never wrested the relics from the ʿAbbāsid caliphs in order to employ them. On the contrary, they were cognizant of the fact that they were symbols of the caliph, who alone had the right to display them on his person. Thus relics became objects in the process of the conferment and establishment of temporal and spiritual authority. Beyond the semblance of the investiture ceremonies and the occasional public display of the relics in battle and on public occasions, these sacred objects never conferred a sacred quality to the persons of the ʿAbbāsid caliphs to the extent that they were regarded as saints or holy persons. However, for the common people relics were sources of divine blessings for their possessors and those who sought *baraka* through them.

Under Ayyūbid patronage, the relics of the Prophet assumed pride of place in the transmission of knowledge in teaching colleges, thus ensuring the continuity of the Prophet's legacy. The sandal became synonymous with religious knowledge, in particular with knowledge of *ḥadīth*. The ʿulamāʾ were the custodians of these relics, responsible for maintaining their historical memory, imparting their history, vouchsafing their authenticity, urging their veneration, and propagating a culture of learning and scholarship. Relics associated with cures such as the sandal and the Prophet's hairs never became legitimators of sovereignty in the sense the mantle, staff, and ring of the Prophet did.

In Islam as in Christianity, relics conferred divine blessings on their possessors and those who came into contact with them seeking relief from adversity, cures, and the fulfilment of supplications. Within the context of the veneration of saints and holy persons relics helped to transform cities from seats of power into pilgrimage centres. Above all, they brought Muslims and Christians closer to the divine.

APPENDIX
Typology of relics

1. Relics associated with the prophets and personages from monotheistic tradition.
   a. Portable and non-portable
      i. Sacred traces in rock such as footprints and handprints (sometimes portable), belonging to the prophets, usually Moses and Muḥammad
   b. Heads of St John the Baptist and of the Prophet Muḥammad's grandson Ḥusayn b. ʿAlī (d. 61/680)
   c. Staff of Moses and objects associated with Jesus
   d. Relics of the Prophet Muḥammad
      i. Hair (beard and head) (*shaʿrāt*)
      ii. Sandals (*naʿl*, pl. *niʿāl*)
      iii. Shoes (*khuff*)
      iv. Cup (*qadaḥ*)
      v. Toothpick (*miswāk*)
      vi. Seal (*khātim*)
      vii. Staff (*qaḍīb*)
      viii. Mantle (*burda*)
      ix. Head covering (*ʿimāma*)
      x. Prayer mat (*muṣallā, khumra*)
      xi. Kohl applicator
      xii. Letters (incl. to the Byzantine Emperor Heraclius and the Coptic ruler of Egypt the Muqawqas)
      xiii. Armour, weaponry, battle gear
         1. Sword Dhū'l-Fiqār which he gave to his cousin ʿAlī b. Abī Ṭālib
         2. Standards employed in battle
      xiv. Minbar (pulpit where the preacher gives the Friday prayer sermon)
2. Relics associated with the Family of the Prophet, including the Shiʿi imams.
   a. Venerable copies of the Qur'an
      i. ʿUthmānī codex of the Qur'an, (named after the 3rd rightly-guided caliph ʿUthman b. ʿAffān)
      ii. Copies owned and/or copied by notable persons such as ʿAlī b. Abī Ṭālib were revered by the Fāṭimids[90]

---

[90] See Petersen, 'Masd̲j̲id', *EI2*; Maqrīzī, *Khiṭaṭ*, IV.

3. Relics of other holy persons, namely saints (Arab. *awliyā'*), mainly men renowned for their exemplary piety and learning.
   a. Cloaks, tunics, or garments
      i. Never assumed the level of veneration as the relics of the Prophet Muḥammad
   b. Venerable copies of the Qur'an
      i. Almohad ruler and spiritual founder Ibn Tūmart (d. 1130 CE)
   c. Other portable objects
      i. Personal effects of a holy person. E.g., the fragment of an enchanted saw that the Damascene saint Shaykh Arslān had in his workshop was buried with the ruler of Damascus Nūr al-Din b. Zankī (r. 541/1146–569/1174)[91]

[91] Meri, *Cult of Saints*, 108–9.

Skeletons in the Cupboard: Relics after the English Reformation

Alexandra Walsham

Devotion to relics, declared the Genevan reformer Jean Calvin in an unusually scurrilous tract translated into English in 1561, was a most 'execrable sacrilege', a 'filthy polution the which ought in no wise to be suffered in the church'. He spared not an ounce of withering contempt and acerbic wit in cataloguing the vast reservoir of counterfeit bones, blood, shirts, caps, and assorted other 'baggage' and 'geare' that filled the churches of Europe and was cunningly manipulated by the devil and the papists to pervert the simple. Among 'the seae full of lyes' he sought to expose was the brain of St Peter, which was actually a pumice stone, and the improbable proliferation of relics of Christ's Cross and Mary's milk: if a man gathered together all the splinters of the former that were said to exist 'there would be inough to fraighte a great ship', while the quantity of the latter could scarcely have been produced 'if the holye virgyne had bene a cowe' or a wet nurse throughout her life. Had it not been for her assumption into heaven, 'they woulde have made the world beleve, that she had a body sufficient to fell a great poudryng fatte'. As for the morsel of broiled fish presented to Jesus by one of his disciples after his resurrection from the dead, Calvin commented cuttingly, this must have been 'wel spiced' or 'merveylously well soussed' to have been preserved for such a long time. The ease with which the populace had been deceived by these tricks was itself a just punishment from God for its gullibility and natural addiction to 'this most perverse kinde of superstition' and to a carnal religion that revolved around visible, physical things.[1]

Beneath Calvin's vicious outburst against relics was a violent rejection of the assumptions about the immanence of the holy that underpinned traditional Catholic devotion to them. The notion that the body parts and

---

[1] John Calvin, *A very profitable treatise . . . declarynge what great profit might come to al christendome, yf there were a regester made of all Sainctes bodies and other reliques, which are aswell in Italy, as in Fraunce, Dutchland, Spaine, and other kingdomes and countreys,* trans. Steven Wythers (London, 1561), sigs A5v, H5v, B4v-B5r, D5v, A7r, C2r-v, E5r, E4r-v, D6v, D8v, A6r, and passim.

possessions of Christ and the saints were sources of supernatural power and conduits of heavenly grace ostensibly flew in the face of a system of faith that powerfully re-emphasized the transcendence of the sacred and the incorporeality of the divine. This essay explores the afterlife of relics in the wake of the English Reformation. It considers the impact of the Protestant campaign to discredit the cult of relics and the significance of the survival and apparent resurgence of this phenomenon in subsequent generations. Rather than dismiss instances of the latter as uncomfortable anomalies and ostensible contradictions with Calvinist theology, I want to investigate what they reveal about the contours and texture of reformed practice and belief, and the transmutation of cultural forms following a major moment of ideological rupture. I shall argue that they provide insight into the confessionalization of material culture in post-Reformation society and illuminate the processes by which objects that were emblems and tokens of memory became implicated in the politics of religious identity formation. My discussion will turn on the various ways—literal and metaphorical—in which relics became skeletons in the cupboard in the later sixteenth and seventeenth centuries.

I

On the eve of the Reformation many hallowed bones, fragments of flesh, droplets of blood, and scraps of fabric remained in the safe-keeping of monasteries, cathedrals, and churches, where they attracted a steady stream of pilgrims to gaze upon, kiss, and even lick them. They were early and conspicuous targets of attack by the Henrician regime and its evangelical allies. In the mid-1530s the royal commissioners for the dissolution of the greater and lesser religious houses sent Thomas Cromwell a series of mocking inventories of the relics they had uncovered in the course of their visitations: at the Benedictine Abbey of Bury in Suffolk these included the coals over which Saint Lawrence was roasted, the parings of St Edmund's nails, St Thomas Becket's penknife and boots, and various pieces of the True Cross, while at the chapel of Our Lady of Caversham near Reading they discovered the 'holy dagger' allegedly used to kill King Henry VI and a shred of the halter with which Judas was hanged. At Hyde in Hampshire they declared their determination 'to swepe awaye all the roten bones that be called reliques . . . lest it shuld be thought we came more for the treasure thenne for avoiding of thabomynation of ydolatry'.[2] Some of these items were sent down to the

---

[2] Thomas Wright (ed.), *Three Chapters of Letters Relating to the Suppression of the Monasteries*, Camden Society, 1st ser. 26 (1843), 85, 221, and quotation at 219. On the destruction of relics, see Ronald C. Finucane, *Miracles and Pilgrims: Popular Beliefs in Medieval England* (London, 1977), ch. 12; Helen L. Parish, *Monks, Miracles and*

Tower of London or ended up in Cromwell's wardrobe of beds in Westminster; others were smashed or burnt on the spot in compelling spectacles of desacralization. Whether Thomas Becket's bones were buried in an unmarked grave in Canterbury or incinerated remains a mystery to this day: contemporary claims that the episcopal martyr was subjected to a mock trial in 1538 before his relics were set alight and the ashes scattered to the wind may be an urban myth 'invented' and propagated by Cardinal Reginald Pole, which gave expression to deep-seated outrage at the barbarity of Henry VIII's proceedings against the saint and his cult.[3]

The exposure of medieval relics as forgeries and fakes was another centrepiece of the propaganda war that Cromwell launched against the Church of Rome.[4] Rumours that the Blood of Christ preserved at Hailes Abbey in Gloucestershire was really that of a duck had already reared their head in the fifteenth century, but were revived in 1538 in an open-air sermon preached in London by John Hilsey. Further investigation by Hugh Latimer, bishop of Worcester, proved the famous blood to be merely an unctuous gum, probably honey coloured with saffron. In an ironic parody of the solemn ritual of exposing hallowed remains on ecclesiastical feast days, the notorious false relic was paraded through the streets and displayed to the crowds assembled at Paul's Cross.[5] Designed to dispel the aura of reverence that surrounded such objects, this too was a strategy for disenchantment. The future Archbishop Thomas Cranmer likewise suspected that relics of Becket's blood were 'but a feigned thing and made of some red ochre' and Latimer dismissed saints' bones as the remnants of pigs and scoffed at the miracles reputed to have been wrought by St Blaise's heart at Malvern as 'juggling deceits'.[6]

Magic: Reformation Representations of the Medieval Church (London and New York, 2005), 79–81.

[3] John Butler, _The Quest for Becket's Bones: The Mystery of the Relics of St Thomas Becket of Canterbury_ (New Haven and London, 1995); Thomas F. Mayer, 'Becket's Bones Burnt! Cardinal Pole and the Invention and Dissemination of an Atrocity', in Thomas S. Freeman and Thomas F. Mayer (eds), _Martyrs and Martyrdom in England, c.1400–1700_ (Woodbridge, 2007), 126–43.

[4] Peter Marshall, 'Forgery and Miracles in the Reign of Henry VIII', _Past and Present_, 178 (2003), 39–73.

[5] See Ethan H. Shagan, _Popular Politics and the English Reformation_ (Cambridge, 2003), ch. 5, esp. 166–71.

[6] George Elwes Corrie (ed.), _Sermons and Remains of Hugh Latimer, Sometime Bishop of Worcester, Martyr, 1555_, Parker Society (Cambridge, 1845), 53–4, 55; John Edmund Cox

Elevated into polemical commonplaces, these claims echoed not only Chaucer's *Pardoner's Tale* and Lollard denunciations of the veneration of 'worme eten bonys' and grubby 'olde raggis' as harmful to the soul's health, but also humanist critiques of religious materialism epitomized by the colloquies of Desiderius Erasmus.[7] This reformist rhetoric converged with an apocalyptic tirade against the lying wonders of Antichrist that was flowing from the pens of men like the Bible translator William Tyndale and the former Carmelite friar John Bale, who reviled relic worship respectively as 'a cloke of advantage against the precepte of God' and as a manifest example of 'the whoredom of the spirit'.[8] Both strains of sentiment fed into the ecclesiastical injunctions issued by the king, which moved from prohibiting abuse of sacred items for 'superstition or lucre' in 1536 to completely outlawing devotion to them two years later, as works 'devised by men's phantasies beside Scripture', which drew down the 'threats and maledictions of God'.[9] These ringing phrases were reiterated in Bishop Nicholas Shaxton's articles for the diocese of Salisbury, which inveighed against the cult as a source of 'intolerable superstition and abominable idolatry' and supplied a list of the spurious relics he had encountered, from 'mucky combs' and 'rotten girdles' to 'locks of hair', 'gobbets of wood', and other 'such pelfry beyond estimation'.[10] They also continued to resonate in the ecclesiastical legislation issued by Edward VI and Elizabeth I and in a key passage of the Church of England's official homily on the sin of idolatry, which waxed indignant against the 'wicked, impudent, and most shameless men' who substituted horse bones for the limbs of saints and encouraged credulous laypeople to pay homage to the tail of a donkey.[11]

(ed.), *Miscellaneous Writings and Letters of Thomas Cranmer,* Parker Society (Cambridge, 1846), 378.

[7] Geoffrey Chaucer, *The Canterbury Tales,* ed. and trans. Nevill Coghill (Harmondsworth, 1977 edn), 244–58, esp. 249, 257–8; Anne Hudson (ed.), *The Works of a Lollard Preacher,* Early English Text Society, OS, 317 (London, 2001), 231; Desiderius Erasmus, 'The Religious Pilgrimage', in *The Whole Familiar Colloquies,* trans. and ed. Nathan Bailey (London, 1877), especially 238–59.

[8] Tyndale, cited in John Foxe, *Actes and Monuments* (London, 1563), 1336; Henry Christmas (ed.), *Select Works of John Bale, D.D. Bishop of Ossory,* Parker Society (Cambridge, 1849), 524.

[9] Gerald Bray (ed.), *Documents of the English Reformation* (Cambridge, 1994), 177, 180.

[10] W. H. Frere and W. M. Kennedy (eds), *Visitation Articles and Injunctions of the Period of the Reformation,* Alcuin Club 14–16 (London, 1908–10), ii. 59.

[11] Edward Cardwell (ed.), *Documentary Annals of the Reformed Church of England; being a Collection of Injunctions, Declarations, Orders, Articles of Inquiry, &c,* 2 vols (Oxford,

The very language of such texts demystified venerated remains and reduced them to mundane objects and bodily detritus.

Later Protestant writers continued to attack reverence for relics as an unscriptural innovation inveigled into the Church by the papacy and clergy.[12] Nowhere in the Bible, they declared, had the Lord sanctioned the offering of reverence to the dead bones or belongings of the holy men of old. On the contrary, the passage in Deuteronomy 34:6 describing the burial of Moses in an unknown place proved that every effort was made 'to cut away occasion of men's idolatry'.[13] Nor was there any foundation for the assumption that they might have thaumaturgic properties, though here the story in Acts 19:22 relating how handkerchiefs and aprons brought from the body of the apostle Paul had healed diseases and ejected evil spirits required careful glossing, together with the episode in Matthew 10:20–22 telling of the woman cured of a bloody flux after she touched the hem of Christ's garment. It was her faith that had made her whole, insisted Latimer, not the fabric of his vestment: to 'run hither and thither' in pursuit of it was 'but foolery'.[14] Emphasizing the precept that God wished to be worshipped in spirit and truth, Protestants saw relic worship as a heinous violation of the first commandment itself. Thomas Rogers, chaplain to Archbishop Bancroft, renewed the assault upon 'the satanical boldness of the antichristian synagogue of Rome' in teaching its adherents 'to give divine adoration and honour unto them' in an exposition of the 39 Articles published in 1607.[15] In a treatise translated into English four years later John Polyander, Professor of Divinity at the University of Leiden, offered a more extended attack on this brand of 'devilish cousenage' devised by 'the great whore of Babylon', in the course of which he mercilessly mocked relics like the feather from the wing of the archangel Gabriel and stones bearing the footprints of Christ and the false miracles 'which the Quacksalvers of the Romane Church' attributed 'to the gownes, dubblets, hose, jackets, shirts, smocks, girdles, and other ragges of the

---

1844), i. 6, 76, 212–13, 243, 340; *Certain Sermons or Homilies Appointed to be Read in Churches in the Time of Queen Elizabeth* (London, 1914 ed.), 245–7.

[12] See, e.g., Thomas Becon, *The reliques of Rome, containing all such matters of religion, as have in times past bene brought into the Church by the Pope and his adherents* (London, 1563), fo. 183v-184r.

[13] James Calfhill, *An Answer to John Martiall's Treatise of the Cross,* ed. Richard Gibbings, Parker Society (Cambridge, 1846), 312–13.

[14] Corrie (ed.), *Sermons and Remains of Hugh Latimer,* 544.

[15] Thomas Rogers, *The Catholic Doctrine of the Church of England: An Exposition of the Thirty-Nine Articles,* ed. J. J. S. Perowne, Parker Society (Cambridge, 1854), 224–5.

departed'.[16] The arguments that reverence for the corporeal remains of mortal creatures was a lingering remnant of paganism and that no sacred power resided in them continued to be rehearsed throughout the seventeenth century alongside the trope that most relics were blatant fabrications.[17]

II

Polemic of this type retained its relevance because, despite the iconoclastic purges of the 1530s and '40s, relics were a continuing presence in post-Reformation England. Some were rescued from destruction or confiscation and lovingly preserved for posterity by religious conservatives confident that the Catholic faith would one day be restored to its dominant status. During the short reign of Mary I, many of these temporarily came out of hiding. Writing in November 1559, John Jewel declared that it was 'hardly credible what a harvest, or rather what a wilderness of superstition had sprung up in the darkness of the Marian times' and described how he had found a forest of 'fragments of the sacred cross', not to mention 'nails with which the infatuated people dreamed that Christ had been pierced'.[18] One such nail, said to have been brought to England by Joseph of Arimathea in the first century AD, had been salvaged from the great Benedictine abbey at Glastonbury by a former employee, who kept it with great reverence. After Jewel took the offensive item away, the old man transferred his attachment to the empty reliquary—to the impression left in the linen case in which it had been enclosed, which itself acquired a reputation for working miraculous cures. The very void left by the Protestant onslaught became the focus of veneration.[19]

A significant side-effect of the Reformation was to transfer relics from the custodianship of monasteries and churches into private hands and domestic settings. For the missionary priests who arrived in England from 1574 to endeavour to reclaim England to Rome, this process was attendant with

---

[16] John Polyander, *A disputation against the adoration of the reliques of saints departed* (Dordrecht, 1611), sig. A2v, pp. 65, 66, and passim.

[17] See, e.g., William Fulke, *Stapleton's Fortress Overthrown. A Rejoinder of Martiall's Reply. A Discovery of the Dangerous Rock of the Popish Church Commended by Sanders*, ed. Richard Gibbings, Parker Society (Cambridge, 1848), 111. For a later attack on relics as 'heathenish' and 'pagan', see the Quaker George Fox's *The man Christ Jesus the head of the Church and true mediator* (London, 1679).

[18] Hastings Robinson (ed.), *The Zurich Letters, Comprising the Correspondence of Several English Bishops and Others, with some of the Helvetian Reformers, During the Early Part of the Reign of Queen Elizabeth*, Parker Society (Cambridge, 1842), 44.

[19] William Weston, *The Autobiography of an Elizabethan*, ed. Philip Caraman (London, 1955), 110–12.

considerable anxiety. The Council of Trent had vigorously defended the cult of relics in its 25th session of 1563 but in Catholic Europe the authentication, transportation, and display of sacred remains was subjected to unprecedented regulation.[20] Against the backdrop of stinging Protestant attacks, the Church also made strenuous attempts to restrain devotion to them within orthodox boundaries. In England, where clerical manpower was scarce, it was exceptionally difficult to exercise control over the relics dispersed after the Dissolution.[21] Like the remains of St Chad which the Staffordshire yeoman Henry Hodgetts stored in his bed-head, many were now in the possession of laypeople, who sometimes employed them in a dubious, quasi-magical fashion. Jesuits like John Gerard strove to bring items like a silver head containing a piece of the skull of St Thomas of Canterbury and the arm bone of the virgin martyr St Vita back into ecclesiastical safe-keeping, but the perilous circumstances in which they worked meant that they had only a limited capacity to achieve this. Relics remained part of a large mobile library of miraculous objects that persistently defied the efforts of the clergy to supervise their use.[22]

These problems were exacerbated by the ever expanding reservoir of new relics engendered by the execution of priests and laypeople who sheltered them. Hanged, drawn and quartered as enemies of the Protestant state, their ritual degradation functioned as a graphic warning: displayed on stakes in conspicuous places, their heads and limbs were 'ghastly bill-boards advertising the awful consequences of treason'.[23] Denied proper burial, their remains

[20] H. J. Schroeder (ed.), *Canons and Decrees of the Council of Trent* (Rockford, IL, 1978), 215–17.

[21] See Alexandra Walsham, 'Miracles and the Counter-Reformation Mission to England', *Historical Journal,* 46 (2003), 779–815, esp. 794–99; and 'Translating Trent? English Catholicism and the Counter Reformation', *Historical Research,* 78 (2005), 288–310, at 307; Raymond Gillespie, *Devoted People: Belief and Religion in Early Modern Ireland* (Manchester, 1997), 158–63.

[22] John Gerard, *The Autobiography of an Elizabethan,* ed. and trans. Philip Caraman (London, 1951), 49–50; Henry Foley (ed.), *Records of the English Province of the Society of Jesus,* 7 vols in 8 (London, 1877–84), ii. 231. See also Anne M. Myers, 'Father John Gerard's Object Lessons: Relics and Devotional Objects in the Autobiography of a Hunted Priest', in Ronald Corthell, Frances Dolan, Christopher Highley, and Arthur F. Marotti (eds), *Catholic Culture in Early Modern England* (Notre Dame, 2007), 216–35.

[23] Peter Lake and Michael C. Questier, 'Agency, Appropriation and Rhetoric under the Gallows: Puritans, Romanists and the State in Early Modern England', *Past and Present,* 153 (1996), 64–107, at 82–3. See also Thomas S. Freeman, '"Imitatio Christi with a Vengeance": The Politicisation of Martyrdom in Early-Modern England', in Freeman and Mayer (eds), *Martyrs and Martyrdom,* 35–69, at 45.

were posthumously shamed and humiliated. Executioners dehumanized their victims as they disembowelled and dismembered them, as did some of those who watched these gruesome exhibitions of annihilation. Officials deliberately disfigured the face of the Franciscan John Jones, by scratching, bruising, and blackening it with powder in 1598. In the case of George Nichols and Richard Naxley, executed at Oxford nine years earlier, however, it was zealots among the spectators who had cut and hacked them with knives. Members of the Dorchester crowd who saw Hugh Green put to death in 1642 played football with his head for the space of six hours and poked sticks in his eyes, ears, nose, and mouth.[24]

Ironically, this only fuelled the spontaneous canonization of these priests as saints and fostered the enthusiastic pursuit of their relics. Their fragmentation and display at the behest of the Tudor and Stuart regime only made the bodies of the martyrs more accessible to the faithful and more available for appropriation. As Cardinal William Allen remarked, the 'godly greedy appetite of holy persons' for their remains was almost insatiable.[25] Catholics scrambled to collect fragments of their flesh, to dip cloths and handkerchiefs in their blood, and to gather up their cassocks, garments, stockings, spectacles, rosary beads, crucifixes, letters, and other possessions, along with the equipment used to put them to death. There was poignant symbolism in the incorruptible index finger and thumb of Father Robert Sutton which was discovered and preserved after his quarters were taken down twelve months after his execution in 1594, these being the digits employed in consecration of the host.[26] Edmund Genings' own anointed thumb had miraculously detached itself and fallen into the hands of Lucy Ridley three years earlier, in another heavenly testimony to the truth of the central Catholic mystery of transubstantiation, a doctrine dismissed by Protestants as a diabolical fiction.[27] Some visitors even ransacked the cells of condemned priests for such articles in anticipation of their martyrdom, convinced that these pious thefts would yield supernatural benefit after their deaths.

---

[24] J. H. Pollen (ed.), *Unpublished Documents Relating to the English Martyrs, vol. I 1584–1603,* Catholic Record Society, 5 (London, 1908), 374; Richard Challoner, *Memoirs of Missionary Priests,* ed. J. H. Pollen (London, 1924), 158, 427.

[25] William Allen, *A briefe historie of the glorious martyrdom of XII. reuerend priests* (Rheims, 1582), sig. C7v.

[26] Pollen (ed.), *Unpublished Documents,* 291.

[27] John Geninges, *The life and death of Mr Edmund Geninges priest, crowned with martyrdome at London, the 10. day of November, in the yeare MDXCI* (St Omers, 1614), 91–4.

Such relics circulated rapidly along the channels of the Catholic underground and supplied a thriving new trade in sacred body parts that was
gathering momentum both in England and on the Continent.[28] This was a
process that the clergy condoned if not actively encouraged: the Jesuits celebrated the miracles of healing and exorcism performed by the hand of
Edmund Arrowsmith, the blood of Henry Morse and Oliver Plunkett, and
fragments of the flesh and bone of Robert Southwell in their Annual Letters
and exiled leaders like Allen eagerly received, conserved, and divided these
corporeal specimens to send to their superiors in Italy and Spain.[29] Other
relics travelled in the reverse direction: in April 1591 it was reported that a
small quantity of Christ's blood sent from Rome had miraculously multiplied
during a Mass celebrated in Oxford on Good Friday: recusants were prepared
to pay £20 per drop, believing that those who wore it about their persons
would be protected thereby from bodily harm.[30] Once again, it was hard to
ensure that laypeople utilized relics in appropriate ways and in accordance
with authorized procedures for their application. The careful management
and oversight of sacred objects that characterized Tridentine practice
in Catholic Europe was hard to achieve within a suppressed Church and
many were used in irregular ways that smacked of 'superstition' to the missionary clergy. Stashed away in secret places, like the head of John Cornelius
which fell out of a cupboard while workmen were clearing rubbish after the
Great Fire of London in 1666,[31] a good many relics may have evaded priestly
jurisdiction more or less completely.

The wonders said to have been worked by the remains of these martyred
priests exposed English Catholicism to fresh outbursts of Protestant ridicule.
Polemical defence of belief in the immanence of the holy embodied in devotion to relics by writers like the Irish Jesuit Richard Archdekin was combined
with a prudent wariness about their capacity to cause embarrassment to the

---

[28] See Trevor Johnson, 'Holy Fabrications: The Catacomb Saints and the Counter
Reformation in Bavaria', *Journal of Ecclesiastical History*, 47 (1996), 274–97; Simon
Ditchfield, 'Martyrs on the Move: Relics as Vindicators of Local Diversity in the
Tridentine Church', in Diana Wood (ed.), *Martyrs and Martyrologies*, Studies in
Church History, 30 (Oxford, 1993), 283–94; Luke Clossey, *Salvation and Globalization
in the Early Jesuit Missions* (Cambridge, 2008), 220–3.

[29] Foley (ed.), *Records of the English Province*, i. 602–3, ii. 59–62, 64, 69, iv. 425, v. 85, 1104–6,
VII.ii 1135, 1137–8.

[30] Mary Anne Everett Green (ed.), *Calendar of State Papers Domestic: Elizabeth I, 1591–4*
(London, 1867), 28–9.

[31] Foley (ed.), *Records of the English Province*, vi. 680.

embattled Catholic cause.[32] The risks were made transparent in 1606 after claims that an exquisite image of Henry Garnet's face had been found on an ear of straw stained with his blood. Already fraught with political resonance because of his alleged complicity in the Gunpowder Plot and his advocacy of equivocation under oath, Garnet's 'straw' was the cause of both consternation and merriment among the nation's Protestants, who claimed that this was no work of God but rather the product of either satanic cunning or human ingenuity. Pamphlets mocking the 'new popish wonder' rapidly circulated and it was said that England was 'belittered with the news' of this miracle. Archbishop Richard Bancroft apparently employed painters to produce an artistic facsimile in order to demonstrate that the straw was the latest in a long line of Catholic fakes.[33] The pages of John Gee's *The Foot out of the Snare* (1624) were filled with similar tales of the false relics by which the Church of Rome pulled the wool over the eyes of the laity and long-standing clichés about their 'cheating idolatries' and impostures perpetrated by the papacy were part of the stock-in-trade of later Stuart anti-Catholic propagandists. John Patrick made 'fables' about Christ's foreskin, the lungs of Edward King and Martyr, and other saints' body parts the subject of a derisive digression in a polemical tract of 1674 and a 'cart load' of the 'cheats' and 'fopperies' the Catholic priesthood imposed on unsuspecting simple papists, including St Joseph's breeches and the comb of St Anne, had been exposed in a short penny-priced pamphlet the previous year.[34] The ejection of the Catholic king James II from the throne and the so-called Glorious Revolution of 1688–89 provided the incentive for more satire in the same ebullient vein, such as a broadsheet advertising the relics for sale at the Savoy—from St James' bottle to the Prayer of Pope Joan and Our Lady's old shoe.[35]

---

[32] Richard Archdekin, *A treatise of miracles. Together with new miracles and benefits obtained by the sacred reliques of S. Francis Xaverius* (Louvain, 1667), esp. 42–4.

[33] See Foley (ed.), *Records of the English Province*, iv. 121–33, 195–201; Gerard, *Autobiography*, 202, 274–6; [Robert Pricket], *The Jesuits Miracles, or new popish wonders. Containing the straw, the crowne, and the wondrous child, with the confutation of them and their follies* (London, 1607); Thomas Fuller, *The Church History of Britain* (London, 1655), bk. 10, 40–1; British Library, London, Add. MS 21, 203, fos 22r-23r.

[34] John Gee, *The foot out of the snare* (London, 1624), 53–6, 66–7. John Patrick, *Reflexions upon the devotions of the Roman Church ... Also two digressions concerning the reliques and miracles in Mr Cressy's late church-history* (London, 1674), sigs A4v-5v, pp. 232–75; *Room for miracles; or miracles from Room. A cart-load for a penny* (London, 1673).

[35] *Religious reliques, or, the sale at the Savoy; upon the Jesuits breaking up their school and chappel* (London, 1688).

A touchstone and lighting paper for anti-popery, by the seventeenth century relics had become charged with significance as a confessional badge and
marker. Their mere discovery in the homes of recusants incriminated their
owners and to wear them on one's person was a tell-tale sign that one adhered
to the illicit Catholic religion. John Harrison of Shropshire, prisoner in the
Bridewell, was evidently captured in 1596 with several in his clothing, which
he said he had received as bones from his brother, ground into a sweet
powder, and carried around with him 'these five years'.[36] The English state
papers are full of letters regarding raids on private houses in which such items
were uncovered[37] and their interception and incineration on bonfires of
vanities was a priority of Elizabethan and early Stuart governments, especially
in the years of high panic and alarm about the political machinations of the
papists and, in the context of the Civil War, their royalist allies. In 1645, a box
of relics found built into the wall of the porch of Tiverton church by the
Cavaliers further convinced some that King Charles I's supporters were the
'champions of Antichrist'.[38] Sources of solace and power to Catholics in the
midst of their tribulations, to Protestants such objects epitomized the inherent idolatry of the popish faith and the meretriciousness of its clerical agents.

III

This is the backdrop against which we must set the development of what looks
on the surface remarkably like a reformed relic culture. Many of the examples
that follow arose in the context of persecution and dissent. Respect for those
who made the ultimate sacrifice or suffered corporeal mutilation for their
religious convictions fostered an instinct to collect physical remnants and
tokens of their heroism. Protestants may have envisaged these 'martyrs' and
'saints' as godly exemplars and witnesses to the truth rather than celestial
intercessors,[39] but the behaviour of some of those who were present at their
deaths and punishments bears, at first glance, a striking resemblance to that of
their 'popish' adversaries. We may begin with instances relating to members

---

[36] *CSP Domestic: Elizabeth 1595–97* (London, 1869), 180.

[37] See, e.g., *CSP Domestic 1581–90* (London, 1865), 68, 155, 198, 223, 244, 345, 351, 384,
644.

[38] *A true and strange relation of a boy, who was entertained by the devil . . . with a coppie of a
letter from maior generall Massie, concerning these strange and wonderfull things, with a
certaine box of reliques and crucifixes found in TIVERTON Church* (London, 1645), 6.

[39] Brad Gregory, *Salvation at Stake: Christian Martyrdom in Early Modern Europe*
(Cambridge, Mass., 1999), ch. 5, especially 140. See also Carol Piper Heming,
Protestants and the Cult of Saints in German-Speaking Europe, 1517–1531 (Kirksville,
Mich., 2003).

of the heretical sect which Protestants heralded as their forerunners, the followers of John Wyclif. Devotees of the relapsed lollard Richard Wych, who was burnt on Tower Hill in 1440 carried away his ashes (sweet-smelling thanks to the efforts of a local apothecary) and erected a cairn of stones and cross at the site, which became renowned for working miracles, until the authorities sought to suppress the shrine by turning it into a dunghill.[40] Half a century later in 1494 the remains of the octogenarian heretic Joan Boughton were removed under cover of night and 'kepydd ffor a precious Relyk, In an erthyn pott'.[41] Posthumously exhumed from their grave in Lutterworth and burnt by order of the bishop of Lincoln in 1428, Wyclif's own bones may have been annihilated but, according to a story first recorded in 1531, where one of them fell a spring had burst forth from the ground. An echo of an ancient aetiological trope of shrine formation, his remains seemingly functioned in the same way as many medieval relics.[42]

Those who watched Protestants perish at the stake during the reign of Mary I in the 1550s exhibited similar instincts: in May 1555 two men were reported to be carrying around bones of the martyr Pygott and showing them to people to encourage steadfast adherence to the Protestant cause and after John Hullier's execution by fire on Jesus Green in Cambridge in July 1557, people fought for pieces of bone and other body parts: 'one had his hart, the which was distributed so farre as it would go: one tooke the scalpe and looked for the tong, but it was consumed except the very roote'. The same scenes accompanied the death of Nicholas Ridley in Oxford, who distributed his possessions to people before the fire was lit. Others 'plucked the poyntes of hys hose: happye was he that mighte gette anye ragge of hym'. John Bradford also gave away his velvet nightcap and other personal belongings to his friends on the way to the stake and had anything survived of the shirt in which he died (a 'wedding garment' made for him by a Protestant follower, over which he had earnestly prayed), it too would probably have been preserved by his disciples.[43] A Catholic account from around the same time described how the heretics gathered together 'the burnt bones of these stynkyng martyrs', 'wallowyng like pygges in a stie to scrape' them up from the pyre, and then

---

[40] For this episode, see Richard Rex, 'Which is Wyche? Lollardy and Sanctity in Lancastrian London', in Freeman and Mayer (eds), *Martyrs and Martyrdom*, 88–106.

[41] John A. F. Thomson, *The Later Lollards 1414–1520* (Oxford, 1965), 156.

[42] See my 'Wyclif's Well: Lollardy, Landscape and Memory in Post-Reformation England', in Angela McShane and Garthine Walker (eds), *The Extraordinary and Everyday Life in Early Modern England: Essays in Celebration of the Work of Bernard Capp* (Basingstoke, 2010), pp. 142–60.

[43] John Foxe, *Actes and Monuments* (London, 1570), 2196–7; (1563 edn), 1377 and 1175.

wore them next to their hearts or grated them into a cup of ale for medicinal purposes.[44] A generation later in 1587, the Jesuit Robert Southwell wrote to his superior in Rome regarding the execution of the Arian Francis Kett: 'a little while after, there was nothing to be seen of his bones and even of his ashes; these foes of holy relics were so eager to get possession of his remains'.[45] When the puritan triumvirate William Prynne, John Bastwick, and Henry Burton were punished for their outspoken attack on Laudian innovations in 1637 by the slicing off of their ears, sympathizers eagerly dipped their hand-kerchiefs into the blood that flowed from the heads of these 'holy living martyrs' 'as a thing most precious'.[46] A woman present at the deathbed of John Reeve, co-founder of the Muggletonian movement, in 1658 cut off a lock of his hair to keep 'for a Memorial of one of the two last Prophets that God will ever send while his World endureth'.[47] The seven bishops imprisoned for refusing to read the declaration of indulgence to Catholics in 1688 were also the subject of an adulation that had the same logical outcome: when they were released on bail people flocked to see and touch them thinking it 'a blessing to kiss any of [their] hands or garments'.[48]

It is important to underline the frequency with which our knowledge of such episodes comes from hostile sources and is refracted through the dis-torting lens and rhetorical conventions of confessional polemic. They were weapons in a war of words in which protagonists on both sides of the Reformation divide sought to undermine the integrity of their rival's faith and unveil the inner contradictions that beset it. Spokesmen for the Church of Rome like the Marian writer Miles Huggarde made much of the ostensible hypocrisy of Protestant relic hunters. How could such behaviour be recon-ciled with a theology that revolved around fierce opposition to the localiza-tion and materialization of the holy? The charge of inconsistency was also levelled against the 'upstert sectaries' by Thomas Stapleton in 1565, who contrasted Protestant attacks on the miracles in Bede's *Ecclesiastical History* with those that could be found in the pages of John Foxe's famous *Actes and*

[44] Miles Huggarde, *The displaying of the Protestantes, and sondry of their practises, with a description of divers their abuses of late frequented within their malignaunte churche* (London, 1556), fos. 54–55.

[45] Philip Caraman (ed.), *The Other Face: Catholic Life under Elizabeth I* (London, 1960), 79.

[46] *A briefe relation of certaine speciall and most materiall passages, and speeches in the starre-chamber* ([Leiden], 1638), 3.

[47] T. L. Underwood (ed.), *The Acts of the Witnesses: The Autobiography of Lodowick Muggleton and Other Early Muggletonian Writings* (New York and Oxford, 1999), 77.

[48] John Spurr, *The Restoration Church of England, 1646–1689* (New Haven, 1991), 96–7.

Monuments, better known as the 'Book of Martyrs', including the claim that the heart of the Swiss reformer Huldrych Zwingli had been found intact in the ashes following an attempt to incinerate it.[49] In a similar vein, the Catholic convert Sir Kenelm Digby sneered at the veneration which puritans accorded the bloody sponges and cloths employed by the executioner who had cut off the ears of Prynne, Bastwick, and Burton: 'you may see how nature leads men to respect relics of martyrs'.[50]

Historians have perhaps been too apt to follow suit and to see these incidents as examples of survivalism and syncretism that attest to the obstinate resistance of popular culture to attempts to reform it, and as evidence of the fundamental failure of the Reformation to eradicate ingrained habits and to transform traditional mentalities. For Bob Scribner such phenomena attest to cultural continuities that question claims of radical disjuncture and point to the existence of 'a covert evangelical sacramentalism'.[51] Such insights help to illuminate the episodes described above, but these apparently dissonant and paradoxical elements deserve closer scrutiny.

Without doubt the artefacts associated with these Protestant martyrs and victims operate in a grey area of reformed thought and experience, but there is often little to suggest that their collectors believed them to be imbued with intrinsic sacredness. In many cases, they appear to have had a simple semiotic rather than sacramental function—almost, but not quite like the bread blessed during the liturgy of the Eucharist itself, they were merely memorials or commemorative tokens. The charisma these keepsakes carried was spiritual and emotional rather than material and miraculous in character. Early evangelical and later Protestant discussions of relics often made precisely this distinction: William Tyndale intimated that where they were regarded as 'signs of remembrance only', they could serve a useful didactic purpose.[52]

---

[49] Bede, *The History of the Church of Englande,* trans. and ed. Thomas Stapleton (Antwerp, 1565), sig. C1r.

[50] The National Archives, London, SP 14/364/68 (27 July 1637).

[51] R. W. Scribner, 'The Impact of the Reformation on Daily Life' and 'The Reformation, Popular Magic, and the "Disenchantment of the World"', in Lyndal Roper (ed.), *Religion and Culture in Germany (1400–1800)* (Leiden, 2001), 275–301, at 289, and 346–65, at 354. Even more ingeniously and gymnastically, Richard Rex has sought to explain away the cult of Richard Wych as a manifestation of orthodox rather than lollard piety, this being a solution that more neatly fits the laws of historical 'rationality': 'Which is Wyche?'.

[52] William Tyndale, *Expositions and Notes on Sundry Portions of the Holy Scriptures, together with the Practice of Prelates,* ed. Henry Walter, Parker Society (Cambridge, 1849), 216; William Tyndale, *An Answer to Sir Thomas More's Dialogue, The Supper of the Lord . . . and William Tracy's Testament Expounded,* ed. Henry Walter, Parker Society (Cambridge, 1850), 60.

This was also implicit in reformed exegesis of two episodes in the Old and New Testaments often marshalled in support of the Catholic doctrine of relics: the resurrection of a dead man when his corpse touched the bones of the prophet Elisha in 2 Kings 13 and the cure of the woman who felt the edge of Christ's garment in St Matthew's Gospel. The former miracle, declared Tyndale, Calfhill, and Polyander, had been done to confirm his calling and served as 'a preaching of penance' to the Israelites and not 'to enforce a worshipping of the body'. The latter had been designed to testify that Jesus was the son of God and not to foster veneration of his clothes, 'though to keep the coat reverently in the memorial of the deed, to provoke unto the faith of Christ, were not evil of itself'.[53] Implicit in the writings of other divines, this differentiation between relic and pious memento casts the incidents we have been exploring in a new light. Just as hot Protestants like the London turner Nehemiah Wallington saved fragments of stained glass broken during the iconoclastic purges of city churches in 1641 'to keep for a remembrance to show to the generation to come what God hath done for us, to give a reformation that our forefathers never saw the like',[54] so too might they legitimately preserve remains of the men and women who had played a seminal part in the process by which England had regained the Gospel and spoken out against overt and crypto-popery. In this sense, these objects in which memory was crystallized and sublimated were entirely compatible with a Protestant outlook. It is also in this context that the pursuit of fragments of the oak in Boscobel Park in Shropshire in which the future Charles II had sheltered after the battle of Worcester in 1651 is perhaps best interpreted. During the Restoration, visitors almost killed it in their eagerness to carry off bits of the bough and bark of the tree in which their king had hidden from the Roundheads.[55] The same fate nearly befell the Holy Thorn at Glastonbury said to have sprung from the staff of Joseph of Arimathea. Its mangled state in the mid-seventeenth century was not simply due to the efforts of a tiny radical minority to destroy this abominable idol, but also to the tourists who broke off twigs and branches as reminders of the place where Protestants believed Christianity had first been planted in England.[56]

[53] Tyndale, *Answer to Sir Thomas More's Dialogue*, 124; Calfhill, *Answer,* 313; Polyander, *Disputation,* 106.

[54] Paul S. Seaver, *Wallington's World: A Puritan Artisan in Seventeenth-Century London* (London, 1985), 151.

[55] Thomas Blount, *Boscobel: or the compleat history of his sacred majesties most miraculous preservation after the battle of Worcester, 3 Sept 1651* (London, 1662), 67.

[56] See Sir William Brereton, *Travels in Holland and the United Provinces, England, Scotland and Ireland M.DC.XXXIV-M.DC.XXV,* ed. Edward Hawkins, Chetham Society (London,

The problem was that the potential for slippage between souvenir and sacramental, sign and receptacle of supernatural virtue was high. '[T]he desire to have relics', wrote Calvin, was 'almost never without suspition'; it was 'the mother of ydolatry, which is ordinarely connexed and joined therwith': human beings could not help themselves in the 'beholdyng and handling' of material objects from offering honour to them.[57] The discomfort that the conduct of some Protestant relic hunters caused to godly ministers cannot therefore be ignored. The 'subtle idolatry' that disturbed Lutheran pastors in late seventeenth-century Germany, where people collected splinters of the Wittenberg reformer's bed,[58] also created unease in the minds of their English Calvinist colleagues. It can be detected, for instance, in the somewhat equivocal comments John Foxe made in the 1563 edition of his *Actes and Monuments* on the 'fervent desire' of the primitive Christians who had collected the ashes of the early martyrs, 'kissed even the verye chaynes wherewith they were tyed', and preserved the swords used to behead them as 'a precious juell, or relique'. He could not disapprove of the piety of an era Protestants upheld for its purity, 'howbeit I allow not the superstition that dyd after degenerate from sincere religion'. By 1570 he modified this passage in a more cautious direction, to reprove the excess of zeal that had led them to revere such remnants, remarking on the 'admiration, and almost superstition' into which they had fallen.[59] He may well have suppressed other evidence of Protestant relic behaviour for the same reason—in a mirror image of the worries of his Tridentine rivals, it carried the risk of exposing the new religion to the allegation that it sanctioned no less dubious practices than those of which it accused the Romanists.[60]

1844), 174–5, and Alexandra Walsham, 'The Holy Thorn of Glastonbury: The Evolution of a Legend in Post-Reformation England', *Parergon*, 21 (2004), 1–25.

[57] Calvin, *Very profitable treatise,* sig. A3r-v.

[58] R. W. Scribner, 'Incombustible Luther: The Image of the Reformer in Early Modern Germany', in *Popular Culture and Popular Movements in Reformation Germany* (London and Ronceverte, 1987), 323–53, at 351–2.

[59] John Foxe, *Actes and Monumentes* (London, 1563), sig. B6v; (1570), sig. *3v.

[60] On Foxe's editorial strategies, see Patrick Collinson, 'Truth and Legend: The Veracity of John Foxes Book of Martyrs', in A. C. Duke and C. A. Tamse (eds), *Clio's Mirror: Historiography in Britain and the Netherlands* (Leiden, 1985), 31–54 and 'Truth, Lies, and Fiction in Sixteenth-Century Protestant Historiography', in Donald R. Kelley and David Harris Sacks (eds), *The Historical Imagination in Early Modern Britain: History, Rhetoric, and Fiction 1500–1800* (Cambridge, 1997), 37–68; Thomas S. Freeman, 'Fate, Faction, and Fiction in Foxe's *Book of Martyrs*', *Historical Journal*, 43 (2000), 601–24.

The case of the Scottish Covenanter James Guthrie, who was executed as a rebel against the king in Edinburgh in 1661, is equally revealing. Various ladies of 'good quality' and impeccable Calvinist credentials took napkins and dipped them in the profusion of blood which issued when his head was severed from his body, following its deposition from the gallows. They were challenged regarding their conduct by the Registrar Archibald Primrose who declared that 'it was a peece of the superstition and idolatry of the Romish Church, to reserve the relicts of the saints!' To this reproof he received the reply that they intended no such abuse and sought only 'to hold up the bloody napkine to heaven in their addresses, that the Lord might remember the innocent blood that was spilt'. According to another account they said that they did so 'that it might cry for vengeance against those that had most cruelly shed it'.[61] This, then, was an invitation to, indeed an invocation of divine intervention. These Scottish presbyterians did not regard relics as a source of the saintly intercession of Guthrie himself, but they did think that they could operate as a kind of lightning conductor to pull down the wrath of God upon their enemies' heads.

It is also worth noting that there are remarkably few cases in which Protestants are said to have imputed thaumaturgic powers to the human remains they gathered. In the 1550s Miles Huggarde made much play with the gospellers who used powdered bones of the Marian martyrs 'to preserve them from the chyncoughe, and suche other maladyes incident to such hoote burnynge stomakes',[62] but we may well wonder how far this was a polemical slur, an embellishment of the facts for the purpose of point-scoring, or alternatively the product of a period in which confessional identities were still in a state of considerable flux. Thereafter, miraculous cures effected by Protestant relics are conspicuous by their absence. Notable exceptions are those reported to have been done by handkerchiefs soaked in the blood of the executed Charles I. Not long after he was beheaded in January 1649 a young maid from Deptford by the name of Mary Bayly was said to have been relieved of blindness and other side-effects of scrofula by one such piece of cloth. According to a pamphlet published about this 'miracle of miracles' that year, 'through Heavens providence' she thereby recovered her eyesight and became as 'lusty and strong' as other girls of her age. For all its 'popish' overtones, this wonder was consistent with the ongoing belief that English monarchs had the capacity, by virtue of their sacred hereditary office, to heal

---

[61] Robert Wodrow, *Analecta: or, materials for a history of remarkable providences; mostly relating to Scotch ministers and Christians,* 4 vols, Maitland Club (Edinburgh, 1842–3), i. 107–9; iii. 103–4.

[62] Huggarde, *Displaying of the Protestantes,* fo. 54v.

this disease by their royal touch. Protestantism accommodated this doctrine, even if some incumbents of the throne were rather wary of putting it into practice. Once the king was dead and could no longer exercise what one propagandist called his 'princely fingers', it was only natural that God would display his anger and vindicate Charles by transferring this gift to the vestiges of him that remained. The accession of Charles II in 1660 largely drew an end to claims of this kind. They were not so much peculiar departures from, as expressions of, Anglican theology, though this does not exclude the possibility that some of those who experienced or witnessed such cures understood them in ways that were marginal to it.[63]

Popular Protestantism sometimes accorded healing power to other material objects, notably the Bible, but also catechisms and prayer books. On one level this reflected the idea articulated by Henry Bullinger that Scripture, together with the Lord's Prayer, Apostle's Creed, and Ten Commandments, were the only true and 'holy reliques' left in the Church of Christ.[64] The inverse of the notion that Jesus was the word made flesh, this may help to illuminate the way in which the Bible replaced the bones and other encased body parts of saints in the process of post-Reformation oath-swearing, itself a solemn procedure that called upon the Lord to punish providentially any person who committed perjury. It also sheds light on folklore regarding the utilization of the Bible as a medical aid and amulet. The nineteenth-century lady from Hampshire who ate pages of the Old Testament leaf by leaf between two sides of bread and butter as a remedy for fits is just one example of a wider practice that illustrates the point that the word was not just communicative sign: 'it could mediate the divine'.[65] Ministers like Barten Holyday may have regarded the utilization of the Bible to ease the pains of childbirth and to tranquillize restless patients as troubling and warned that it was not to be regarded as 'Physique for the Body'. But 'superstitions' of this kind were manifestations of genuine

---

[63] *A Miracle of Miracles: Wrought by the Blood of King Charles the First, of Happy Memory, upon a Mayd at Detford* (London, 1649), 5; J. G., *A letter sent into France to the Lord Duke Buckingham His Grace of a Great Miracle Wrought by a Piece of Handkerchefe, Dipped in his Majesties Bloud* (London, 1649); Andrew Lacey, *The Cult of King Charles the Martyr* (Woodbridge, 2003), 62–6.

[64] Henry Bullinger, *The Decades*, ed. Thomas Harding, 4 vols, Parker Society (Cambridge, 1849–52), i., 212.

[65] David Cressy, 'Books as Totems in Seventeenth-Century England and New England', *Journal of Library History*, 21 (1986), 92–106, at 99; Ulinka Rublack, *Reformation Europe* (Cambridge, 2005), 157, and 157–69 *passim*. See also Rublack's essay in this volume.

reformed devotion and piety.[66] They highlight points of intersection between the external forms of pre- and post-Reformation religious culture even as they reveal the ways in which material objects became badges of adherence to the Protestant faith.

IV

Finally, we must examine the ways in which some medieval relics were absorbed into the Protestant world. Not all hallowed remains were victims of the reformers' holocaust. The dual status of Anglo-Saxon and Norman monarchs as sovereigns and saints made it difficult, indeed politically dangerous, to slight and denigrate their remains, which survived undisturbed in cathedrals and minsters like Westminster, Winchester, and York. The fact that many of the bones and skeletons removed from shrines at the time of the Dissolution were re-interred rather than destroyed reflected the Protestant conviction that the body was the mansion of the soul, which deserved a decent Christian burial in joyful anticipation of its resurrection at the last judgement. Even those of one's deluded popish ancestors were not to be treated, in Henry Bullinger's words, 'like a dead dog', for who could know which of them might have been saved by divine decree from damnation in hell?[67] Degradation of human remains was only appropriate in the case of people who had placed themselves beyond the spiritual pale, such as suicides, who were conventionally buried in unconsecrated ground with a stake through their hearts, and heretics and traitors, whose corpses were made to bear the marks of their disgrace. Hence the posthumous punishment meted out to the mid-seventeenth-century regicides Henry Ireton, John Bradshaw, and Oliver Cromwell, whose 'odious carcasses' were exhumed on the anniversary of the death of the royal martyr in January 1661, dragged to Tyburn on a sledge and hung on the gallows. Cromwell's head was cut off and placed on a stake, where it stayed for more than two years as a grim warning of the consequences of king-killing.[68]

The Protestant assumption that the body was the temple of the holy ghost also dictated the determined efforts of the Elizabethan authorities to ensure

---

[66] Barten Holyday, *Motives to a Good Life in Ten Sermons* (Oxford, 1657), 129–30.

[67] Henry Bullinger, *The Decades*, iv. 523. On Protestant attitudes to death, see Peter Marshall, *Beliefs and the Dead in Reformation England* (Oxford, 2002).

[68] On suicides, see Michael MacDonald and Terence Murphy, *Sleepless Souls: Suicide in Early Modern England* (Oxford, 1990), esp. 18–20, 44–9. On the exhumation of the regicides, see James Heath, *Flagellum: or the life and death birth and burial of O. Cromwell. The late usurper. Faithfully described* (London, 1655), 200; Samuel Butler, *Hudibras*, 3 vols (London, 1793), iii. 379–80 (transcript of a manuscript diary of Mr Edward Sainthill).

that the victims of Marian Catholic rites of symbolic defilement were reverently reinstalled in proper graves after 1558. The German Protestants Martin
Bucer and Paul Fagius who had taken up academic posts in Cambridge under
Edward VI and died there were subjected to posthumous trials for heresy and
their decaying cadavers disinterred and burnt on Market Hill; this was
reversed in July 1560, when a ceremony was held to restore their honour.[69]
In Oxford, the body of Catherine, a former nun who had cast off her vows and
married the Italian reformer and Regius Professor of Divinity, Peter Martyr
Vermigli, was likewise removed from its tomb in Christ Church Cathedral on
the instructions of Cardinal Reginald Pole and dumped on a dunghill. When
the theological tide once again turned, it was recovered and reinstated in its
original place. Probably at the instigation of the puritan subdean James
Calfhill, her bones were mingled with those of the medieval saint
Frideswide and an edifying plaque placed over them declaring in Latin
'Here lies religion with superstition'. By this means Frideswide's relics were
'paradoxically preserved for posterity by Protestant fanaticism'.[70]
Simultaneously a lesson about the evils of idolatry and the legitimacy of
clerical marriage and a memorial to a godly Protestant lady, this was an act
of iconoclasm and preservation rolled into one.

Other ancient Catholic relics seem to have gradually migrated into the
realm of the historical artefact. Daniel Woolf has argued that the official
abolition of relic worship in the 1530s helped to nurture a more 'secular'
interest in antiquities. These filled the empty space left behind by the evacu-
ation of devotion to sacred fragments of Christ and the saints.[71] While the
speed with which such relics cast off their religious associations should not be
exaggerated, there is certainly evidence to suggest that as the passions that had
fired the Reformation waned people came to contemplate medieval skeletons
with greater detachment and in a more neutral fashion as archaeological
objects. For example, when a body was discovered beneath the aisle of a
parish church in Buckinghamshire in 1619, the bones were kept on display
and shown to strangers as 'reliques of admiration' and local gentlemen dismembered it and took the pieces home with them. Domestic travellers like a

---

[69] Foxe, *Actes and Monuments* (1563 edn), 1537–52.

[70] Foxe, *Actes and Monuments* (1563 edn), 1558–9 (vere 1570–1); Brett Usher, 'James
Calfhill', in *Oxford Dictionary of National Biography*, http://www.oxforddnb.com
[accessed 5 Sept. 2008]. James Bentley, *Restless Bones: The Story of Relics* (London,
1985), 146. On the politics of disinterment in Ireland, see Clodagh Tait, *Death, Burial
and Commemoration in Ireland, 1550–1650* (Basingstoke, 2002), ch. 5.

[71] Daniel Woolf, *The Social Circulation of the Past: English Historical Culture 1500–1700*
(Oxford, 2003), 191–7.

Norwich lieutenant who toured the west country in 1635 could speak with equanimity about how they had 'tossed and tumbled' saints' bones in the vaults of Glastonbury Abbey and relics encountered by the wealthy in the course of their grand tours of Europe also excited more curiosity than they did fear, anger, or awe.[72] The same cast of mind allowed a drawing of Becket's shrine and bones to be preserved in an antiquarian manuscript and the insertion of an account of the upright bodies discovered by a gardener in the crypt of Ambresbury nunnery into the minute book of the Society of Antiquaries in 1718.[73] It is symptomatic of these shifts that the word relic itself was increasingly losing its more explicitly Catholic connotations and coming to be used to denote things kept for the remembrance of persons, places, periods, and even residues of past belief.[74] The prank played by a Scottish gentleman who created a walking stick out of the knotted wood of a crab tree three years later and in jest gave out that it was Joseph of Arimathea's legendary staff is no less suggestive of the processes of desacralization that Woolf describes. Purchased as an authentic relic by a 'bigotted papist', after which it was placed in a case in Naples and became famous for miracles,[75] it also indexes the confessionalization of rival religious cultures that intensified in the later phases of the long Reformation.

Denuded of the aura of holiness by which they had previously been surrounded, some relics ended up in contemporary cabinets of curiosities like those of John Tradescant at Lambeth, which later passed into the hands of Elias Ashmole. Among Tradescant's treasures were a piece of the stone of John the Baptist's tomb, the Padre Guardian's staff of Jerusalem, Edward the Confessor's knit gloves, and a vestal nun's head-dress 'of tiffany curiously crisped'. These shared space on his shelves with the stirrups and hawkshood of King Henry VIII and Anne Boleyn's embroidered night veil. Merton College, Oxford, was still showing off one of the thorns 'which they say our Saviour was crowned with al' in the later seventeenth and early eighteenth

[72] John Weever, *Ancient Funeral Monuments* (London, 1631), 30; L. G. Wickham-Legg (ed.), *A Relation of a Short Survey of the Western Counties, Made by a Lieutenant of the Military Company in Norwich in 1635,* in *Camden Miscellany,* 16, Camden Society, 3rd ser., 52 (1936), 79.

[73] British Library, London, MS Cotton Tiberius E. VIII, fo. 313v; Society of Antiquaries, London, MS 265 ('Minute Book of the Antiquarian Society, London, 1718. January'), fo. 124v (p. 24).

[74] The evolution in meanings of the word and its increasing use in a metaphorical sense can be traced in the *Oxford English Dictionary,* http://dictionary.oed.com [accessed 25 Aug. 2008].

[75] Wodrow, *Analecta,* iii. 350.

century. Ralph Thoresby's private collection included 'Manna gathered in the Wilderness, where the Children of Israel travelled' and a 'Fragment of the Royal-Oak at Boscobell, where King Charles II was miraculously preserved'. Intended to provoke wonder at the manifold mysteries of Creation in the viewer, the attitude of Protestants towards such 'rarities' still incorporated an element of religious amazement.[76] But it also attests to a reconfiguration of the matrix within which objects hitherto regarded as sacred were comprehended by contemporaries: it bears witness to the birth of the museum. In this institutional setting material artefacts were valued not for their ability to transcend time and provide a conduit to the divine, but on the contrary because of their historicity—because of their capacity to open a window into a past that was slipping into oblivion. Similarly, human remains became objects of scientific scrutiny and empirical observation rather than pious veneration.

This was a society in which the same item could simultaneously be a focus of spiritual reverence, an historical object that could arouse the intellectual interest of those who repudiated relic worship, and a source of aesthetic pleasure. The point is illustrated by two incidents that occurred at the court of Charles I in the 1630s. In the first his French Catholic consort Queen Henrietta Maria arranged for a small piece of the Cross on which Christ had suffered to be transferred from the Tower of London to her private chapel at Somerset House, after the king's servants decided to display it with other treasures in one of the royal palaces. In the second Cardinal Francesco Barberini presented a reliquary containing a bone of the virgin martyr St Martina to the queen. She was delighted with the gift and chose the saint as her future patroness; her husband, by contrast, was impressed by the exquisite workmanship of the beautiful case in which it was placed.[77]

Relics thus carried multiple meanings in the religiously pluralistic and culturally diverse society that was post-Reformation England. The advent of Protestantism prompted a series of complex but decisive transpositions

---

[76] John Tradescant, *Musaeum Tradescantianum: or, A Collection of Rarities Preserved at South-Lambeth neer London* (London, 1656), esp. 42–9; Michael Hunter, 'The Cabinet Institutionalised: The Royal Society's Repository and its Background', in Oliver Impey and Arthur MacGregor (eds), *The Origins of Museums: The Cabinet of Curiosities in Sixteenth and Seventeenth Century Europe* (Oxford, 1985), 159–68, at 160; Katie Whitaker, 'The Culture of Curiosity', in N. Jardine, J. A. Secord, and E. C. Spary (eds), *Cultures of Natural History* (Cambridge, 1996), 75–90, at 85–6.

[77] Philip Caraman (ed.), *Years of Siege: Catholic Life from James I to Cromwell* (London, 1966), 99, 125.

of the sacred which have much to tell us about the nature and shape of this religious revolution, its theological tenor, and its long-term cultural repercussions. The robust scepticism and iconoclastic rejection that marked its earlier stages did not prevent the resurgence of forms of behaviour towards human remains that were outwardly reminiscent of the discredited Catholic cult of relics and which attracted charges of Protestant hypocrisy. Such polemical taunts, however, carry the risk of deceiving us. The reverence some contemporaries displayed for the vestiges of reformed heroes and heroines did sometimes slide across the porous and fuzzy border between 'superstition' and piety, but on many other occasions it seems to have remained merely commemorative in character. The evidence analyzed in this essay may tell us less about manifestations of subconscious resistance to the Reformation than about the development of a Protestant culture of memory and identity centred as much on material objects as on distinctive dogmas and rituals. This developed against the backdrop of persisting assumptions about the physical body as a receptacle for the soul and in the context of a surge of antiquarian interest in historic remains that was itself a complex by-product of the religious upheavals of the era. Finally, it was the way in which relics were caught up in the heated confessional conflicts of the era that transformed them, on both sides of the theological divide, into proverbial skeletons in the closet, sources of ideological anxiety and potential scandal.

Grapho-Relics: Lutheranism and the Materialization of the Word

Ulinka Rublack[*]

I

Religions are historically specific ways of investigating what cultures take to be the supernatural. But how do beliefs resolve into gestures, habits, and temperament, ingrained by rituals of spiritual preparation, communication, or of learning?[1] Religious identities hinge on practices, which embody and build up specific ideals about the way in which communities of believers locate themselves on earth in relation to the divine. In Lutheranism they implicate the religious self physically as well as intellectually, because ideas are always embodied or materialized in verbal and non-verbal communication or objects. They are spoken and performed, written down, inscribed, or visualized. As they merge with the body through the modulation of a voice, posture, or gesture, or with matter, such as a desk, ink, and paper, and thereby proclaim particular ideals of writing, they become part of a display which is embedded in cultural assumptions about how ideas are represented as truthful and as leading to salvation. It is therefore misleading to think of Lutheranism as a disembodied, interiorized religion of the word, located in a 'rationally reasoning' mind, in contrast to an equally generalized 'sensuous Catholicism'.[2] The problem before us is to reconstruct just how the senses were implicated in different ways in Protestant traditions. How did Lutherans, in particular, invest word-related practices with spiritual meaning and emotional resonances to provide accounts of a truthful religion?[3]

[*] I wish to thank Sachiko Kusukawa, Trinity College, Cambridge, for her initial help in working towards the paper presented at the *Past and Present* conference, as well as Alex Walsham, Lyndal Roper, and Francisco Bethencourt for their perceptive comments.

[1] This paraphrases Lorraine Daston and Peter Galison's immensely useful approach to scientific objectivity, and thus the interaction with the natural, in *Objectivity* (New York, 2007), 52.

[2] For a summary of this position see Ulinka Rublack, *Reformation Europe* (Cambridge, 2005) ch. 4 and Epilogue.

[3] This is all the more important for a period which 'lacked a systematic bifurcation between real and thought objects, and consequently apprehended matter not as that which is

By inquiring more deeply into word-related practices for what is often rather casually typified as 'the religion of the word', this article seeks to contribute to an emerging history of Lutheran identities and memory culture. It draws particular attention to the importance of Luther's and other leading reformers' handwritten autographs and inscriptions as mediated physical remains which were intensely treasured by their followers. These 'grapho-relics' need to be integrated into our understanding of the distinct spiritual as well as cultic nature of Lutheranism, which was developed by Luther and adapted by Lutherans for generations to come. In order to understand their relevance, we first need to look at the transition of Wittenberg relic culture from Frederick the Wise, the ruler, to Martin Luther, the reformer.

II

Martin Luther was born in 1483, became an Augustinian monk in Erfurt, and found a position in the nearby newly founded University of Wittenberg in his late twenties. The small town of Wittenberg to Luther seemed at the margin of civilization; yet Frederick the Wise, who had ruled over this part of Saxony since 1486, attempted to make the town a cultic centre, a centre of learning, and a centre of arts and courtly life. The university was to turn it into a centre of learning, his court artist Cranach and burgeoning workshop were to turn it into a centre of arts, while religious foundations and relics were to make it a cultic centre. In 1493, Frederick had made his pilgrimage to the Holy Land and had brought back key pieces, such as St Anne's thumb from Rhodes. At the Imperial Diet in 1507, Frederick used papal support to request other imperial representatives, the estates, to hand over further relics to him.[4] By 1509, Cranach's workshop had finished the most detailed ever printed catalogue of a relic collection, the *Heiligthumsbuch*.[5] It initially included 108 woodcuts, and in a second edition printed in the same year there were already

---

deprived of meaning but as a principle of structure that underpins all meaning': Juliet Fleming, *Graffiti and the Arts of Writing in Early Modern England* (London, 2001), 21, and 25 for the following definition of cultural graphology in Derrida's *Of Grammatology*. This is difficult for us to grasp, but Protestants, for instance, could take words to visualize things. On a sixteenth-century altar painting the words spoken during the Eucharist thus created a chalice and host, Wolfgang Brückner, *Lutherische Bekenntnisgemälde des 16. bis 18. Jahrhunderts. Die illustrierte Confessio Augustana* (Regensburg, 2007), 106.

[4] Martin Brecht, *Martin Luther: Sein Weg zur Reformation 1483–1521* (Stuttgart, 1981), 121.

[5] Livis Cárdenas, *Friedrich der Weise und das Wittenberger Heiltumsbuch: Mediale Repräsentation zwischen Mittelalter und Neuzeit* (Berlin, 2002); Lucas Cranach, *Wittenberger Heiligthumbsbuch* (Munich, 1884).

117 illustrations of reliquaries. Of these, only the glass of St Elisabeth with particles of her dress, hair, and bones still exists. It was said to have awakened sixteen people from death, healed a blind man, and helped pregnant women. The *Heiligthumsbuch* featured this reliquary first in order to visualize the house of Wettin's connection with a saint. It likewise proclaimed dynastic traditions through a key relic from the Askanian heritage: a thorn from Christ's crown at his Crucifixion. Its title-page was the first among the *Heiligthumsbuch*s to memorialize a ruler as relic collector through a portrait, rather than to represent a patron saint.[6] In addition, the book emphasized not just the spiritual value of its pieces to glorify Frederick's territorial rule, but also documented the material and artistic value of goldsmiths' work through extremely detailed descriptions of precious materials which had gone into the making of reliquaries and other objects.[7] Precise woodcuts and extraordinarily detailed lists of particles allowed those looking at the book to meditate on and appreciate with full information the relics after the brief moments of an actual encounter. In Wittenberg, the relics could only be seen in the midst of policed crowds and guides shouting out what they were.[8] The *Heiligthumsbuch*, as one art historian puts it, can therefore be regarded as the first precursor of the exhibition catalogue.[9] Alongside the collection itself, it lured locals and people from far away to spend on the remission of their sins in Wittenberg, and thus to finance Frederick's ambitious building plans.

One year before the *Heiligthumsbuch* was published Frederick moreover commissioned an advertising brochure for prospective students. It was written by Andreas Meinhard, the later Wittenberg town scribe, and described Frederick's art and relic collections at length. It was structured around the dialogue of two students, Reinhard and Meinhard. Meinhard gradually convinced Reinhard of the excitement of studying in the new University of Wittenberg: this, then, was the precursor of the student prospectus. Reinhard was shown a perfume shop disseminating sweet smells above a bath-house; he was assured that all Jews had been driven out of Wittenberg; he was taken around beautiful colleges, and introduced to the pleasures of the nearby countryside.[10] But above all, this fictive prospective student was impressed

---

[6] Cárdenas, *Heiltumsbuch*, 116–17.

[7] Ibid., 110. Alongside Cranach, the local goldsmith Christian Düring was one of the richest and most influential men in Wittenberg.

[8] Ibid., 117–18.

[9] Ibid., 120.

[10] *The Dialogus of Andreas Meinhardi: A Utopian Description of Wittenberg and its University, 1508*, ed. and trans. Edgar C. Reinke (Ann Arbor, 1976), 307–8.

by the fact that Wittenberg internationally ranked so highly through distributing so many and special indulgences through its castle church:

> On each day in the morning and evening . . . the person who has uttered three angelic salutations earns a hundred days of indulgences. Similarly, while at solemn mass the words are chanted, 'Ex Maria Virgine', the person who says 'Verbum caro factum est', earns just as many days; in the case of the chant which commences with the words, 'Rogamus te, Domine,' just before the elevation of the host, one hundred days.[11]

This list went on extensively, and all the relics and vestments were described in detail, leaving Reinhard heaving with awe about this 'regal and divine' assemblage of things.[12] The text vividly conveyed Frederick's dynamism as an ardent collector, who was said to rarely enter 'our famous city without some new acquisition'; acquisitions from 'all parts of the globe.'[13] By 1520, there were more than 19,000 particles, which were exhibited during All Souls Day. Print was therefore used to draw the faithful and students to Wittenberg, but also to construct the idea of Wittenberg as cultic centre for a wider audience. Frederick thus belonged to the long line of rulers who made relics central to their prestige. Yet he was the first skillfully to use the media and artistic knowledge available at the time to disseminate its propagation. This keen awareness of the importance of medialization strategies left an imprint on the Reformation, as Luther and his Wittenberg team continued to work closely together with Cranach's workshop and with printers. Frederick's activities moreover had shown that even this small town, so undistinguished when compared to large cultic centres such as Cologne, could display its ambition through the triad of avant-garde artistic production, learning, and the claim that it was specially connected with the holy.

III

This, then, was the local setting in which Luther in 1520 began to develop his ideas that the papacy was the arch-enemy of Christ, the Anti-Christ, who was rising from hell during the last days on earth. Luther was excommunicated by Leo X soon after. He now saw his role as that of a prophet, like Daniel, a man through whom God worked, and a prophet for these last days on earth, to spread the true evangelical belief. Frederick's relic collection was still on show in autumn 1521, while Luther had been taken to the Wartburg under

[11] *Dialogus*, 253.
[12] Ibid., 255.
[13] Ibid., 254.

Frederick's protection and was translating the New Testament. No indulgences were handed out and no papal flags were shown. But the relics were still exhibited, the final occasion being in 1522, the year in which Luther managed to convince Frederick to let him return to Wittenberg. From then on, the 19,000 relics, including drops of Mary's milk, no longer made Wittenberg a cultic centre; they had no place in the new Jerusalem Luther wished to see here. The collection was melted down, re-used, or sold by the debt-ridden duke John the Steadfast, in the years following Frederick's death in 1525.[14]

Meanwhile the largest German treasure of relics remained in nearby Halle, built up by Frederick's rival collector Albrecht of Brandenburg, to whom Luther initially sent his 95 theses against the indulgence trade. This collection was twenty times the size of Frederick's, and its indulgence promised 39 million days of release from purgatory! One of Luther's last and characteristically brilliant pieces of popular satirical writing dates from 1542 and was entitled 'News from the Rhine', *Neue Zeitung vom Rhein*. It was occasioned by the move of Albrecht's relic collection from Halle, which had become Protestant, to Mainz, where Albrecht now fully resided as archbishop. Luther anonymously published this broadsheet to profane and unmask the allegedly sacred through laughter and drive away the devil with his trickery:

> our lovely people from the Rhineland want to give these poor, naked bones new clothes. For the gowns they had in Halle are torn. And if they had to stay there longer, they would soon have been frozen. . . . There are many new particles, and a great new indulgence from our holiest father pope Paul III, such as . . . three flames from Moses' bush on mount Sinai, two feathers and an egg, from the Holy Ghost, . . . a whole pound of the wind which gushed before Elia in the cave.[15]

Yet Luther did not do away with relics. He opposed false relics and a false belief in relics, but endorsed the notion that there were new relics, summing up true evangelical belief. He retained the noun 'relic' as an idiom through which his followers could express reformed belief. The first indication of this came in February 1522 during the negotiations on what would happen to the Wittenberg relic collection, when Luther congratulated Frederick that he could now acquire a 'new relic' for free: 'a whole cross with nails, speers and flagellation instruments'. This was only partly ironical. It actually summed up Luther's theology, built on Romans 3:23–28: only belief in the

---

[14] Cárdenas, *Heiltumsbuch*, 126.
[15] *Martin Luthers Werke, (WA)*, vol. 53 (Weimar, 1920), 404.

death of Christ, who had taken on the sins of the world, made the believer just. Luther also made clear that he held on to the notion of relics as sacred media in his important 1538 treatise 'On the councils and church'. He rejected the concept of an institutionalized church, and wished to replace it with a sense of a Christian people (*Volk*) or holy community, in whom the Holy Spirit dwelt. God's word was the new sacred medium, which brought fruit wherever it was preached to believers. This word worked wonders, fixed everything and sustained everything. It drove evil away.[16] And yet this was no easy religion, or something like going on a shopping spree for redemption set out by a greedy papacy, as buying indulgences was in Luther's view. Suffering, doubt, and persecution were part of the fate of God's people. Luther had long declared these spiritual experiences to be the 'new relics'.[17]

IV

We can therefore turn to the question of how this religion not just of 'the word', but of the *wondrous, holy word* became concrete in religious practice. The centrality of the word corresponded to the notion of religious doubt and despair, Luther's *tentatio, Anfechtung*, assaults by the devil, as new relics and a spiritual cornerstone. Only Christians meditating on the biblical word were challenged by the devil, until they finally received the comforting word of God.[18] Those who went through such tribulations were assured of their eternal life. It was thus advisable for the pious to collect and store fortifying biblical prophecies and promises for these times through writing or marking practices. These ideas turned words and books into a treasure replacing the treasure of traditional relics, and made the ability to at least have access to books and read crucial for an individual's struggle for faith and hope. Collecting words therefore became central to managing the uncertainties involved in attaining grace.

Luther thus frequently opposed the sacred word to the dead letter. Biblical words were directly related to God. Luther conceived scriptural words as sacrament and the sacrament as visible word and sacred sign through which God worked in believers. They were signs which held the signified within them and made it work.[19] So did the very name 'God' in writing. This view related to long established ideas about the salvific power of the Holy Name, which was often rendered as a holy monogram and pressed onto

[16] Martin Brecht, *Martin Luther: Die Erhaltung der Kirche 1532–1546* (Stuttgart, 1987), 197.

[17] Brecht, *Martin Luther: Sein Weg*, 156.

[18] Thomas Kaufmann, *Martin Luther* (Munich, 2006), 62.

[19] Heinrich Bornkamm, *Luther: Gestalt und Wirkung,. Gesammelte Aufsätze* (Gütersloh, 1975), 157–8.

wafers, for instance.[20] Luther, of course, opposed the old custom of wearing amulets of sacred words to which protective or miraculous powers could be attributed, but only because this seemed to be done without sincere faith and was calculated in its efficacy.[21] The power of faith was primarily bound to the biblical word: 'verbum suum, SUUM verbum, Dei verbum', and yet it was enduringly difficult for humans to believe in the certainty and truth of God's word.[22] The act of inscribing biblical words rendered this belief manifest. It was linked to the expectation that this truly believing writer would be protected. Luther thus immediately wrote the verses of Psalm 118, 17 in red letters onto the walls of his rooms in Coburg castle to ward off Satan, with notes for a tune: 'I shall not die but live, and I shall declare the words of God.'[23] Yet this was no ritualized practice to be repeated with just one psalm. Luther also held that any cognition of the sacred transcended human reason and apprehension, even necessitating a believer's loss of consciousness (*Ohnmacht*).[24] It had to be given by the Holy Ghost at God's will.[25] This further explains why it was necessary to assemble a whole collection of biblical words to manage uncertainty: for Lutherans it was unpredictable which of these would 'fall into' the heart at any particular time. Veit Dietrich's 1548 edition of consolatory sentences (*Trostsprüche* or *Sententiae consolatoriae*) put together by a Coburg pastor, Johann Grosch, thus referred to Luther's own experience that even well known sentences might lose their power (*sich verlieren*) and not 'sink in'. Hence only a collection enabled one to find sentences *at any time* which spoke clearly and with certainty to believers.[26] The word took part in God's omnipotence, and its effects could be seen: it was the only weapon for Protestants and had felled the papacy. The word 'Christ' alone, as Luther wrote in his most famous hymn 'A mighty fortress', composed around 1528, could slay the devil. Luther, moreover, seems to have combined such beliefs in the power of the sacred word with the common contemporary belief that spiritual words had a different efficacy when spoken

[20] See Susan Wabuda, 'The Name of Jesus', in *Preaching during the English Reformation* (Cambridge, 2002), 147–77. I am grateful to Alexandra Walsham for this reference.

[21] Don C. Skemer, *Binding Words. Textual Amulets in the Middle Ages* (Pennsylvania, 2006), 67.

[22] *WA*, vol. 48/1, 58/76.

[23] A doctor noted them down twenty years later; WA, vol. 48/1, 283–4, 4.

[24] Thus, Luther commented on Psalm 118, 14 in the following way: "Nicht ehe kann Christus unser Macht sein, wir werden denn inn uns selbst onmechtig und gecreuziget mit allerley leyden. Als denn wird er auch unser Psalm, Lied und Gesang, Darauff folget der Sieg und Heil inns ewige Leben, Amen." Anno 1544, *WA*, vol. 48/1, 65/84.

[25] Bornkamm, *Luther: Gestalt und Wirkung*, 150.

[26] *WA*, vol. 48/1, 326.

while the thresholds of rooms were crossed. According to Justus Jonas's famous account of the reformer's death, published immediately in March 1546, Luther several times rose and as he stepped over the threshold, on his way to bed, he uttered these words: 'In manus tuas commendo spiritum meum, Redemisti me Domine DEUS veritatis. (I place my soul in thy hands, for thou, God, hast truly redeemed me)'. He crossed and re-crossed his room, once or twice. As he put himself down to rest, he complained of very severe pressure on his chest.[27]

Yet, it is suggested as a result of Luther's ritual incantation, 'his heart did not pain him'.[28] In this sense then, Lutherans held that embodied practices of saying biblical words by true believers could have concrete bodily efficacy and retain the ancient function of religious belief as healing.

Within Lutheran cultures in Germany, a whole genre of tales soon dwelt on Luther and the supernatural power he as prophet could wield through the efficacy of the word.[29] Stories recounted how Luther as God's instrument and 'miracle-man', *Werkzeug* and *Wundermann*, had fought off the devil with hymns or biblical quotations, how his prayers had restored Melanchthon's health, how psalms spoken by him had extinguished fires or how his prayers had alleviated a community's dearth.[30] The scene of Luther 'rescuing his friend Melanchthon from death through his prayers' as a privileged intercessor in 1540 remained a regular theme on lithographs into the nineteenth century.[31] Miraculous stories of Lutheran sacred places, Bibles, or images were experienced, told, and noted down by clergymen until the eighteenth century. A key publication was one Lübeck superintendent's work entitled *De reliquiis Lutheri*, published in 1703, which described not only commemorative remains of the reformer, but linked them to stories of their supernatural power.[32]

It is against this specific background of Lutheran beliefs in Germany, rather than any generalized European Protestant culture, that Bob Scribner argued that such objects and stories 'promoted piety, confessional solidarity and

---

[27] *The Last Days of Luther, by Justus Jonas, Michael Coelius, and Others*, trans. and ed. Martin Ebon (New York, 1970), 64–5; 68–59.

[28] Ibid., 69.

[29] R. W. Scribner, *Popular Culture and Popular Movements in Reformation Germany* (London, 1987), 301–54.

[30] On Johannes Mathesius' influential 1566 History of Luther and the *leitmotif* of him as *Werkzeug* and *Wundermann* within it see Irena Backus, *Life Writing in Reformation Europe: Lives of Reformers by Friends, Disciples and Foes* (Aldershot, 2008), 11.

[31] Cat., *Luthers Leben in Illustratonen des 18. und 19. Jahrhunderts* (Coburg, 1980), 115–16.

[32] Scribner, *Popular Culture and Popular Movements*, 329.

self-confidence' in a culture characterized by 'syncretism with Catholic forms'.[33] That is, Scribner did not repeat Catholic polemicists, who of course had argued right from the sixteenth century that Luther himself wished to be revered as a saint.[34] Scribner rather emphasized that the Lutheran Reformation fused innovation and tradition. This fusion, it is now widely agreed, was integral to important strands within Lutheran belief and sustained through an oral, written, and visual culture right into modernity. Robert Kolb, by contrast, has explicitly argued that the German Lutheran Reformation 'left in place more remnants of medieval respect for saints than did other Protestant movements', but had one 'contemporary saint': 'No single Puritan hero, no Calvinist saint, stood so tall among sixteenth-century Protestants as Luther.' Because of his concept of the living voice of the Gospel,

> Luther's disciples were prepared to hear God's power exhibited in the mouths of the proclaimers of the Word. Among their contemporaries in his category, they knew of no one comparable to Luther. Among the prophets of God throughout history, they recognized few comparable to Luther.[35]

The challenge remains neither to homogenize this tradition, nor to overstate its 'Catholic' connections. Instead we need to reconstruct plural Lutheran cultures, which adapted and continued to re-make the reformer's legacy with different balances of innovation and selections of equally plural medieval traditions in different milieux.

V

One innovation surely lay in the way in which this new religion rooted its authority in a university it could control. The vitality of a distinct Lutheran memory culture, which finds no close parallel in the reformed parts of Europe, clearly evolved through the fact that Luther and the tightly knit team of men with whom he worked in Wittenberg fostered the notion that the city was the only legitimate centre of true Christian belief through the work of its scholars. Luther was presented as a divinely inspired scholar during his lifetime, and Luther made it absolutely clear from early in his

---

[33] Ibid., 353.

[34] Peter Burschel, 'Das Monster. Katholische Luther-Imagination im 16. Jahrhundert', in Hans Medick and Peer Schmidt (eds), *Luther zwischen den Kulturen: Zeitgenossenschaft—Weltwirkung* (Göttingen, 2004), 33–48.

[35] Robert Kolb, *For all the Saints: Changing Perceptions of Martyrdom and Sainthood in the Lutheran Reformation* (Macon, 1987), 157.

career that he wished to be addressed as 'Doctor Martin Luther'. His name on many prints and pictures became shortened to the monogram D.M.L. This was unique among the reformers, and a clear strategy on Luther's part to insist on the legitimacy of his standing through the notion that he was to be identified as the 'Doctor of Holy Scripture', as broadsheets regularly introduced him (*der Heiligen Schrift hochgelehrter Doktor*). This learning itself was not grounded in the dead letter either, but through the way in which the Holy Ghost worked in him. Luther, the ousted heretic, therefore defiantly commanded to be addressed and thus recognized as infused and enlightened by the Holy Ghost and scriptural knowledge, so much so that even his wife had to address him as *Doktor*. He assumed for himself the words of Psalm 119:99: 'I have more understanding than all my teachers: for thy testimonies *are* my meditation', or rather, in Luther's own translation, 'my speech'. This entitled him to be a judge of all human and devilish knowledge, and legitimized the authority of Luther and his generation over the power of tradition claimed by the Roman Church.[36] The mode of address as highly learned doctor, then, was essential for the account Luther wished to give of himself and his singularity.[37] Luther, for example, told the peasants and cobblers of his colleague Karlstadt's rebellious parish in Orlamünde in no uncertain terms never to write to him as a 'brother' again. He aggressively accused them: 'You have written a letter to me like an enemy, for you have not given me my title, which many princes and lords, who are my enemies, give and do not break away.'[38] The mayor justified this mode of address by saying that this had been a secret letter from them to him in a brotherly spirit. Luther in response threw a tantrum. The mayor could only save the situation by formally addressing Luther as 'honourable highly-learned *günstiger Herr Doctor*'. Only then did Luther deign to stay. Yet he refused to take his red doctoral beret off to honour anyone. This had become his visual mode of address, to perform his authority and command instant respect from those he regarded as spiritualists. 'Spiritualists' defied the importance of learning and meditating on scripture.[39]

---

[36] *WA*, vol. 48/1, 74–6.

[37] For this understanding of the importance of modes of address see Judith Butler, *Giving an Account of Oneself* (New York, 2005).

[38] *WA*, vol.15, 345: "Ferner ir habt mir einen feindeßbrief geschryben, ir gebt mir meinen title nicht, den mir doch etliche fürsten und herrn, so meine feinde seindt, geben und nicht abbrechen."

[39] For an exploration of this theme see Ulinka Rublack, *Dressing Up: Cultural Identity in Renaissance Europe* (Oxford, 2010), ch. 3.

Luther, then, had not just created a monogram, but also an epithet for himself as a sacred man. To change it could consequently come close to sacrilege. This made his status analogous to the pope, of whom Erasmus had critically remarked in his famous 1522 treatise on letter writing:

> The Roman pontiff is addressed as 'Most blessed father'; if you write 'Father most blessed', the document is torn up. He is called 'Most holy father'; if anyone should write: 'Father most holy', the meaning has changed. . . . Suppose I refer to the pontiff of Rome, who does not covet ambition, gain, pleasures, and tyranny, but serves Christ's glory and the well-being of the Christian flock, with the appellation 'evangelical shepherd'; would not that be more fitting than if I said 'most blessed father, 'since the epithet 'blessed' is equally appropriate for a man of wealth? If the pontiff is really such as I have described him, I have given him a worthy title; if he is not, I have given him a subtle reminder of what he should be.[40]

By addressing Luther as 'dear brother', the humble people of Orlamünde had given Luther a reminder of how, in their view, he should act. In Johannes Mathesius's 1566 lauding history of the reformer, by contrast, Luther mostly appeared entitled 'Doctor', and this 'closely connected' his description of him as a prophet with Luther as a doctor of the holy scripture.[41] It made him special, rather than brotherly, and inspired awe. This reverence to his name lent Luther's signature and inscriptions their particular cultic relevance as mediated remains.

VI

Yet what exactly were Luther's physical remains, apart from handwriting? Was their possession taken as a means to communicate with the holy? It is assumed that when Luther died, as in the case of Albrecht Dürer in 1528, casts of his head and hands were taken by the artist Lukas Furtenagel in Halle from the reformer's body.[42] In the humanist culture of the Renaissance, these two body parts were believed to emphasize a person's identity. This idea led to the

---

[40] 'On the Writing of Letters', in J. K. Sowards (ed.), *De conscribendis epistolis; Formula; De civilitate,* in *Collected Works of Erasmus* (Toronto, 1985), 25:61.

[41] Kolb, *For all the Saints,* 118.

[42] Uta Kornmeier, 'Luther in effigie, oder: Das "Schreckgespenst von Halle"', in: Stefan Laube, Karl-Heinz Fix (eds), *Lutherinszenierung und Reformationserinnerung* (Leipzig, 2002), 347–51.

proliferation of two genres: portraiture and personal correspondence. A person's handwriting was said to reflect the uniqueness of the writer. As Erasmus wrote: 'a man's handwriting, like his voice, has a special, individual quality', just as the artist's hand, *maneira*, began to signify a recognizable, individual style.[43] Erasmus moreover pressed the artist Holbein faithfully to render his hands in the act of writing for his famous portrait of the humanist. Indeèd, the only sketch studies of hands Holbein seems to have made are of Erasmus.[44] Dürer, too, cultivated this notion through inscribing images, or at least adding his monogram. The fact that something had been written in someone's own hand was increasingly lent emphasis, while signatures were usually still regarded as part of a piece of writing, rather than of value in themselves. Italian humanists, for instance, do not seem to have collected autographs.[45] Yet there was a tremendous sense of surprise and esteem when Charles V himself wrote and signed his Worms declaration that he would fight Luther, because normally secretaries did such work. Charles thereby underlined that these were his very own convictions.[46] Humanism with its veneration of scholarly knowledge and the competition of rulers building up different universities in German territories, who expected fees and needed attractions, had moreover fostered the new social role of the star scholar. Star professors embodied their knowledge in personalized ways—their knowledge, too, did not appear to be an assemblage of dead letters and removed from life, but they gave it force and contemporary relevance with their singular voice, body, experience, and in their writing.

Hence in Wittenberg as a new cultic centre, Lutheran relics innovatively turned out to be grapho-relics. The signature in Luther's or Melanchthon's or other professors' hands under a biblical quotation mediated the spiritual presence of the reformer and the authenticity of a piece of writing. Such practices of inscription circulated God's word as a new sacred medium through the body of Luther and Wittenberg professors in whom the Holy Spirit evidently dwelt. Luther and Melanchthon, and other Lutheran professors after them, therefore cultivated an innovative practice of inscription, which circulated the word as graphic remains from Wittenberg and fostered a sense of friendship and belonging among adherents. The signatures

[43] Béatrice Fraenkel, 'La signature comme exposition du nom propre', in Anne-Marie Christin (ed.), *L'écriture du nom propre* (Paris, 2000), 215–33.

[44] Cat., *Erasmus von Rotterdam: Vorkämpfer für Frieden und Toleranz* (Basel, 1986), 123.

[45] I have not found any literature on this theme, and wish to thank Peter Burke for his advice on this point.

[46] Fritz Reuter (ed.), *Der Reichstag zu Worms von 1521: Reichspolitik und Luthersache* (Worms, 1971), 235, "mit aigner hand".

encapsulate the beginnings of a lasting phenomenon a French scholar has termed 'la performativité du nom propre signé'.[47]

Some wrote to Luther just to ask for his signature. 'You asked for my hand, here you have it!' (*manum meam petiisti, ecce manum habes*): thus read Luther's shortest ever letter of reply.[48] Comforting sentences (*Trostsprüche*) were handwritten into a particular book, Bible, or album. A commentary on them, a signature, place name, and date typically rounded off the inscription. Melanchthon, as his contemporary biographer noted, apparently spent an 'incredible' amount of time and effort on these entries; and would usually sign 'Scriptum manu Philippi'.[49] Luther's biographer Mathesius likewise reported that he spent the last years of his life 'inscribing himself in many people's books'. Luther had certainly started off the practice in 1534, which began to spread rapidly from 1542.[50] It enjoyed a broad social reach among the middling and upper ranks of society. Many texts were written in the vernacular.[51] The first autograph inscription was thus in German and included a long rhymed warning about the work of the devil. It was for Luther's Wittenberg barber and friend Peter Beskendorf.[52] Luther gave other inscriptions to people such as a Halle organist, the mayor of Halle, the painter Furtenagel, a Zwickau magistrate, Paul Tucher of Nürnberg, or a merchant's wife.[53] Three hundred and five books with Luther's inscriptions, or separate *alba amicorum*, which started as a new genre in Wittenberg in the 1540s specifically to collect autographs and inscriptions, are still preserved. Leather-binders were keen to earn money by pressing portraits of Luther and Melanchthon on the front and back of alba, while others entered widely circulating woodcut images of the key reformers.

A student called Nicolaus Zeitlos, for example, bought the Wittenberg Bible. Luther and Melanchthon both entered biblical quotations and some prose in it. Zeitlos added to this a portrait of Luther by Cranach as well as a double portrait of Luther and Melanchthon, framed by angels and the four

---

[47] Fraenkel, 'La signature', 231.

[48] Werner Wilhelm Schnabel, *Das Stammbuch. Konstitution und Geschichte einer textsortenbezogenen Sammelform bis ins erste Drittel des 18. Jahrhunderts* (Tübingen, 2003), 276.

[49] Hans-Peter Hasse, 'Wittenberger Theologie im "Stammbuch": Eintragungen der Wittenberger Professoren im Album des Wolfgang Ruprecht aus Eger', in: M. Beyer/ G. Wartenberg (eds), *Humanismus und Wittenberger Reformation* (Leipzig, 1996), 88.

[50] Schnabel, *Das Stammbuch*, 246–7.

[51] See also ibid., 249.

[52] *WA*, vol. 48/1, 149–52.

[53] Ibid., 36; 56; 12; 267; 24; 265.

evangelists.[54] We know that Zeitlos also acted as intermediary, and obtained an autograph of Luther and Melanchthon for one Johan Kaler. Many used Lufft's 1541 costly 'Median' edition of the German Bible to paste in or bind in images and inscriptions. Luther was usually the first person to be asked, after whom other professors such as Bugenhagen and Melanchthon would write. This underlined Luther's singular status in the hierarchy of Wittenberg theologians. A copy of the 1541 Lufft Bible which the reformers presented to the Danish king likewise contained inscriptions and autographs, first by Luther, followed by Melanchthon, and finally Bugenhagen.[55] Bourgeois and noble people who did not receive presentation copies travelled to Wittenberg to obtain inscriptions and autographs.[56] Psalm verses were particularly popular, and the practice of inscriptions as such strengthened the role of the Wittenberg theologians as shepherds of the soul through biblical exegesis.[57] Popular Lutheran spiritual treatises, such as Johann Spangenberg's 1542 *Booklet for the Comfort of the Sick* already praised biblical passages of this kind as a shield 'to quench all the flaming arrows of the Evil One'. Spangenberg specified in successive paragraphs which inscriptions worked particularly well as comfort for illness, against assaults by the devil, terror in the face of death, or even assaults from hell.[58] This affirmed their deeply reassuring qualities and the notion that only a collection helped to confront a whole range of spiritual worries which haunted believers throughout their lives.

For generations to come, authentic autographs and handwritten inscriptions of leading reformers thus easily retained their particular value. A student called Christoph von Teuffenbach, for instance, bought a copy of Melanchthon's *Loci Communes*. In the blank leaves bound in front of this book he gathered inscriptions with autographs from Melanchthon, Bugenhagen, Major, and Winsheim. Inside the front cover, underneath an engraving of the Last Supper, a clipping of a paper with a biblical inscription and signature by Martin Luther was pasted in. Luther had died in 1546, two years before Teuffenbach had even matriculated. A note added that Justus Jonas had given Luther's signature on 3 March 1548 to Johannes Martinus of

[54] Werner W. Schnabel (ed.), *Die Handschriften der Stadtbibliothek Nürnberg: Die Stammbücher und Stammbuchfragmente*, Part I. (Wiesbaden, 1995), 3.

[55] These have been digitalized by the Royal Library in Copenhagen and can be viewed on the web under the keywords 'Luther and the Reformation in Denmark'.

[56] Schnabel, *Stammbuch*, 250.

[57] See also ibid., 264.

[58] Johannes Spangenberg, *A Booklet of Comfort for the Sick, & On the Christian Knight*, trans. and ed. Robert Kolb (Milwaukee, 2007), 62–3.

Antwerp, who himself had entered Wittenberg University in 1546. Martinus
testified underneath the clipping that he had then given Luther's autograph to
his fellow student Teuffenbach as a gift. These testimonies proved the signature's authentic provenance.[59] Decades later still, a man called Georg Werner
who had matriculated in Wittenberg in 1584 acquired the seal of a letter by
Zwingli addressed to Philip of Hesse for his *liber amicorum*, and also a page
with twenty-five lines written by Luther's hand, as authenticated by
Melanchthon's son, seventeen lines written by Melanchthon, and his son's
autograph.[60] Zeitlos' bible autographs from Luther and Melanchthon had
been authenticated by the notary Thomas Hertinger.

   Authentication obviously became a key issue, because just as relics could be
forged, so handwriting and signatures could be copied.[61] One student who
put together a friendship album with signatures, inscriptions and pictures
from his stays at Nördlingen, Wittenberg and Augsburg between 1582 and
1617 thus pasted two paper fragments into the album: a quote from Horace
with Melanchthon's signature (Phillipus), and a small piece of paper, written
on both sides by Luther, without his signature, but with an inscription that it
was the hand of Luther. Small cuts of printed portraits of each reformer were
pasted next to their fragments. Practices of this kind show why neat distinctions between a Lutheran culture of memory and forms of relic-worship are
sometimes hard to draw. Yet these Protestant remains could be collected by a
far wider circle of people than Catholic relics, and, in an age of widening
university education, drew on the identification of people who admired academic knowledge-making with religious reformers who were professors as
well.

   Students' energy, in turn, could easily become limitless. Johann Spon, a
student from Augsburg, for instance, gathered entries in an album in
Wittenberg between 1554 and 1559, that is, after Luther's death. He himself
copied quotes from Luther and Melanchthon as well as their praises of
Wittenberg as a place where the light of the Gospel shone. Wolfgang Kren,
meanwhile, was the son of an Austrian cloth dealer, who studied in
Wittenberg between 1568–1573. He not only managed to still obtain an
autograph of Luther, as well as an eight-year-old letter from the professor
of medicine Vitus Örtel Winshemius the Elder, but also gathered a total of

[59] Richard G. Salomon, 'The Teuffenbach Copy of Melanchthon's 'Loci Communes',
Renaissance News, 8 (1955), 79–85.
[60] Karlheinz Goldmann, *Nürnberger und Altdorfer Stammbücher aus vier Jahrhunderten*
(Nürnberg, 1981), 298.
[61] See Schnabel, *Stammbuch*, 247, fn.15; 249, fn.24 as well as the attempts by the editors of
the *WA* themselves to identify forgeries.

fifty-eight entries from Wittenberg professors and colleagues in 1571. *Ora et labora* was printed into the front of the album, *Honour to God* on its back.[62] Georg Vogtherr, the son of a Lutheran parson, who matriculated in 1578, had a coloured full-length portrait of Luther after a popular broadsheet by Lucas Cranach (Fig. 1) on the front and a full-length portrait of Melanchthon on the back of his copy of Camerarius' biography of Melanchthon, in its first 1566 edition. He pasted in a partly coloured Cranach woodcut of Melanchthon. Vogtherr collected 56 inscriptions in Wittenberg.[63] One woman called Ursula Resch, on the other hand, bought a 1541/2 edition of Luther's German Psalter and completed it just with a pasted-in autograph from Luther in the front and Melanchthon in the back. She gave it to her future spouse as a New Year gift when he first came to eat at her parents' house, for a year full of luck and happiness, '*ein vilglückseliges Neues Jahr*'. Books and autographs could thus be appropriated in a completely new way, by a woman to wish for earthly happiness in a life with her love. I loved this book, noted this man, because of the 'autograph of the honourable highly illuminated men', '*hocherleuchten Menner*'.[64] Books with these inscriptions often remained in a family for generations. In 1665, a sermon in north Germany referred to the Bible of a Wittenberg student which Luther had inscribed with psalm words and a commentary. The student had become a pastor back home, and one century later his family still kept his Bible as a 'spiritual treasure'.[65]

VII

In these ways Wittenberg became the production centre of new 'relics' and treasures, Lutheran grapho-relics, whose power was sustained by a new religion of the word and cultic portraiture. Immediately after Luther's death, collections of comforting biblical quotations and commentaries Luther (and sometimes other Wittenberg professors) had inscribed into Bibles multiplied in different German towns and regions. Johann Aurifaber and Georg Rörer, in particular, published sizeable editions of Luther's inscriptions as spiritual testimony in 1547.[66] Even the titles of these books provide an answer to the question of how Lutheranism was spiritually distinct, and how Lutheranism set out to construct not just a negative identity—binding people together through anti-papalism—but a community of the fortified faithful. Two Nuremberg editions from 1548, for instance, advertised the following

---

[62] Schnabel, *Stammbücher Nürnberg*, 26–30.

[63] Ibid., 45–50.

[64] *WA*, vol. 48/1, 17/21; *WA*, vol. 48/2, 37.

[65] "*geistlicher schatz*", *WA*, vol 48/2, 47.

[66] Schnabel, *Stammbuch*, 264.

Fig. 1. This popular woodcut encouraged its audience to memorize key points of Luther's biography. Portrait of Martin Luther, Lucas Cranach the Younger, *c.*1540–1550. British Museum AN49788001. © Trustees of the British Museum

'beautiful' sayings (*schöne sprüche*) on their title page, which Luther and others had entered into many Bibles. The psalm words 'Do not leave me when I shall be grey and old' were answered with the biblical promise 'Yes, I shall carry you until you are old and grey. I will lift and carry you, and save you'. At the end of the book, psalm words encouraged 'Glory to the people who can rejoice'.[67] Luther's later inscriptions could highlight a surprisingly simple, accessible message of assurance. He thus commented on Psalm, 1:1: 'If someone wants to be pious, do good things and gain salvation, then he should mainly abstain from wrong teaching and just busily keep to God's word alone. Thus he will be safe. Martinus Luther D. 1545'.[68]

There was no emphasis here on tribulations as new relics. Yet such words were ascribed healing powers as spiritual medicine by later Lutherans, following the old assumption that they would only be sought by true believers who were afflicted by spiritual anxiety and doubt. Christian Scriver's (1629–1693) popular 'Treasure of Souls' thus praised God's words as a 'pharmacy' for times of sadness and despair. He recommended parishioners to assemble books with biblical quotations and fortifying phrases from sermons and godly conversations. When believers were overcome by doubt or melancholy, they could leaf through such collections or the Bible, and wait for the Holy Ghost to infuse them with strength when they read or even slept upon particular passages. Scriver thus recounted the exemplary story of a God-fearing man who would take his Bible when he was saddened 'in his head and heart' until he found some comforting lines, then he would lie his head on the book, think about the phrase so often and move it in his heart until he fell asleep; when he woke up his worries were usually gone, he gave himself into God's sacred and fatherly will, and therein found comfort and peace for his soul.[69]

Scriver moreover told the story of a simple-minded, and perhaps only partially literate, pious man who would mark such fortifying phrases with crosses in red stone. Scriver had seen another man, who had marked in black ink with his initials those passages in which he had felt the power of the Holy Ghost in his heart.[70] The archivist of a 'great man', finally, had shown Scriver this man's Weimar Bible, where he had inscribed his 'name, place of birth, fatherland, as well as honourable offices on the pages of the 14th, 15th and 16th chapter of John the evangelist'. There was no doubt for Scriver that his

---

[67] *WA*, vol. 48/2, 26–7.

[68] *WA*, vol. 48/1, 11.

[69] M. *Christian Scrivers Seelen-Schatz: Darinnen von der menschlichen Seelen hohen Würde, tiefen und kläglichem Sünden–Fall, Busse und Erneuerung durch Christum . . . fürgezeiget,* (Magdeburg and Leipzig, 1731), 119.

[70] Ibid., 119.

sad and troubled soul had found comfort in these sentences.[71] Personal
inscriptions in collections of biblical inscriptions thus provided spiritual testimony, which could literally reinstate one as a person, with a name, country,
and offices. They marked out a personal history of an experience of the divine
from within the experience of doubt and made it legible to others.

The reassurance to be gained from such labours nonetheless was embedded
in the certainty that the world would disastrously come to an end through the
raging Antichrist. The owner of a 1556 edition of Luther's German works, for
example, in 1593 inscribed the following prophecy into the first volume,
which Luther had inscribed with chalk on the wall of his Wittenberg study
just behind his Bible, shortly before his death: 'Millesimo Sexcentesimo venit
turcus Totam Germaniam devastaturus'. Other reports on this prophecy
included Italy in the total devastation to be brought on by Turks in 1600.[72]
The owner of Luther's German works moreover reported that a board had
been placed in front of the Wittenberg inscription, which could be pushed
away to reveal Luther's original writing. This gave ritual presence to the whole
notion of the Reformation as the beginning of a time of revelation through
Luther as a new prophet Daniel. Prophetic secrets would be revealed before
the end of the world. Daniel had not understood the 'words he was told to
write; rather they were "closed up and sealed till the time of the end" (Dan.
12:9)'.[73] Luther's words were closed up and revealed, rather than sealed.

VIII

Luther himself described his study as the 'poor' place from which he had
nonetheless stormed the papacy (*mein armes stublein, daraus ich doch das
babstumb gesturmet habe*).[74] He immediately designated his study as another
'remain' for memory: '*propter quam causam dignum esset perpetua memoria*'
('for which reason it merits permanent memory'). His study did indeed
become the key element of the new cultic topography Lutheran Wittenberg
successfully established. The iconography of Luther's divinely inspired work
as a scholar in his study developed alongside a vigorous veneration
of St Jerome in his study as well as a new cult of the scholarly study as a
'virtuous room' separated from worldly concerns and thus a place of privileged, divinely sanctioned individual knowledge-making in Renaissance

[71] Ibid., 119.
[72] The prophecy was first announced by a Franciscan called Johann Hilten.
[73] Robin Bruce Barnes, *Prophecy and Gnosis: Apocalypticism in the Wake of the Lutheran Reformation* (Stanford, 1988), 95.
[74] *WA*, vol. 48/2, 134–6.

humanism.[75] A woodcut in the 1530 Wittenberg edition of the New Testament, for instance, depicted Luther as the evangelist Matthew, writing on a beautiful desk, next to an angel and inspired by the Holy Ghost (symbolized through the dove hovering above him). By any scholar's standard, this desk was miraculously tidy.

A particularly intriguing element of the Lutheran memory culture soon to emerge from this matrix of religious and scholarly reverence was a Luther effigy. Twentieth-century critics were the first to deride it as a 'terrifying ghost' and finally dismantled it in its largely disintegrating state. Its origins can be traced back to the seventeenth century, when, it is presumed, the casts of Luther's face and hands after his death were remodelled in wax.[76] They were then coloured, the face was finished with glass eyes, eye-lashes, eyebrows and hair, to be integrated into a life-size doll of the reformer, mounted on wood and dressed with a large black gown, white shirt, doublet, and a doctor's cap. It was seated on an ornate chair in front of a small desk with a large book on it. Luther's hands were prominent in this display, as they were held to reflect his authentic remains. This doll was displayed in the library of the Marien-church in Halle, which owned a major collection of the reformer's writings and opened a new library building in 1612. Perhaps the doll was made for the opening. It would therefore have been the first European effigy for display purposes which was not linked to a funerary ritual, or of a ruler. The figure was first repaired and referred to in 1663.[77] Its purpose was to intensify the presence of the reformer for the memory of those who visited the library next to a church through a realistic display of his work, in a public place akin to his scholarly environment. Its location did not invite the direct relationship of reverence leading to the expectation of a personal mediation of the divine, which characterized the relationship of Catholic believers and images of saints. In this sense, it was designed to make memory rather than the sacred real. Around 1680, the first copper engravings were issued depicting Luther after his effigy, and these depictions were replicated in different formats. In contrast to one final twentieth-century photograph of the doll, however, Luther was shown in each of these depictions sitting upright and looking into the distance or even directly at the onlooker, rather than into his books. After 1891 there was even an attempt to sell plaster-casts of Luther's face taken from the doll, but this was quite unsuccessful.[78] In 1917, to

[75] Dora Thornton, *The Scholar in his Study: Ownership and Experience in Renaissance Italy* (New Haven, Conn., 1997), 176.

[76] For the following see Kornmeier, 'Luther in Effigie', 343–73.

[77] Ibid., 346–7.

[78] Ibid., 361.

celebrate the 400th 'anniversary' of the Reformation, postcards of the Luther effigy were sold, which now depicted the reformer engrossed in his Bible. From 1924 the figure was exhibited in the sacristy, while Halle scientists in 1926 authenticated that the casts were originally taken from Luther at his death. The 'original' casts were now displayed separately from the doll, which was furnished with copies. In 1927, a debate arose about whether this doll was a residue of Catholic hero-worship and cultic devotion, to which people still brought flowers, or merely an 'artistic rarity' and piece of memory which nobody worshipped in any way. Mathilde Luddendorf, a woman closely connected to Hitler, objected with particular vigour to the way in which the doll had been displayed even in the Marien-library so as to confront visitors unexpectedly and at least entertain for a little while the shocking sense that Luther had come alive. To counter this position, a brochure about the value of the effigy as an object which would serve to honour Luther's memory was issued in 1931. This, apparently, was to be the last trace of the Luther doll.

Today the mask and the hands are on a permanent exhibit in the Marienkirche in Halle. They are described as 'original', and displayed in a large glass case as if Luther sat in an upright position. It is explicitly suggested that the reformer faces spectators as if he were raised from his deathbed. The further descriptions then admit that this display was probably made after a plaster cast made by the Halle painter Lukas Furtenagel in 1546, but assert that the death mask was received by the Marienkirche through its pastor Justus Jonas, a close friend of Luther. The mask is described as belonging to the 'treasures and witnesses from the Reformation that Halle is amply equipped with'.[79] The hands now clearly possess secondary importance, as they are no longer linked to a religious imagination invested in the power of the writing hand, which this article has traced as a central element of Lutheranism. The hands now are mounted on a piece of black cloth, without any book, so as to help spectators re-imagine the deathbed scene, rather than Luther as a religious scholar of the wondrous word. The emphasis on the authentic nature of both casts nonetheless is crucial to make modern audiences 'witnesses' of Luther's implicitly peaceful death, rather than his alleged sudden, anguished death from one of his regular bouts of over-eating and drinking. The manner of Luther's death had immediately become a key element in his contested legacy across Europe, and it continued to be taken as

---

[79] See the information under http://www.marktkirche-halle.de: 'Die Original–Totenmaske Martin Luthers gehört zu den Schätzen und Zeugnissen der Reformationszeit, mit denen die Marktkirche zu Halle reich ausgestattet ist'.

proof of whether or not he was revealing divine truth.[80] If part of the function of relic collection was to make present and preserve for memory particles connected to the bodies of long dead saints, apostles, Mary, or even Christ himself, then this same function is preserved in the Halle display, and with it the prestige it accords to Halle as a specific place which possesses these treasures and thus 'fame by association'.[81] The casts and their presentation testify to a particularly striking concern for 'material continuity' in the same 'remarkable persistence' Caroline Bynum has identified for the 'Catholic' relic cult, 'even where it seemed almost to require philosophical incoherence, theological equivocation, or aesthetic offensiveness'.[82] The adult admission fee to see the death mask in Halle is two euros. No blind man will be healed, no dead person be awakened. The masks and hands are not said to work miracles and mediate the sacred. Yet they are valued as significant bodily bearers of the reformer's individuality. They thus confront us with questions about the enduring place of the 'pious memento' in a Lutheran culture of memory and belief, a process which has revolved around the gradual redefinition of a 'relic' as a mnemonically potent, treasured remain.[83]

IX

Meanwhile, Luther's final inscription into an estate manager's book of sermons was the last authentic remain eternalized by his followers. These words, as Justus Jonas concluded in his account of the reformer's death, had come true and alive in Luther's un-pained death, when he had joined God in 'peaceful sleep'. Once more, these words could never be just a dead letter, a dead remain, but had become redemption and eternal life, since they, rather than Catholic relics, were the real *Heilthumb*, holy objects. Jonas wrote:[84]

> With him, the words of John came true: 'Verily, verily, I say unto you, If a man keep my saying, he shall never see death' (John 8:51). This phrase represents his last writing, he inscribed it, as a

[80] See, in particular, Adolf Herte, *Das katholische Lutherbild im Bann der Lutherkommentare des Cochläus*, 3 vols (Münster, 1943); *Luther's Lives: Two Contemporary Accounts of Martin Luther*, trans. Elizabeth Vandiver, Ralph Keen, and Thomas D. Frazel (Manchester, 2002); *The Last Days of Luther*.

[81] Just as Castle Krottdorf in Siegerland, which exhibited a bed in which Luther slept, until the beginning of the twentieth century; see Scribner, *Popular Culture and Popular Movements*, 314–15.

[82] Caroline Walker Bynum, *The Resurrection of the Body in Western Christianity, 200–1336* (New York, 1995), 11.

[83] See also the contribution by Alexandra Walsham in this volume, 121–43.

[84] Spangenberg, *On the Christian Knight*, 127.

memento, into a Postil (A Family Book of Sermons) in his own handwriting, commenting on it in a dedication to Hans Gasman, an estate administrator from Ellrich, in (the country of) Hohenstein. The dearly beloved Father (Luther, U.R.) interpreted it as follows: Never see death. 'Truly, these words are beyond belief, and contradict general, every day experiences; and yet, they are quite true: If a man contemplates God's word with sincerity, from his heart, believes in Him and falls asleep with his thought, or dies, then he fades and passes on before he recognizes faith or is aware of it, then he must surely pass on with a certainty in the Word he believed and valued.' Under this was written: 'Martinus Luther, Doctor 1546, done on the 7th day of February.'[85]

Luther in this way and through the use of his motto *Vivit* ('He lives'), turned himself into the embodiment of one of the most potent forces of religious belief: he could triumph over death, and so could those who believed in his truth. Lutheranism thus remains ill understood as an anti-sensual, disembodied religion of the word. Rather, it saw true belief rooted in a writing hand as well as a heart and mind mediating sacred biblical words. It was grounded in an experience of spiritual struggles and assurance, which ultimately was affirmed not through introspection, but by losing consciously reasoning personhood in deep sleep. Word collecting instead of traditional relic worship among literate people hence became built into strategies to assure oneself of attainable grace.

The reformers' autographs were not priceless: they had an exchange value. A market developed for them, in which several of the reformers' sons acted as intermediaries for their fathers' remains. Nowadays, Luther autographs cost enormous sums. Of their spiritual value to owners we know little. An investigation of this phenomenon would be part of the anthropology of Protestant religions, which naturally follows on from the historical anthropology of Lutheranism attempted here.

---

[85] *The Last Days of Luther*, 78–80. For Cochläus's commentary on this see *Luther's Lives*, 547.

Tongues, Toes, and Bones: Remembering Saints in Early Modern Bohemia

Howard Louthan

Nearly fifty years ago John Pocock noted:

> If a traditional relationship with the past has been ruptured, the first instinct of society's intellectuals may be to restore it and this may be attempted by reshaping myth, by historisation or by the construction of a new image of the past in terms of some new continuity of which society has become aware in the present.[1]

Though Pocock was writing in general terms, his observation has special relevance for Central Europe. For Catholics the revolution launched by Luther and his allies was the greatest challenge their church had faced since the initial period of Christianization. To use Pocock's terms the Protestant revolt constituted the most significant rupture with the past Central European Catholics had ever experienced. Though the historiography of the Counter-Reformation is decidedly more extensive and sophisticated than it was even two decades ago, there are significant questions that have only been examined cursorily if considered at all. How did the church respond on an intellectual level to the Central European crisis? How did Catholic scholars grapple with the problems of rupture and memory? What practical strategies did they implement to bridge the church's triumphs of the past with its difficulties of the present? These types of questions lie at the heart of the Catholic resurgence in Central Europe. One of the key facets of this revival was a renewed interest and heightened emphasis on sacred relics and remains. These tangible tokens of memory were not only one of the most effective tools Catholics had at their disposal to counter the Protestant challenge, but more profoundly, they reflected a new understanding of the church's past and its relationship with the present.

In marked contrast to the historiography of Late Antiquity and the Middle Ages, the study of sacred remains in the Catholic Reformation is in its

---

[1] John Pocock, 'The Origins of Study of the Past: A Comparative Approach', *Comparative Studies in Society and History*, 4 (1962), 217.

infancy.[2] Until recently, the relic collection of a prince such as Spain's Philip II was simply seen as evidence of the ruler's overweening piety. Those studying early modern Catholicism, however, are now beginning to examine relics, their acquisition and strategic deployment, in more sophisticated fashion. A recent study on Philip II and his cache of nearly 7,500 holy artefacts has illustrated how the king manipulated these items to bolster royal authority and help construct a coherent spiritual and territorial identity for his realm.[3] Leading statesmen such as the Duke of Lerma or the archbishop of Valencia, Juan de Ribera, also used relics to further their own political or ecclesiastical ends. Cities competed with each other as they feverishly sped to recover the remains of their respective patrons. Philip II flexed his diplomatic muscles on behalf of Toledo to compel religious houses in France and the Low Countries to relinquish the putative bones of St Eugenio, the city's first bishop, and St Leocadia, an early virgin martyr.[4] In Rome, the 1578 discovery of 'Priscilla's catacombs' and the remains of what were presumably early Christian martyrs triggered a great trade in relics. Martyrs were on the move, and when a Polish diplomat requested a relic from Pius V before returning to his homeland, the pope merely bent to the ground, dug up a handful of earth and passed it over to his visitor calmly assuring him that the very soil beneath his feet was mixed with the blood of martyrs.[5]

In contrast to the Mediterranean world, far less work has been done examining the place and role of relics north of the Alps. To be sure, initial impressions from this region are not promising for such an investigation. There is Luther's thunderous attack on the cult of St Benno, Calvin's withering assault on relics and the seemingly omnipresent crowds of iconoclasts eager to sack the closest church at hand. But when the dust had settled, and the Catholics had regrouped, sacred relics and remains became a focal point in Rome's

---

[2] There is no survey of relics and their use in the Catholic Reformation. For a general overview see Arnold Angenendt, *Heilige und Reliquien: die Geschichte ihres Kultes vom frühen Christentum bis zur Gegenwart* (Munich, 1994).

[3] Guy Lazare, 'Possessing the Sacred: Monarchy and Identity in Philip II's Relic Collection at the Escorial', *Renaissance Quarterly*, 60 (2007), 58–93.

[4] A. Katie Harris, *From Muslim to Christian Granada: Inventing a City's Past in Early Modern Spain* (Baltimore, 2007), 38; Ben Ehlers, 'Negotiating Reform: Juan de Ribera, Archbishop of Valencia, and the Colegio de Corpus Christi', *Archiv für Reformationsgeschichte*, 95 (2004), 186–209.

[5] Central here is the work of Simon Ditchfield, 'Text before Trowel: Antonio Bosio's *Roma sotterranea* Revisited', in R. N. Swanson (ed.), *The Church Retrospective, Studies in Church History* 33 (1997), 343–60; 'Martyrs on the Move: Relics as Vindicators of Local Diversity in the Tridentine Church', in Diana Wood (ed.), *Martyrs and Martyrologies* (Oxford, 1993) (Studies in Church History, 30), 283–94.

efforts to re-establish the church in Central Europe. Cologne emerged as a key centre. With Ursula and her 11,000 virgins, the martyrs of the Theban legion and the bones of the Three Magi, city leaders aggressively promoted their massive trove of sacred artefacts. Antiquarian literature celebrating the city's sacred past poured from its presses. Aegidius Gelenius devoted more than half of his weighty history of Cologne to its sacred monuments and relics. On its elaborate frontispiece the artist depicted the city as a *sacrarium*, a massive repository of holy relics collected over the course of nearly 1500 years.[6] Cologne of course was not unique. To the east in Fulda the enterprising monks publicized the remains of St Boniface, the Apostle of the Germans.[7] To the south Duke Maximilian I of Bavaria (1597–1651) styled himself as Germany's Catholic champion and mounted a well-coordinated propaganda campaign against the Protestants. He commissioned the Jesuit Matthias Rader to eulogize the duchy's holy past. In his multi-volume hagiography, *Bavaria sancta*, Rader cried out against those 'who have declared eternal war on the saints, dug up their relics like dogs and destroyed them with fire and water'.[8] At the same time Maximilian helped supervise the translation of approximately one thousand catacomb saints who had been brought north from Rome for deployment in Bavaria.

To probe this issue more closely, I will focus on one specific region where relics played a critical role in the Catholic resurgence. Our area of consideration, the kingdom of Bohemia, however, differed in two substantial ways from the other regions I have mentioned. Geographically, it lay beyond the Rhine/Danube axis, an important boundary both for Roman settlement and early Christianization. While Aegidius Gelenius boasted that in a village not far from Cologne, Constantine had his famous vision predicting victory over Maxentius and the triumph of Christianity, Bohemian antiquarians could make no comparable claim concerning the antiquity of the faith in their homeland. It was not until the ninth century that Saxon monks penetrated the region with Byzantium's missionary brothers, Cyril and Methodius, coming a few years later to Moravia. The second and more important difference relates to the issue of heresy. While Cologne may have wobbled during the Reformation with the defection of its archbishop, Hermann von Wied, ultimately it did not fall. The same is true of course for Bavaria, Mainz, and Fulda, that island of Catholic orthodoxy in hostile territory. Bohemia was

---

[6] Aegidius Gelenius, *De admiranda, sacra, et civili magnitudine Coloniae Claudiae Agrippinensis Augustae Ubiorum Urbis* (Cologne, 1645).

[7] Christoph Brower, *Fuldensium antiquitatum Libri III* (Antwerp, 1612).

[8] Cited in Trevor Johnson, 'Holy Fabrications: The Catacomb Saints and the Counter-Reformation in Bavaria', *Ecclesiastical History*, 47 (1996), 284.

markedly different. During the Hussite revolution the Bohemians defied the threats of Rome and the armies of the emperor to create a semi-autonomous church. By the sixteenth century the situation had deteriorated to such an extent that in his debate with Luther, Johann Eck merely had to mention the word Bohemia to conjure the spectre of heresy. More than two centuries of religious rebellion, however, came to an abrupt end in November 1620 when a Habsburg coalition defeated an army of the Bohemian estates at the Battle of White Mountain. Though Catholicism was restored by royal fiat, the church's leaders had a daunting task before them. Unlike Rader in Bavaria or Gelenius in Cologne, Bohemia's learned clerics confronted a rupture with the past that had begun not with the Reformation but over a century earlier with Hus.

What role did relics play in this process? The first point to note is their centrality. When one of the kingdom's most treasured objects, the Madonna of Stará Boleslav, was captured by the Swedes during the Thirty Years War, its release became a high priority of state and was one of the critical issues of the peace negotiations. Patriotic clerics were quick to point out that Prague boasted one of the largest collections of sacred artefacts on the continent. The Czech musician and cleric, Mauritius Vogt, claimed that after Rome and Cologne, Prague's collection was the most extensive. The dean of St Vitus Cathedral, Tomáš Pešina, went even further by asserting that Prague had more relics than any European metropolis save Rome.[9] Hyperbole aside, there was undeniably a massive if scattered sampling of holy remains across the region. In the fourteenth century Emperor Charles IV and his ally Archbishop Arnošt of Pardubice scoured the continent to assemble an enormous collection that the antiquarians later highlighted.[10] In calendrical fashion Tomáš Pešina worked his readers through the history of the church by simply drawing attention to some of the most significant relics of St Vitus. Pešina featured the jaw and five teeth of St Luke on October 18, a small arm bone of Emperor Constantine on May 21, the head of Basil the Great on June 14, the entire body of martyred Duke Wenceslas on September 28 and a shoulder bone of St Thomas Becket on December 29.[11]

For a closer examination of relics and their function in historical literature of the period, let us turn to the most prolific of Bohemia's antiquarians, the

---

[9] V. Schwarz (ed.), *Město vidím veliké: cizinci o Praze* (Prague, 1940), 59; Tomáš Pešina, *Thesaurus in lucem protractus* (Prague, 1675), A2v-A3r.

[10] Bohuslav Balbín, *Vita venerabilis Arnesti primi Archiepiscopi Pragensis* (Prague, 1664), 179–81; Tomáš Pešina, *Phosphorus septicornis, stella alias matutina* (Prague, 1673), 501–24.

[11] Pešina, *Thesaurus*, D1r-F2r.

Jesuit Bohuslav Balbín. During his busy lifetime the industrious Balbín produced an extensive corpus of texts examining various aspects of the region's
ecclesiastical heritage. His most influential monograph was the *Epitome historica rerum Bohemicarum* (1677), a treatise a modern Czech scholar has
described as the 'first standard survey of Czech history'.[12] Balbín's text
begins with a preface celebrating the ancient city of Boleslav, which at its
height surpassed Prague in power and influence. Though forgotten today,
this early settlement according to the Jesuit was the 'altrix infantiae
Christianorum in Bohemia'.[13] It was the site of so many critical events of
the kingdom's sacred past. Here in the tenth century Duke Wenceslas,
Bohemia's future patron, was martyred by his treacherous brother. A few
decades later it was an important setting for Prague's third bishop, St
Adalbert, who worked a series of celebrated miracles in the town. It was
also home of the Madonna of Stará Boleslav. The recovery of its history
was of such importance for the Jesuit that he devoted the final two of the
Epitome's seven books to the city and its famous treasure. Though the first five
books of the text were in some respects a more conventional history of
Bohemia chronicling major events from the founder of the Přemyslid dynasty, Duke Bořivoj in the ninth century, to Emperor Ferdinand II in the
seventeenth, Balbín approached his subject matter in a fashion that emphasized the kingdom's spiritual heritage with frequent reference to its relics.
While historians today focus on powerful Přemyslid princes such as the
swashbuckling Otakar II (1253–78) who for a short time made Bohemia
the strongest state in Central Europe, Balbín placed greater emphasis on
more obscure figures such as Boleslav II (972–99) who established the
region's first bishopric or Břetislav I (1034–55) who invaded Poland and
returned with the holy remains of St Adalbert. When discussing Vladislav
II (1140–72), the Jesuit underplayed his role in the crusades and subsequent
coronation as Bohemia's first king and instead focused on the discovery of the
Madonna of Stará Boleslav, which was unearthed during his reign by a peasant tilling his field.[14] During the Hussite wars Balbín laid special stress on the
lance of St Longinus, which was recovered from the heretics, and in the late
sixteenth century he noted that in his dealings with his Spanish cousins,
Emperor Rudolf II was shrewd enough to grease the wheels of diplomacy
with a large shipment of relics to the Iberian peninsula.[15]

---

[12] Jan Kučera, Jiří Rak, *Bohuslav Balbín a jeho místo v české kultuře* (Prague, 1983), 124.

[13] Bohuslav Balbín, *Epitome historica rerum Bohemicarum* (Prague, 1677), 1.

[14] Ibid., 146–51; 237–9.

[15] Ibid., 419, 605.

Balbín's treatment of relics in the *Epitome* was typical for the period and reflects their new importance in this society. At this juncture, however, let us move beyond this more basic observation and return to the questions with which the article began. How did relics actually function? What was distinctive about their use in the Czech lands? How were they employed by Catholic elites to repair a break with the past? Three points, here, should be particularly noted. From the chains of the Apostle Peter to the arm of St Ludmila, Bohemia was well stocked with sacred artefacts that could be deployed at a moment's notice. The attentive historian should pay careful attention to what items were being dusted off and put to conspicuous public use. It is all the more interesting, then, that in the decade after White Mountain the relic that featured most prominently in the civic life of Prague was the body of Norbert of Xanten, a twelfth-century saint who had never visited the city during his lifetime and whose remains were only recently 'liberated' from Lutheran Magdeburg.

Norbert, the founder of the Premonstratensian order, arrived in Prague in May 1627. His acquisition was actually quite a coup for the Bohemian church. Apart from the difficulties of prying his bones loose from the grip of the jealous Magdeburgers who were reluctant to part with the body of the city's patron, there was intense competition within the order, especially with the Low Countries, to house the remains of the saint.[16] Even when Prague did win out, the local Premonstratensian community was inundated with requests for bits and pieces of his body. After placating St Michael's Monastery in Antwerp with a portion of mummified skin and a segment of his small toe, church leaders in Bohemia were able to persuade Pope Urban VIII to issue the bull, *Non licet dare,* to help preserve what remained of Norbert's earthly remains in Prague.[17]

Norbert's arrival in the city was commemorated with an elaborate eight-day festival that cost the hefty sum of 11,000 *Reichsthaler*.[18] Why such a fuss for the bones of a cleric who had never been active in Bohemia? Succinctly put, Norbert was a saint with a usable past. Those who celebrated what was curiously called his 'homecoming' highlighted two distinct aspects of his life

---

[16] For a fuller consideration of the 1627 translation see Howard Louthan, 'New Perspectives on the Bohemian Crisis of the Seventeenth Century', in Philip Benedict and Myron Gutmann (eds), *Early Modern Europe: From Crisis to Stability* (Cranbury, NJ, 2005), 52–79.

[17] The bull is reproduced in *Octiduum S. Norberti triumphantis* (Prague, 1627), s5r-v.

[18] C. Straka, 'Litteratura de translatione S.P. Norberti a. 1627 eiusque iubilaeis', *Analecta Praemonstratensia,* 3 (1927), 336.

and career.[19] The first were his efforts combating heresy. Norbert had successfully dispatched the heretic Tanchelm who according to legend distributed bathwater in lieu of the Eucharist. Catholic leaders seized on this aspect of his ministry as a means to address the errors of the Hussites whose most prominent sign of apostasy was their misuse of this sacrament. The second was his role as bishop. Norbert had ended his career as archbishop of Magdeburg and in this capacity helped Emperor Lothair III (1133–37) expand the authority of the German *Reichskirche* eastward into Slavic lands. With the defection of Konrad von Vechta to the Hussites in 1421, Prague's archiepiscopal see had been vacant for nearly 150 years. Though Emperor Ferdinand I finally named a new archbishop in the second half of the sixteenth century, the position remained weak during the Protestant interlude. It was only now after White Mountain that there was a more serious attempt to recover the power and prestige of this office with the appointment of the energetic and effective Ernst von Harrach. What better model could Emperor Ferdinand II and his new archbishop aspire to than Norbert and his imperial patron Lothair!

Tomáš Pešina had similar criteria in mind as custodian of the cathedral's relics. When Pešina began this position, he was confronted with a massive but disorganized collection of artefacts. One of the items that he found was the 'manus et brachia' of an unknown Greek saint first mentioned in an old catalogue compiled during the reign of Vladislav II. The bone-collecting prelate used his skills of detection (or perhaps the arts of fabrication) to declare that he had discovered the remains of the soldier Mercurius, a third-century warrior-saint from Cappadocia. Despite an impressive record of military service, Mercurius was martyred by Emperor Decius for his refusal to offer sacrifices to pagan gods. Again, why all the effort or even possible prevarication for a set of dusty bones with obscure Greek lettering? As with Norbert, Mercurius was a useful saint for this particular setting. Many in the Catholic world publicly grumbled that Bohemian believers had offered little resistance and quickly capitulated to Hus and his minions. Even the kingdom's beloved Wenceslas could be seen as a weak and passive patron who meekly allowed his brother to kill him. Bohemia desperately needed a muscular, militant and even bellicose saint who would stand up to the heretics. This Mercurius could offer, for his most famous exploit was his posthumous encounter with Julian the Apostate. According to one legend when Basil the Great was imprisoned by the pagan emperor, he had invoked Mercurius who

---

[19] According to Jan Sixt of Lerchenfels, a 'righteous son of God' had been delivered from the 'fire of the heretics to be worthily greeted by Prague with drums, trumpets, songs and great rejoicing'. Jan Sixt of Lerchenfels, *Přenešení sv. Norberta*, *ivr.

appeared in a vision and informed the troubled bishop that he had dispatched Julian with a spear. As dean of the cathedral, Pešina was especially sensitive to this issue. Only half a century earlier the followers of Bohemia's Winter King, the Calvinist prince Frederick, had ransacked St Vitus in a spree of iconoclastic violence. Now faithful Catholics could view the remains of a saint who even in death could confront and punish pagan princes. Interestingly enough, at the same time Pešina was promoting the Mercurius cult, a new and more militant image of Wenceslas was emerging who like the Cappadocian returned after death to wreak violence on those who had failed to embrace the new Christian faith.

My second observation directly addresses the issue raised by Pocock. How do intellectuals in a specific society understand breaks and ruptures with the past? In many ways this was the central question of the Counter-Reformation in Bohemia. The kingdom's Catholic leaders were faced with the formidable task of creating or re-creating a Catholic culture that had been interrupted by more than two centuries of heresy and rebellion. A Jesuit antiquarian, Jiří Kruger, may have captured this dilemma best in his multi-volume work, *Sacri pulveres*. Kruger's image of sacred or holy dust, the remains of a once resplendent ecclesiastical culture, visually encapsulated the quandary facing the church. Relics were the most effective means this society had of literally bringing the past into the present. For one example we can turn to St Procopius, an eleventh-century hermit, a confessor of Duke Oldřich I († 1034) and later founder of the important Sázava monastic community. Even before White Mountain there were attempts to revitalize his cult. His remains were brought to the Prague castle in 1588, and after the Thirty Years War church authorities began an important renovation of the monastic complex in the Sázava valley aggressively promoting it as an important pilgrimage site. Those who journeyed there could see relics that had been preserved from Procopius' time. One in particular merits special attention. A cup purportedly carved by Procopius himself and from which the hermit had served Oldřich was now used as a chalice for the Eucharist. This relic was intended to be more than a holy object to be marvelled at or meditated on. Through the central act of Christian worship, it entered the believer's world in a real and tangible manner. By participating in the sacrament, faithful Catholics were able to experience a suspended sense of time where a holy past helped sanctify a more problematic and complicated present.[20]

[20] Pablo Jiménez Diaz, 'Spain, Prague, and the Habsburg Ideology: Some Aspects of the Architecture of Rudolf II', in Lubomír Konečný, Beket Bukovinská, and Ivan Muchka (eds), *Rudolf II, Prague and the World* (Prague, 1998), 13; Jaroslav Kadlec, 'Svatý Prokop',

At the end of the Thirty Years War Bohemia celebrated the return of what was arguably the kingdom's most important relic, the Madonna of Stará Boleslav. During the war it had been captured twice, first by the Saxons and then later by the Swedes. Its recovery was an important military objective for both the imperial house and the Bohemian church. Why was this copper relief of the Virgin and child such a beloved object? There were of course a series of miracles connected with it, but that is true for nearly all relics. The issue of continuity is critical here. No other relic in the kingdom could be connected to so many holy men and women. According to one legend it came originally from Byzantium. Cyril and Methodius had brought it with them to Bohemia where it was passed down and connected with the first Christian princes of the region, Duke Bořivoj and his wife Ludmila. It later passed through the hands of Wenceslas and his faithful servant, the Blessed Podiven who had hidden it to protect it from the duke's pagan enemies. It was miraculously recovered in the twelfth century and then survived Hussite marauders, Saxon infantry, and Swedish soldiers. Now finally with peace secured, this relic, which embodied Bohemia's embattled but ultimately triumphant Catholic community, was with much acclamation reinstalled in Stará Boleslav. The iconography of the church where the object was housed reflected the theme of continuity. Statues of the kingdom's patron saints who had made the pilgrimage to see the icon were prominently displayed in the niches of its façade.[21] Indeed, this object was invested with such emotional energy that Empress Maria Anna of Spain insisted that the icon be brought to Vienna's *Hofburg* and placed in her room while she was giving birth to the future emperor, Leopold I. In later life Leopold, himself, made at least 15 trips to Stará Boleslav to see the relic![22] This issue of continuity was also seized upon by Bohemian clerics in their campaign to reinvigorate the Marian cult. The most visible sign of their efforts were the many Marian columns across Bohemia and Moravia that seemed to appear like mushrooms after rain. By the accession of Maria Theresa in 1740 there were nearly two hundred of them in city squares and town plazas.[23] The most famous one was raised in 1650 in Prague's Old Town Square where weekly processions and other worship rituals transformed this site into one of the city's most important devotional

---

in J. Kadlec (ed.), *Bohemia Sancta* (Prague, 1989), 126–39; A. Podlaha, *Posvátná místa* (Prague, 1907), I:117–26.

[21] Kašpar Arsenius z Radbuzy, *Pobožná knížka o blahoslavené Panně Marii* (Prague, 1629).

[22] Thomas Winkelbauer, *Ständefreiheit und Fürstenmacht* (Vienna, 2003), II:222.

[23] See the data of A. Šorm and A. Krajča (eds), *Mariánské sloupy v Čechách a na Moravě* (Prague, 1939), 84–7.

spaces. As a means to link an older form of Marian piety with the new, a copy of the Madonna of Stará Boleslav was installed at the base of the column.[24]

Not all relics that specifically bridged past and present were material. Bohemia's antiquarian literature was full of ghost stories. Though there was certainly an entertainment value to these tales of the supernatural, the discussion of phantoms and apparitions also served a more serious purpose. They were an effective literary device by which chronology could be suspended and the past literally brought into the present. Balbín and others devoted special attention to the White Lady, a benevolent ghost of a medieval noblewoman. When Swedes occupied the town of Telč and interrupted the established customs and practices of the municipality, she appeared to remind the townspeople to continue a long-standing annual tradition of feeding sweet porridge to the poor.[25] Though antiquarians assigned ghosts a variety of social functions in this literature, they were frequently cast as the spectral custodians of Bohemia's holy sites. When the iconoclasts descended on St Vitus during the reign of the Winter King, Jan Tanner claimed that Wenceslas himself called out from his tomb rebuking those who dared destroy the cathedral's precious relics.[26] The spirits of more ordinary men and women also stood guard over the kingdom's sacred remains. Balbín told the story of a well-meaning nobleman who planned to renovate a church that had fallen into disrepair. The appearance of a doleful ghost halted the project midstream. The phantom, who identified himself as the original builder of the church, informed the enterprising noble that workmen threatened his long forgotten tomb. Plans were altered accordingly and the ancient bones were honoured appropriately.[27]

My final point is concerned with the traffic and flow of relics. A critical transition took place in Bohemia over the course of the seventeenth and early eighteenth centuries. At one end of the chronological spectrum were the festivities surrounding the arrival of St Norbert in 1627. Here we have a translation, a set of relics imported to Prague. The translation of holy remains had been a traditional means of building an ecclesiastical identity ever since the days of Wenceslas in the tenth century. The strategy was mastered by

---

[24] Susan Tipton, '"Super aspidem et basiliscum ambulabis . . .": Zur Entstehung der Mariensäulen im 17. Jahrhundert', in Dieter Breuer (ed.), *Religion und Religiosität im Zeitalter des Barock* (Wiesbaden, 1995), I:383.

[25] Bohuslav Balbín, *Miscellanea historica regni Bohemiae* (Prague, 1681), 185–6 (I, 3).

[26] The story is in Jan Tanner, *Trophaea sancti Wenceslai Bohemiae regis ac martyris* (Prague, 1661). Cited in Robert Pynsent, *Questions of Identity: Czech and Slovak Ideas of Nationality and Personality* (Budapest, 1994), 197.

[27] Bohuslav Balbín, *Miscellanea historica regni Bohemiae* (Prague, 1687), 111 (I, i).

Charles IV who seems to have left no sacred site unplundered.[28] The need for imported relics, however, was even more acute in the years immediately following White Mountain. Bohemia required assistance from the wider Catholic world to address two centuries of heresy. It was through translation in particular that the church sought to reclaim lost territory. Norbert was only the beginning of a far broader campaign to bring the holy back to Bohemia. Prague's young and dynamic archbishop, Cardinal Ernst von Harrach, was quick to grasp the potential of this approach. Though rebuffed in his attempt to extract the bones of St Clement from Rome, he did manage to acquire the remains of early church martyrs while orders such as the Capuchins initiated their own aggressive program of importing relics.[29]

If 1627 marked one end of the spectrum, the remarkable events of 1729 signified the other, for by this date the balance of trade had moved definitively in Bohemia's favour. The Czech lands were no longer a region starved for holy imports but had now become a net exporter of piety. This momentous shift was in large part dependent on the historic canonization of John Nepomuk. Nepomuk was the fourteenth-century confessor of Queen Sophie, the wife of dissolute Wenceslas IV whose jealousy led him to dispose of the priest one dark night in the Moldau's chilly waters. Though a local cult had developed around Nepomuk and his tomb in St Vitus Cathedral, he was still relatively unknown outside this immediate area at the beginning of the eighteenth century.[30] Less than thirty years later, however, Nepomuk was undeniably Bohemia's best known celebrity and the kingdom's only saint canonized during the Counter-Reformation. The campaign that culminated in the celebration of 1729 was a well orchestrated drive spearheaded by the elites—an aggressive archbishop in Prague, key Bohemian operatives inside the Roman curia, and timely imperial support. Although efforts to secure his canonization had begun in the late seventeenth century, a crucial turning point was reached in 1719. Medical examiners exhumed his body and discovered what

---

[28] David Mengel, 'The Emperor's New Bones: Charles IV and the Cult of Relics in Prague', in 'Bones, Stones and Brothels: Religion and Topography in Prague under Emperor Charles IV (1346–78)', Ph.D. dissertation, University of Notre Dame, 2003, 263–372.

[29] Národní archiv, ŘK, 52/I: 6, 8, 9, 11, 13, 24–6, 33–5, 37, 49; Johannes Miller, *Historia Beatissimae Virginis Glacensis* (Glatz, 1690), 140–2; Alessandro Catalano, *La Boemia e la riconquista delle coscienze* (Rome, 2005), 168.

[30] When the archbishop of Salzburg canvassed his territory in 1701, he discovered that although the nobility were aware of his cult, the common folk had little knowledge of Nepomuk. Vít Vlnas, *Jan Nepomucký, česká legenda* (Prague, 1993), 104, 106.

they believed was his miraculously preserved tongue. His beatification quickly followed with that final step to sainthood not far behind.[31]

Nepomuk truly was a global figure in the first half of the eighteenth century. Jesuits eulogized him through their drama in the steamy jungles of Brazil while he became patron of the new university in Mexico. In the Pacific his biography was translated into both Tagalog and Chinese. In Europe his statue could be found perched atop bridges from Poland to Portugal.[32] Within Bohemia Nepomuk reflected the new confidence of a church that had successfully expelled heresy, re-established the old faith and could now export its own forms of sanctity. Nepomuk also reflects a changing understanding of relics and the holy within this society. With Nepomuk sacrality breaks its bounds, and the holy is not restricted to a specific relic or a local pilgrimage site of historical significance. The situation in the early eighteenth century stands in decided contrast to the era of Charles IV. In the late fourteenth century the Luxemburg emperor used relics to 'anchor Prague's sacred topography'.[33] Charles's capital did not have the advantages of cities within the boundaries of the former Roman Empire that with easier access to the great relic repository of the Italian peninsula had amassed their collections of sacred remains at an earlier date. The emperor quickly made up for lost time. Of the 450 relics catalogued in St Vitus Cathedral in the seventeenth century, Charles was most likely responsible for more than two thirds of these acquisitions.[34]

While Charles IV imported relics into Prague to enhance its spiritual prestige, in the eighteenth century Bohemian officials were exporting the sacred out of Prague to promote the kingdom's standing within the Catholic world. Though there was no major campaign to distribute his body parts across the continent, Nepomuk was a saint intended for mass production. His famous statue on the Charles Bridge in Prague was replicated countless times and often acquired talismanic properties. In one Styrian hamlet Nepomuk's feast day was celebrated with a procession that reached a climax when the villagers threw his statue into a stream with the intent of purifying the water.[35]

---

[31] For an overview of the proceedings see Vlnas, *Jan Nepomucký*, 98–127.

[32] Best on the Nepomuk cult as an international phenomenon is Yves Larfargues, 'Le culte mondial de Jean Népomucène aux XVIIe et XVIII siècles: histoire, mythe et spiritualité', Ph.D. dissertation, Paris, 1965.

[33] Mengel, 'The Emperor's New Bones', 265.

[34] Ibid., 268.

[35] J. Mezler-Andelberg, 'Bemerkungen zur Verehrung des hl. Johannes von Nepomuk', in H. Wiesflecker and O. Pickl (eds), *Beiträge zur allgemeinen Geschichte* (Graz, 1975), 34–5; Hans Koren, *Bauernhimmel* (Graz, 1974), 53–8.

Wax likenesses also appeared in churches and were a special means of physically bringing the saint before the people.[36] Then there were the amulets, medals, and rosaries intended for private devotion. Eighteenth-century tourists visiting Prague were regularly accosted by hawkers eager to sell pendants and charms engraved with the saint's likeness.[37] More significant was the fact that Nepomuk invaded the most ordinary of spaces. From the furniture of burgher homes to the jugs and gingerbread moulds of peasant kitchens, the saint penetrated life at its most basic level.

Though Nepomuk was certainly an exceptional figure, there were other developments that indicated Prague had become an important 'producer' of baroque piety in this period. There was Marie Elekta, a Discalced Carmelite who had arrived in the city in 1656. A mystic nun, she was regarded in many circles as a living saint. After her death, there were reports claiming that her body resisted putrefaction.[38] More curious still is the story of Prague's Jewish saint. In 1694 Simon Abeles, a spirited adolescent who had recently returned home after an altercation with his father, died in mysterious circumstances. Abeles was a member of a prominent Jewish family but had evinced some interest in Christianity in the months prior to his death. His father and a family friend were interrogated, tortured, and eventually convicted of his murder. The case became a *cause célèbre* with publications on this affair appearing as far afield as Amsterdam, Florence, and Königsberg. Though Abeles had never been baptized, Bohemia's Catholic leaders were quick to act. They cast the boy as a young martyr and staged an elaborate funeral with the archbishop at the head of a procession worthy of a Habsburg prince. According to contemporary reports massive crowds filed by the open coffin while opportunistic relic hunters eagerly sought some physical token from this event that would vouchsafe divine favour. With great pomp and ceremony, the body was laid to rest in an elegant tomb of the Týn church, Old Town's most important house of worship. An informal cult developed around this site as believers reported miracles at the tomb well into the eighteenth century.[39]

---

[36] Franz Matsche, 'Sekundärleiber des heiligen Johannes von Nepomuk', *Jahrbuch für Volkskunde*, n.f. 6 (1983), 107–48.

[37] 'The Travels of Three English Gentlemen, in the Year 1734', *Harleian Miscellany* 5 (1810), 349.

[38] Zdeněk Kalista, *Ctihodná Marie Elekta Ježíšova* (Rome, 1975); for the legends see Josef Svátek, *Pražské pověsti a legendy* (Prague, 1997), 93–4.

[39] Howard Louthan, *Converting Bohemia: Force and Persuasion in the Catholic Reformation* (Cambridge, 2009), 300–16.

If we take a small step back for a broader view of Bohemia's ecclesiastical landscape, relics were in many respects at the very heart of the kingdom's Catholic revival both literally and metaphorically. Catholic antiquarians saw themselves as a special type of archaeologist committed to the excavation of a Christian past that had been covered in thick layers of debris left by successive generations of Hussites, Calvinists, and Lutherans. The relic was at the centre of this quest, for it authenticated their confessional vision of the past. It is not surprising then that a former rector of the university in Prague spent his spare hours digging up his country estate searching for the foundations of what he believed was one of the oldest Christian monuments in Bohemia, a tenth-century church he took special pains to restore.[40] These holy remains were not inanimate objects of mere admiration or wonder but infused with a spiritual energy that could transform the present. Bohuslav Balbín once led a mission to north-east Bohemia, in a region that had been a Protestant bastion. In one village, he visited the local church and began poking through its jumbled collection of old and discarded items dating from a period long before the arrival of the Hussites. In the course of his search he came across a dusty altar, long forgotten and abandoned. This object, he believed, was definitive proof that the building had originally belonged to an ancient monastic order. The enthusiastic missionary gathered the village's inhabitants, displayed the altar and explained its significance. According to Balbín, all promptly converted.[41] For the antiquarians the discovery of the past through its relics and remains, the unearthing of a Christian antiquity, ultimately led to a Catholic *renovatio* of their society.

Conclusion

From this brief survey of baroque Bohemia, what broader conclusions can we reach concerning the function of relics and remains in the early modern world? Pocock reminds us that societies are constantly reshaping their relationship with the past. Sacred artefacts were a critical part of this process in Catholic Europe. Though Rome's apologists claimed that they were a tangible, constant, and enduring witness of the church's heroic past, relics have never been immutable objects resistant to time and change but are fashioned and refashioned according to society's shifting needs. They are also multivalent. The same object can be viewed in radically different ways. While Habsburg emperors deployed Nepomuk's relics to express their dynastic

---

[40] Kučera and Rak, *Bohuslav Balbín*, 196. Balbín captured this sentiment visually in the frontispiece of the *Epitome* where a figure enters a dark grotto with a lantern held high to shed light on the forgotten remains of the kingdom's ancient civilization.

[41] A. Rejzek, *Bohuslav Balbín T.J., jeho život a práce* (Prague, 1908), 113.

ambitions, Czech patriots seized upon the image of his tongue as a symbol of their resistance to Vienna. Relics, as well, could be constructed from all sorts of surprising elements of the past and fused together into a new synthesis. Jan Středovský noted in his history of Moravia that the Madonna of Stará Boleslav was actually composed from the shards of broken idols.[42] In similar fashion, the blood of a Jewish boy was used by the church to help solidify Catholic identity in late seventeenth-century Prague. Doctors who examined the corpse of Simon Abeles weeks after his death were purportedly amazed by the freshness of his injuries. Many who filed by his body dipped handkerchiefs into his bloody wounds or chipped pieces from the coffin. Even an act of desecration could be transformed into a holy object. In 1620 a Carmelite chaplain accompanying Bavarian troops entered the ruined town of Strakonice in southern Bohemia. Picking through the rubble, he discovered a Nativity Scene ritually mutilated by the retreating Protestant soldiers. The charismatic friar made the wounded image a rallying point for the troops and wore it into battle at White Mountain. Accredited with supernatural powers, the icon was copied many times over and placed in churches across Bohemia. At papal insistence the original was ultimately installed as the prized trophy of Santa Maria della Vittoria in Rome.[43]

Relics can also complicate our grand religious narratives. Despite Calvin's critical treatise or Luther's attack on the unhappy Benno, there was undeniably an appeal to sacred remains that crossed confessional lines. When Abraham Scultetus, the Calvinist chaplain of Bohemia's Winter King, organized a team of labourers to destroy the art and relics of St Vitus, he elicited a significant response from the Prague citizenry. Utraquists and Lutherans joined the small Catholic minority to protest against the demolition of the Wenceslas Chapel, the centre of the royal saint's cult. So substantial was the outcry that the chapel with its beautiful wall paintings, inlaid gems, and tomb of the saint was spared the hammers and chisels of the workmen.[44] In similar fashion one of the great promoters of the Madonna of Stará Boleslav was not Catholic at all. In the years before White Mountain, Adam Rosacius z Karlsperka, a Protestant professor at the Charles University, was among the cult's most prominent supporters.[45] It should also be remembered that the

---

[42] Jan Středovský, *Sacra Moraviae Historia sive Vita SS. Cyrilli & Methudii* (Solisbach, 1710), 271.

[43] Louthan, *Converting Bohemia*, 153–5.

[44] See the edited collection of primary sources in Vincenc Kramář, *Zpustošení Chrámu svatého Víta v roce 1619* (Prague, 1998).

[45] See his *Oratio panegyrica de Boemiae reviviscentia* (Prague, 1615), 56.

campaign to bring the remains of St Norbert to Prague was frustrated for many years by the stubborn Magdeburgers. In fact, one visiting delegation from Prague had been literally blocked by members of a Lutheran mob who despite their new confessional allegiance had no intention of surrendering their saint to the Bohemian interlopers. It was only through the pressure of Emperor Ferdinand II and a timely military victory of his generalissimo Albrecht von Wallenstein that the bones ever saw their way south.

Similar stories come from the villages as well. Before White Mountain the Church of the Visitation in the tiny mountain town of Bozkov was the focus of a regional cult centred on a miraculous statue of the Virgin. Without a priest for many years Bozkov was finally visited by an ecclesiastical deputation in 1651. Catholic authorities found the cult still thriving though its principal custodian was a heretic according to the clerical inspector.[46] It seems clear, then, that in the early modern world relics possessed a type of ecumenical appeal. Despite the rhetoric of the reformers, they continued to creep into the worship of Protestants especially in Central Europe. More than two decades ago Robert Scribner highlighted the fascinating phenomenon of the 'incombustible Luther', miraculous images of the reformer that could not be destroyed. Scribner saw this modest Luther-cult as a form of confessional syncretism that was developing in popular Lutheran culture.[47] Scribner's 'incombustible Luther' is but one example of a pattern characteristic of Central Europe as a whole. Polish Calvinists observed days of patron saints and promoted a mild Marian piety. Their anti-Trinitarian neighbours considered them little better than Catholics.[48] In Hungary the Sabbatarians reflected an even stranger admixture of belief and practice. For their day of worship, this radical sect of Anabaptists rejected Sunday in favour of the Jewish Sabbath.[49] The continuing appeal of relics reflected this same general dynamic. Popular religious culture in Central Europe was characterized by its hybridity, not surprising for the most confessionally diverse region of the continent. In this light, then, it seems appropriate to close with a final example that returns to Simon Abeles. Many had come long distances to see the martyred youth and if possible collect a physical token from his

---

[46] Zdeněk Kalista, 'Bozkov čili Maria na hory putující', in Zdeněk Kalista, *Ceská barokní pout'* (Žd'ár nad Sázavou, 2001), 25–66.

[47] Robert Scribner, 'Incombustible Luther: The Image of the Reformer in Early Modern Germany', *Past and Present*, 110 (1986), 38–68, especially 66–8.

[48] Janusz Tazbir, *A State Without Stakes* (New York, 1973), 128.

[49] The definitive source remains Samuel Kohn, *Die Sabbatharier in Siebenbürgen* (Budapest, 1894).

coffin or even body. The greatest prize was the boy's blood, which according to various accounts still lay miraculously fresh in his wounds. One of those hunting for relics was a dentist from Protestant Saxony. We can only speculate if any in the crowd that day noted the great irony of the scene before them as the man stood over the body and reverentially bent down to touch the dead boy. Here was a German Lutheran who had made the arduous journey to Catholic Prague all in an effort to obtain the blood of a Jewish boy.[50]

[50] Louthan, *Converting Bohemia*, 311.

'The Devil was in that Little Bone': The Portuguese Capture and Destruction of the Buddha's Tooth-Relic, Goa, 1561

John S. Strong

It is safe to say that relics in Buddhism are just as numerous and cultically just as important as they are in Roman Catholicism.[1] However, the comparative study of relics across cultures is, in many ways, still in its infancy. In the case of Buddhist and Christian relics, for instance, most studies have been carried out in rather abstract, general terms.[2] What are lacking are discussions of specific concrete situations in which Buddhist and Christian notions of relics—both competing and coinciding—actually come together. In this paper, I would like to focus on one such instance: the reported capture and destruction of the Buddha's tooth relic by the Portuguese in the sixteenth century.

According to an ancient Pali text, the *Mahāparinibbāna sutta* [Discourse on the Great Extinction], after the Buddha's cremation, nothing was left of his body except for a large number of relics.[3] The Commentary on the text specifies that these came in three sizes; they were as big as mustard seeds, broken grains of rice, and split green peas and were said to resemble jasmine

---

[1] On Buddhist relics in general, see Gregory Schopen, *Bones, Stones, and Buddhist Monks* (Honolulu, 1997); Kevin Trainor, *Relics, Ritual, and Representation in Buddhism* (Cambridge, 1997); Brian D. Ruppert, *Jewel in the Ashes: Buddha Relics and Power in Early Medieval Japan* (Cambridge, Mass., 2000); David Germano and Kevin Trainor, *Embodying the Dharma: Buddhist Relic Veneration in Asia* (Albany, 2004); John S. Strong, *Relics of the Buddha* (Princeton, 2004); Peter Skilling, 'Cutting Across Categories: The Ideology of Relics in Buddhism', *Sōka Daigaku Kokusai Bukkyōgaku Kōto Kenkyū-jo Nenpō/Annual Report of the International Institute for Advanced Buddhology at Soka University*, 8 (2005), 269–322; Johannes Bronkhorst, 'Les reliques dans les religions de l'Inde', in Lars Göhler (ed.), *Indische Kultur im Kontext: Festschrift für Klaus Mylius* (Wiesbaden, 2005), 50–85.

[2] For two perceptive reflections on Buddhist relics in a comparative context, see Robert H. Sharf, 'On the Allure of Buddhist Relics', *Representations*, 66 (1999), 75–99; Gregory Schopen, 'Relic', in Mark C. Taylor (ed.), *Critical Terms for Religious Studies* (Chicago, 1999), 256–68.

[3] *Thus Have I Heard: The Long Discourses of the Buddha*, trans. Maurice Walshe (London, 1987), 275–6.

buds, washed pearls, and nuggets of gold.[4] More like little jewels or gems than ashes or bones, these relics were seen as testimonials to the ongoing 'presence' of the Buddha in this world. Hence they were thought of as powerful objects and, much in demand, they were quickly divided among eight North Indian kings, each of whom took away his share for enshrinement in his own country.[5] Subsequently, according to legend, these relics were collected and redistributed by the Mauryan emperor Aśoka (third century BCE) who enshrined them in 84,000 shrines throughout the Indian continent and beyond.[6]

At the same time, other traditions developed about other bodily relics of the Buddha—his collarbone, his finger bones, and in particular his four eye-teeth. In addition, objects that he once used or touched (his robe, his bowl, the Bodhi tree under which he attained enlightenment) came to be considered as secondary relics.[7] Thus, in due course, pilgrims and devotees throughout the Buddhist world, could visit and venerate a great number and variety of relics. Indeed, in South and Southeast Asia today, virtually every Buddhist temple or monastery will enshrine what are held to be some physical remains of the Buddha, some object that once belonged to him, some trace of his presence enlivened by association with his body or his teaching. Simply put, Buddhist relics, broadly defined, were and are 'everywhere', causing one scholar to describe this proliferation as a 'hemorrhage of the sacred'.[8]

Within this plethora of relics, the Buddha's tooth, which is presently enshrined in Kandy, Sri Lanka, is quite famous. Several texts recount its legendary saga.[9] One of four famous eye-teeth of the Buddha, it was originally kept in the kingdom of Kalinga in India, enshrined in a city appropriately called Dantapura ('Toothville'). Eventually, after multiple adventures (some of which will be recounted below), it made its way to the island of Sri Lanka, where, in the late fourth century CE, it was kept in a temple in the royal palace and came to be seen as a palladium of power. From then on, for centuries, whenever the king moved his capital, the tooth moved with him, and possession of it was thought not only to grant legitimacy to him as ruler but to

---

[4] See Strong, *Relics of the Buddha*, 117. The word used for relics here is 'sarīra' which literally means 'body'.

[5] *Thus Have I Heard*, 276.

[6] John S. Strong, *The Legend of King Aśoka* (Princeton, 1983), 219–21.

[7] Strong, *Relics of the Buddha*, chs. 6 and 7. On the Buddhist classification of relics and its relationship to Roman Catholic categorization, see Strong, *Relics of the Buddha*, 8, 46–7.

[8] Bernard Faure, *Visions of Power* (Princeton, 1996), 163.

[9] See, e.g., Bimala Churn Law, *The Dāṭhāvaṃsa (A History of the Tooth-relic of the Buddha)* (Lahore, 1925).

insure adequate rainfall, abundant crops and victory in war.[10] In this light, the reported capture of the tooth by the Portuguese during their invasion of the Jaffna peninsula (in Northern Sri Lanka) in 1561, and its subsequent supposed destruction by the Viceroy of Goa, Don Constantino da Bragança may be seen as events of major importance and significance.

The saga of the tooth-relic's destruction is told in several sources, but its basic narration is found in the work of Diogo De Couto, the sixteenth-century Portuguese historian who completed the great chronicle of his country's advance into Asia that had been started by his fellow scholar and compatriot, Joaõ de Barros.[11] There we are told:

> The Viceroy, D. Constantino da Bragança, having conquered the kingdom of Jaffna, went back to Goa with the king of that country fettered in irons that were covered over with crimson velvet, and carried along with him also the sacred tooth . . . [for] amongst the spoils of the principal temple [was] a tooth mounted in gold, which was generally said to be the tooth of an ape, but which these idolaters regarded as the most sacred of all objects of adoration. The Viceroy was immediately made aware that its value was inestimable, as the natives would be sure to offer vast sums to redeem it. They believed it to be the tooth of their great saint Buddha.[12]

The initial thought, then, seems to have been to hold the tooth for ransom, and to sell it back to the Sri Lankans. Soon, however, things grew more complicated. The king of Pegu, in Burma, heard that the Portuguese had acquired the relic, and, having long desired to acquire it for himself, decided

---

[10] On the role of the Sri Lankan tooth-relic, see A. M. Hocart, *The Temple of the Tooth in Kandy* (London, 1931); Victor Goloubew, 'Le temple de la dent à Kandy', *Bulletin de l'Ecole Française d'Extrême-Orient*, 32 (1932), 441–74; H. L. Seneviratne, *Rituals of the Kandyan State* (London, 1978); Dharmaratna Herath, *The Tooth Relic and the Crown* (Colombo, 1994). On the other tooth relics of the Buddha, see Strong, *Relics of the Buddha*, 190–205.

[11] Joaõ De Barros and Diogo De Couto, *Da Asia. Dos feitos, que os Portuguezes fizeram na conquista, e descubrimento das terras e mares do Oriente* (Lisbon, 1783) 17:316–17, 428–33. This account was translated into English in James Emerson Tennent, *Ceylon: An Account of the Island* (London, 1859), 2:213–16. Tennent's translation was reprinted with some changes and no proper acknowledgement in J. Gerson Da Cunha, 'Memoir on the History of the Tooth-relic of Ceylon', *Journal of the Bombay Branch of the Royal Asiatic Society*, 11 (1875), 127–31. I have generally followed Tennent's translation, slightly altering it at times with an eye on Da Cunha and on the Portuguese original, and an ear on current English usage.

[12] Tennent, *Ceylon*, 213.

that this might be his chance to do so. Working through an intermediary, a Portuguese merchant named Martin de Mello, he sent some envoys to Goa, with an offer to buy the tooth for a sizeable fortune (the sum of three to four hundred thousand cruzados is mentioned), and, as a sweetener to the deal, 'a proposal for a perpetual alliance with Portugal, and an undertaking to provision the fortress of Malacca at all times when called upon; together with many other conditions and promises'.[13]

The viceroy was inclined to accept the offer since it would help replenish the depleted coffers of the colonial regime (not to mention his own personal accounts). However, just as he was about to conclude the agreement, the archbishop of Goa, Don Gaspar, got wind of the affair; together with some members of the inquisition who were then present in the colony, he approached the viceroy and 'warned him that he was not to permit this tooth—this relic of the devil (*reliquia do demonio*)—to be ransomed for all the treasures of the universe, since it would be dishonouring to the Lord, and would afford an opportunity to these idolaters to pay to that bone the homage that belonged to God alone'.[14]

This caused Don Constantino to pause, and eventually to capitulate. After some back and forth, he agreed to a resolution that the relic should be destroyed, that 'it was not proper to give up the tooth [to the Peguans], since its surrender would be an incitement to idolatry and an insult to the Almighty, crimes [lit., 'a sin'=pecado] which could not be contemplated, though the state, or even the world itself, might be imperilled'.[15]

Accordingly, the viceroy, Don Constantino, formally handed the tooth over to the archbishop, Don Gaspar, who 'placed it in a mortar, and with his own hand reduced it to powder, and cast the pieces into a brazier which stood ready for the purpose; after which the ashes and the charcoal together were cast into the river, in sight of all those who were crowding the verandahs and windows which looked upon the water'.[16]

The reactions to this, both in Goa and back home in Portugal, were mixed. Some protested against the archbishop's act, and lambasted the viceroy as a fool, saying that the gold that had been turned down would have solved the state's cash flow problems and that the 'pagans' would probably just make another tooth to worship out of a piece of bone or something. On the other hand, the viceroy, Don Constantino, was also praised as a conscientious and religious man who had chosen to stand against idolatry, and to resist the

---

[13] Ibid., 214.
[14] Ibid., 214.
[15] Ibid., 215.
[16] Ibid., 215.

temptations of avarice, an image that he actively sought to propagate. Indeed, once the act of destroying the relic was completed, he had a commemorative medallion struck. This showed 'the Viceroy and Archbishop surrounded by the prelates, monks, and divines who had been present on the occasion, and in their midst. . .the burning brazier, together with Buddhists offering purses of money, and above [it all], the letter C, being the initial of Don Constantino, was repeated five times, thus: C C C C C, standing for the five words "Constantinus, caeli, cupidine, cremavit, crumenas".'[17] This was taken to mean: 'Constantino, out of yearning for heaven, consigned the cash to the flames!' Here the emphasis seems to be on the viceroy's faith and his doing the proper thing and getting credit for it.

If, however, the Portuguese expected that their destruction of the tooth would put an end to the saga of the relic, or that it would result in the capitulation and humiliation of the Sri Lankans, they were sorely disappointed. Instead, in the years that followed, at least two sorts of reactions among Sri Lankan Buddhists seem to have taken place, both of them implying the survival of the Buddha's relic (which, after all, is still to be found in its temple in Kandy).

First of all, there was the claim that what the Portuguese had mortarized was actually not the tooth of the Buddha, but something else. It should be said that the tooth itself, at the popular level, had multiple identities. As Paul Courtenay put it:

> This fetish was an object of veneration for the whole population of Ceylon. . . . In the eyes of the Sinhalese Buddhists, it had an inestimable value because. . .it was a tooth of the Buddha. . . . [but] the [Muslims], who surrounded [the mountain they called] Adam's Peak with legends concerning our primal ancestor, considered it to be a tooth of Adam. [And] the Śaivite Tamils worshipped this old piece of ivory as a tooth of the monkey-king Hanuman.[18]

Picking up on the latter point, some Buddhists claimed that these multiple identifications reflected the fact that there were actually multiple teeth and so maintained that what the Portuguese had destroyed was actually a relic Hanuman, the divine monkey king of *Rāmāyāna* fame.[19] Thus, it was not

---

[17] Tennent, Ceylon, 216.

[18] Peter Courtenay, *Le Christianisme à Ceylan* (Lille, 1900), 1: 207.

[19] See the argument in K. Vajira's *Daladā Itihāsaya Saha Samskrtiya*, as reported in Aloysus Pieris, 'The Cult of the Sacred Tooth Relic—its Origin and Meaning', *Dialogue* (Colombo), n.s. 10 (1985), 67.

their Buddha's tooth that was destroyed but a Hindu or 'folk' relic. This would explain the anomaly of its being captured in Jaffna (never a Buddhist stronghold), near the presumed endpoint of the legendary causeway (the present day 'Adam's Bridge') which Hanuman's 'monkeys' were said to have built for Rāma connecting India and Lanka.

Alternatively, there was the claim that what had been destroyed was a replica of the tooth of the Buddha, not the original real thing that had been secreted away ahead of time.[20] We know, from epigraphical and other evidence that such replicas existed.[21] Indeed, a mid-fifteenth-century monarch used to wear one as an amulet on his person; and, in times of crisis, it was common to hide the tooth away and replace it with a facsimile. For instance, this is said to have been the case throughout the Second World War,[22] and, even today, it is maintained that, for security reasons, what is paraded on elephant back in the great annual festival of the tooth-relic in Kandy is not the actual tooth but a replica.

The second Sri Lankan Buddhist reaction to the Portuguese destruction of the tooth was to deny it ever happened. This view admitted that the Portuguese did manage to capture the genuine tooth-relic of the Buddha but claimed that, just as it was about to be pulverized in the mortar, it miraculously slipped through the bottom of the vessel and, passing through the earth itself, re-emerged on a lotus blossom in its original shrine.[23] This, as we shall see, reflects more ancient legends about the tooth-relic.

Both of these claims, of course, opened the way for a number of individuals to assert that they had been in possession of the real tooth all along and indeed had preserved it from destruction. For example, Don Juan Dharmapala, the semi-Christianized king of Kotte, soon announced that he had hidden away the 'real' tooth in his capital. Always the opportunist, he promptly offered this relic to the same king of Pegu who had been snubbed by the Portuguese. He then sent it to Burma, along with his supposed 'daughter' in marriage—a girl who turned out to be no relation at all—in order to seal a marital and

---

[20] The common claim was that at the time of the Portuguese invasion, the relic was hidden away at Delgamoa in Saffragam, in the hill country (near Ratnapura). See George Turnour, 'Account of the Tooth Relic of Ceylon, supposed to be alluded to in the opening passage of the Feroz lât inscription', *Journal of the Asiatic Society of Bengal*, 6 (1837), 867.

[21] See Herath, *Tooth Relic*, 82; Goloubew, 'Temple de la dent', 354n.

[22] Herath, *Tooth Relic*, 81.

[23] Francisco De Sousa, *Oriente conquistado a Jesus Cristo* (Porto, 1978 [1710]), 1:189.

commercial alliance.[24] Not long after Don Juan's shenanigans, Konnappu Bandāra, who had attacked Kandy for the Portuguese but then turned against them, claimed possession of another 'real' Buddha's tooth that had been hidden away. He then used it, as well as his marriage to a Kandyan princess, as part of his attempt to legitimize his usurpation of the Kandyan throne.[25] This, significantly, is the first mention of the tooth's being enshrined in Kandy, where it remains today.[26]

It is difficult to know how to evaluate these various claims, and I do not propose, in what follows, to resolve the issue of whether what the Portuguese destroyed in Goa in 1561 was 'a' tooth of the Buddha, or 'the' tooth of the Buddha, or something else altogether. Instead, I would like to re-examine the account of the Portuguese action in the context of the history of relics—both Roman Catholic and Buddhist—for it is important to read this story in the dual perspective of sixteenth-century Portuguese religious emotions as well as of Sinhalese Theravāda Buddhist traditions.

The care with which the Viceroy sought to clarify his motivations in having his medallion struck, and the emphasis he placed on the rejection of the gold that was being offered in exchange for the tooth are noteworthy. The ransom money, it should be pointed out, was not the only sum at stake here. There was also a plan afoot for the Portuguese to take the tooth on a great money-raising tour of South and Southeast Asia before delivering it to the king of Pegu.[27] The idea of purchasing or selling or exhibiting relics in exchange for money or other benefits would have been perfectly familiar to the Roman Catholic Portuguese of the time. Indeed, De Couto indicates that Don Constantino's fidalgos (and many of his compatriots back home in Portugal) were amazed that he did not seize this opportunity to gain as much as possible from his good fortune.[28]

Historically, the Church had had mixed feelings about the merchandizing of its own relics, but the practice was widespread, the most spectacular

---

[24] Tennent, *Ceylon*, 2:218–19. This tooth is thought to have later been enshrined in a pagoda in Ava, and was the subject of some controversy in the mid-19th century, when some visiting Sri Lankan monks questioned its authenticity (see Alfred Jacobs, 'Le bouddhisme et son législateur', *Revue des deux mondes*, 26 [1860], 129).

[25] Tennent, *Ceylon*, 2:220–1.

[26] M. H. Sirisoma, 'Temples for the Tooth Relic in Sri Lanka', *The Buddhist Vesak Annual*, (1988), 46.

[27] This is according to Lafiteau (see Da Cunha, 'Memoir', 130n). The Portuguese would not be the last to think of this; on modern tours of Buddhist relics sponsored by the British, the French, and the Chinese, see Strong, *Relics of the Buddha*, 205–9.

[28] Tennent, *Ceylon*, 2:215.

instance, perhaps, being Saint Louis's purchase, for a huge sum, of the Crown of Thorns (and other relics) from the Byzantine Emperor Baldwin II, in 1241.[29] At the same time, the exhibition of relics for the purpose of fund-raising, coupled with the granting of indulgences to pilgrims, was commonplace.[30]

By the sixteenth century, however, things were beginning to change. Along with money-making indulgences, relics themselves were one of the targets of the voices of reform, whether Protestant or not. In 1543, Jean Calvin virulently ridiculed the excesses of venerating dubious relics in his *Treatise on Relics*, a propagandistic pamphlet that, within a few decades, helped change many Europeans' outlook on relics in general.[31] On the Catholic side, the Church, it is true, reaffirmed the cult of relics at the Council of Trent in 1563, but, in the same breath, it condemned its excesses and established a commission to verify the authenticity of relics that were questionable.[32] It is in this context, perhaps, that we should understand the actions of the bishop of Goa and of the Viceroy, Don Constantino—not only in their destruction of the tooth which was clearly seen as a pagan, and so inauthentic, relic, but also in the medallion they had struck which seems to aim at the greed and this-worldliness of fellow Christians.

There is another aspect to this story, however. That is the description of the way in which the tooth was destroyed. Don Gaspar is said first to crush it in a mortar, then to burn the powdery residue in a brazier, then to scatter the ashes—not only of the tooth but of the charcoal fire itself—into the flowing waters of the local river. This, clearly, is a man who knows his relics. He is aware, from his own tradition, that even the tiniest fragment—of the wood of the True Cross, of the bone of a saint, of the milk of the Virgin—suffices to embody the power of the relic. To destroy the relic, he must thus destroy it completely. Just pulverizing the tooth is not enough, for then there will remain the powdery pieces; burning those pieces is not enough, for then there will remain the ashes; dissolving those ashes and having them carried

---

[29] See Nicole Hermann-Mascard, *Les reliques des saints: formation coutumière d'un droit* (Paris, 1975), 350–4; Anatole Frolow, *La relique de la vraie croix: recherches sur le développement d'un culte* (Paris, 1961), 427–9.

[30] For several 15th-century examples of indulgences intended to help finance the reconstruction, for instance, of the Cistercian abbey of La Boissière in France, see J. B. Barrau, *Notice historique sur la vraie croix de Baugé* (Angers, 1874), 80. More generally, see G. J. C. Snoek, *Medieval Piety from Relics to the Eucharist* (Leiden, 1995), 250ff.

[31] For the treatise, see John Calvin, *Three French Treatises*, ed. Francis M. Higman (London, 1970). On its influence, see Hermann-Mascard, *Les reliques*, 413.

[32] Hermann-Mascard, *Les reliques*, 413.

out to sea—hopefully—will suffice. Don Gaspar also knows that anything brought into contact with the relic may be imbued with its power; hence he disposes also of the charcoal with which he burned the relic, and though it is not stated, one suspects he consigned the mortar and pestle to the flames as well. This is a man who wishes to take no chances.

Don Gaspar's actions are presumably informed by his familiarity with Christian relics, but they make sense within the Buddhist context as well. For there too the rules of 'contagious magic' were applied to relics. Two examples, one ancient and one modern, will suffice to illustrate this. In the *Mahāparinirvāṇa sūtra*, the tale is told how, after all the bodily relics of the Buddha were distributed to various kings after his funeral, and the urn in which they had been momentarily placed was taken to be venerated in its own right, there arrived a man who also wanted to claim a share. Alas, he was too late to receive any bodily relics of the Buddha, but, significantly, he was quite content to be given and to worship the ashes from the Buddha's cremation fire—the equivalent, perhaps, of Don Gaspar's charcoal. These too, clearly, were seen as worthy embodiments of power.[33]

The second example concerns the very tooth Don Gaspar supposedly destroyed, but in its later incarnation in Kandy. In the late nineteenth century, according to a tale that may well have been embellished, the King of Siam sent some envoys to Kandy asking for permission to borrow the tooth and take it to Bangkok, in exchange for an offering of 50,000 pounds. Their request was denied. They then asked for permission to dip the tooth in oil which they could then take back to their king. This too was refused. Finally, with the intercession of British authorities, they were able to lightly touch the tooth with a piece of cloth which was then put into a vial of oil, which was then taken back to Thailand where it was used to consecrate still more oil that was distributed throughout the kingdom.[34]

In the context of both Christian and Buddhist relics, then, it is admittedly important for Don Gaspar to have been as meticulous and thorough as he was in attempting to destroy the Buddha's tooth. Both the Portuguese and the

---

[33] See Ernst Waldschmidt, *Das Mahāparinirvāṇa sūtra, Abhandlungen der deutschen Akademie der Wissenschaften zu Berlin, Philosophisch-historische Klasse*, 1949, no. 1 and 1950, nos. 2–3 (Berlin, 1950), 450.

[34] This story, said to have taken place 'some twenty years ago', is recalled in C. F. Gordon Cumming, *Two Happy Years in Ceylon* (New York, 1892), 320–1. There may be some confusion here with the similar tale of Burmese envoys getting, in 1858, a facsimile of the tooth for deposit in the walls of the new palace in Mandalay. See Jacobs, 'Le bouddhisme et son législateur', 129.

Buddhists present would have readily understood his actions, for both recognized secondary relics and the rules of contagious magic.

At the same time, Don Gaspar would seem to have been aware of South Asian funerary practices. In India, the four traditional means of disposing of the dead were cremation, burial, breaking up and exposure, and sinking in water. The Portuguese here, in what they do to the relic, employ three of these techniques. Their message would seem to be clear: this relic is dead and gone! The fact that this message was not taken by the Sri Lankans who promptly asserted that the relic was alive and present reflects, of course, their pressing desire to continue to possess the tooth. But there is something else at work here: a conviction about the indestructibility of relics. Generally speaking, for Buddhists, relics can be stolen, but they cannot be destroyed. What the Portuguese destroyed, then, could not possibly have been the tooth of the Buddha for it, by definition, was thought to be indestructible.

This was not just an abstract claim; it was backed up by a specific legend about the very same tooth the Portuguese said they had captured. In the eyes of the Buddhists, 1561 was not the first time some non-believer had tried to smash, burn, and sink the Buddha's tooth. According to the *Dāṭhāvaṃsa* [the Chronicle of the Tooth], a thirteenth-century Pali text that traces the legendary history of the tooth-relic, long ago, before its arrival in Sri Lanka in the fourth century CE, the tooth was enshrined in the kingdom of Kalinga, in India, in a town called Dantapura. The local ruler of Dantapura was a Buddhist devotee but his lord and emperor, Paṇḍu, who ruled in Pāṭaliputra, was not. At the instigation of some 'heretics', Paṇḍu ordered the local ruler to come to the capital with the 'dead person's bone' that he worshipped, angry that his vassal was reportedly maligning the Hindu gods. When the princeling arrived bearing the holy tooth on his head, the heretics requested that it be destroyed. First a big pit of charcoal was prepared, and the relic was thrown into it. Instantly, according to this text, the flames were cooled and the relic was seen to rest, unburned, on a lotus blossom. Then the heretics had it placed on a chopping block and smashed with a hammer; un-fractured, the tooth merely slipped into the wood, intact. Later, attempts were made to sink it in a moat, and to bury it in the earth and have it trampled by elephants. In each case, it resurfaced unscathed.[35] Eventually, the relic was sent to Sri Lanka, which it reached after a series of other adventures. But, in

[35] Law, *Dāṭhāvaṃsa*, 18–22 (text), 23–30 (trans.)

the meantime, one moral of the story had been made: the Buddha's tooth-relic cannot be destroyed, at least not by heretical non-Buddhists.[36]

The Buddhists, however, were not the only ones to believe in the indestructibility of relics. The Portuguese themselves shared this faith, though they applied it only to Christian relics. Indeed, in the Roman Catholic tradition, there were a number of ways of asserting the authenticity of a relic, but one of the more spectacular, in the Middle Ages at least, was that of trial by fire. This was a recognized ceremony, with its own established liturgy, whereby the relic was placed in a specially prepared charcoal brazier; if the flames died down and went out and the relic remained intact, its genuineness was confirmed; if not, its counterfeit nature was exposed.[37]

It is noteworthy that what is most emphasized in the Portuguese accounts of the destruction of the Buddha's tooth is the use of fire in doing so. On Don Constantino's medallion, for example, it is the brazier—the fire—that is featured, and not the mortar or the river. In this light, it is possible that Don Constantino's actions should be viewed not simply as being aimed at destroying the relic, not simply as devoutly rejecting the money he would have received for the relic, but also as submitting it to a trial by fire—a test

---

[36] For multiple other examples of unsuccessful attempts to destroy Buddhist relics, in China, Korea, and Japan, see Strong, *Relics of the Buddha,* 142. In addition, there were a number of other 'historical' precedents informing the loss of the tooth to the Portuguese. Towards the end of the 13th century a South Indian general invaded Sri Lanka, seized the tooth and sent it back to his home country where it was kept by the Pandyan king Kulasekhara. According to Sinhalese sources, several years later, it was supposedly recovered by a subsequent Sri Lankan king, as a result of what the island's chronicle calls 'skillful negotiation (*Cūḷavaṃsa* 90:46–55, trans. Wilhelm Geiger, *Cūḷavaṃsa being the More Recent Part of the Mahāvaṃsa* [London 1929], 2:204–5). See also Herath, *The Tooth Relic,* 72–3; Goloubew, 'Le temple de la dent', 450. (On the suggestions that actually the Jaffna peninsula was given to the Pandya as a ransom for the tooth, see Herath, *The Tooth Relic,* 180n.181.) Then again in 1411, the Chinese Ming Dynasty admiral, Zheng He, is said, in Chinese sources, to have captured the tooth during his incursion into Sri Lanka and to have returned with it to China (Li Ronxi, *The Great Tang Dynasty Record of the Western Regions* [Berkeley, 1996], 353–5). Contemporary Sri Lankan sources are silent on this, and later ones paint a very different picture of the whole episode and suggest that if Zheng He did steal anything, it might have been a replica of the Tooth (Herath, *The Tooth Relic,* 81).

[37] For the ritual, see Eugene A. Dooley, *Church Law on Sacred Relics* (Washington, 1931), 26–7. On its usage, see Snoek, *Medieval Piety,* 329–32; Hermann-Mascard, *Les reliques des saints,* 135; Thomas Head, 'Bodies of Truth: The Genesis and Abandonment of the Ritual Proof of Relics by Fire', unpublished paper delivered to the Davis Seminar, Princeton University, 1993.

which, in the eyes of his co-religionists, would definitively confirm the spurious nature of this tooth.

But the test of fire was not only used to ascertain the genuineness of a relic (or lack thereof); it was also an exorcism designed to root out the presence of the Devil. Focusing on the western hemisphere, Fernando Cervantes has pointed to the importance of demonology for our understanding of sixteenth-century colonial encounters.[38] It is in this context that we can appreciate that the thoroughness with which the archbishop destroyed the Buddha's tooth may have been informed not only by his knowledge of the nature of relics, but also by his worries about what possessed it. Little is said overtly about this in Diogo De Couto's account, although the tooth is called a 'reliquia do demonio'. A somewhat different picture is presented, however, in Fernaõ de Queyroz's account of this episode in his *Temporal and Spiritual Conquest of Ceylon* (1687). There it is recalled that, immediately after the tooth's capture, in Jaffna itself, Don Constantino was urged by the Franciscans who were with him, and by another bishop, Don Jorge Temudo, to do away with the relic immediately by burning it in a brazier. He refused to do so and decided to take the tooth with him back to Goa, declaring that this was a matter for some deliberation given the fact that the sale of the relic might solve some of the empire's financial problems. To this the Franciscans objected strenuously, not because of their desire to score points against paganism, but because they were convinced that 'the Demon was in that little bone,' and they were afraid that to keep it would have unfortunate consequences for the fleet (i.e., shipwreck) on its return trip.[39] Don Constantino did not, as we know, follow the Franciscans' advice on this occasion and destroy the tooth immediately, but their words are reminders that, when he did do so later, his actions may have been reflections not only of faith but also of fear.

Conclusion

'If there ever was a point where two extremes met, it is this. The burning of a tooth for the glory of the Almighty was the point of contact between the sublime and the ridiculous'.[40] As this quote suggests, the Portuguese destruction of the tooth of the Buddha in 1561 is sometimes cited as an example of the irreconcilable clash of two world views. We have seen enough, however, to understand that, in terms of relics at least, these two world views shared a lot

---

[38] Fernando Cervantes, *The Devil in the New World* (New Haven, 1994).

[39] Fernaõ de Queyroz, *The Temporal and Spiritual Conquest of Ceylon*, trans. S. G. Perera (Colombo, 1930), 1:365.

[40] Da Cunha, 'Memoir', 131.

of common ground. For the Buddhists, this was not the first time the tooth had been threatened by antagonistic non-Buddhists: the 'heretics', in actions almost identical to those of the Portuguese, had tried, unsuccessfully, to destroy it long ago. The fact that the Portuguese, this time around, were apparently successful did not rock the Buddhists' faith at all; it merely convinced them that this was not the genuine relic of the Buddha but some other relic. The Portuguese, moreover, shared views with the Buddhists on the nature and importance of relics. They shared views about their being sellable or purchasable commodities of great value. They shared views about their being testable by fire and possibly indestructible. And they shared views that the only relics that could be destroyed—i.e., the only relics that were not genuine relics—were other people's relics. Thus, when the viceroy destroyed the Buddha's tooth, the Christians had it confirmed in their minds that it was not a real relic but a 'reliquia do demonio', and the Buddhists concluded likewise that it was not a real relic but a duplicate or a tooth of Hanuman. It may be argued, of course, that the Portuguese and Buddhists were here viewing things from the opposite ends of a tunnel, but at least they were seeing the same tunnel.[41]

It has become standard when talking about certain features of post-eighteenth-century Theravāda Buddhism, especially though not exclusively in Sri Lanka, to speak of 'Protestant Buddhism'—a Buddhism so affected and infected by British colonial images of it, as rational, non-ritualistic, non-superstitious—that its own self-perception has become transformed.[42] Indeed, some have claimed that Buddhism, as a historical tradition, was invented in Britain in the nineteenth century, and that an image of the historical, human Buddha as a sort of Martin Luther protesting against the excesses of Brahmanism was formed 'in the 1850s, during an especially virulent outbreak of anti-Catholicism in England'.[43] The study of the destruction

[41] Friedrich Max Müller, in an often quoted passage, has asked why the Portuguese navigators recognized at once some of the objects they saw among the populations they visited as *feitiços* (fetishes)? Because, he says 'they themselves were fetish-worshippers' they themselves were 'perfectly familiar with a *feitiço* . . . and probably all carried with them some beads or crosses, or images, that had been blessed by their priests before they started their voyage.' See Friedrich Max Müller, *Lectures on the Origin and Growth of Religion* (London, 1880), 61.

[42] See Richard Gombrich and Gananath Obeyesekere, *Buddhism Transformed: Religious Change in Sri Lanka* (Princeton, 1988), 202–40. For an interesting critique of their view, see John C. Holt, 'Protestant Buddhism?', *Religious Studies Review*, 17 (1991), 1–6. See also Gregory Schopen, 'Archaeology and Protestant Presuppositions in the Study of Indian Buddhism', in Schopen, *Stones, Bones*, 1–22.

[43] Philip C. Almond, *The British Discovery of Buddhism* (Cambridge, 1988), 73.

of the Buddha's tooth takes us back to 'pre-Protestant', 'pre-Orientalist', 'pre-British' perceptions of Buddhism that preceded and informed later perceptions—both Sri Lankan and British. Moreover, it suggests that we need to be much more attuned to important distinctions between different types of colonialism in the study of Sri Lankan culture, and not lump together the Portuguese, Dutch, and British rules into some generic form of western oppression.

In this light, it is interesting to examine the reactions of nineteenth-century largely Protestant British scholars and officials to the story of the Portuguese destruction of the tooth. They generally seem to have held ambiguous attitudes. On the one hand, being for the most part rational post-enlightenment Protestants and sceptics of a stripe not inclined to take relics of any kind seriously, they often treated the whole episode humorously, joking especially about the plethora of 'new' 'fake' tooth relics that suddenly appeared in different places in the wake of the Portuguese action. On the other hand, ironically, the British had a vested interest in the genuineness of the tooth in Kandy since they were enthusiastic asserters of the claim that, with their seizure of that tooth, all native resistance to their rule had ceased and that they were henceforth perceived as legitimate sovereigns over the island. Sir William Colebrooke, for example, declared that 'the possesssion and exhibition of the Tooth relic of Bhood is regarded by the natives of the Kandyan provinces as the most important of the prerogatives of the Kings of Kandy to which the British government has succeeded'.[44] John Davy, the British governor's physician who toured Kandy in 1817 put it this way: 'The effect of [the tooth's] capture was astonishing and almost beyond the comprehension of the enlightened. Now the people [say] the English are indeed masters of the country; for they who possess the relic have a right to govern'.[45] In that light, the British could hardly maintain that the Portuguese had destroyed the relic 250 years earlier! So it comes as no surprise to find the prominent Pali scholar, T. W. Rhys Davids claiming even in 1874 that the Portuguese were confused as to what they had captured, that no Sinhalese king would have ever sent the tooth relic to Jaffna (where they captured it), and that 'we have every reason to believe that the very tooth referred to [in the *Dāṭhāvaṃsa*—the Pali Chronicle of the Buddha's tooth] is preserved to this day in Kandy'.[46]

---

[44] Kitsiri Malalgoda, *Buddhism in Sinhalese Society 1750–1900* (Berkeley, 1976), 117.

[45] John Davy, *An Account of the Interior of Ceylon and of its Inhabitants* (Dehiwala, 1969 [1821]), 275.

[46] See Da Cunha, 'Memoir', 139.

Willy-nilly, then, (but mostly willy) the British found themselves to be custodians of the Buddha's tooth, and thus the official sponsors of its cult. The British resident in Kandy kept the keys to the inner sanctuary of the temple of the tooth in his library (keys which had previously been kept by the Kandyan kings), dutifully releasing them every day for the regular occasions of worship; and, on more solemn occasions, he personally participated in processions honouring the tooth, walking barefoot (shocking for a nineteenth-century Englishman) up to the altar and making offerings (on one occasion, a musical clock) to the relic on behalf of the colonial government.[47] In other words, the British consciously took over—vis-à-vis the tooth relic—the responsibilities and prerogatives of ancient Sri Lankan royalty.[48]

But this did not last very long. Succumbing to increasing pressure from missionaries on the island and Christian societies in England, the colonial rulers gradually gave up their role as custodians of the Buddha's relic. Thus, in 1847, the British finally divested themselves of all official and ceremonial relations to it, leaving those to a committee of elders from prominent monasteries, much to the objections of the Kandyan chiefs and monks who unsuccessfully petitioned the governor and the Queen not to do so. Since the committee had no claims to any kind of temporal sovereignty over the island, the identity of the tooth as a palladium was dead.[49]

In fact, this action did more harm to the tooth-relic than the Portuguese had done in trying to destroy it. Today, Sri Lankans, thinking about their oppression by successive European powers, tend to be more bitter about the attitude the British took towards the tooth-relic than about the attitude of the Portuguese. For the Portuguese, at least, were operating in the same context as the Sri Lankans. They destroyed the tooth in such a way that it could be recovered. But the British, after initially entering into the Sri Lankan context, soon withdrew from it, and left the Buddha's tooth in a limbo from which no recovery has yet been possible.

[47] Malalgoda, *Buddhism in Sinhalese Society*, 119n.

[48] Da Cunha, 'Memoir', 144.

[49] Malalgoda, *Buddhism in Sinhalese Society*, 117–20.

The Strange Business of Memory: Relic Forgery in Latin America

Paul Gillingham

This essay surveys assorted cases of relic forgery from colonial and modern Latin America, to argue that such forgeries are (a) particularly widespread in the region; (b) part of a quite formalized sector of the region's informal economies; and (c) commodities produced by a wide range of elite and non-elite actors. To explain why this should be, it suggests a very schematic typology of relic forgery in Latin America (taken here as a broad, Chicano construct, encompassing parts of California and upstate New York) and attempts a superficial political economy of relic forgery. This last focuses particularly on the modern period, and on the role of archaeology in a strange business: the materialization of memory through fraud.

Forging relics is, as other essays in this volume suggest, a practice that spans a whole range of times, places, and cultures. Some relics, like Mohammed's toothpick or splinters of the One True Cross—usefully interchangeable, one might think—became ubiquitous precisely because of the ease with which they could be mass-produced. Three hundred men, Luther mocked ponderously, would not have sufficed to carry off all the fragments of the One True Cross.[1] Such forgery is merely a subset of the broader category of artefact and antiquity fraud. There is surprisingly little historical literature on this exotic trade; yet it is, as any curator or collector knows, extremely commonplace. Museum director Thomas Hoving estimated that thirty per cent of the objects offered to the Met were fakes. Even the most knowledgeable collectors, he wrote, would purchase some forgeries over a career's span, for fakes abounded in every market; antiquity fraud was a 'massive, truly monumental industry'.[2] Hoving's choice of 'industry' was neither verbal sloppiness nor

---

[1] David Lowenthal, 'Authenticity: Rock of Faith or Quicksand Quagmire?', *The Getty Conservation Institute Newsletter*, 14 (1999), 5–8.

[2] One favoured, moreover, by at least two long-standing traits of collectors and curators: i) the drive to unearth rarities, usually of high intrinsic value and easily squared with a western aesthetic sense, and ii) the assumption, as Hoving's mentor taught him, that 'although it was a mistake to collect a fake, an error every adventurous connoisseur had

hyperbole, but a reasonable definition of a complex business bound tightly to the laws of supply and demand. Thus post-war Rome, for example, became a centre of forgery due to a potent combination of strong American demand for antiquities, their relative scarcity and the poverty of restorers, sculptors, and the academics who verified and gave provenances for their fakes.[3] (This was not Rome's first period of notoriety for art fraud: in the first century AD Seneca the Elder found half a dozen workshops forging Greek jewels and intaglios, while 'painters' galleys' in the seventeenth and eighteenth centuries mass-produced old masters.)[4] Forgeries can have impacts well beyond a misleadingly labelled display case or a stung collector. The Donation of Constantine lent medieval popes a theocratic claim to temporal jurisdiction that legitimized sweeping land grabs: Pope Adrian IV's grant of Ireland to England, Pope Alexander VI's division of the non-European world into Spanish and Portuguese territories.[5] Yet for all that the historical significance of forgeries has been minimized, while the production of fake antiquities has been universal, ubiquitous, and unusually intense in the late nineteenth and twentieth centuries.

Certain characteristics of Latin American societies in both colonial and modern periods favoured comparatively widespread artefact fraud. Material incentives for forgers were consistently powerful, whether afforded by fluid property rights or by the proximity of monied consumers in North America. Opportunities for forgers were likewise strong: historically low literacy levels have magnified the power of the inventive, forging minorities, while conquest and *kulturkampf* in the sixteenth century generated a relative ignorance of the pasts of complex indigenous societies with highly sophisticated material cultures. Artefact fraud has been consequently commonplace. Its production ranges from the banal—Aztec black pottery, a form of deceptive, unlabelled tourist art since at least the 1820s—to the spectacular, such as the Aztec crystal skulls; and from the micro—the Ica stones of Peru, say—to the distinctly macro, whether the pyramid of the sun in Teotihuacán, to which the lead archaeologist added an extra level for aesthetic reasons, or the lost city of Quechmietoplican, a Mesoamerican fantasy dreamed up by

made, *it was an absolute sin to brand as a forgery an authentic work of art!*': Jane Walsh, 'What is Real? A New Look at PreColumbian Mesoamerican Collections', *Anthronotes*, 26 (2005), 17; Thomas Hoving, *King of the Confessors* (New York, 1981), 38, 44, 173.

[3] Hoving, *King of the Confessors*, 83, 171–3.

[4] Thomas Hoving, *False Impressions: The Hunt for Big-Time Art Fakes* (New York, 1996), 31, 62.

[5] Mark Jones, 'Why Fakes?' in Mark Jones (ed.), *Fake? The Art of Deception* (Berkeley, 1990), 12.

nineteenth-century tourist guides on the basis of abandoned mine-work-ings.[6] By the late nineteenth century forgery was quite literally an industrial process in Mexico, where artisans used high-speed rotary wheels to cut and polish stone and crystal, softened obsidian in petrol baths, soldered together filigree goldwork and, most impressive of all, used galvanization to transform waxwork dummies into copper moulds for production-line baking of 'pre-hispanic' pottery. (The government's Inspector of Monuments collected over 80 such moulds.)[7] Given the lack of competitiveness in Mexico's more formal industries—it cost nineteen per cent more to produce a piece of cloth in Veracruz than it did in Manchester—artefact forgery may have been the country's most successful export industry.[8] By the 1930s, at any rate, pur-portedly prehispanic artefacts were so ubiquitous in the United States that one archaeologist claimed one of his 'most frequent sources of Mexican objects' to be Irondequoit Bay in New York State, where the 'housewives and widows' of collectors dumped them.[9] *Gringos* were not the only dupes: Diego Rivera's vast collection of pre-Columbian art was 'riddled with fakes'.[10]

Given such a rich hoard of stories of artefact fraud, it is tempting to blur categories and to define a relic as vaguely as possible: as, perhaps, 'something which remains or is left behind, particularly after destruction or decay'.[11] This is clearly analytically unsatisfactory, reducing both the precision and the cumulativity of any comparative studies. An exacting, functionalist definition of relics—as uniquely religious inventions, specifically body parts, intimate personal possessions and contact materials that are thought to provide

[6] William H. Holmes, 'The Trade in Spurious Mexican Antiquities', *Science*, 7:159 (19 Feb. 1886); Jane Walsh, 'Crystal Skulls and Other Problems; Or, "Don't Look It in the Eye"', in Amy Henderson and Adrienne L. Kaeppler (eds), *Exhibiting Dilemmas: Issues of Representation at the Smithsonian* (Washington DC, 1997), 116–39; Massimo Polidoro, 'Ica Stones: Yabba-Dabba-Doo!', *Skeptical Inquirer* (Sept.-Oct. 2002); author's interview, Eduardo Matos Moctezuma, Mexico City, 20 July 2000, *Periódico Oficial del Estado de Guerrero*, XXI:34 (25 Aug. 1897).

[7] Leopoldo Batres, *Antigüedades Mejicanas Falsificadas: Falsificación y Falsificadores* (México DF, 1910?), 24.

[8] Steven Haber, *Industry and Underdevelopment: The Industrialization of Mexico, 1890–1940* (Stanford, 1989), 37–8.

[9] Arthur C. Parker, 'The Perversion of Archaeological Data', *American Antiquity*, 5 (1939), 57–8.

[10] Michael D. Coe, 'From Huaquero to Connoisseur: The Early Market in Pre-Columbian Art', in E. Hill Boone (ed.), *Collecting the pre-Columbian Past: A Symposium at Dumbarton Oaks, 6th and 7th October 1990* (Dumbarton Oaks, 1993), 273.

[11] Lesley Brown (ed.), *The New Shorter Oxford English Dictionary*, 2 vols (Oxford, 1993), II:2537.

supernatural means to pragmatic ends—is the easiest defended. There are, admittedly, frequent linguistic attempts to sacralize secular artefacts: deeming national heroes 'martyrs', their bones 'relics', their graves 'altars to the *patria*', their memories the objects of 'cults'.[12] A handful of the most successful—the bones of Emiliano Zapata, or the would-be bones of Cuauhtémoc, or the Aztec crystal skulls—seem to attain for some followers the sacral function of religious relics, becoming objects that wield magical as well as mnemonic power.[13] The overwhelming majority do not. Yet if non-religious artefacts are generally not believed to possess the numinous power of religious relics, they do share other key characteristics. What we might call 'secular relics' satisfy David Hume's actor-centred description of the miraculous, namely materials which generate 'the passion of *surprise* and *wonder* . . . an agreeable notion [that] gives a sensible tendency towards the belief of those events from which it is derived'.[14] Relics religious and secular all work at the intersection of credulity and power; both types are examples of what Pierre Nora described as a material *lieu de mémoire*, namely 'any significant entity . . . which by dint of human will or the work of time has become a symbolic element of the memorial heritage of any community'.[15] Such symbolic capital is readily converted, as Pierre Bourdieu has argued, into economic or

---

[12] See, e.g., the report on commemoration of Obregón's death, Mexico City, 17 July 1945, AGN/DGIPS- 79 exp 2–1/130/633, *Periódico Oficial del Gobierno del Estado de Guerrero* XXVI:34 (21 Aug. 1903), report on parade . . . of 5 Feb. 1949, Mexico City, AGN/DGIPS-102/JNM.

[13] Zapata is regularly invoked as a revenant who will come down from the hills on a white horse to protect his people in their hour of need; Cuauhtémoc is the object of literal prayers for intercession, and is simultaneously rumoured to wield a mortal curse against non-believers in his cult; the crystal skulls are variously believed capable of projecting holograms, promoting healing, and remote control killing. Pancho Villa is also the object of a religious cult in Chihuahua, but one without many relics. Villa's skull was stolen in the 1920s, and his bones lie in Mexico City. Samuel Brunk, 'The Mortal Remains of Emiliano Zapata' in Lyman L. Johnson (ed.), *Death, Dismemberment and Memory: Body Politics in Latin America* (Albuquerque, 2004), 146–53; John Womack, Jr, *Zapata and the Mexican Revolution* (London, 1969), 330; Paul Gillingham, *Cuauhtémoc's Bones: Forging Identity in Mexico* (forthcoming, 2010), ch.3; Robert Todd Carroll, 'Crystal Skull' at http://skepdic.com/crystalskull.html; Friedrich Katz, *The Life and Times of Pancho Villa* (Stanford, 1998), 789–93.

[14] Adding sceptically that 'if the spirit of religion join itself to the love of wonder, there is an end of common sense; and human testimony, in these circumstances, loses all pretensions to authority'. David Hume, 'Of Miracles', in Hume, *An Enquiry concerning Human Understanding* (Illinois, 1988), 150–1.

[15] Pierre Nora, *Rethinking France: les lieux de mémoire*, 3 vols (Chicago, 2001) i, xvii.

political capital.[16] The relationship is old enough to be recognized in some etymologies; thus the root of the word for relic in Serbian—*mošti*—is *moć*, or power.[17] In widening our focus beyond the purely religious we lose some precision; but in exchange we may gain some analytical insight, for relics religious and secular are surrounded by many similar social relationships and practices.[18] Hence, in this essay, relics will be broadly defined as artefacts of widely accepted charismatic power, whether they serve as the sign for a famous individual or as the sign for a major, transformative idea.

There are assorted approaches that might be used here: the history of magic, religion, or memory, the anthropology of ritual and material culture, the sociology of community, instrumentalist theories of nationalism. The latter, perhaps an obvious choice for the analysis of secular relics at least, suffers however from a double weakness. Constructivist readings of hero/relic cults tend to assume a top-down flow of production, in which these signifiers of identity are invented by narrow coteries of metropolitan elites and artlessly consumed by their gullible subjects. Instrumentalist readings of symbolic manipulation further tend to assume that the mere existence of a statue, a reliquary, a grave, a postage stamp, or any other place of memory constitutes in itself conclusive proof that the represented symbol is central to both producers and consumers of that memory. I am unconvinced that either of these assumptions works everywhere, all the time. Some straightforward quantification of the resources invested—by both producers and consumers of symbols—would be a useful rule-of-thumb gauge of those symbols' significance in the everyday scheme of things. It is worth remembering, moreover, that Pierre Nora's 'entirely symbolic' history, or 'history of the second degree', was originally deeply reliant on an older, more positivist historiography which he and his followers effectively cannibalized. Without such older historiographical traditions to relate to, it becomes impossible to 'point up the links between the material base of social existence and the most elaborate productions of culture and thought'. How does an 'entirely symbolic' historiography know what that material base looks like? How could we assess the 'reuse and misuse' of historical narrative in the utter absence of a professional historical narrative?[19] Cultural analyses which overly despise the material can

---

[16] Pierre Bourdieu, *Outline of a Theory of Practice* (Cambridge, 1977), 47–67.

[17] Ivan Čolović, 'Relics' in *The Politics of Symbol in Serbia* (London, 2002), 166.

[18] See, e.g., Lyman Johnson's argument that the representational conventions and the narrative structures of nationalist relic cults are 'clearly derived from the earlier cult of saints'. Lyman L. Johnson, 'Why Dead Bodies Talk: An Introduction' in Johnson (ed.), *Death, Dismemberment and Memory*, 20.

[19] Nora, *Rethinking France*, xx, xxiv.

produce partial, and eventually sterilely interchangeable, understandings of the past—understandings of the sort which Nora, at base an empiricist whose *meisterwerk* filled seven volumes, might despise. Hence, in this survey, the use of culture and political economy as twin organizing concepts in attempting a relic-centred brand of the history of memory. An understanding of a relic's cultural context is essential to understand the sources of its power; but a grasp of a relic's political economy is also essential to understand why and how people fetishize, materialize, and trade these symbols across the world.[20]

This is not a contrarian's effort to graft a *marxisant* analysis onto a primarily cultural field of history; it is merely following the lead of specialists in artefact forgery. Such specialists repeatedly stress the business side of relic fraud. Leopoldo Batres, a prominent and politically able archaeologist of late nineteenth-century Mexico, put it particularly clearly: 'One of the industries that has reached the greatest sophistication since long ago has been the falsification of antique objects.'[21] (He should have known, as something of a participant-observer: it was Batres who wittingly added a level to the Pyramid of the Sun in Teotihuacán, and Batres who tried to sell one of the first fraudulent Aztec crystal skulls to Mexico's National Museum.)[22] Batres was quite right: some two thousand years earlier the mummy sellers of Hawara in Egypt had defied pharaonic decree and sold worshippers crocodile mummies that CT scans show to be wholly crocodile-free.[23] His contemporaries agreed with him. William Holmes, director of the Smithsonian at the time, warned of how the 'increased demand' of his 'museum-making era' had 'led to many attempts, on the part of dishonest persons, to supply the market by fraudulent means'.[24] A century later the stress on forgeries as the end products of classical economics endures. As the curator Mark Jones observes,

> Fakes are . . . only secondarily a source of evidence for the outlook of those who made and uncovered them. They are, before all else, a response to demand, an ever changing portrait of human desire.

[20] And may even provide 'an ideal if somewhat unusual microcosm in which to examine the creation, evaluation, and circulation of commodities'. Patrick Geary, 'Sacred Commodities: The Circulation of Medieval Relics' in Arjun Appadurai, *The Social Life of Things: Commodities in Cultural Perspective* (Cambridge, 1986), 169.

[21] Batres, *Antigüedades Mejicanas Falsificadas*, 1.

[22] Author's interview, Salvador Rueda, México DF Oct. 1995, Walsh, 'Crystal Skulls and Other Problems', 127.

[23] The prior existence of the decree establishing that animal mummies should actually contain animals is suggestive. Maev Kennedy, 'Massive Mummy Fraud Discovered after 2,000 Years', *The Guardian* (21 June 2006).

[24] Holmes, 'Spurious Mexican Antiquities', 170.

> Each society, each generation, fakes the thing it covets most . . .
> Where there are fakes it is clear that there was a booming market in
> the things thus imitated: fakers are above all creatures of the
> market.[25]

What follows, then, is a typology of relic fraud in Latin America; some case
studies to illustrate each category; and two final questions: how big a business
has relic production really been? And who are the producers, who are the
consumers, and how are they connected?

Relics reflect what societies need to find or forge. As such, production
fashions shift nimbly to keep pace with shifting belief systems. On this
basis we might propose four types of relic forgery in Latin America: religious,
monarchic, nationalist, and scientific. These types show a certain evolution
over time: thus religious and monarchic frauds tend to occur in the colonial
period, while nationalist and scientific forgeries are more characteristic of the
modern period. The labels are more roughly indicative than tight, mutually
exclusive categories, as distinct relic frauds often fall into more than one class.
Thus the enterprising Antonio Tandazo Montoya y Minchala, who used a
blend of fake royal charters and papal bulls to set himself up as a *cacique* in
several indigenous villages in highland Ecuador, created a set of forged text
relics both religious and monarchic.[26] And the bones of the last Aztec
emperor Cuauhtémoc, a nineteenth-century production, were primarily
nationalist relics; but were also to some extent monarchic (he was indigenous
royalty), scientific (the forger aimed to substantially recast a central narrative
of Mexican historiography) and religious (assorted authors and public speak-
ers developed the parallels between Cuauhtémoc and Christ; communist
schoolteachers devised prayers to the last *tlatoani*).[27]

This last was a striking tribute to the enduring influence of baroque
Catholicism in Latin America. An Augustinian concern with conversions in
quantity rather than doctrinal quality had allowed the first churchmen in
Latin America to build a large church with real speed: in Mexico alone there
were an estimated four million converts by 1540, served in 1559 by some 160
monasteries.[28] There were over a hundred missions in Peru by 1600; Lima's

---

[25] Jones, 'Why Fakes?', 13. See also Hoving's systematic use of industrial metaphors in
Hoving, *False Impressions*, 26, 30, 51.

[26] Joanne Rappaport and Thomas B. F. Cummins, 'Literacy and Power in Colonial Latin
America', in George C. Bond and Angela Gilliam (eds), *Social Construction of the Past:
Representation as Power* (London, 1994), 95–6.

[27] Juan Campuzano, *Cinco héroes de Guerrero: Galeana, Guerrero, Cuauhtémoc, Álvarez,
Altamirano* (México DF, 1961), 23; *El Universal* 4 Oct. 1949.

[28] Alan Knight, *Mexico: the Colonial Era* (Cambridge, 2002), 33–5.

(rather worldly) large convents housed over a thousand nuns apiece.[29] That speed was fuelled, in part, by the early Franciscans' apocalyptic interpretation of the conquest. By the late sixteenth century this had been supplanted by a baroque Catholicism that centred on the doctrine of purgatory. In this religious framework saints' relics were a critical source of both sacred and temporal power, instruments to harness the magical intercession of their referents. Such beliefs stretched back to Cortés himself, who carried an image of the Virgin Mary on his standard, told the Indians of Cempoala that she would serve as their new 'intercessor' and instructed the Nahuas of Tenochtitlán to pray to her for rain.[30] 'Relichood' lies in the eye of the beholder, and paintings, crosses, tapestries, clothes, statues, and their adornments could all be constituted as relics; magical objects that were expected, when appropriately propitiated by the deserving, to perform miracles for both individuals and communities in need.

A broad range of social practices could catalyze those miracles. Some were rigorously programmed, such as the annual saint's day processions around a settlement's centre, or an individual's prayer to their eponymous saint on his or her day, or the persignation required on crossing a relic's path. Others were more *ad hoc*, ranging from personal invocation, accompanied by physical contact with the relic if possible, to the grim parades of relics that desperate communities mounted as last-ditch defences against drought or plague. A broad range of fabricated images—sometimes containing body parts or contact relics, occasionally containing prehispanic idols—were believed to take on the life and the numinous power of the saint in question, and were worshipped with intimacy: lovingly dressed, petitioned, chatted with, and offered food. While this was a universal medieval lay belief, in Mexico the associated practice was probably helped by the Nahua faith in *ixipitla*: statues or humans who impersonated the gods, and in their ritual disguise lured the referents into temporarily possessing them.[31] The miracles that were sometimes believed to result were central to baroque cosmology, providing something of a counterweight to what Weber called 'the problem of theodicy', or why a just God should permit the existence

[29] Charles H. Lippy, Robert Choquette, and Stafford Poole (eds), *Christianity Comes to the Americas, 1492–1776* (New York, 1992), 58, 62.

[30] William B. Taylor, 'The Virgin of Guadalupe in New Spain: An Inquiry into the Social History of Marian Devotion', *American Ethnologist*, 14 (1987), 10–11.

[31] Jeanette Favrot Peterson, 'Creating the Virgin of Guadalupe: The Cloth, the Artist, and Sources in Sixteenth-Century New Spain', *The Americas*, 61 (2005), 571–610; Geary, 'Sacred Commodities', 176.

of evil.[32] They were also critical to any religious institution's balance sheet, attracting the local (and in cases long-distance) faithful and ensuring financial support for convents, monasteries, and churches. Cash was not the only material benefit of relics. Relics and the saints' cults they underpinned were also used to promote political autonomy for villages, or to provide legal protection for community lands in the form of confraternities. In Tonalá, Oaxaca, for example, the miraculous discovery of a cross inside a cave backed up the town's claim to the regional dominance it had enjoyed before the conquest.[33] Relics were key instruments in what Claudio Lomnitz has called 'a popular culture built at every point on the domestication and popularization of the death cult'.[34]

There was, however, a key problem with relics in early colonial Latin America: their scarcity. European churches had been stockpiling relics of the saints and martyrs since the fifth century, and had taken the logical next step in adding value—transferring their thaumaturgic power to reliquaries—around the tenth century. During the key early stages of evangelization missionaries in Latin America, on the other hand, lacked both their own saints and their own relics.[35] The mere passage of time can lend gravitas and 'relichood' to all sorts of community belongings. For the first generations of conquerors and conquered, however, little or no time had passed, and the signifiers of foreign saints were all too newly crafted. One response to the shortage was to import: in 1617 the Jesuits sent a monk relic-hunting in the graveyards of the Basque country, explaining to their guardians that 'I need relics of saints and in these chapels there are few or none of them'.[36] Another was to forge. In 1648 the Inquisition opened a case against one Domingo de Robles, who had entered Valladolíd, Yucatán,

> with some skins that he claimed were of saints and other pieces of
> paper and bits of wax or [illegible] like pieces of Agnus and a rosary
> with a little wood cross and a Christ, and with all of this he went

---

[32] Richard Swedberg, *The Max Weber Dictionary: Key Words and Central Concepts* (Stanford, 2005), 274.

[33] *Historia de Tonalá, Oaxaca coleccionada por el Sr. Pbro. D. Avelino de la T Mora López para Conmemorar el III Centenario del Hallazgo de La Santa Cruz En la Gruta del Río de Santa María Tindu, Oax.* (Sant Domingo Tonalá, 1957), 56. With thanks to Ben Smith.

[34] Claudio Lomnitz, *Death and the Idea of Mexico* (New York, 2005), 261.

[35] David A. Brading, *Mexican Phoenix: Our Lady of Guadalupe: Image and Tradition across Five Centuries* (Cambridge, 2001), 19–20.

[36] Lomnitz, *Death and the Idea of Mexico*, 247.

around healing and using these things to rub the women, saying that his relics had the virtue of healing.[37]

Such early colonial wide boys were clearly commonplace, as both the ecclesiastical and civil authorities drew up regulations to control relics. Their forgery devalued one of the papacy's traditional currencies of power, namely the central reserves of relics that were the catacombs, filled with the bones of early Christian martyrs.[38] The Santo Oficio attempted to physically vet all relics; the colonial authorities passed an edict declaring that 'no trader or merchant can sell [relics], and if traders possess any such objects, they must declare them, so that they can be repossessed and placed in a convenient destination'. Yet by hook or by crook the urgent demand for relics was satisfied. By 1728, the *Gaceta de México* recorded, the relics displayed on All Saints Day in the cathedral included 'the body of Saint Primitivo, that of Saint Hilaria, two heads of the Eleven Thousand Virgins, of Saint Anastasio, of Saint Gelacio, of Saint Vito, and others'.[39]

Relic production was more than a local business centred on local concerns and local politics. Two religious cults attained continental significance, namely those to St Thomas the Apostle and the Virgén de Guadalupe. Both were strongly politically charged arguments that creoles deployed in the battle against peninsular discrimination. (An all-encompassing prejudice, as Jorge Cañizares Esguerra shows, which damned not only the lands and peoples of the Americas but even their stars, imagined as the source of baleful influence and collective inferiority.)[40] One response was to argue for pre-evangelization, the theory that the Americas had been converted to Christianity at the very beginning. The *Acta Thomae* claimed, after all, that St Thomas the apostle had proselytized far 'beyond the Ganges'. He had reputedly been a stonemason, and his name meant 'precious twin'; both characteristics of the pale-skinned Mesoamerican god Quetzalcóatl. The easily made identification was further strengthened by the crosses that bewildered the conquistadors and by assorted rumours and fragments; it resolved, moreover, the theological dilemma of how the Son of God could have overlooked a vast proportion of humanity. The St Thomas cult could function simultaneously as an

---

[37] Ibid., 248.

[38] Geary, 'Sacred Commodities', 182.

[39] Stafford Poole, *Our Lady of Guadalupe: The Origins and Sources of a Mexican National Symbol, 1531–1797* (Arizona, 1996), 30, 59, Lomnitz, *Death and the Idea of Mexico*, 248.

[40] This, Cañizares Esguerra argues, may be the earliest manifestation of scientific racism. Jorge Cañizares Esguerra, 'New World, New Stars: Patriotic Astrology and the Invention of Indian and Creole Bodies in Colonial Spanish America, 1600–1650', *The American Historical Review*, 104 (1999), 33–68.

instrument for proselytization in the Americas and for Creole self-defence in Europe. The outcome, in short order, was the rapid emergence of the relics necessary to substantiate such a useful idea. In Peru the Augustinians alleged St Thomas to have been the Inca founder-god Viracocha, his path remembered in the indigenous shrines, the *huacas*, that criss-crossed the Andes. In Brazil his footprints were discovered in rock, worshipped as the tracks of a great prophet by the Tupinamba. In Chile both footprints and letters in rock were interpreted as further traces of the apostle, leading one father to send rock samples to Rome for substantiation.[41]

The various footprints of St Thomas may well have been straightforward strides of faith. The apparition of the Virgin Mary in the Valley of Mexico, on the other hand, was attacked as a knowing invention from the start.[42] The story is widely known: Mary is held to have appeared three times on a hill outside Mexico City, Tepeyac, to a poor and pious Nahua named Juan Diego. The soon-to-be bishop Zumárraga disbelieved the story; and so, the earliest account tells us, the Virgin instructed the Indian to gather flowers in his cloak and to present them to the Franciscan. When the cloak was opened and the flowers fell, however, they had left fixed on the material the 'Virgin Mary, Mother of God, in her holy image which today is preserved, guarded and venerated in her sanctuary of Guadalupe of Mexico' (Fig. 1).[43] The relic was extremely successful, drawing intense veneration from first Spanish and, much later, indigenous pilgrims. By the 1680s Jesuits were promoting it as unique in the world, powerful even beyond St Luke's supposed paintings of Mary, for the Mexican image, they claimed, had been painted by God or Mary herself.[44] This earliest account, however, comes over a century after the apparition of virgin and relic, and was founded on oral histories; as the author straightforwardly owned up, 'I searched for papers and writings regarding the holy image, but I did not find any'.[45] This may have been because the sixteenth-century devout seem to have considered the relic

---

[41] Jaques Lafaye, *Quetzalcóatl y Guadalupe: La formación de la conciencia nacional en México* (México DF, 1995), 232–65.

[42] And has continued to generate controversy to the present. The recent canonization of Juan Diego met with protests from, among others, the abbot of the Basilica of Guadalupe himself. *Reforma* 2 Dec. 1999.

[43] Miguel Sánchez, *Imagen de la Virgen María madre de Dios de Guadalupe, milagrosamente aparecida en la ciudad de México [1648]*, cited in Brading, *Mexican Phoenix*, 63.

[44] Brading, *Mexican Phoenix*, 99. For a convincing rebuttal of the myth that the Virgin of Guadalupe was instantly powerful among indigenous populations see Taylor, 'The Virgin of Guadalupe in New Spain'.

[45] Brading, *Mexican Phoenix*, 56–7.

Fig. 1. The painted cloak with the iconic Virgen de Guadalupe, Valley of Mexico, sixteenth century. By permission of the Museo de la Basílica de Guadalupe

nothing more than a rather good painting (Bernal Díaz compared the puta-tive artist to Michelangelo).[46] The first record of the cult comes in September 1556, when Archbishop Montúfar lavishly praised the Virgin of Guadalupe and her image's miraculous cure of a stockbreeder. The iconodule bishop drew a stinging rebuttal from the iconoclast Franciscan provincial, Francisco de Bustamante, which in turn sparked an investigation into the cult. This investigation revealed that the cult's material centrepiece, the painted cloak, was held to work miracles but was also believed to have been made by one of the great indigenous painters, Marcos Cipac de Aquino; a finding that no one challenged.[47]

To the inventive historian Edmundo O'Gorman the answer was clear: the archbishop had planted the image to promote conversion in the Valley of Mexico. Without evidence for such a Machiavellian interpretation, however, it seems more likely that this was a collective progression into fraud.[48] For Serge Gruzinski the authors of the 'irrefutable construct' were clearly the three authors of the mid-seventeenth century who successfully transmuted a sixteenth-century painting into a miraculous image.[49] For seventeenth-century creoles there was the same solid ideological motive to invest the painting of the virgin with magical power as there had been to find traces of Thomas the Apostle, namely a defence against metropolitan discrimin-ation. And there was also a powerful material motive. As Jaques Lafaye has argued, converting a cult to the Spanish Virgin of Guadalupe into a domestic apparitionist movement had a major economic effect. The alms collected in her name had hitherto been remitted to the Jeronymites in charge of the mother house of Guadalupe in Extremadura; after 1600 they stayed in New Spain. The impact was immediate. Even as the relic was subjected to repeated archdiocesan inquiries it drew in large sums from the faithful. On at least one occasion, the visit of 1653, the two phenomena were connected, the arch-bishop concerned to track down where the abundant alms were actually going.[50] As early as 1576 the chapel generated a surplus that could be set aside for orphans' dowries; a new building, opened in 1622, was part-financed by alms-givers who received, in return, copper-plate certificates worth 40 days' remission of sins; by 1749 the cult was wealthy enough to invest

---

[46] Cited in Peterson's detailed reconstruction of the actual process of painting the image. Peterson, 'Creating the Virgin of Guadalupe', 588.

[47] Poole, *Our Lady of Guadalupe*, 60–4; Serge Gruzinski, *La guerra de las imágenes: De Cristóbal Colón a 'Blade Runner' (1492–2019)* (México DF, 1995), 111.

[48] Poole, *Our Lady of Guadalupe*, 7–8.

[49] Gruzinski, *La guerra de las imágenes*, 124.

[50] Ibid., 123.

nearly half a million pesos in further building works.[51] In 1757 the Indians of nearby Zacualpan protested that their priests had initiated feast days in honour of Guadalupe to increase their incomes.[52] The Virgin of Guadalupe, above all other Latin American relic cults, has been extraordinarily 'good to think'; she has also been extraordinarily good business.[53]

Largely coeval with religious relics were monarchic relics. Given the theocratic nature of contemporary European rule, it is unsurprising that the two categories sometimes overlap. Thus the councilmen of Puebla, for example, were offered relics to kiss on the feast day of Saint Teresa as a mark of her special favour to these local arbiters of distant royal power.[54] While the bones of Spanish royalty were unavailable, those of their indigenous counterparts were theoretically to be had; but in a relic-aware culture, their politically driven disappearance was over-determined. Cortés left Cuauhtémoc, the last Mexica emperor, hanging from a tree on Tabasco Plain; the viceroy had Tupac Amaru, the self-identified Inca who led the 1780 indigenous rebellion, dismembered and scattered across the Andean Highlands. Contact relics may have been more common, and were clearly sometimes forged. In the mid-seventeenth century the Andalusian adventurer Don Pedro de Bohorques Girón re-invented himself as 'Huallpa Inca', and, equipped with serviceable Quechua and a faked silver diadem of the sun, persuaded 25,000 Andeans in the remote Calchaquí valley to accept him as their lord.[55] Yet monarchic relics were most commonly textual, and took above all the form of royal land grants to communities across Latin America.

The power of these *títulos*, which proliferated in the mid-seventeenth century, may have drawn in part on the universal, carefully constructed charismatic sway of kings, expressed in beliefs such as the royal touch; but it was also rooted in earthier considerations. In a period of sometimes chaotically

---

[51] Lafaye, *Quetzalcóatl y Guadalupe*, 374–80; Brading, *Mexican Phoenix*, 54; Poole, *Our Lady of Guadalupe*, 227–35.

[52] Taylor, 'The Virgin of Guadalupe in New Spain', 14–15.

[53] She remains so to the present: Marian apparitions multiplied in Mexico's chaotic *fin de siècle*. Squatters in Mexico City in the late 1990s, threatened with eviction, found an image of the Virgin in the cross-section of a tree they felled; underground travellers read Marian outlines into a damp stain in the Hidalgo metro station that became '*la virgen del metro*', *Reforma* (30 Jan.1999); Juan Villoro, 'El testigo innecesario' in *La Jornada Semanal* (19 Dec. 1999).

[54] Except when they fell out with the church. Frances L. Ramos, 'Succession and Death: Royal Ceremonies in Colonial Puebla', *The Americas*, 60 (2003), 192–3.

[55] Bohorques was deeply aware of the power of relics, and on one occasion chose to meet the Spanish governor of the province at Indian ceremonial sites; Robert Ryal Miller, 'The Fake Inca of Tucumán: Don Pedro de Bohorques', *The Americas*, 32 (1975), 196–210.

fluctuating property rights, such grants were the main source of clear title for indigenous villagers. They were, as such, subject to frequent forgery throughout the colonial period and beyond. The Ecuadorian forger Montoya, arrested in 1803, confessed to his inquisitors 'that he carried with him seven royal charters and that he managed to be the *cacique* of many villages and that he could live wherever he liked'.[56] Forgeries were not just the work of entrepreneurial individuals like Montoya: across Mexico both Spanish and indigenous kings were invoked in villages' primordial titles, which were systematically forged by indigenous communities.[57] 'It seems', James Lockhart reports,

> that somewhere in the orbit of Mexico City there existed what amounted to a factory or studio for false titles, where towns in need could have a document made to order, complete with pictures in a pseudo-sixteenth-century style, indigenous-style paper, and a final smoking to give the appearance of age . . . The antiquing process extended to the (often rather skeletal) texts themselves . . . the fabricators bent over backwards to use indigenous vocabulary.[58]

Forged titles were not, finally, restricted to out-of-the-way places in the countryside. In 1753 petitioners claiming descent from the last Mexica emperor, Cuauhtémoc, produced a royal grant signed by Philip II, dated 1523, which ceded those heirs extensive lands in the central Mexico City *barrio* of Tlatelolco. The *Audiencia de México* declared it false without too much trouble; Philip II had yet to be born in 1523.[59] Yet the faked Tlatelolco grant was not just ambitious; it was also an accurate reflection of the clout of both Spanish and indigenous royalty in text relics, instruments potentially more powerful than any other in Spain's litigious colonies.

Such relics endured well beyond the monarchy they represented (forged *retablos*, tin *ex votos* with deliberately naïve paintings and homilies, are easily found in the markets of modern Mexico City, while *títulos primordiales* have

---

[56] Rappaport and Cummins, 'Literacy and Power in Colonial Latin America', 95–6.

[57] Serge Gruzinski, *Le colonisation de l'imaginaire. Sociétés indigenes et occidentalisation dans le Mexique espagnol. XVIe –XVIIIe siècle* (Paris, 1988), 139–188.

[58] James Lockhart, *The Nahuas After the Conquest: A Social and Cultural History of the Indians of Central Mexico, Sixteenth Through Eighteenth Centuries* (Stanford, 1992), 413–15.

[59] Hector Pérez Martínez, *Cuauhtémoc: vida y muerte de una cultura* (Campeche, 1982), 261–3.

Fig. 2. 'We thank you little Virgin because this year there was good fishing. Lusio M.
1974'. Tin ex voto, La Lagunilla Market, Mexico City. Photograph courtesy of
Paul Gillingham

commonly been invoked in twentieth-century land disputes) (Fig. 2). Yet as
the colony receded into the past so forgers tended to eschew its symbols in
favour of new classes of relic forgery, namely the nationalist and the scientific.
Between *c.*1850 and *c.*1950 two social phenomena coincided in Latin
America: the rise of modern nationalism and the rise of modern archaeology.
The two were deeply interrelated. Some of the roots of archaeology in Latin
America were exogenous, as the United States and Europe found in lost
indigenous cities a focus for their own Rousseauian romanticism, and
indulged it by commodifying the cultures and pasts of the Other. As the
playwright Rodolfo Usigli put it to an American academic, 'You buy everything . . . the codices, the manuscripts, the incunabula, Mexico's

archaeological treasures; you'd buy Taxco, if you could only get it home'.[60] Yet archaeology also flourished for endogenous reasons: archaeologists provided many of the skeletons on which the flesh of a modern nation-state could hang. Ruins and artefacts bore witness to the antiquity and urbane sophistication of prehispanic culture, which lent Latin American nations legitimating identities. Bones—if they could just be found—would provide secular, nationalist relics to tie contemporary populations to would-be founding fathers. And when neither ruins, artefacts, nor bones were forthcoming, they could always be manufactured.

Before stratigraphy, before radiocarbon dating, before thermoluminescence or electron microscopy, before in fact the professionalization of archaeology or history, it was rather difficult to tell the difference between genuine and fake. A double illiteracy was at work: the long-term high incidence of quite literal illiteracy in Latin America, which strongly favoured fraud, and the more immediate cultural illiteracy of foreign consumers, which led them to buy into the systematic mass production of forged prehispanic artefacts.[61] The anthropologist Edward B. Tylor found the manufacture of sham antiquities to be 'a regular thing' in 1850s Mexico.[62] It was not just laymen, but also Tylor's colleagues who fuelled the business, falling victim 'so often . . . [to] money-making tricksters'.[63] Archaeological fraud became sufficiently widespread in the late nineteenth century that the 1878 world fair had a special section devoted to notable forgeries, while Mexico's National Museum dedicated an exhibit space to exposing fake prehispanic pottery, and the journal *Science* published articles warning of the vendors' sophistication.[64] Perhaps the most far-reaching frauds of all, however, were those aimed at the domestic market: the nationalist relics.

Some of these cases matched classic instrumentalist models, and were the products of elites at the very top of the state, backed by the cultural managers of a complicit academy. Such was the case of the relics of Mexico's *niños héroes*, the child heroes: six cadets believed to have been the last defenders of Mexico City against the United States Army in 1847, who fought with

---

[60] Through characters in his *meisterwerk*, *El gesticulador*. Rodolfo Usigli, *El Gesticulador* (México DF, 1985), 44–5.

[61] Holmes, 'Spurious Mexican Antiquities', 170; Ignacio Bernal, *A History of Mexican Archaeology* (London, 1980), 160–7.

[62] Cited in Walsh, 'What is Real?', 2. Walsh dates the expansion of the fraudulent antiquities market to the immediate post-Independence period.

[63] L. P. Gratacap, 'An Archaeological Fraud', *Science*, 8 (5 Nov. 1886), 403–4.

[64] Batres, *Antigüedades Mejicanas Falsificadas*, 5, 2; Gratacap, 'An Archaeological Fraud'; Holmes, 'The Trade in Spurious Mexican Antiquities'.

bayonets when their ammunition ran out, and who died one by one, until the last remaining cadet wrapped himself in the flag and jumped from the castle walls to his death. The story is magnificent but questionable. Only three of the six cadets are documented as having been in Chapultepec Castle at the time. The gesture of suicide rather than surrendering the flag was attributed to various soldiers before settling on Juan Escutia, a cadet of whom we know nothing, whose passage through the Colegio Militar left no trace whatsoever. American reports of the battle record Major Seymour of the Ninth Regiment as capturing the Mexican flag. Finally, and perhaps most suggestively of all, the first commemorations of the war dead failed to mention the six cadets.[65] The story as every Mexican now knows it, a central plank in the strongly sacrificial metanarrative of Mexican nationalism, is a late nineteenth-century invention. Yet it was long a cult without relics. In 1944 a General claimed to know where they were buried, and within five days soldiers had dug up the necessary six skeletons in Chapultepec forest.[66] There was, however, a problem: the remains came from a mass grave, which contained bodies of the numerous dead from both sides. Positive identification of the cadets was out of the question: on request, however, the National Institute of Archaeology and History produced a report concluding that the skeletons were of young males and might be those of the *niños héroes*.[67] The Secretary of Education—backed by a group of undistinguished 'official' historians—then converted conditional to definitive and pronounced them the *niños héroes*. Proof positive in hand, the government made extensive use of the remains in commemorating the invasion's centenary.[68]

Other nationalist relic forgeries are private initiatives, and non-elite private initiatives at that. Such was the case of Cuauhtémoc, the last Mexica emperor, whose tomb and relics were discovered in Ixcateopan, a remote village in Guerrero, in the late 1940s. This was a highly sophisticated three-part forgery, consisting of a tomb, concealed beneath the altar of the parish church; a legend, encoded in both colonial documents and contemporary diaries of the 'living letter', the villager who incarnated four centuries of secret memory; and an oral history, in which peasants reproduced signs to the tomb through rumours and customs such as the doffing of hats behind the church to salute

[65] E. Plasencia de la Parra, 'Conmemoración de la hazaña épica de los niños héroes: su origen, desarrollo y simbolismos', *Historia Mexicana*, 45 (1995), 247–50, 274; Ernesto Fritsche Aceves, 'Los Niños Héroes o el olvido', *Nexos*, 285 (2001), 78–80.

[66] Plasencia de la Parra, 'Conmemoración de la hazaña épica de los niños héroes', 264–7.

[67] *Excélsior*, 10 Sept. 1947.

[68] Author's interview, Salvador Rueda, (México DF, Oct.1995); Plasencia de la Parra, 'Conmemoración de la hazaña épica de los niños héroes', 267–8.

the king hidden within. It was also, to the disbelief of scholars, the creation of the 'living letter' himself, an autodidact rancher named Florentino Juárez. Juárez was a self-made man, literate, politically powerful, and in local terms wealthy, who found himself on the losing end of village politics in the early 1890s. Out of favour with the regional elite, he watched as they removed over half of the municipality that his faction ruled; the half containing, moreover, many of his properties. Small-scale absentee landowners were often forced to sell up cheap or lose their lands at this time; so driven by reasons affective, political, and materialist, Juárez led a vigorous campaign against municipal amputation. He wrote letters to the regional warlord and the bishop; he petitioned the state congress; and he forged Cuauhtémoc's tomb. It was a typical instance of instrumentalist nationalism in every way but one: the non-elite identity of its creator, who gave Mexicans who believed one of the greatest nationalist relics, and gave us a well-documented case of grassroots instrumentalism.[69]

Our final category of relic forgery, the scientific, is a further product of the global commodification of culture and the spread of archaeology, in part to satisfy that demand. Scientific relic forgeries might be defined as those that materialize objects of pronounced charisma, rooted in a claim to radically reshape scientific understandings of the world. These may be subdivided by the ambition—of both input and outcome—that fuels their creation. Some are relatively modest. The Calaveras skull, for example, was a purportedly Pliocene skull, dug out of a Californian mine in 1866 and presented to J. D. Whitney, Professor of Geology at Harvard. Whitney used it to posit a wholly original interpretation of the descent of man, whereby *homo sapiens* had emerged first, and far earlier than hitherto suspected, in the Americas.[70] Other scientific relic forgeries are medium-range, raising teasing questions about established narratives without taking the risk of establishing categorical counter-narratives of their own. Such are the 'Aztec crystal skulls', life-size rock crystal skulls owned by the Smithsonian (Fig. 3), the British Museum and the French *Musée de l'homme*. Genuinely startling objects, they were

[69] Paul Gillingham, 'The Emperor of Ixcateopan: Fraud, Nationalism and Memory in Modern Mexico', *Journal of Latin American Studies*, 37 (2005), 561–84. Another study of grassroots instrumentalism is afforded by Claudio Lomnitz's work on Tepotzlán; see, e.g., Lomnitz, 'Center, Periphery, and the Connections between Nationalism and Local Discourses of Distinction' in Lomnitz, *Deep Mexico, Silent Mexico. An Anthropology of Nationalism* (Minneapolis, 2001), 165–93.

[70] Ralph W. Dexter, 'Historical Aspects of the Calaveras Skull Controversy' in *American Antiquity*, 51 (1986), 365–9.

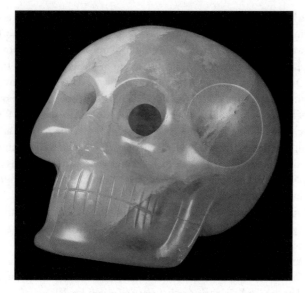

Fig. 3. 'Aztec' crystal skull, Smithsonian Institution, Washington DC. By permission of James DiLoreto, Smithsonian Institution

promoted as masterpieces of their culture, expressions of a technological ability beyond that of the twentieth century (which has proved fertile ground for a host of new age readings, ranging from the myth that the skulls, once reunited, will end the world, to the Indiana Jones story that they are the remnants of Prometheus-like aliens.)[71] In reality, Jane Walsh has convincingly posited a sophisticated, transnational, nineteenth-century origin. The rock crystal was Brazilian; the carvers German, from the declining lapidary centre of Idar-Oberstein; their salesman, the entrepreneurial Frenchman Eugène Boban.[72] The skulls constituted exemplary scientific relics. They were aesthetically powerful, they were worked from comparatively rare and valuable material, and they purported to recast quite fundamental opinions on the past, in this case the technological reach of indigenous societies.

[71] An idea promoted by, among others, one 'Illinois' Shapiro. Robert Todd Carroll, 'Crystal Skull' at http://skepdic.com/crystalskull.html.

[72] Having traced the skulls to Boban, the self-described 'antiquarian to the Emperor Maximilian', Walsh suggests this origin on the basis of Boban's reported claim that the skulls were German, and the efforts of Idar-Oberstein's carvers to stay afloat at the time by importing rock crystal from Brazil. Walsh, 'Crystal Skulls and Other Problems', 116–39.

The Aztec crystal skulls were not, however, the most messianic of scientific relic forgeries. At least two cases posit that man and dinosaur coexisted, disproving Darwin and the long chronology in favour of either divine or alien genesis, and consequently star on websites with names like 'creationresource.org', 'bibleandscience.com' or 'forbiddenarchaeology.com'. The first is the set of clay figurines collected by German émigré Waldemar Julsrud in Guanajuato, Mexico, in the 1940s. A huge collection of these—over 30,000— were sold to Julsrud by a family who claimed to have dug them up in a genuine Tarascan ruin. The figurines are not, however, classically Tarascan. They represent instead Brontosaurus, Tyrannosaurus Rex, and other well-known Mesozoic reptiles, interspersed with the odd Egyptian sarcophagus. Their message is clear: dinosaurs and (all sorts of) humans coexisted, throwing either archaeological or paleontological dating out of court.[73] The second, similarly themed fraud is that of the Ica stones: similarly anachronistic etchings, jumbling spaceships, kangaroos, dinosaurs, and Indians, on andesite rocks from the desert town of Ica in Peru. As in Acambaro, the site proved extraordinarily generous, yielding more than 15,000 of the stones between the 1960s and the early 1990s. Their collector, Dr. Javier Cabrera, interpreted them as the record of an extraterrestrial occupation of Earth, by the so-called Gliptolithic Man, who coexisted with the great reptiles and genetically engineered *homo sapiens* before jetting off from the nearby Nazca Lines spaceport.[74] Both of these scientific relic forgeries drew heavily on popular culture to challenge the elite consensus; both have done well in the age of the internet; both are eloquent of a substantial divide between academy and public, or of the predictable antagonism that Nora describes between the 'sacred context' of memory and the 'prose' of history.[75]

Why do people go to so much trouble to forge relics? It is difficult, as Michael Coe observes, to quantify systematically just how lucrative archaeological fraud actually was. Documents are confined to the odd gem such as the Robert Woods Bliss letters; annotated auction catalogues are comparatively rare before 1960, and even known auction prices must be treated with care due to mechanisms such as secret reserves. Isolated cases, though, give some idea of the incentives which brought forgers into production in such large numbers.[76] At the high end of the market Walsh has traced French dealer

---

[73] Charles C. Di Peso, 'The Clay Figurines of Acambaro, Guanajuato, Mexico', *American Antiquity*, 18:4 (Apr. 1953), 388–9.

[74] For more, see Javier Cabrera Darquea, *The Message of the Engraved Stones of Ica* (Ica, 2000).

[75] Nora, *Rethinking France*, 3.

[76] Coe, 'From Huaquero to Connoisseur', 288; Jones, 'Why Fakes?', 13.

Eugène Boban's repeated attempts to sell rock crystal skulls in Mexico, France, and New York. One crops up first—billed as 'a masterpiece of lapidary art', explicitly not included among the pre-Colombian artefacts—in a sales catalogue Boban published in 1881, where it is valued at 3,500 francs. The glass skull he attempted to pass off on Mexico's national museum in 1886 (in cahoots with Batres) was priced at $3,000; the crystal skull he managed to sell to Tiffany's of New York, which ended up in the British Museum, went for $950.[77] The Wari Forger, a restorer of Andean pottery with a profitable sideline in fakes, sold a single ceremonial urn to an American collector in 1943 for $5,000.[78] These were relatively large sums for their time. On the periphery, however, prices were low. William Henry Holmes of the Smithsonian found elaborate 'modern-antique' black pottery vases going at five dollars apiece at the railway station in Teotihuacán (Fig. 4).[79] In nearby Atzcaputzalco Scottish prospector and antiquities dealer William Niven was hoaxed by villagers who created, buried, and then dug up clay tablets, relics which he read as the remains of a forgotten culture (later popularized by Colonel Churchward as 'the Lost Continent of Mu'); a labour-intensive way of earning diggers' salaries.[80] Waldemar Julsrud in Acambaro only paid a peso for each figurine.[81] Brígido Lara, a brilliant modern forger of Totonac and Maya pottery, rarely made much more than a thousand pesos for his pieces, which his dealers sold on for tens of thousands of dollars, and which Sotheby's passed as authentic.[82] Forgers did not, generally, realize huge profits: why did they bother?

In cash-poor peripheral economies, however, even the promise of regular salaried employment can be significant, and a little cash will consequently buy a lot of fraud. The five dollars that Holmes was asked for his gaudily worked vase was the equivalent of some twenty days of a miner's wages, or a month's

---

[77] Walsh, 'Crystal Skulls and Other Problems', 124–9.

[78] Alan R. Sawyer, 'The Falsification of Ancient Peruvian Slip-decorated Ceramics' in Elizabeth H. Boone (ed.), *Falsifications and Misreconstructions of Pre-Columbian Art* (Dumbarton Oaks, 1982), 27.

[79] Holmes, 'The Trade in Spurious Mexican Antiquities', 171. Forged black pottery from the Chimu and Inca periods has recently grown plentiful in Peru. Robert Sonin, 'The Art Historian's Dilemma: With Remarks Upon the State of Art Falsification in the Central and North Andean Regions' in Boone (ed.), *Falsifications and Misreconstructions*, 3.

[80] Robert S. Wicks and Roland H. Harrison, *Buried Cities, Forgotten Gods: William Niven's Life of Discovery and Revolution in Mexico and the American Southwest* (Lubbock, 1999), 213–25, 237–40.

[81] Di Peso, 'The Clay Figurines of Acambaro, Guanajuato, Mexico', 389.

[82] Minerva Vacio, 'De falsificadores y reproductores: Brígido Lara, Inventor del nuevo arte prehispánico', *Arqueología Mexicana*, IV (1996), 56–61.

EXAMPLE OF MODERN-ANTIQUE MEXICAN VASE (HEIGHT, 11 IN.).

Fig. 4. 'Aztec' black pottery vase purchased by William Henry Holmes in Teotihuacán in the 1880s. Reprinted by permission of the American Association for the Advancement of Science from *Science*, 7:159 (19 Feb. 1886)

pay for a domestic servant, or up to a ton or so of maize.[83] Niven paid five pesos on his first contact with the people of Atzcaputzalco, to be shown 'the real source' of their terracotta finds; this was the equivalent of twenty days' wages for a field labourer at the time; and for years thereafter he gave the villagers rents for their fields and cash salaries, otherwise unobtainable, for their men. Julsrud may have paid over 30,000 pesos to the father and son who forged the Acambaro relics in the early 1940s. Mexican GDP per capita at the time was only 8,000 pesos, and this was moreover a sideline for the family of forgers, occupying the long winter days when their fields lay idle.[84] Forgers' price strategies need evaluating, in short, in terms of Purchasing Power Parity (PPP) rather than through the relatively low gains they made in metropolitan currencies, or by comparison to the large margins made by dealers.

Relic producers could, moreover, compensate for low margins with high volumes. Lara's earnings per fraud were comparatively low, but he turned them out in industrial quantities: some 3,000 Totonac sculptures and pots, at least 500 Olmec works, hundreds of Maya pieces.[85] Holmes estimated that his vendors shifted at least one piece per day, which for all their (possibly tactical) appearance of poverty would have placed them among the wealthiest of contemporary villagers (Fig. 5).[86] The Ica stones have attained the ultimate expression of global commodification, internet sales of reproductions at $75 each.[87] In Latin America, where economies traditionally relied on commodity extraction and export, forged relics have consequently constituted very successful commodities. There is sometimes little else to sell. Ica lies in the Atacama Desert, its people heirs to centuries of deforestation, one of its main modern industries consisting in further deforestation to produce black-market charcoal.[88] Rocky slopes and a remote location make Ixcateopan one of the poorest municipalities in one of the poorest states in Mexico.[89] Such places always had paltry natural resources, losing tickets in the commodity lottery. It was the genius of some of their inhabitants to realize that history,

---

[83] González y González, *El indio en la era liberal*, 408, 412; *Periódico Oficial del Gobierno del Estado de Guerrero*, XVII:64 (30 Sept. 1893).

[84] In 1940. INEGI, *Estadísticas históricas de México* CD–ROM (México DF, 2000); Di Peso, 'The Clay Figurines of Acambaro, Guanajuato, Mexico', 388.

[85] Vacio, 'Brígido Lara', 58.

[86] Holmes, 'The Trade in Spurious Mexican Antiquities', 171.

[87] At www.mtblanco.com, where staff are 'Digging up the facts of God's Creation: One fossil at a time'.

[88] Simon Romero, 'Ecosystem in Peru is Losing a Key Ally', *The New York Times* (7 Nov. 2009).

[89] Moisés T. de la Peña, *Guerrero Económico*, 2 vols (México DF, 1949), II: 612–14.

Fig. 5. The Barrios brothers' display moulds for forged prehispanic pottery in their Teotihuacán workshop: Leopoldo Batres, *Antigüedades Mejicanas Falsificadas: Falsificación y Falsificadores* (Mexico City, 1910). By permission of the Randall Library Special Collections, University of North Carolina, Wilmington

too, can be a natural resource; and, using that realization, to try and turn economic peripheries into symbolic centres.[90]

To do that these producers needed consumers, which raises a final question: why do people buy, in both literal and metaphorical terms, forged relics? There are three principal reasons. Forged relics are, to be sure, not advertised as such, although many consumers must have suspicions that they manage to quiet long enough to consume. Yet as Geary notes, dubious provenances often act counter-intuitively to help construct relics' value. Saints' relics too precious to obtain without theft and its corollary, clandestine dealing, were among the most sought-after medieval relics: a relic 'once stolen (or said to be stolen) was valuable because it had been worth stealing'.[91] Similar rationales add value to nationalist and scientific relics. Latin American states began to legislate export controls on artefacts from the late nineteenth century onwards, and consequently relics of evident high value—whether rarity or intrinsic—could often only be obtained by questionable means.

---

[90] For more on this idea and its limits see Arjun Appadurai, 'The Past as a Scarce Resource', *Man*, 16 (1981), 201–19.

[91] Geary, 'Sacred Commodities', 187.

Prominent dealers such as John Wise might return from Panama with a Veraguas gold eagle under their shirts. The Olmec jade mask in the American Museum of Natural History was smuggled out of Mexico under an eminent Harvard archaeologist's coat.[92] The self-fulfilling, closed logic of conspiracy theory, meanwhile, empowers scientific relics such as the Ica stones precisely on the grounds of the massed opposition of 'official' scholars. Such tautological reasoning only facilitates the forgers' work.

Second, consumers initially enter the market for relics, forged or authentic, in great part because of the power they lend their possessors. As we have seen, religious relics combined magical and very material power, attracting pilgrim donations, legitimizing communities, their lands, and their political sway. Monarchic relics, whether crowns or royal grants, lent owners second-hand divine right, with all the controls over humans and resources this implied. Nationalist and scientific relics could be sold directly in both domestic and increasingly global markets, or could prove profitable in more roundabout ways. The intense social practices that surround all classes of relics allowed owners to readily convert the symbolic capital of ownership into a wide range of economic and political rents. The Ica and Acambaro forgeries have both underpinned the creation of local museums, run, in at least one case, by the initial collector's family; the Rodríguez Juárez family, 'owners' of Cuauhtémoc's bones, asked the government to return their ancestral home, collected funds in the last emperor's name, pitched their story as a radio drama and installed several generations in local political office.[93] Closer to home, it takes no great imagination to hypothesize the benefits beyond aesthetic pleasure that prehispanic relics afford wealthy collectors, who in lending them to museums also extend lucrative business or political networks. To revert to Bourdieu's useful schema, relics offer both very concentrated and surprisingly liquid symbolic capital.

The final reason that people buy forged relics lies in the intricate relationship that links producers and consumers. Coe has described the social networks that conveyed archaeological frauds, alongside authentic artefacts, out of Latin America between the First World War and the 1960s. At their base were the diggers; these passed their finds on to 'runners', who traded to 'residents', long-term, often foreign, city-dwellers with legitimizing alternative careers; internationally mobile dealers then passed the objects to the dealers and museums who were the relics' end-users.[94] These are the links of a typical commodity chain, along which information and influence flows

---

[92] Coe, 'From Huaquero to Connoisseur', 284, 288.

[93] Gillingham, *Cuauhtémoc's Bones*, ch. 8.

[94] Coe, 'From Huaquero to Connoisseur', 273–7.

in both directions. Forgers produced a blend of what their history permitted and what the market demanded, and their market research influenced their creations in three areas. First, the design of the objects forged often followed prevailing western tastes and interests, and was fine-tuned by the feedback of art books, dealer opinions and even peer-reviewed journals.[95] Second, the materials chosen—at the top end of the market—were those offering the greatest intrinsic appeal, such as gold, silver, jade, or rock crystal; those most likely to elevate a forgery, such as the fake gold pendant of the emperor Tizoc, to uncontestable 'relichood', its possessor to the first rank of entrepreneurial aesthetes.[96] Third, the provenance stories of forgeries tended to combine realism with high romance—artefacts were often 'discovered' in the course of standard rural activities, such as ploughing or well-digging.[97] The consumer, in the end, was caught in an effective pincer movement. If an object fitted well with an established corpus of authentic relics, then its authenticity was easily assumed. And if it did not, if it seemed exceptional, then its rarity value could only increase its desirability as a unique masterpiece.

Forgery is a universal human pursuit, relatively commonplace even in scholarland. The renowned archaeologist Shinichi Fujimura salted his digs with stoneware to argue for sophisticated ceramic-producing cultures in the far Japanese past.[98] Professor Reiner Protsch von Zieten's discovery of a missing link between humans and Neanderthals proved to be his very own, Germanic, Piltdown Man.[99] In Latin America, though, relic forgery has been particularly widespread. Three of Mexico's central symbols of national identity, namely the last Aztec emperor Cuauhtémoc, the Virgin of Guadalupe and the *niños héroes*, have fake relics as their central signifiers. This is in part due to the democratic nature of Latin American relic forgery, as much a popular pursuit as it has ever been an elite enterprise. Many relics, from saints' skins to alien portraits, have been created by 'grassroots instrumentalists'—ranchers, peasants, itinerant mining speculators, indigenous communities, and backstreet antiquity vendors—who by inventing the material remains of the past also co-authored its narrative.

[95] Esther Pasztory, cited in Jane Walsh, 'What is Real? A new Look at PreColumbian Mesoamerican Collections' in *Anthronotes*, 26 (Spring, 2005), 6; Frederick Peterson, 'Faces That Are Really False' *Natural History* (Apr. 1953), 176–80.

[96] Walsh, 'What is Real?' 7, 17–18.

[97] Holmes, 'The Trade in Spurious Mexican Antiquities', 171.

[98] 'Archaeologist Exposed as Fraud', *BBC News Online* (5 Nov. 2000).

[99] Luke Harding, 'History of Modern Man Unravels as German Scholar is Exposed as Fraud', *The Guardian* (19 Feb. 2005).

Grassroots instrumentalists, like their elite counterparts, were quick to appreciate the tactical and economic possibilities of religious devotion or the prehispanic past, whose symbolic capital was readily convertible into economic capital. Some, like their elite counterparts, also held affective motives for their work.[100] It is impossible to believe otherwise in considering the life of Pedro de Bohorques, who led his Andean constituency in rebellion against Spain; or Florentino Juárez's lovingly faked Cuauhtémoc myth, with its emotive prose; or Brígido Lara's career, which took him from fraudulent genius to conservator of the prehispanic objects he clearly loved.[101] Yet primordialist interpretations of relic forgery can only be taken so far. While it clearly helps to have a taste for the work, it is extremely difficult to find materially disinterested relic fraud in Latin America. Of the cases we have surveyed, the Calaveras fraud is the only one with no evident pay-off; the entire creation was the practical joke of miners who disliked the aloof Professor Whitney.[102] It is all too easy, on the other hand, to trace the economic significance of these forgeries. Materializing memory by fraud was good, if strange, business; and as case studies from the Andes and Mexico demonstrate, it was a business open to entrepreneurs of all classes. The recent wave of forgeries discovered in leading museum collections evinces such entrepreneurs' lasting success.[103]

---

[100] Just as medieval relic promoters could hold genuine beliefs in their power at the same time as they tactically constructed their value. Geary, 'Sacred Commodities', 181.

[101] Miller, 'The Fake Inca of Tucumán', 202–6; Silvio Zavala, 'Dictamen acerca de los hallazgos de Ichcateopan', *Revista Mexicana de Estudios Antropológicos*, II (1950), 258–91; Vacio, 'De falsificadores y reproductores'.

[102] And without ethnographic detail, it is difficult to say that the ringleader of the jokers did not gain significant prestige, with all its associated benefits. Dexter, 'The Calaveras Skull Controversy', 365–9.

[103] Walsh, 'What is Real?'.

The Several Legs of Santa Anna: A Saga of Secular Relics

Alan Knight

When it comes to relics, sacred and secular, Latin America seems a promising field. It is the largest Roman Catholic bloc in the world; moreover, those processes—such as nationalism and state-building—which tend to spawn secular relics have a longer history in Latin America than in most places. Catholicism had a 1500-year head-start in Europe, but in Latin America it faced no iconoclastic Reformation, hence the region's rich heritage of 'baroque' religion: the cult of the saints, shrines, pilgrimages, *cofradías*, and *ex-votos*.[1] Indeed, the cult of the saints, derived from Spain, but hybridized by its contact with pre-Columbian religion, was stronger in Latin America than in Europe, since clerical and papal control was weaker.[2] Regarding relics, Latin America was short on originals. Old relics arrived sporadically—like the bone of St Felix, sent as a gift by Pope Urban VIII to the infant town of Atlixco (Mexico);[3] but, compared to Europe, Latin America's arsenal of relics was neither extensive nor ancient. By far the most potent Catholic symbol, certainly in Mexico, has been the 'brown' Virgin of Guadalupe whose appeal, evident on altars, flags, placards, badges, T-shirts and windscreens, is ubiquitous. But these images are not relics, since they claim no direct material link to the Virgin herself. The cult does possess a 'secondary' relic: the *tilma* (cotton cloak) on which the Virgin's image was imprinted—a sort of Mexican Turin shroud.[4] But, despite the strength of Marianism in Mexico, there are no

---

[1] William B. Taylor, *Magistrates of the Sacred: Priests and Parishioners in Eighteenth-Century Mexico* (Stanford, 1996); Terry Rugely, *Of Wonders and Wise Men. Religion and Popular Cultures in Southeast Mexico, 1800–76* (Austin, 2001).

[2] William Christian, *Local Religion in Sixteenth-Century Spain* (Princeton, 1981); Pierre Ragon, 'Los santos patronos de las ciudades del México central (siglos XVI y XVII)', *Historia Mexicana*, 52/2 (2002), 383.

[3] Ragon, 'Los santos patronos', 378.

[4] A primary relic consists of a part of a saint, such as St Felix's bone; a secondary relic is something which had contact with a saint, such as 'dust or lamp oil or candle wax from their tombs': Valerie Flint, *The Rise of Magic in Early Medieval Europe* (Oxford, 1998),

major relics claiming a closer affinity with the Virgin; nor is this surprising, if we consider European precedent.[5] Indeed, it may be that Marianism was strong in Mexico, as it was in some parts of Europe, precisely because indigenous saints and relics were rare.[6]

Eventually, Latin America produced its own saints but, compared to Europe, very few martyrs; hence they usually lacked the cachet of a gruesome death. (How important is the blood-and-guts of martyrdom when it comes to investing relics with power and appeal? Intuitively, there seems to be a link.) Mexican images of martyrdom abound, but they depict distant 'foreign' scenes, like St Laurence being griddled, or St Sebastian being shot full of arrows. Many Mexican churches contain the corporeal remains of worthy prelates, but most are post-1800 and, usually, they died with their boots on. After the Mexican Revolution of 1910 church-state conflict produced a fresh crop of Catholic (usually 'Cristero') martyrs, whom Pope John Paul II, the greatest of papal saint-makers, set about beatifying and sanctifying. The most celebrated was Father Pro, executed in 1927, whose tomb soon attracted 'sick pilgrims', seeking 'candle stubs and droplets of holy oil'; and, as 'these minute traces of sacrality scattered like pollen across the land', so miracles began to occur.[7] Thus, by an odd chronological inversion, Mexico's martyr-saints are

---

183. Some sources also refer to tertiary relics. Thus, spiritual power somehow correlates with proximity to the saint. As an 'old Indian' told a traveller who visited the shrine of Chalma, famous for its image of Christ, in 1926, 'the real saint [*sic*] is buried under the altar': Todd Downing, *The Mexican Earth* (Norman, Okla., 1996 [1940]), 302. The presence of a body—of a primary relic, over and above the image—was therefore important. At the lowest level we find, in Mexico, amulets which resemble relics in their utility, but which lacked saintly contact: an 'ill-mannered Spaniard' explained to the Inquisition that the 'small bag of bones' he regularly carried on his person had been stolen from a cemetery, since 'everyone knows [that] human bones prevent fatigue': Pamela Voekel, *Alone Before God: The Religious Origins of Modernity in Mexico* (Durham, 2002), 209.

[5] In Europe, primary relics of the Virgin Mary were rare: Diarmaid MacCullough, *Reformation. Europe's House Divided, 1490–1700* (London, 2004), 18, states that there were none, although Flint, *The Rise of Magic*, 304, refers to Charlemagne having a hair of the Virgin.

[6] 'Marian shrines were common throughout Europe, *particularly in regions which had bred few native saints*': MacCullough, *Reformation*, 18 (my emphasis).

[7] Matthew Butler, 'Trouble Afoot? Pilgrimage in Cristero Mexico City', in Matthew Butler (ed.), *Faith and Impiety in Revolutionary Mexico* (Basingstoke, 2007), 158–9, which also mentions the (secular) Cristero martyr Juan Tirado, similarly executed, and soon a producer of miracles. Of Father Pro's four cited 'miracles', one clearly fits the bill: a blind child healed. But the three others—involving a reformed thief, drunk, and adulterer—do not seem to constitute 'miracles' (supernatural intervention in the

of recent vintage. As I also note in conclusion, new visionaries and saints (but not martyrs) continue to spring up, spawning cults which, in Darwinian fashion, struggle to survive and reproduce, some successfully.[8]

José Antonio López de Santa Anna was, despite his name, no saint. As a charitable acquaintance put it, he had 'a great many faults and some vices, both as a public and private man'.[9] He—and his several legs—enter our discussion in the guise of secular heroes and relics, within the context of baroque Catholic culture. Historical 'heroes' are ten-a-penny, but some have a distinct 'reliquary' association: a material object which carries their imprint or, better, is a surviving bit of the heroic body, if not the whole thing. Again, there are plenty of Latin American examples. Some involve exiles' bodies: San Martín may still languish in Boulogne and Porfirio Díaz in Montparnasse, Paris;[10] but the embalmed body of Eva Perón was, after a long cloak-and-dagger history, returned from Madrid to be buried in downtown Buenos Aires.[11] In Mexico, where 'the dead are still a force in politics',[12] bodies have been regularly moved about according to political fashion. Over time, the massive Monument of the Revolution acquired the mortal remains of the heroes of the Mexican Revolution, 'each entombment [being] . . . the occasion for a massive popular tribute', the most recent being the re-interment of the partial body of Pancho Villa in 1976.[13] Likewise the heroes of independence: Miguel Hidalgo, whose head had rotted in a cage on the walls of the Guanajuato granary for a decade, was finally laid to rest in a crypt under the Column of Independence, alongside his ally José María Morelos (both, as it happens, patriot-priests).[14] Even more redolent of

---

normal working of the laws of nature) but rather 'born-again' phenomena, of the kind President Bush supposedly experienced. Perhaps the miraculousness of the event is proportional to the incorrigibility of the sinner.

[8] Edward Wright-Rios, *Revolutions in Mexican Catholicism: Reform and Revelation in Oaxaca, 1870–1934* (Durham, 2009).

[9] Waddy Thompson, *Recollections of Mexico* (New York, 1846), 80–1.

[10] David Merchant and Paul Rich, 'A Policy toward the Dead: Repatriating Controversial Political Leaders', *Review of Policy Research*, 21 (2004), 129–35.

[11] Nicholas Fraser and Marysa Navarro, *Eva Perón* (New York,1980), 168–92.

[12] Merchant and Rich, 'A Policy toward the Dead', 131.

[13] Thomas Benjamin, *La Revolución. Mexico's Great Revolution as Memory, Myth and History* (Austin, 2000), 134. Villa's body was 'partial' because, three years after his assassination and burial in 1923, his body was clandestinely dug up and the head removed: Friedrich Katz, *The Life and Tmes of Pancho Villa* (Stanford, 1998), 789–90.

[14] Hugh M. Hamill, *The Hidalgo Revolt* (Gainesville, 1966), 216; Benjamin, *La Revolución*, 122. Similarly, Vicente Guerrero, the first elected president of the independent Republic,

religion is the trade in heroic body parts. Apart from Santa Anna's leg(s), we could cite Alvaro Obregón's arm (blown off at the battle of Trinidad in 1915, then pickled in alcohol and placed in the Monument to the Revolution); or Pancho Villa's head, stolen from his grave in 1926 and, despite several rumoured finds, still lost to posterity.[15]

Of course, lumping together sacred and secular relics may be spurious; perhaps Obregón's pickled arm and the withered arm of St Simeon Stylites have nothing in common apart from their anatomy. Some scholars, however, have assumed a closer kinship, at least regarding function: sacred and secular relics share a common purpose, inspiring veneration, promoting solidarity, providing solace, even working 'miracles' (at which point the sacred/secular distinction dissolves).[16] Latin America's Catholic heritage perhaps favoured secular practices which cannibalized religion: secular heroes struck Christlike poses; political cults emulated their saintly predecessors; Catholic ritual was replicated in secular ceremony.[17] Does the story of Santa Anna's legs—or Obregón's arm or Villa's head—reflect an enduring brand of Catholic and corporeal imagery, transposed from a sacred to a secular context? I shall first tell the story, then reflect on its significance.

Making a relic

Santa Anna, born in 1794, was eleven times president of Mexico between 1833 and 1855. He was the central figure in Mexico's turbulent post-independence politics; historians have called this 'the age of Santa Anna', when Mexico was 'the country of a single man', and Santa Anna was 'the product and

---

having been treacherously 'executed' down on the Pacific coast of Oaxaca in 1831 was 'exhumed and buried in the cathedral [of the City of Oaxaca] following an elaborate procession and funeral' some two years later: Peter F. Guardino, *The Time of Liberty: Popular Political Culture in Oaxaca, 1750–1850* (Durham, 2005), 207.

[15] Jürgen Buchenau, 'The Arm and Body of a Revolutionary: Remembering Mexico's Last Caudillo, Alvaro Obregón', in Johnson (ed.), *Death, Dismemberment and Memory*, 179–206. Obregón's arm, much deteriorated, was finally taken back to his home state of Sonora for burial in the 1980s: an interesting reversal of secular-relic-centralization which, perhaps, was linked to the decline of the revolutionary myth/project and the reassertion of state (i.e., provincial) identity during that decade.

[16] Miracles being 'violations of the laws of nature' (Hume), events 'contrary to the order of nature' (Spinoza) or 'outside the order of nature' (Aquinas): John Earman, *Hume's Abject Failure. The Argument Against Miracles* (Oxford, 2000), 8–9.

[17] Alan Knight, 'Popular Culture and the Revolutionary State in Mexico, 1910–40', *Hispanic American Historical Review*, 74 (1994), 406–13.

personification of the period'.[18] Contemporaries drew comparisons with mythical and world-historical heroes: Hercules, Hannibal, Cincinnatus, Caesar, Nero, Attila, Cortés, Cromwell, and—the most common, Santa Anna's preferred comparison—Napoleon.[19] He first made his name as a royalist officer in the Mexican War of Independence (1810–21). Bold, brave, impetuous, fond of gambling and cockfights, willing to engage in harsh repression and occasional embezzlement, he belatedly switched sides and joined the insurgents on the eve of Independence (1821). With the defeat of the Crown, Mexico acquired a new fluid political system in which the norms of government remained uncertain, experimental and contested. The early republic suffered from factional strife, regional tension, fiscal fragility, and praetorian intervention. At the same time there were serious political debates, genuine popular participation, and meaningful elections, initially based on manhood suffrage. Crucially for Santa Anna's career, Mexico was also vulnerable to foreign aggressors: a revanchist Spain, a belligerent France and—the biggest threat—an expansionist United States. Santa Anna won his major laurels fighting the Spaniards at Tampico in 1829; he lost his leg to the French in the 'Pastry War' of 1838; and he lost another leg to the American invaders in 1847. These encounters built the Santa Anna myth and, perhaps, turned his leg, sacrificed for the country, into a form of secular relic, a symbol of Mexican heroism and nationalism.

In 1829, a Spanish invasion force landed near the Mexican Gulf port of Tampico.[20] Down the coast at Veracruz, Santa Anna rang the church bells, patriotically harangued the people, and headed north with a force of some 2,000. After sporadic fighting, the Spanish commander agreed to terms and was allowed to sail away with his army, their numbers thinned by the diseases of the hot lowlands. The encounter, though small-scale, scuppered hopes of a revived colonialism and guaranteed Mexican independence. Santa Anna became a national hero. When a weary courier brought the news to Mexico

---

[18] Enrique González Pedrero, *País de un sólo hombre: El México de Santa Anna*, 2 vols (Mexico City, 1993); Ruth R. Olivera and Liliane Crété, *Life in Mexico Under Santa Anna, 1822–55* (Norman, Okla., 1991), xi.

[19] Fernando Díaz Díaz, *Caudillos y caciques. Antonio López de Santa Anna y Juan Alvarez* (Mexico City, 1972), 138, 153, 202; Madame Calderón de la Barca, *Life in Mexico* (London, n.d., [1843]), 32; Carmen Vázquez Montecón, *Santa Anna y la encrucijada del Estado y la dictadura* (Mexico City, 1986), 59; Will Fowler, *Santa Anna of Mexico* (Lincoln, Nebr., 2007), 116, 119, 142, 179. I return to the Napoleonic parallel below.

[20] What follows is taken from: Wilfrid Hardy Calcott, *Santa Anna. The Story of an Enigma Who Once Was Mexico* (Hamden, Conn., 1964 [1936]), 71–8; Fowler, *Santa Anna*, 120–4; and Antonio López de Santa Anna, *Mi historia militar y política, 1810–1874* (Mexico, 1905), 20–5.

City's Teatro Principal, where President Guerrero was present, 'pandemonium broke out and the production was stopped as the hysterical crowd rushed out to carry the news to the city'.[21] Santa Anna was promoted to General; Congress declared him *benemérito de la patria*; and state legislatures voted him commemorative swords and medals. At Veracruz, he was carried by a jubilant crowd to the cathedral where a *Te Deum* was sung, to be followed by a lavish ball. The captured Spanish flags were displayed from a balcony of the National palace and a monument was erected at Tampico, now renamed 'Santa Anna de Tamaulipas'.[22]

Having thus made his name, Santa Anna would capitalize on his patriotic credentials for years to come; and Mexicans would, repeatedly and rather puzzlingly, call upon him at moments of national crisis for decades to come.[23] The first such crisis—the Texas rebellion of 1835–6—can be briefly treated. When Texas declared its independence in 1835, Santa Anna marched north, crushed the rebels at the Alamo, then suffered an ignominious defeat at San Jacinto, after which he narrowly escaped execution. It was 'the most humiliating moment of his career'.[24] Defeat in Texas stripped him of the laurels won at Tampico; and his barbaric treatment of prisoners-of-war earned him the enduring hatred of the Texans. His politico-military career seemed to be guttering out. His leg would help revive it.

The second crisis occurred in 1838. During the 1830s Mexico became more unstable; liberal federalism lost ground to conservative centralism (Santa Anna went with the flow); and foreign interests suffered, as debts went unpaid, property was seized, and foreign residents experienced violence. One victim was a French pastry cook whose bakery was destroyed by 'roistering Mexican soldiers'.[25] The French government inflated the claim and, when the cash-strapped Mexican government refused to pay, a French fleet blockaded the Gulf coast and bombarded the port of Veracruz. Santa Anna, then enjoying one of his many political sabbaticals on his nearby hacienda, rode down to the coast to take command. In the small hours of 4–5 December 1838, a French landing force, led by the Prince de Joinville,

[21] Calcott, *Santa Anna*, 76.

[22] Ibid., 77.

[23] Shannon Baker, 'Antonio López de Santa Ana's Search for Personalized Nationalism', in Samuel Brunk and Ben Fallaw (eds), *Heroes and Hero Cults in Latin America* (Austin, 2006), 62–4.

[24] Michael P. Costeloe, *The Central Republic in Mexico, 1835–46. Hombres de Bien in the Age of Santa Anna* (Cambridge, 1993), 50. Fowler, *Santa Anna*, ch. 8, tells the Texas story, with an eye to balancing the record in Santa Anna's favour.

[25] Calcott, *Santa Anna*, 155; Costeloe, *The Central Republic*, 144.

King Louis-Philippe's son, attacked the port.[26] Awoken by the blast of a petard against the city gates, Santa Anna fled, half-dressed, through the French lines to the outskirts of town. He regrouped his forces and led a counter-attack. The French, at this point, were disembarking;[27] but they covered their retreat with artillery fire and, as Santa Anna advanced at the head of his men (which was his usual practice: he did not lack valour), he was struck by grapeshot. Santa Anna's horse was killed outright, his left leg was seriously wounded, and the French escaped.

Such wounds were usually fatal. The five doctors who attended decided that the leg could not be saved, gangrene might set in, and they must amputate. Santa Anna composed a grandiloquent account of the action, exaggerating its significance, while prophesying his imminent demise: 'I was wounded ... and probably this will be the last victory that I shall offer my native land'.[28] Distributed as a broadsheet, Santa Anna's premature auto-obituary was read 'in the drawing rooms, cafes and plazas' of Mexico City, where tearful citizens raised up prayers for the stricken national hero. The stain of San Jacinto was washed away 'and enthusiasm for the Hero of Tampico was reborn'.[29] Of course, Santa Anna did not die. The doctors saved his life, but botched the amputation, failing to seal the stump with sufficient skin and leaving two inches of bone protruding.[30] As an amputee, Santa Anna suffered recurrent pain and, at times of exertion, the wound was liable to open up.[31] This, perhaps, contributed to his melancholic countenance; he had an air of

---

[26] Costeloe, *The Central Republic*, 146–7; Fowler, *Santa Anna*, 188–9. While the French Admiral Baudin claimed that, in landing troops, he sought simply 'the disarming of the forts', the British Minister to Mexico reported that 'it is notorious that one [French] party marched directly into the town with no other object than that of capturing the person of General Santa Anna': Ashburnham to FO, 21 Jan. 1839, FO 50/122A.

[27] Santa Anna, *Mi historia*, 48, claims that he drove the French into the sea and Fowler, *Santa Anna*, 188–9, seems to credit him (asking why, if they entered Veracruz in the first place, the French then evacuated the port, if not because of Santa Anna's onslaught). Two plausible answers are available (see previous footnote).

[28] Calcott, *Santa Anna*, 158; Costeloe, *The Central Republic*, 147; Díaz Díaz, *Caudillos y caciques*, 145.

[29] Calcott, *Santa Anna*, 160; Díaz Díaz, *Caudillos y caciques*, 145–6, 148; Costeloe, *The Central Republic*, 154, which observes 'not a word was now said about Texas'.

[30] Oakah L. Jones, *Santa Anna* (New York, 1968), 79; Brantz Mayer, *Mexico As It Was and As It Is* (New York, 1844), 71.

[31] At the Battle of Buena Vista in 1847, when Santa Anna's horse was shot from under him, the fall 'caused the wound on his mutilated leg to open up again': Fowler, *Santa Anna*, 262.

'placid sadness' which gave way to a more 'startling' expression, 'especially when he spoke of his leg', which he did 'frequently'.[32]

Now, a prosthesis was needed, and Santa Anna soon acquired several (though there were two basic models). Usually, a careful eye-witness noted, 'he stumps (*sic*) along on an old-fashioned wooden peg', which he preferred to several 'mock legs', complete with 'patent springs and self-moving inventions, which have been presented to him by his flatterers from all parts of the world'.[33] Two such 'mock legs' were purchased from the specialist prosthetics company of Charles Bartlett of New York for the whopping price of $1,300 in silver (so this was no present), which Bartlett (who, as far as we know, was no flatterer) melted down and turned into a set of spoons.[34] We will encounter these legs again. Meanwhile, however costly or painful, the loss of the (corporeal) leg proved politically invaluable: 'this loss', an observer noted, 'was a gain to the daring chieftain . . . well-worded proclamations and a discreet use of the amputated limb . . . have served to restore him to the authority he so ingloriously lost in 1836'.[35]

After a brief recuperation at his hacienda, Santa Anna travelled by mule-drawn litter to a jubilant Mexico City, where he received a 'rapturous' welcome, not least from an 'enthusiastic rabble'.[36] President Bustamante, distracted by rebellion, named him provisional president. But the daily grind of politics never appealed to Santa Anna. Though said to be too weak to take the presidential oath in person, he rose from his sickbed, returned to his litter, and confronted a rebel army at Puebla. The city was saved; the rebels were defeated; and Santa Anna ordered the summary execution of the rebel general. On his return to the capital, he was again feted as a conquering hero, with cannon fire, fireworks, and pealing of church bells. And, again, 'a swarming yelling mob filled the streets', while the Mexican elite voted Santa Anna a

---

[32] Calderón de la Barca, *Life in Mexico*, 33. Note also Costeloe, *The Central Republic*, 186 on Santa Anna's 'resigned and rather melancholy' expression; and, an eye-witness account, his 'bilious temperament' and the set of his mouth which, 'when at rest, is that of mingled pain and anxiety': Mayer, *Mexico As It Was*, 73.

[33] Mayer, *Mexico As It Was*, 73. Jones, *Santa Anna*, 88, following Calderón de la Barca, *Life in Mexico*, 455, has the legs correctly sorted: an 'unadorned wooden leg', commonly used, and 'a more handsome one, fitted with an attractive boot, for more stately occasions and whenever he reviewed the troops'.

[34] James Bowman, Illinois Central College New Release, 14 Jan. 1968; Lauren R. Pacini to Harold Patton, 29 April 1996: Illinois State Military Museum Archive, Camp Springfield, Illinois, US, Box 1402, General Reference, Leg, Artificial, Santa Anna. Further references to this archive will be given as ISMMA.

[35] Mayer, *Mexico As It Was*, 340. One might query 'discreet'.

[36] Fowler, *Santa Anna*, 194; Calcott, *Santa Anna*, 161; Costeloe, *The Central Republic*, 151.

lavish jewelled plaque.[37] After basking briefly in triumph (and, his critics alleged, making off with a million pesos from the national treasury), Santa Anna again quit politics for rest and recreation at his favourite hacienda.[38] Personal preferences aside—he liked gaming and cockfights better than wrestling with the nation's intractable finances—Santa Anna saw that his popularity was best served by sporadic deeds of derring-do, which reinforced his role as a national hero in moments of crisis, and would be eroded by the daily graft of politics ('graft' in both senses).

Such a crisis occurred in 1841, when revolt again threatened to topple the government. Santa Anna prevaricated, joined the rebels, and was (again) named provisional president. Inaugurated amid the usual noisy ritual, Santa Anna now had to make a fist of government. He set up a centralist administration, packed with cronies and flatterers, which governed busily, introducing a controversial currency reform and planning the re-conquest of Texas.[39] Santanista ritual now became elaborate, systematic and personalist; indeed, as the government's fortunes declined, and a combative liberal Congress confronted the executive, ritual became an antidote to mounting unpopularity. Portraits of Santa Anna proliferated; the Gran Teatro de Santa Anna was inaugurated; at least two statues were erected in the capital—one, in the Plaza del Volador, pointing prophetically towards Texas (so it was said. Critics noted that the presidential finger was really indicating the National Mint).[40] When Santa Anna's wife fell gravely ill, a huge procession—20,000 people, carrying 8,000 candles—paraded through the capital, headed by the Archbishop of Mexico and other dignitaries.[41] Such quasi-regal displays reinforced rumours that Santa Anna was considering

---

[37] Calcott, *Santa Anna*, 163–4; Jones, *Santa Anna*, 80–1.

[38] On Santa Anna's landed empire in Veracruz, centred on Manga de Clavo ('Clove Spike') see Fowler, *Santa Anna*, 86–7, 89–90. This territorial base afforded him not only a safe and comfortable retreat, but also a stream of income and a body of loyal *jarocho* (Veracruzano) retainers who could campaign in the hot morbiferous lowlands. They were bound to their leader by strong and enduring ties, personal and clientelist, which contrasted with the weak and ephemeral 'charismatic' bond which, perhaps, linked Sana Anna to a broader but fickle popular following (as I note in conclusion).

[39] Mayer, *Mexico As It Was*, 344–5; Thompson, *Recollections of Mexico*, 86; Costeloe, *The Central Republic*, 189–95.

[40] Fowler, *Santa Anna*, 224; Díaz Díaz, *Caudillos y caciques*, 166–7; Jones, *Santa Anna*, 87.

[41] Thompson, *Recollections of Mexico*, 102; Fowler, *Santa Anna*, 228. When Doña Inés, having survived this illness, finally died in August 1844, her widower remarried - with a 15 year-old girl - inside six weeks; this 'utter disregard for the social conventions of mourning was looked on with distaste, if not disgust, by the society of the capital'. Costeloe, *The Central Republic*, 241–2.

crowning himself king.[42] On the anniversary of his victory at Tampico (11 September), a massive military parade of over 4,000 men marched to the National Palace, where, amid flowers and mirrors, chandeliers and velvet curtains, the President held court, surrounded by officers, flunkeys, and portraits of Napoleon.[43]

The conversation also turned to Napoleon, and how Santa Anna, at Tampico, had encountered 'the same good fortune which Napoleon enjoyed when he happily disembarked in Egypt', which observation 'filled him [Santa Anna] with inexplicable satisfaction' and prompted the President to mention the inscription which, in Spanish, Latin, English, and French, would adorn the newly built monument to his leg, about to be inaugurated in Mexico City.[44] And, two weeks later, on the anniversary of Mexican independence (27 September), Santa Anna attended a lavish ceremony, at which his amputated leg, brought up from Veracruz, was ceremoniously interred in the Santa Paula cemetery in Mexico City. The chosen orator, contemplating the 'holy and terrible place where we find ourselves' (that is, the cemetery), hailed the 'mutilated remains of an illustrious caudillo of Independence and Liberty' (later, the same remains were deemed 'adorable') and, mixing classical, literary, and historical allusions (Milton, Marathon, Plataea, Thermopylae, Xerxes, Leonidas, Carnot, Turenne, and *dulce et decorum est pro patria mori*), paid tribute to the 'thousand times fortunate General Santa Anna' who, 'with the blood he spilled for his country, could purchase the love of all Mexicans and merit those civic crowns which, unlike the diadems of kings, do not burn the brow'.[45] Napoleon, 'the foremost captain of the century', made another rhetorical appearance, since his compatriots ('a great and powerful nation') had been humbled by Santa Anna; a bouquet was tossed

[42] Costeloe, *The Central Republic*, 205, 209.

[43] These quasi-imperial proceedings provoked the republican censure of observers like the American Brantz Mayer, *Mexico As It Was*, 71–2, 74. Mayer also notes the Napoleonic pictures, which formed part of a stylistic pattern: the preferred white horse; the back-to-front hair-style; and Santa Anna's tendency to draw parallels between his own life and Bonaparte's: Jones, *Santa Anna*, 24, 94.

[44] Carlos María de Bustamante, *Diario histórico de México*, 11 Sept. 1842 (this and other Bustamante citations are taken from the CD Rom compiled by CIESAS, the Colegio de México and INAOE, under the coordination of Josefina Zoraida Vázquez and Héctor Cuauhtémoc Hernández Silva, in 2003. Given its format, I am citing by dates, not page numbers).

[45] 'Discurso que . . . pronunció en el Panteón de Santa Paula el Ciudadano Ignacio Sierra y Rosso', in Bustamante, *Diario histórico de México*, anexos, November 1842. See also *El Siglo XIX*, 2 Oct. 1842 (for a restrained account, the paper being opposed to the Santa Anna government).

to the 'valiant veterans' of 1838; and the younger generation was enjoined to contemplate the monument with 'the fire of a sacred enthusiasm (*entusiasmo santo*)'.[46] The leg (or foot), carried in a glass case 'like a saint's relics', was placed in a funerary urn and buried beneath a 'magnificent monument': a column, complete with cannon, surmounted by the Mexican national symbol, an eagle grasping a snake.[47] It soon became a site of 'veneration' and 'pilgrimages'; although, of those who came, 'some were moved by devotion, others by curiosity'.[48] Where devotion led, commerce soon followed: entrepreneurial street-people—'our smart canaille'—soon began hawking hand carved models of the Santa Anna monument.[49]

However, the cult of Santa Anna coincided with mounting unpopularity: the withdrawal of copper coinage provoked popular protests; the recovery of Texas stalled; the government's chronic insolvency could not be remedied, even by unpopular tax hikes and confiscations of church property; and stories of official corruption gathered strength, while the legislature berated a beleaguered executive.[50] Mounting opposition was often expressed informally but openly ('in the most public places'), by means of flyers, cartoons, graffiti, and songs. At the San Agustín fair, the crowd applauded when the president's fighting cocks lost, while the solemn interment of his leg inspired scurrilous verse, which included a collective poetic protest to Congress on behalf of the corpses in the Santa Paula cemetery:

> Even the tiniest bone / of all the dead / here in Santa Paula together / beg the Congess / to reprove the excess / of whoever, out of adulation / seeks to disturb the sepulchral mansion / wishing to put here / the big bone of Santa Anna.[51]

This intruder—this 'pestilential foot'—will only 'disturb the sleep of the peaceful grave' (say the bones): 'for it is in the nature of a thing to resemble

---

[46] 'Discurso . . . Sierra y Rosso', in Bustamante, *Diario histórico*.

[47] Calcott, *Santa Anna*, 224. Mayer, *Mexico As It Was*, 207, refers to a 'crystal vase'. Although the limb is usually referred to, in English, as a 'leg', the Spanish sources usually prefer 'pie' (foot) or—critics especially—just 'hueso' (bone). See also 'Discurso . . . Sierra y Rosso', in Bustamante, *Diario histórico*; and *Siglo XIX*, 28 Sept. 1842, 2 Oct. 1842, which refers to the leg being lodged in a 'small box' (*pequeña caja*).

[48] Fowler, *Santa Anna*, xxii; Bustamante, *Diario histórico*, 1 Nov. 1842.

[49] 'Nuestros habilísimos léperos': Bustamante, *Diario histórico*, 1 Nov. 1842.

[50] Costeloe, *The Central Republic*, 193–4; Fowler, *Santa Anna*, 236; Calcott, *Santa Anna*, 177.

[51] Calcott, *Santa Anna*, 185; Bustamante, *Diario histórico*, 1 Nov. 1842.

its owner' and, being a 'chip off the old block', it will be a troublemaker, a war-monger, who will subvert the calm of the grave, making a mockery of the old injunction: *'requiescat in pace'*.

The bones did not lie. Santa Anna's rule became more despotic and unpopular, his absences from the capital more capricious. Even his closest cronies complained, while the British Minster, sympathetic to Santa Anna, reported the 'greatest dissatisfaction' with the government and the president's 'total disregard for public opinion'.[52] Congress was forcibly closed, while opportunist generals sniffed the wind and scouted opportunities for personal revenge and promotion.[53] In December, a virtually bloodless rebellion broke out in Mexico City. The garrison mutinied, Congress reconvened, while the city 'mob' took to the streets. Like most 'mobs', this one had clear targets. The new statue of Santa Anna in the Plaza del Volador was torn down; the Santa Anna theatre 'was broken into and badly abused'.[54] To cries of 'death to the cripple', 'kill the lame bastard' and—rather more politically correct—'long live Congress', the rioters made their way to the cemetery and disinterred the leg, after which it was 'dragged through the streets by a howling mob'.[55] Its ultimate fate remains unclear: one account says the leg was 'profaned and burned'; another than it 'was dragged about the streets till at last the bone was rescued by an officer and conveyed to a secure place'.[56] As we shall see, it did—perhaps—reappear thirty years later.

Revolt spread. Even in Santa Anna's home state of Veracruz, the mob seized an official portrait of the President, which was then 'publicly outraged and burnt in the plaza'.[57] The veracruzanos had no leg (no 'primary relic') to desecrate, so they made do with a representational icon. Thus reviled, Santa Anna decided to quit. Though his leg was lost, he could still squeeze some

---

[52] Fowler, *Santa Anna*, 232, 234; Bankhead to Foreign Office, 3 Dec. and 31 Dec. 1844, FO 50/177, no's 108, 110.

[53] Costeloe, *The Central Republic*, 220–1, 249–50.

[54] Fowler, *Santa Anna*, 239; Costeloe, *The Central Republic*, 248–50; Calcott, *Santa Anna*, 208. *El Siglo XIX*, 9, 11 Nov. 1844, which supported the revolt, stressed how rapid, peaceful and orderly it was: 'no crime has stained the people's triumph today' and 'no excesses have been committed'.

[55] Calcott, *Santa Anna*, 208; Shannon Baker, 'Antonio López de Santa Ana's Search for Personalized Nationalism', in Brunk and Fallaw (eds), *Heroes and Hero Cults in Latin America*, 72–3; Bankhead to Foreign Office, 31 Dec. 1844, FO 50/177 no. 110.

[56] Jones, *Santa Anna*, 92; Bankhead to Foreign Office, 31 Dec. 1844, FO 50/177 no. 110.

[57] Calcott, *Santa Anna*, 204.

political capital from it. Bidding farewell to his dwindling army, he struck a Napoleonic pose:

> Companions-in-arms! With pride I sustained the loss of an import-
> ant member of my body, lost gloriously in the service of our Native
> Land, as some of you bore witness; but that pride has turned to grief,
> sadness and desperation. You should know that these remains have
> been violently torn from the funeral urn, which was broken, and
> dragged through the streets to make sport of them.[58]

The most bitter aspect of his overthrow, it was said, was the treatment of his leg; thirty years later, as he penned his self-exculpatory memoirs, the memory of that 'sacrilegious attack by an impious faction' still rankled.[59]

I now address the final relevant episode in Santa Anna's turbulent career. Having achieved independence in 1836, Texas was absorbed into the United States ten years later. President Polk, eager for continental expansion, pro-voked a war of aggression which President Grant, a veteran of the conflict, later called 'one of the most unjust wars ever waged by a stronger against a weaker nation'.[60] Politically factionalized and fiscally desperate, Mexico was hard put to resist, as two American armies invaded, one overland from the north-east, one by sea via Veracruz. The Mexican government—now a loose alliance of liberals—decided to call on Santa Anna, who, having defeated the Spaniards in 1829 and the French (after a fashion) in 1838, would, it was hoped, repulse the Americans in 1846. Indifferent to political labels and ideologies, Santa Anna assumed the presidency and took command of Mexico's defences. He fought two major battles against the two principal American armies: that of Zachary Taylor at Buena Vista, near Saltillo, in February 1847, and that of Winfield Scott at Cerro Gordo, Veracruz, two

---

[58] Ibid., 211, based on Santa Anna, *Mi historia*, 55.

[59] Santa Anna, *Mi historia*, 54, 59; Fowler, *Santa Anna*, 239. Santa Anna's subsequent flight down to the coast—disguised as a muleteer—involved some piquant adventures, not least when he was caught by the Indians of Xico who proposed to boil him in a large cauldron, garnish him with chiles, wrap him in banana leaves, and present him, in the form of a big *tamal*, to the authorities. But the parish priest made them desist. The story, however fanciful, was passed down by oral tradition and remained current in the 1930s; in 1999 a local historian reported (plausibly) that Santa Anna had fathered two illegit-imate children by a woman from Xico and her family 'enjoyed pretending they were going to cook Santa Anna, to avenge his cruel treatment of their relative': Calcott, *Santa Anna*, 214; Fowler, *Santa Anna*, 434.

[60] Ulysses S. Grant, *Personal Memoirs* (London, 1999 [1885–6]), 25.

months later. (Meantime, he also engaged in secret negotiations with the Americans: but that is another story).

Buena Vista was a bloody draw, after which Santa Anna retreated south, allowing the American army to advance into Mexico. Cerro Gordo, fought close to Santa Anna's own Veracruz estates, proved to be a rout, in part because of Santa Anna's careless generalship.[61] And he paid a personal price. As the outflanked Mexican army broke and fled ('the surprise of the enemy was complete', Grant recalled, 'the victory overwhelming'),[62] Santa Anna narrowly escaped to his hacienda of Tuzamapan, with the Americans in hot pursuit. Weary, aching, his amputated leg giving him pain, he was described as 'huddled in his seat, a picture of dejection and misery'.[63]

At some point—probably on the night of the battle itself—soldiers of G Company of the 4th Illinois Infantry nearly captured the defeated general, who made a rapid escape on a mule cut from the traces of his personal carriage. But the carriage remained, and the Illinois irregulars appropriated Santa Anna's dinner (roast chicken), some $18,000 in coin, and his artificial left leg. So, Santa Anna had to beat another hasty and ignominious retreat, while the Illinois irregulars claimed the leg as legitimate booty of war (the chicken they ate and the coin they turned over to the US army command: since, as a disingenuous officer put it, 'we are gentlemen and we did not come to loot').[64] The captured leg soon had a taste of things to come: having been 'held up as a trophy to the view of the [American] troops', it was then (allegedly) used as a bat by the Illinois volunteers in an impromptu game of baseball; a trivial matter in the story of Santa Anna but, it seems, a 'very significant piece of baseball history', it being 'the first time that baseball in any form was played in a foreign country'.[65]

[61] Fowler, *Santa Anna*, 268–9; Calcott, *Santa Anna*, 259–60; Díaz Díaz, *Caudillos y caciques*, 203.

[62] Grant, *Personal Memoirs*, 68–9.

[63] Calcott, *Santa Anna*, 260. Another 'local legend' has him slaughtering and disembowelling a horse so that he and a companion could shelter for the night inside the warm carcass.

[64] James H. Merryman, Jalapa, to 'My Dear Father', 21 April 1847 (transcript) seems the best eye-witness account; further details, including the quote (of Lt. William Duncan) are from 'The Capture of General Santa Ann's Cork leg' (anon. resumé), both ISMMA Box 1402, General Ref.

[65] For which 'the men of the Illinois 4th deserve credit and recognition', according to a historian of baseball: Angus MacFarlane to Illinois State Military Museum, 19 July 2004, ISMMA Box 1402, Newspaper Clippings, with extract from the *San Francisco Chronicle*, May 1929, depicting the scene (in cartoon form, captioned: 'believe it or not, American soldiers played baseball with the wooden leg of Santa Anna').

Santa Anna made a final effort to rally his troops for the defence of Mexico City. But it was too late; the charisma was spent and desertions were now common. In October, Scott's army entered the capital, Santa Anna resigned, and peace was concluded. A final indignity ensued: in January 1848 an American detachment, led by Texas Rangers eager for revenge against the conqueror of the Alamo, attempted to catch—and very likely kill—the retired general, now lodged, with his family, at the spa-town of Tehuacan. Tipped off, Santa Anna narrowly escaped (again), but his family possessions—his gold-braided jackets and jewelled walking stick—were picked over. No leg was found amid the booty this time.[66] Granted a US army safe-conduct, Santa Anna made it to the coast and took ship for Jamaica.

This was not quite the end of Santa Anna's political career. He returned for one last hurrah in 1853, summoned from exile as president-elect-in-absentia. The familiar sequence of events ensued: a noisy welcome at Veracruz, with cannons booming and bells pealing; a *Te Deum* and a military review; a throng of flatterers and job-seekers. The press, tightly censored, flattered the president who, surrounding himself with his old cronies, governed in increasingly autocratic style: he re-established Iturbide's Order of Guadalupe, a sort of gimcrack nobility; he distributed—and received—medals, uniforms, sashes, coats, and capes. After careful debate, he assumed the title of 'His Serene Highness'; he was styled 'el ilustre mutilado de Veracruz'.[67] Under the glitzy exterior, however, the regime was shaky, increasingly seen as corrupt, cliquey, and despotic.[68] In 1854 disgruntled opponents, chiefly liberals, rose in rebellion. Though Santa Anna took the field against them, he could not prevail. On his return to the capital he received a kind of 'Roman triumphal entry', complete with music, fireworks, opera, bullfights, and artillery salvoes; a statue of Santa Anna, clad in the robes of the order of Guadalupe and brandishing a Mexican flag, was hastily erected. Five days later a tropical storm blew down both arch and statue.[69] As rebellion spread, Santa Anna was forced to flee Mexico City, where the celebrating mob again took to the streets and sacked his house, to the now familiar cries of 'death to the crip-ple'.[70] Santa Anna sailed into exile in Colombia. He would never be president again; and when he finally returned to Mexico in 1867, he faced an

---

[66] Calcott, *Santa Anna*, 274; Santa Anna, *Mi historia*, 92–3.

[67] Vázquez Montecón, *Santa Anna*, 50, 58.

[68] Calcott, *Santa Anna*, 290–8; Fowler, *Santa Anna*, 285–311. Fowler, though kinder to Santa Anna than many biographers, concedes that, by now, he had become tyrannous, capricious, and increasingly 'detach(ed) from reality' (309).

[69] Calcott, *Santa Anna*, 309–10.

[70] Fernando Escalante Gonzalbo, *Ciudadanos imaginarios* (Mexico, 1992), 284–5.

ignominious court-martial. Not only had his political career ended; so, too had the 'age of Santa Anna', since the victorious liberals now enacted radical reforms, which in turn provoked a clerical-conservative reaction, an unusually bitter civil war, and the brief creation of a Habsburg monarchy, backed by French bayonets. The result was intense political polarization, popular—and patriotic—mobilization, and a triumphant war of national liberation. A new politics, and a new political generation, supplanted the spent force of Santanismo.

Santa Anna himself, exiled following his court-martial in 1867, was allowed to return to Mexico, under amnesty, seven years later. He travelled on the new train from Veracruz up to the capital, where he could be seen shuffling through the streets west of the Zócalo, powerless, poor, and frail, with 'dim eyes peering toward the ground, trying to find a safe footing for tottering steps made still more uncertain by the worn and splintered peg'.[71] One day—it was said—an 'old man of the people', an army veteran of Tampico and Veracruz, called on the general, whom he found sadly 'decrepit'; the visitor carried a box in which lay the remains of the—real, amputated—leg which, he said, he had rescued from the carousing mob back in 1844. For thirty years 'he and his wife . . . had treasured [the bones] as a sacred trust'; now a widower, he wished to return the severed leg to 'their life-long hero'. Santa Anna, weeping, embraced the man, kissed his forehead, and regretted he could offer neither rank nor gold by way of reward. He died in June 1876, supposedly of his old complaint, dysentery, at the exceptional age of eighty-two, now a 'relic of another age'.[72]

The leg in exile

But the leg—the elegant prosthetic—lived on; since 2006 it has resided in a glass case in the Illinois State Military Museum at Fort Lincoln, Springfield, Illinois, alongside a life-size diorama, which—complete with (imitation) leg, chest of gold coins, and plastic roast chicken—depicts Santa Anna at the moment of the leg's capture. It returned to the US (the site of its manufacture) in 1847 with its Illinois captors, whose names are now to be found inscribed on the shin. Just up the road, in Piatt County, Illinois, lies the community of Cerro Gordo ('Big Hill'), formerly Griswold, named after the battle because of its 'elevated status'. For thirty years the leg remained a private possession in

---

[71] Calcott, *Santa Anna*, 361.

[72] Ibid., 361–4, quoting *El Siglo XIX*, 19 June 1876; see also Baker, 'Antonio López de Santa Ana's Search for Personalized Nationalism', 74; and Fowler, *Santa Anna*, 346–7, which describes a funeral devoid of official honours, but attracting a respectable turnout: 8,000 mourners and 40 carriages.

[73] James Haines to F. K. Rhoades, 3 Aug. 1907, ISSMA, Box 1402, General Ref.

Pekin (Illinois), being hawked around state fairs and even put on show in the Rhoades family house at 10c a look.[73] Several accounts include the leg among the exhibits in the Great Exhibition in London's Crystal Palace and, more reliably, in P. T. Barnum's American Museum in New York, where newspaper adverts billed it along with 'a Magnificent Moving Diorama of the FUNERAL OF NAPOLEON BONAPARTE' and an 'OURANG OUTANG - ANATOMICAL VENUS'.[74] Meanwhile, Santa Anna leg stories spread beyond Illinois, circulated, in part, by war veterans, and displaying the fungibility of such folk memories. Some were mildly scurrilous and racist: a boy who grew up in Washington, Arkansas, towards the beginning of the twentieth century, later (1971) recalled how 'we kids were often told by the old folks that Santa Anna's leg was captured by Illinois troops, not in battle, but at the time when he was bedded down with his mistress, and that he barely escaped in the darkness and that his mistress and leg were captured as evidence of the almost successful foray'.[75]

After thirty years of freelance commercialization, the leg was handed over to the State of Illinois in 1882. It then mouldered in a dusty vault for fifty more years, before being brought out for a brief display at the Illinois State Fair in August 1938 (this 'at the express desire of then-Governor Horner').[76] The fifty year hiatus reflected lack of official interest and resources: the Mexican-American War, though suitably glorious, excited much less interest than the Civil War; the veteran cohort was also much smaller and left a smaller generational-cultural footprint. During the mid-twentieth century, however, interest picked up, propelled by both 'externalist' trends (US-Mexican detente after the Mexican Revolution and National Guard recruitment drives during the Vietnam War), and the ('internalist') growth of a more affluent 'heritage industry' in the United States.[77] These were American trends (or 'push factors'); there was scant Mexican interest in the leg, hence no 'pull' factor (compare Greek demands for the return of the Elgin marbles or Mexican claims to Moctezuma's 'headdress', held by the Museum of Ethnology in Vienna). This is hardly surprising: Santa Anna was not fondly remembered in Mexico and does not figure among the standard canon of

---

[74] Ernest E. East, 'Santa Anna's Cork Leg', *Illinois Archival Information*, April 1954, ISSMA, Box 1402, News Clippings; James Lutzweiler to William Holland, 4 Sept. 1996, citing the *New York Herald*, 26 June, 11 Sept. 1847, ISSMA, Box 1402, General Ref.

[75] Carter Jenkins to Frank Tolbert, 11 Oct. 1971, ISSMA, Box 1402, General Ref.

[76] Thomas Deuel to C. E. Black, 1 Aug. 1938, ISSMA, Box 42, General Ref.

[77] The 'internalist' and 'externalist' explanations of historiographical shifts are taken from Peter Novick, *That Noble Dream. The 'Objectivity Question' and the American Historical Profession* (Cambrige, 1988), 9.

patriotic heroes; after the direct action of the mob in 1844, there have been no Santa Anna statues in Mexico City. As one Mexican put it, when the return of the leg to Mexico was mooted (by the Americans) in 1976: 'the US can either keep his cork leg, or show it off, or throw it away'.[78]

The leg again emerged from its vault in 1942, a brief beneficiary of US-Mexican wartime collaboration. As the conflicts generated by the Mexican Revolution of 1910 receded, the US embraced Mexico in its 'Good Neighbor Policy', and further cemented the relationship in opposition, first, to the Axis Powers, then to Soviet Communism. Cultural policy—the promotion of so-called 'soft power'[79]—complimented traditional diplomacy; a classic example being the return of Mexican war trophies, including 69 captured flags sent south of the border by President Truman in 1950. These trophies did not include the leg. However, eight years before, at the height of the Second World War, three Illinois state Representatives—all Democrats—had formally proposed the return of the leg to Mexico, 'as a gesture of friendship and unity', with a view to 'promoting continental and hemispheric solidarity'. To which resolution a Republican added: 'although we realize that this action may leave the Democratic Party . . . without a leg to stand on'.[80] Though passed, the resolution carried no weight (it was not a law) and so the leg stayed in Springfield.

The leg saw daylight again in the 1970s, when it figured in a mobile exhibit—the 'Grand Heritage Mobile'—which 'traveled all over the state enticing youg men to gawk [sic] at the history of the Illinois National Guard . . . and to put their names on the dotted line'—in other words, to join the military.[81] Thus, denied a role in the Second World War, the leg did its bit during Vietnam. For two more years, 1976–8, it was also on loan to the Historical Museum of the Militia and National Guard in Washington DC. Such a loan raised knotty legal and semantic questions. The leg had had several labels slapped on it: for some it was, indeed, a 'relic'; for others, a 'souvenir'; but, most commonly, it was called a 'trophy', specifically a 'war

[78] Raúl Avitia, quoted by Shelley Epstein, *Peoria Journal Star*, 12 March 1986, ISSMA Box 1402, News Clippings.

[79] Joseph S. Nye, *Soft Power. The Means to Succeed in World Politics* (Cambridge, 2004).

[80] East, 'Santa Anna's Cork Leg'.

[81] Mick Cochran, 'The Adjutant's Antiques', *The Springfied State Jounal-Register*, 10 May 1975, ISSMA, Box 1402, photocopies.

[82] Numerous references in ISSMA, Box 1402. It was also called a 'wooden leg' (though the cognoscenti sometimes alluded to its cork composition); one expert, perhaps influenced by Santa Anna's encounter with Andrew Jackson, turned it into a 'hickory limb': C. E. Black to Milton Howe, 21 July 1932, ISSMA Box 1402.

trophy'.[82] As such, however, the leg could be considered either 'a personal trophy of the soldier who captured it' or an official 'military trophy of war' covered by statute law; in which case the Illinois State Government had the right to oppose any loan, which it did (unsuccessfully). Soon, however, the leg's status was resolved in favour of State (of Illinois) ownership; an indication, perhaps, of the state's (small s) appropriation of such historico-cultural artefacts, in defence of its collective 'heritage'.

Like a medieval monastery jealous of its splinter of the True Cross, Illinois recurrently reasserted its claim on the leg: for example, when the state of Texas sought to borrow it for the 1986 Sesquicentennial celebration of Texan Independence.[83] Legalism aside, the tussle between Texas and Illinois involved rival state 'heritage' industries ('Santa Anna's leg uncorks [sic] two-state feud', reported the *Desmoines Register*), even if Illinois's refusal was based on the utilitarian argument that the leg was 'too deteriorated' to travel (hardly a tribute to its custody of the artefact).[84] The dispute followed established (American) tradition by generating a stream of feeble puns: 'Texas can't pull Santa Anna's leg away from Illinois Guard'; 'Illinois stands firm on Santa Anna's leg'; the leg 'won't be hoofing its way to Texas any time soon'.[85] Indeed, the plethora of pedal-and-prosthetic puns in the (American) primary literature—letters and newspaper reports alike—indicate that, by the later twentieth century, Santa Anna's leg had become a kind of comic curio.[86]

Thus, an ugly mutilation, suitably sanitized by time and distance, became an item for comic banter—banter that cannot even qualify as black humour, which would be more consciously transgressive; this is mainstream,

---

[83] The request came from the Witte Museum in San Antonio, not the official museum of the Alamo, whose curator explained that, since the latter already possessed Santa Anna's 'ceremonial robes, his traveling cot, religious medallion, silver candlesticks from his private altar, a saddle and a small solid gold snuff box (which) he gave Sam Houston for sparing his life at San Jacinto', the leg was surplus to requirements: Amy Wilson, 'Illinois Has a Leg Up on Santa Anna Artefact', *Texas Weekly Magazine*, 13 July 1986, ISSMA, Box 1402, Ref. News Clippings.

[84] *Desmoines Register*, 11 Feb. 1986, ISSMA, Box 1402, News Clippings.

[85] Further examples from the American sources: 'the leg stands on its own merits'; the leg 'has its foothold in Illinois history'; the 'leg is our legacy'. In seeking the leg for the Washington exhibition of 1976, Adjutant-General Patton was going 'out on a limb', while state policy sought to 'hobble Santa Anna's leg'.

[86] In fact, the punning tradition is much older: in 1842 Fanny Calderón de la Barca, wife of the Spanish Minister, 'saw Santa Anna's leg lying on the counter' of a shoemaker (where, one assumes, it was being refurbished): 'with this leg', she explained, 'he reviews his troops next Sunday, putting his *best foot foremost*; for generally he wears an unadorned wooden leg': *Life in Mexico*, 455.

middle-American jocosity, Bob Hope rather than Lenny Bruce. While it is true that Mexican revolutionary General Alvaro Obregón, 'el manco de Celaya', made jokes (rather better ones, as it happened), about his missing arm, quite soon after he had lost it, his was self-deprecating—and politically astute—black humour, ostensibly directed against himself. But for late twentieth-century American commentators, the leg was neither sacred, nor even sombre: when it came out of storage in 1942, it was photographed being cradled in the arms of two radiantly smiling young ladies.[87] Had the artefact come from closer to home, spatially, temporally, or ethnically, the response might have been different and more respectful (consider, for example, FDR's wheelchair and calipers). The point is obvious, but worth underlining: relics, including secular relics, are entirely dependent on their cultural context for their supposed power.[88]

The burgeoning American—especially Texan—heritage industry continued to generate proposals for swaps and purchases. A 'pretty well-off' private lawyer from Texas sought to buy the leg for his state, while a Texas heritage-historian floated the idea of returning the leg to Mexico in return for the flag of the New Orleans Greys, lost at the battle of the Alamo.[89] Recently, it was suggested that the leg be returned to Mexico and a 'reproduction' placed on show in Illinois; the argument—a reasonable reflection of recent thinking—being: 'how would you like it if Mexico had the Bill of Rights on display in their Museum?'[90] Two final incidents also reflect changing American mores. In 2006 an episode of the animated TV series *King of the Hill* (set in Texas) 'urged viewers to "return the leg to the Mexican people"' (this advocacy, a Fox TV Network spokeswoman carefully explained, was 'made in jest': perish the thought that Fox should stray from its usual chauvinistic stance).[91] The Illinois National Guard and Militia Historical Society responded: 'we, not Santa Anna, are King of the Hill'. And when the Texas State History Museum made a final attempt to borrow the leg in 2003 the (Texas) curator explained

---

[87] Patricia Reese to Mark Whitlock, n.d., with (1942) cuttings: ISSMA, Box 1402, Ref. Photocopies.

[88] 'Although symbolic objects, [relics] are of the most arbitrary kind, passively reflecting only exactly so much meaning as they were given by a particular community': Patrick J. Geary, *Furta Sacra. Thefts of Relics in the Central Middle Ages* (Princeton, 1990), 5.

[89] Kirby Pringle, 'A Leg Up On History', *News Gazette*, n.d. (1994?); Diane Jennings and Brendan Case, 'Flags Battle Never Ends', *Dallas Morning News*, 6 March 2005, ISSMA, Box 1402, Ref. News Clippings.

[90] Terence C. Jackson to Mark Whitlock, 12 Sept. 2005, ISSMA, Box 1402, News Clippings.

[91] 'We Not Santa Anna are King of the Hill', Illinois National Guard pamphlet, ISSMA, Box 1402, Ref. News Clippings.

that they wanted the leg not just to 'interpret Santa Anna's role in the US war with Mexico' but also, he stressed, 'as a story representing people with disabilities'.[92]

So, having replaced an emotive—if ephemeral—patriotic symbol (the real leg), the prosthetic made its way from New York to Mexico, accompanied Santa Anna through several political vicissitudes, returned to the US, thanks to the victorious, baseball-loving Illinois Volunteers, and then became a circus exhibit, a dusty entombed relic, a brief bargaining chip in the making of the Good Neighbor Policy, a running joke, an item in the burgeoning American heritage industry, an object of inter-state rivalry, and, finally, a symbol of politically-correct policy towards the disabled. The leg had long ceased to matter in Mexico; but it had become an interesting bit-player—could we call it a footnote?—in American cultural history.

Interpretation

In colonial Mexico, the crown enjoyed a genuine—if declining—legitimacy, underpinned by a powerful Catholic hegemony, both ideological and institutional. A kind of colonial throne-and-altar regime prevailed, until the late-Bourbon reforms began to undermine this usually happy union. The Independence movement revealed growing tensions: priests were prominent on both sides, while the popular cry of 'long live King Ferdinand and death to the gachupines (Spaniards)' exemplified a schizoid popular-political culture, infused with both anti-Spanish xenophobia and a kind of 'naïve monarchism'. After the bloody War of Independence there followed a long period of political experimentation and instability; Mexico was, in the full sense of that overworked term, a 'postcolonial' state (and society). In socio-political terms, two founts of potential legitimacy were involved: the nation and the state. Of course, these intertwined: according to the imperious logic of 'modern' nationalism, any self-respecting nation deserved and needed a coterminous state, without which it risked extinction. By 1821, notions of Mexican nationhood were fairly pervasive (though how far they penetrated, say, Indian and popular groups is debatable). If the nation existed, a state had also to exist. But what sort of state: monarchical, republican, representative, authoritarian, clerical, liberal, centralist, federalist? There was scant consensus, hence the

---

[92] Tom Wancho to ISSMA, 12 Nov. 2003, ISSMA, Box 1402, General Ref. Even back in 1942, when the return of the leg to Mexico was mooted, the secretary of the Association of Limb Manufacturers of America, on the look-out for some free publicity for the prosthetics industry, inquired whether 'it would be possible for this Association to take some part in the presentation': J. Korrady to Leo Boyle, 24 Jan. 1942, ISSMA, Box 1402, General Ref.

chronic instability, which made possible Santa Anna's convoluted and opportunistic career. In other words, Mexico suffered an acute legitimation deficit—perhaps, in Habermasian terms, a prolonged legitimation crisis.

The newly independent regime, briefly imperial, then republican (and often 'Santanista'), brought a genuinely new form of politics, premised on a potentially new, postcolonial legitimacy. The new politics involved elections—initially based on universal male suffrage—and a vigorous print media. A narrow elitist colonial-bureaucratic politics gave way to a more rambunctious, mass-based, popular politics, which, even in provincial towns, could be 'fierce[ly] partisan'.[93] Quite quickly, royal subjects became republican citizens. They also resorted to riot (which, though hardly new, was now more severe and threatening); and, in the form of the militia, the popular classes were mobilized behind ambitious political leaders. The latter were often radical liberals and federalists, like Juan Alvarez; but conservative leaders, like the Emperor Agustín and Santa Anna, could also count on mass, sometimes 'mob', support. Indeed, Santa Anna combined an appeal to both elite vested interests and the urban poor: Santanismo embodied a loose alliance of 'plebeyos y ... alcurnia' ('plebs and patriciate').[94] Furthermore, while it is true that this dramatic political opening later gave way to—partial— closure (hence the conservative, even authoritarian, governments of Santa Anna in the 1840s and '50s), there was no going back to the colonial regime (Santa Anna's defeat of the Spanish expedition of 1829 helped to confirm that). Amid the experimental politics of the period, aspiring leaders had to build effective coalitions, usually involving mass support.[95] And they sought new forms of legitimation to fill the vacuum created by the collapse of the colony.

Traditional monarchical legitimacy could not be replicated. True, Iturbide flirted with monarchism in the 1820s, as Santa Anna did in the 1840s and '50s; and Maximilian briefly essayed an imperial regime in the 1860s. But even had monarchism succeeded, it would necessarily have succeeded in the form of liberal-constitutionalism, or Bonapartist imperialism, or 'popular Caesarism'.[96] Since traditional monarchism, 'sacred and quasi-sacerdotal', premised on Divine Right and even endowed with 'thaumaturgic' powers,[97] was defunct, Mexico's postcolonial rulers had to tap alternative sources of

---

[93] Guardino, *The Time of Liberty*, 220.

[94] Díaz Díaz, *Caudillos y caciques*, 167.

[95] Torcuato S. di Tella, *National Popular Politics in Early Independent Mexico, 1820–47* (Albuquerque, 1996), offers an illuminating analysis.

[96] Di Tella, *National Popular Politics*, ch. 4.

[97] Christopher Dawson, *Medieval Essays* (London, 1953), 77.

legitimacy: democratic, nationalist, and religious. Thus, they had to convince Mexicans that they responsibly represented the people; that they embodied and protected the *patria*; and that they enjoyed the support and favour of Mexico's powerful Catholic Church (and thus of God?).

Here we can reintroduce relics, including Santa Anna's egregious leg. Santa Anna sought to play a 'populist' role, stressing his rapport with the common people, but he was no democrat: he despised the plebs, and his political style became increasingly autocratic (in which he resembled his hero, Napoleon). He therefore had scant claims to democratic legitimacy. There remained nationalism and religion. There is no doubt that Santa Anna's rise to power depended on his patriotic exploits and image; like Napoleon—or, later, General Boulanger—Santa Anna could capitalize on the intimate link between nation and army, nationalism and militarism.[98] His leg, lost in defence of his country against the might of France, was a potent symbol, sedulously exploited by Santa Anna and his cronies; it went beyond mere military memorabilia. Hence Santa Anna was repeatedly 'called upon' in times of national crisis, be it foreign invasion or domestic conflict. The 'idea that a revolution involving Santa Anna could not lose' was surprisingly durable.[99] But, while he twice succeeded in repelling foreign invaders, in 1829 and, with qualifications, in 1838, his response in 1836 (Texas) and 1847 (the Mexican-American War) was disastrous; Buena Vista, followed by Cerro Gordo, gravely damaged his political reputation. An effective nationalist appeal depended—one could generalize, 'depends'—on a measure of nation-alist success. Speeches, medals, uniforms, drums, parades, cannon fire, and bones-in-glass-boxes do not convince if the outcome is ignominious defeat and massive loss of territory (especially when this is compounded by suspicious dalliance with the enemy). Nationalism, in other words, is not just a question of symbols and tropes; like economic policy, it has a utilitarian quality, and those who do not generate some nationalist 'utility', however many limbs they may lose in the service of their country, risk forfeiting their nationalist appeal. They are also likely to leave no institutional legacy—that is, no network of *adictos* (die-hard supporters), dedicated to preserving the memory and the 'cult' (the secular *cofradía*, we might call it). Today, Santa Anna scarcely figures in the pantheon of Mexican heroes; he cannot compete with Juárez (a sober civilian, but a patriot and a winner) or Pancho Villa (who shares with the British Army and Al Qaeda the distinction of directly attacking the US mainland).

[98] Will Fowler, *Tornel and Santa Anna. The Writer and the Caudillo, 1795–1853* (Westport, Conn., 2000), 214.

[99] Díaz Díaz, *Caudillos y caciques*, 158.

What of religion? Religious legitimation of the secular state is not a medieval monopoly. Islamic theocracies aside, there have been plenty of 'Christian' regimes bolstered by religious legitimation. In the case of Santa Anna and his leg, religious connotations are suggested by the recurrent use of terms like 'relic', 'veneration', and 'pilgrimage'; Santa Anna, we are told, was seen as a 'Messiah' by some (but also as an 'Antichrist' and a 'vile Lucifer' by others).[100] Can we therefore consider the leg a 'secular relic', which contributed to a form of religious, or quasi-religious, perhaps 'charismatic' legitimation? In my view, probably not.

In personal terms, Santa Anna appears to have been charming. He had a 'sweetly wooing smile' which offset his melancholic appearance, and he could turn on the tears; but he was a poor public speaker, his voice 'timid and subdued', hence no rabble-rousing demagogue.[101] However, 'charisma', to the extent it means anything, does not reside in individual virtues or talents: it requires a reciprocal bond between leaders and followers and is highly subjective and circumstantial (one man's charismatic leader is another man's posturing crackpot).[102] Hence it is to circumstances—events and structures—that we must look. There is good evidence that Santa Anna sought to build a political cult; and that that cult had some ostensibly religious features (including the leg-as-relic). Did it work? Did religious legitimation rub off on Santa Anna?

Religious legitimation is a complicated concept and it can take several forms: I shall refer to these as (i) alliance (ii) plagiarism (or 'mimesis') and (iii) genuine secular/religious hybridization. To anticipate my conclusion, we can see, in the case of Santa Anna (and other secular rulers), clear evidence of (i) and (ii) but not (iii). While the intimate bond between church and state (i.e., crown) was strained through the later eighteenth century and irreparably broken with Independence, post-1821 governments could still strike useful alliances with the Catholic Church, as did Santa Anna himself. He seems to have been a Catholic believer (not a Deist or freethinker); his speeches and writings are littered with conventional Catholic allusions; and he repeatedly enlisted the sanction of the institutional church, with celebratory *Te Deums*, archiepiscopal blessings, and massive religious processions. When he returned to Mexico City after the battle of Buena Vista, he was met at

---

[100] Fowler, *Santa Anna*, xxii; Fowler, *Tornel and Santa Anna*, 168–9; Costeloe, *The Central Republic*, 151, 258; Baker, 'Antonio López de Santa Ana's Search for Personalized Nationalism', 75; Díaz Díaz, *Caudillos y caciques*, 241; *El Siglo XIX* (15 Dec. 1844).

[101] Mayer, *Mexico As It Was*, 72–3; Vázquez Montecón, *Santa Anna*, 25.

[102] Douglas Madsen and Peter G. Snow, *The Charismatic Bond. Political Behavior in Time of Crisis* (Cambridge, Mass., 1991), ch. 1.

the Villa of Guadalupe by the 'polko' leaders, wearing their 'scapularies and relics on their chests' (something which many Mexican leaders, convinced anti-clericals, would never have stomached).[103] This did not stop him squeezing the Church when he needed money; but that was also standard medieval and early modern practice, even in colonial Mexico. In other words, Santa Anna conformed to the standards of the lay Mexicans of his time: avowed Catholics, attached to Catholic liturgy and ritual, rather less attached to Christian morality (hence Santa Anna's Rabelaisian sex and social life), and self-interested when it came to the Church's massive material wealth. He did not share the stern anticlericalism of Juárez, still less the dogmatic Jacobinism of later revolutionary anti-clericals like Obregón and Calles. However, Santa Anna's alliance with the Church was mutually tactical and pragmatic; given the ideological power of the Mexican Church, it clearly lent him support (as he no doubt calculated); but such a tactical alliance did not invest Santa Anna, or his leg, with any religious, numinous, or supernatural aura.

It is true that some Santanista public ritual emulated older Catholic practices: the 'pomp and circumstance . . . pictures, statues, processions and imposing rituals' which impressed even censorious Protestant visitors.[104] The recovery, display, and interment of the leg borrowed from religious precedent (no previous secular ruler of Mexico attempted such a performance; but colonial viceroys rarely fought battles, certainly not against foreign invaders). Colonial Mexico was familiar with relics, including body parts; and, following Independence, church burials continued, even as the secular state sought – for reasons of public health and decency – to concentrate interments in designated 'suburban' cemeteries. In 1845 General Barrera's body parts—'heart and entrails'—were 'publicly displayed' in the Convent of San Diego, where they produced 'an extraordinary stench' until the new Board of Public Health ordered them to be speedily buried.[105] So there was nothing bizarre or unprecedented about the story of Santa Anna's leg.

We do not know whether Santanista quasi-religious ritual represented deliberate performative plagiarism, or unconscious cultural mimesis. Did Tornel – Santa Anna's organic intellectual and spin-doctor—sidle up to his boss and whisper: 'I have this great idea for your leg'? Or did Mexicans, after generations of baroque Catholic acculturation, naturally think of putting revered limbs in glass cases, making the switch from saintly to Santanista relics a kind of subconscious segue? A century later, Mexico's revolutionaries, engaged in a bitter struggle with the Church, attempted a similar

[103] Benito Juárez, *Apuntes para mis hijos* (Mexico, 1955), 40.
[104] Thompson, *Recollections of Mexico*, 101.
[105] Voekel, *Alone Before God*, 204–17.

performative plagiarism, devising socialist weddings, baptisms, and catechisms, while depicting revolutionary 'martyrs' in Christlike poses. In this
case, emulation was deliberate; in the former (Santanista) case, it is hard to
say. But regarding consequence, rather than cause, we can be more confident:
it didn't work very well. It had a contrived quality, hence it did not last. Just as
socialist rites of passage soon fizzled out, so the Santanista relic cult came to a
dramatic and ignominious conclusion, at the hands of what Santa Anna
himself called the 'impious mob' in December 1844. In contrast, some thoroughly secular rituals endured and prospered: the Grito ('Cry') of 15/16
September, which celebrates the tocsin of Independence (a secular patriotic
anniversary, though one which commemorates the heroic action of a parish
priest, Father Hidalgo), remains a powerful ritual in the Mexican nationalist
calendar. The date of Santa Anna's triumph – 11 September – now signifies a
quite different anniversary.

So Santa Anna clearly allied with the Church and plagiarized Catholic
ritual, albeit with scant success. Are there, finally, any grounds for believing
that he or his cult acquired 'religious' status, that they transcended secular
limits, turning Santanismo into a form of 'secular religion'? The answer, I
think, is clearly, 'no'; but why not? After all, there is plenty of talk of modern
'secular religions', arising in the French Revolution, supposedly evident in
twentieth-century totalitarian regimes (Nazism, Stalinism, Maoism, and
Fidelismo), and apparent even in revolutionary Mexico.[106] In some cases,
secular relics have been involved, like the embalmed body of Lenin.

In my view—shared, it seems, by some students of Nazism and
Peronism—this interpretation is mistaken.[107] It confuses metaphor and
description. Secular 'religions' may emulate religious (e.g., Catholic) rituals;
that is the plagiarism (witting or unwitting) which I mentioned. To call such
practices 'religious'—thus, by extension, to refer to Santa Anna's leg as a
'relic' which is 'venerated' by 'pilgrims'—is to employ a series of metaphors.
There is nothing wrong with that, so long as we are aware that these are
metaphors (just as it would be to say 'he walks his dog religiously every

---

[106] Adrian Bantjes, *As If Jesus Walked On Earth. Cardenismo, Sonora and the Mexican
Revolution* (Wilmington, 1998), 15–18, draws interesting parallels between Mexican
and French 'secular religions'. For a recent unconvincing attempt to stress the religious
legitimation of Fidel, see Lillian Guerra, ' "To condemn the Revolution is to condemn
Christ": Radicalization, Moral Redemption and the Sacrifice of Civil Society in Cuba,
1960', *Hispanic American Historical Review*, 89 (2008), 73–109.

[107] Fraser and Navarro, *Eva Perón*, 182; Stanley Stowers, 'The Concepts of "Religion",
"Political Religion" and the Study of Nazism', *Journal of Contemporary History*, 42
(2007), 9–24.

day'). So, metaphorically, the Santanista cult showed some 'religious' borrowings (as did the Nelson or Napoleon cults). But real religion involves, apart from ritual, a supernatural or transcendental quality (and in most cases, a strongly normative ethical dimension, which, it is hardly necessary to add, Santanismo lacked: there is not much of the Sermon on the Mount to be found in his self-serving, power-hungry, militaristic career). There is no evidence of Santanismo displaying such a supernatural or transcendental quality. The leg wrought no miraculous cures; its 'pilgrims' (whose numbers remain uncertain) may have come to gawp, or to pay homage to a national hero, but they did not come to seek spiritual solace, miracles, or moral guidance. Nor is this surprising. The same is true of most 'secular religions' and 'secular relics'. Marat was a French-revolutionary martyr, around whom a kind of cult developed; but it was not a supernatural or miraculous cult like that at Lourdes in nineteenth-century France.[108] Mexican-revolutionary martyrs, like Obregón, who lost first his arm, then his life, in the service of the Revolution, enjoyed a kind of cult—that is, a dedicated following, affectively tied to the caudillo in both life and death (the Mexican term *adictos* sums it up well). But there were no miracles associated with, and nothing supernatural or transcendental about, the Obregonista 'cult'. It was resolutely secular, as befitted a secular and strongly anticlerical *político*/general. In none of these cases could secular and nationalist heroes—Marat, Obregón, Santa Anna—make the transition across the entrenched boundary which demarcated the secular and the religious, the this-world and the other-world, at least in the period under consideration.

This does not mean that new religious cults could not spring up. On the contrary, they sprang up all the time in nineteenth- and twentieth-century Mexico. But the objects of really religious cults were not generals or politicians, people who operated in the sordid world of Realpolitik. The new cults were created by adolescent girls (mentored, sometimes, by elderly religious women – *beatas*); by oddball male adolescents (like El Niño Fidencio); by anonymous bandits and soldiers like Jesus Malverde and Juan Soldado; and, of course, by Cristero priests and martyrs, like Father Pro, already mentioned.[109] The only secular or revolutionary leaders who acquired a whiff

---

[108] Albert Soboul, *Understanding the French Revolution* (London, 1988), 141, 144.

[109] We may compare these to the few French-revolutionary 'saints' who achieved culthood: young women like Perrine Dugué, martyred by the Chouans, who continued to work miracles and receive ex-votos down to the twentieth century: Soboul, *Understanding the French Revolution*, 134–5. For a distinctly sympathetic account of modern Mexican cults, see Paul J. Vanderwood, *Juan Soldado: Rapist, Murderer, Martyr, Saint* (Durham, 2004).

of supernatural status in Mexico were popular leaders who never achieved power and who were cut off, usually tragically and treacherously, in their prime: leaders like Emiliano Zapata and Pancho Villa.[110] But even in those cases, the supernatural 'value-added' was, I would say, quite small: these were primarily secular popular heroes whom a very small heterodox minority invested with supernatural or religious status. The majority 'revered' them, but not in any religious sense., Politics usually prohibits sanctity, at least in the 'modern', post-Enlightenment world. In Mexico today, politicians enjoy low esteem (as they have for decades); priests—not least because they stand aside from politics—are contrastingly well regarded.[111]

There is, finally, a functional or utilitarian dimension. In Mexico, as in many Catholic countries, the cult of the saints (of which relics are an important part) offers practical, this-worldly benefits: timely rainfall, a good harvest, health, prosperity, a lasting marriage, children, and long life. Devotees of the cult make specific requests (hence the ex-votos and *milagros*); if requests are not answered, the saint may be spurned, even physically chastized. Saints had to prove their worth: in colonial times, they had to come—like secretaries or au pairs—with 'solid and verifiable references';[112] and new cults sprang up, in modern times as before, in response to particular practical demands. In the past, the agricultural cycle dominated, while natural disasters such as floods and earthquakes were important catalysts of cults. Recently, the growth of the cult of Jesús Malverde (or Colombia's Virgen de los Sicarios) reflects the boom in drug trafficking and associated violence. Secular heroes—Santa Anna, Obregón, Zapata, Villa—may inspire 'veneration'; they may acquire 'cults' and 'shrines'; but they rarely, if ever, offer practical (supernatural) benefits in hard times. Again, we risk being misled by metaphor.

Finally, the real spiritual, supernatural saint has one big advantage over his secular rival. Notwithstanding the functional dimension just mentioned, saints, cults, and relics operate in something of a win-win situation. If a good outcome ensues—the rains come, the harvest is bountiful, the illness abates—then saintly power is confirmed and the cult thrives. But even if it does not, there may be a 'logical' explanation. Perhaps the invocation was wrongly done; perhaps the bad outcome was the work of an inscrutable Providence; perhaps it was a justified punishment for past sins. Clearly, members of the cult are not endlessly forgiving (hence the occasional

[110] Samuel Brunk, 'The Eyes of Emiliano Zapata', in Brunk and Fallaw (eds), *Heroes and Hero Cults*, 115, 118; Katz, *The Life and Times of Pancho Villa*, 793.

[111] Gabriel A. Almond and Sidney Verba, *The Civic Culture: Political Attitudes and Democracy in Five Nations* (Boston, 1965), 68–78.

[112] Ragon, 'Los santos patronos', 371.

chastisement of useless saints). But saints—and their relics—have a good get-out when things go wrong, since they are not constrained by the hard-and-fast evidence of daily reality. (The same get-out helps maintain the fiction of astrology, of course).

Secular politicians do not enjoy these advantages. The criteria of success and failure are more clear-cut, evident, and terrestrial; and if they regularly fail to deliver, they will eventually be voted out, forcibly ousted, or, at the very least, grudgingly resented. They cannot usually appeal to an inscrutable Providence. It is true that some secular ideologies emulate religion by claiming higher purposes and lofty criteria: nationalism would be the best example, in whose name a great many bad outcomes can be justified. Neo-liberal orthodoxy—that the free market always knows best—shares some of this quality, as did the dogmatic Marxism of the past. But secular ideologies, including nationalism, Marxism and neo-liberalism, are still perilously dependent on evidential and utilitarian outcomes: if the nation loses, if the Party fails, if the market implodes, then there is no supernatural ace hidden up the secular sleeve. Thus, even if they seek to plagiarize religion, secular leaders are vulnerable to here-and-now, this-worldly refutation and de-legitimization in a way that religious authorities are not. To put it differently, drawing on James Scott's formulation: the 'public transcript' of the state is more easily shown to be hypocritical and at odds with reality than the 'public transcript' of religion, whose 'reality' is more detached, subjective, and inscrutable.[113] Hence secular leaders stand or fall by events; Santa Anna experienced 'enormous fluctuations' in popularity and reputation, which depended not just on battles won and lost, but also on more mundane considerations, such as whether the streets of Jalapa flooded on his watch.[114] As a result, secular cults, like Santanismo, have proven much more ephemeral and context-dependent than religious ones, like that of the Virgin of Guadalupe, which continue to flourish. And their associated 'relics' have not done the business in the way that religious relics have. Therefore, it may be best to draw a sharp line between the two and conclude that talk of secular saints, cults, and relics is, at best, metaphorical and, at worst, seriously misleading.

---

[113] James Scott, *Domination and the Arts of Resistance: Hidden Transcripts* (New Haven, 1990).

[114] Baker, 'Antonio López de Santa Ana's Search for Personalized Nationalism', 65.

Mao's Travelling Mangoes: Food as Relic in Revolutionary China*

Adam Yuet Chau

A relic is usually a small thing that is a fragment or concentration of something larger, an inanimate thing reminding one of a previously live thing or person; it has power and therefore is revered and worshipped. Well known examples of relics include the Buddha's remains (*sarira*) and the remains of Jesus Christ and Christian saints. Things used or touched by high religious personages are often treated by worshippers as powerful relics. For example, it is rumoured that when the Dalai Lama travels and stays in hotels, the hotel management is often bombarded by requests from Tibetan Buddhists to give or sell to them the (unwashed) towels and toiletries used by His Holiness. Because the Dalai Lama is considered the reincarnation of a bodhisattva, the things he has touched or used become something similar to the Buddha's relics.

A relic is usually small, hard, and rare (e.g. a bone fragment, a tooth, or a piece of bloodied cloth from a martyred saint). But can food be relics? The usual qualities of food do not lend themselves to becoming relics. Food is perishable, and rotten food stinks. Food is meant to be consumed, therefore it is more likely to end up in someone's stomach than on an altar or in a relic collection. A food item is seldom unique, therefore it does not possess one of the necessary qualities of relics: rarity. Because food is usually commonplace, it is difficult to endow a food item with extraordinary qualities. But this article is about one unusual moment in history when a few mangoes acquired relic-

* I wish to thank Alexandra Walsham for inviting me to give a paper at the 'Relics and Remains' conference held at the University of Exeter, on which this article is based. I am grateful to the conference participants for their helpful feedback, especially John Strong, and colleagues who read and commented on earlier drafts: Isabelle Charleux, Paul Cohen, Henrietta Harrison, John Moffett, Alexandra Walsham and three anonymous reviewers for *Past and Present*. My thanks also go to Stefan Landsberger and Dwight McWethy, who graciously gave permission for using images from their Mao poster and memorabilia collections. This study drew much inspiration from Michael Dutton's article 'Mango Mao' and Nikolai Ssorin-Chaikov's works on gifts to Soviet leaders.

like qualities. The mangoes were from Pakistan. But the 'relicking' of these mangoes took place in Mao Zedong's revolutionary China. This article will attempt to explore the mango relics through the lenses of changing political winds during the Cultural Revolution, Maoist revolutionary material-cultural practices, the cultural idioms of gift giving and hosting, Buddhist relic worship practices in traditional China, and what I call 'relic dialectics'. By 'relic dialectics' I mean the intriguing relationship between uniqueness and sameness, authenticity and inauthenticity (or fakery and replica-making), convergence and dispersal, immobility and mobility, secrecy and display, proximity and distant yearning, and corruptibility and incorruptibility. Even though the mango relics were specific to their historical, cultural, and sociopolitical context, it is hoped that this analysis will shed light on certain general qualities of relic-making (or 'relicking') that are found across cultures and historical periods.

The broad outline of the mango story is well known, though divergent accounts appear in later days about the details.[1] On 5 August 1968, Mao received the Pakistani foreign minister Mian Arshad Hussain,[2] who brought with him a basket of golden mangoes as gifts for the Chairman. Instead of eating the mangoes, Mao decided to give them to the Capital Worker and Peasant Mao Zedong Thought Propaganda Team (*shoudu gongnong Mao Zedong sixiang xuanchuandui*) that had earlier been sent to the Qinghua

---

[1] The mango-giving event has been recounted and briefly analysed in a number of works: Richard Baum, 'China: Year of the Mangoes', *Asian Survey*, 9 (1969), 1–17; Robert Benewick, 'Icons of Power: Mao Zedong and the Cultural Revolution', in Harriet Evans and Stephanie Donald (eds), *Picturing Power in the People's Republic of China Posters of the Cultural Revolution* (Lanham, 1999), 123–37; Michael Dutton, 'Mango Mao: Infections of the Sacred', *Public Culture,* 16 (2004), 161–87. [Despite the title of the article, Dutton's piece is not primarily an analysis of the mango fever but rather of Maoist political culture in general through the lens of George Bataille's concept of the 'general economy of desire'.]; Jennifer Hubbert, '(Re)collecting Mao: Memory and Fetish in Contemporary China', *American Ethnologist*, 33 (2008), 145–61; Afreda Murck, 'Golden Mangoes—The Life Cycle of a Cultural Revolution Symbol', *Asian Art*, 57 (2007), 1–22; *Wenge bowuguan* (Cultural Revolution Museum), 1966–1976 *Zhongguo baixing shenghuo shilu* (A Real Record of the Lives of the Chinese Masses, 1966–1976*), Jingguan jiaoyu chubanshe* (Police Academy Education Publisher), 40–4; Xu Ben, '*Maozhuxi zeng mangguo de yizhong jiedu: chongjian zhongguo shehui de liwu guanxi*' (One way of interpreting Chairman Mao's gift of mangoes: rebuilding the gift relationship in Chinese society), online article available at http://www.huachengnz.com/article/-view_3090.html [accessed 19 Sept. 2007]. See also Zhai Hua's blog entry on this topic at http://blog.sina.com.cn/s/blog_48670cb20100aqwe.html [accessed 26 March 2009].

[2] Mian Arshad Hussain was Pakistan's foreign minister from May 1968 to April 1969.

University in Beijing to rein in the rival Red Guard gangs. Two days later, on 7 August, the *People's Daily*, the official news organ of the Communist Party-state, carried a report on the mango gift that included the following extra-long headline in extra-large font: 'The greatest concern, the greatest trust, the greatest support, the greatest encouragement; our great leader Chairman Mao's heart is always linked with the hearts of the masses; Chairman Mao gave the precious gifts given by a foreign friend to the Capital Worker and Peasant Mao Zedong Thought Propaganda Team'. The article includes the following description of the events that took place on 5 August:

> In the afternoon of the fifth [of August], when the great happy news of Chairman Mao giving mangoes to the Capital Worker and Peasant Mao Zedong Thought Propaganda Team reached the Qinghua University campus, people immediately gathered around the gift given by the Great Leader Chairman Mao. They cried out enthusiastically and sang with wild abandonment. Tears swelled up in their eyes, and they again and again sincerely wished that our most beloved Great Leader Chairman Mao lived ten thousand years without bounds, ten thousand years without bounds, and ten thousand years without bounds! They all made phone calls to their own work units to spread this great happy news; and they also organized all kinds of celebratory activities all night long, and arrived at Zhongnanhai despite the rain to report the good news, and to express their loyalty to the Great Leader Chairman Mao.[3]

One eye-witness of the mango-giving event provides the following account:[4]

> Mao gave the mangoes to Wang Dongxing, who divided them up, distributing one mango each to a number of leading factories in Beijing, including Beijing Textile Factory, where I was then living. The workers at the factory held a huge ceremony, rich in the recitation of Mao's words, to welcome the arrival of the mango, then sealed the fruit in wax, hoping to preserve it for posterity. The mangoes became sacred relics, objects of veneration. The wax-covered fruit was placed on an altar in the factory auditorium, and workers lined up to file past it, solemnly bowing as they walked

---

[3] Zhongnanhai is Mao's residence by the Forbidden City in the centre of Beijing, which is several miles from Qinghua University, situated in the north-western corner of Beijing.

[4] The events recounted here are based on the memoir of Mao's personal physician Dr. Li Zhisui. See Li Zhisui, *The Private Life of Chairman Mao: The Memoirs of Mao's Personal Physician* (London, 1996), 503. Wang Dongxing was Mao's chief bodyguard and director of the Central General Office.

by. No one had thought to sterilize the mango before sealing it, however, and after a few days on display, it began to show signs of rot. The revolutionary committee of the factory retrieved the rotting mango, peeled it, then boiled the flesh in a huge pot of water. Mao again was greatly venerated, and the gift of the mango was lauded as evidence of the Chairman's deep concern for the workers. Then everyone in the factory filed by and each worker drank a spoonful of the water in which the sacred mango had been boiled.

After that, the revolutionary committee ordered a wax model of the original mango. The replica was duly made and placed on the altar to replace the real fruit, and workers continued to file by, their veneration for the sacred object in no apparent way diminished.

In order to share the honour with workers and the revolutionary masses elsewhere, more replicas of the mangoes were made and sent around the country. All over the country welcoming parties were organized to receive the mangoes, and many work units enshrined the mango replicas for the masses to view in order to partake in the Chairman's gift. Mao badges with the platter of mangoes and posters with revolutionary messages illustrated with the mangoes began to appear; a cigarette factory in the city of Xinzheng in Henan Province began producing a line of mango-brand cigarettes (still in production today); a film was made on class struggle using the Mao mango gift as a key symbol in the story line. In the months following Mao's giving of the mangoes a mango fever descended upon China.

How may one explain the mango fever? Were the mangoes simply the right fruits that appeared at the right time in the right place to be endowed with such relic-like qualities? First we need to look at the mango fever in the historical and political context of revolutionary China. Mao Zedong (1893–1976) led the Chinese Communist Party and the People's Liberation Army to victory after defeating the Nationalists in the Civil War (1945–49) and proclaimed the establishment of the People's Republic of China on 1 October 1949. In the first decade or so of the People's Republic, Mao's power and authority went unchallenged. With the help of the Soviet 'older brother' (*Sulian laodage*) and following the Soviet model of five-year plans, revolutionary China adopted aggressive programmes of industrialization and collectivization. But the Sino-Soviet falling out of 1959 and the three-year famine following the Great Leap Forward Campaign of 1958 greatly weakened Mao's credibility and his philosophy of revolutionary voluntarism and he was, for a while, losing control of the situation. It seemed that Mao's revolutionary charismatic authority was to be replaced and succeeded by routinized, bureaucratic authority. But Mao staged a surprise comeback by launching the Great Proletarian Cultural Revolution (*wuchanjieji wenhua dageming*) in the summer of 1966, mobilizing young people, especially students, to 'bombard the headquarters' of Party leadership. The Red Guard (*hongweibing*) Movement swept the entire country, as young men and women in secondary schools and universities formed Red Guard organizations and brought the message and practice of perpetual class struggle to all corners of the country.[5] The Red Guards resorted to violence and brutality as they struggled against 'capitalist-roaders' and revisionists within the Party, 'counter-revolutionary academic authorities', and other 'bad elements'. They were also eradicating the 'four olds' (*sijiu*) (old culture, old customs, old morality, old thoughts) and establishing the 'four news' (*sixin*).

But factionalism quickly developed, and rival Red Guard gangs fought one another with not only words (in the forms of big character posters, political slogan murals, and shouting revolutionary messages in processions, struggle meetings, and through public address systems) but also real weapons. Usually there were two large opposing factions on each school campus, and they would clash with each other in group battles involving rocks, bricks, roof tiles, sticks, knives, shovels, axes, metal chains (e.g. from bikes), and sometimes even guns, small cannons, grenades, and bombs that they either had manufactured themselves in the campus machine shops or had raided from nearby People's Liberation Army military compounds or militia ammunition storage facilities. The violence escalated quickly and anarchy reigned supreme for a few months. Finally Mao decided to put a stop to this and sent propaganda teams to the different campuses to rein in the rival groups and bring back order.

The first Worker and Peasant Mao Zedong Thought Propaganda Team was sent to Qinghua University on 27 July 1968.[6] Thousands of workers from Mao's 'personally directed factories' in Beijing were dispatched in trucks to the Qinghua University campus.[7] At first they encountered fierce opposition from the Red Guards, who attacked the unwanted visitors with rocks and bombs. A few workers died and a few hundred were injured. But with the help of the People's Liberation Army 8341 Corps and Mao's personal intervention through meeting with the top leaders of the Beijing Red Guard factions the

---

[5] For a sociological account of the Red Guard Movement, see Andrew G. Walder, *Fractured Rebellion: The Beijing Red Guard Movement* (Cambridge, Mass., 2009).

[6] The events recounted here are based on Li, *The Private Life of Chairman Mao*, 499–503.

[7] One report claims that hundreds of trucks carrying loads of workers converged at Qinghua, and the number of worker participants might have reached 30,000 strong. Li, *The Private Life of Chairman Mao*, 500.

propaganda teams quickly took control of the Qinghua and other university and secondary school campuses in the capital. Similar takeovers took place all over China, when the propaganda teams occupied schools, universities, research institutes, and hospitals, disarmed rival gangs, and quelled violent conflicts. When Mao gave the mangoes to the Capital Worker and Peasant Mao Zedong Thought Propaganda Team stationed in Qinghua University on 5 August (i.e. about a week after the propaganda team first marched into Qinghua), it was perceived as a huge as well as timely token of support for the propaganda teams, the legitimacy of whose mandate was not acknowledged or accepted by the students at first.

Lest there are conspiracy theorists out there who think that Mao planned and orchestrated the whole mango fever phenomenon, they should be disabused of such thoughts. According to Li Zhisui, Mao's private doctor, who was very close to Mao during the period in question, Mao was surprised to hear that his gift of mangoes had received such royal treatment by the workers. He was amused by the feverish response to the mangoes but did not seem to care to put a stop to the fever.[8] In other words, we may say that Mao had at most consented to the mango fever but did not plan it. Mao and other top Chinese Communist leaders shared food items with members of their security guard service and party subordinates quite frequently,[9] so this particular gift from Mao's perspective was no more than a gesture of attention and care for the propaganda team members who had suffered initial setback. I believe he did intend the mangoes to be eaten by members of the propaganda team, though perhaps he was not being terribly considerate as there were clearly too few mangoes for too many people. It was the workers who took the initiative to interpret the mangoes as something more than simply a gesture of attention and care, something more than a few fruits to be eaten to satisfy one's thirst, hunger, and curiosity for the exotic.

Here we need to consider the mangoes' intrinsic qualities. The most important quality of the mangoes that stood out in the mango fever is their golden colour. In all of the Chinese source descriptions of the mangoes the

---

[8] Li, *The Private Life of Chairman Mao*, 503: 'When I told Mao about the veneration accorded to his mango, he laughed. He had no problem with the mango worship and seemed delighted by the story.'

[9] In fact, giving food to subordinates was a common practice for the Chinese emperor during dynastic times. Typically an emperor's meal consisted of dozens if not over a hundred dishes, so he could only eat a small portion of them. The leftovers would be sent to his favourite ministers, princes, princesses, etc. as a gesture of benevolence. See Evelyn S. Rawski, *The Last Emperors: A Social History of Qing Imperial Institutions* (Berkeley, 1998).

'golden yellow' colour (*jinhuangse*) is emphasized. 'Golden yellow' is a colour traditionally associated with the colour of the robe and other regalia of the emperor. People could be executed for having purposefully or inadvertently used this imperial colour. In other words, the associations of this colour are emperor-ness, augustness, elegance, and supremeness. Another image evoked by the golden yellow colour is of course gold itself, which is a precious metal much to the liking of the Chinese traditionally. Jewellery in gold is common in Chinese tradition, and images of gold nuggets and gold coins are common decorative motifs. The gold-related traditional motifs and beliefs were of course condemned during the Maoist era as remnants of the feudal past, but they were transferred to new contexts related to Mao or the Communist Revolution. Mao was always portrayed as the rising sun with red and golden rays beaming from behind his head. Communism was the 'great road beaming with golden lights' (*jinguang dadao*) down which all Chinese should tread. Ripe and golden crops waving in the mild wind at harvest time as well as golden coloured sunflowers beaming happily towards the sun were common images and metaphors (the sun being Mao and his thoughts, and the sunflowers being the Chinese people and the revolutionary masses). In other words, the mangoes' golden colour might have greatly facilitated their incorporation into revolutionary symbolic play in Mao's China.

The exoticism of the mangoes is another important quality that must have contributed to the mango fever. Because the mango (*Mangifera indica*) is a tropical fruit commonly grown in South Asia and Southeast Asia but not at all common in China, most Chinese in 1968 had not seen or heard of mangoes.[10] An elderly woman who was a secondary school teacher in Beijing at that time related to the author that most of her colleagues had never seen a mango and went to see Mao's gift of mangoes also out of curiosity. The description of the mangoes at that time followed a formulaic expression ('the gift given to the Worker and Peasant Mao Zedong Thought Propaganda Team by the Great Leader Chairman Mao—mangoes'), and the fact that the mangoes were given to Mao by a foreign diplomatic visitor was not emphasized. Michael Dutton argues that this is to make Mao into the original giver of the gift.[11] But the fact that the mangoes were from a foreign land was not hidden from the masses

---

[10] Nowadays southern China has become a major mango growing region and most urban Chinese have, if not tasted the fruit, at least seen mangoes in the markets. Mangoes are no longer as exotic as they were in the Maoist era.

[11] Michael Dutton, 'Mango Mao'. See also Donald S. Sutton, 'Consuming Counterrevolution: The Ritual and Culture of Cannibalism in Wuxuan, Guangxi, China, May to July 1968', *Comparative Studies in Society and History*, 37, (1995), 136–72.

either. The receivers of the mangoes (i.e. the propaganda team members at Qinghua) as well as subsequent recipients of the distributed real and replica mangoes knew that the mangoes were given to Mao by a 'foreign friend' (*waiguo youren*), even though who this foreign friend was and where he or she was from became obscured or were considered irrelevant, which is why there were divergent accounts of these details. Some thought the mangoes were from Pakistan (which was correct), some thought they were from Congo, and others thought they were from the Philippines or some other Southeast Asian country. Though agreeing with Dutton about the import-ance of placing Mao as the original gift giver so as to reaffirm his moral superiority (in addition to acknowledging the fact that he liberated the Chinese people from feudalism and imperialism), I argue that the fact that the mangoes were from abroad and from the exotic tropics was an important factor in contributing to the mango fever. The exoticism of the mangoes might be compared with the exoticism of the Buddha and his relics when Buddhism was first introduced into China in the first century after Christ.

In 1968, when the mango fever broke out in China, most Chinese had never heard of or seen a mango (or a picture of a mango), therefore when they read about Mao's mango gift or heard about it they could not possibly have known what exactly this fruit looked like. Even after they had seen the real mangoes or their replicas they would not have known how the fruit tasted, what the fruit's texture was like, or indeed how to eat such a strange-looking fruit. For almost all Chinese involved in the mango fever, the mangoes were an aural and visual experience. They heard and read the word '*mangguo*'—Mandarin Chinese for mango, literally '*mang*', a family of tropical and sub-tropical plant, and 'fruit', most likely a transliteration of a South Asian original word for mango[12]—over and over again and saw the *mangguo* or their repli-cas either on the altar or as depicted in posters and Mao badges. But their understanding of Mao's gift *mangguo* was not comparable to our modern-day experience and understanding of mangoes since most of us have eaten the fruit and can see them being sold in supermarkets every day. For us mangoes cannot possibly be made into a sacred object, a relic, whereas for the Chinese in 1968 the exotic *mangguo* could very well become a relic. But of course it had to be first touched by Mao and gifted by Mao at a politically momentous time. The power of *mangguo* to spark Chinese fancy was illustrated by a story on the mango widely spread during the mango fever period.[13] Some people believed

---

[12] The '*ang*' in '*mangguo*' should be pronounced as the '*ang*' in the English word 'angst' but with a rising tone.

[13] See a version of the story in Yao Xiaoyuan's blog at http://blog.sina.com.cn/s/blog_47368a060100a1xm.html.

that, in ways that are reminiscent of the legendary 'ginseng fruit' (*renshenguo*) described in the classic novel *Journey to the West*, it would take a mango tree sixty years to flower, another sixty years to bear fruit, and sixty further years for the fruits to ripen, and the fruits have magical qualities. The story went that these magical mangoes would only grow in Africa, and an African president came to visit Mao and brought one of these magical mangoes as a gift, and that Mao, instead of eating it himself, gave the fruit to the Capital Worker and Peasant Mao Thought Propaganda Team, and that the team members, instead of eating the fruit, shared it with the revolutionary masses of the whole country.[14]

For the members of the propaganda teams and members of the working class (*gongren jieji*) in particular and for the Chinese revolutionary masses in general, Mao's mango gift had become a 'key symbol'.[15] It was able to garner the attention, 'regard' (as object of intense viewing), energy, and devotion that previously only Mao's portrait had been able to garner.

The ways in which the mango relics were 'worshipped' and displayed followed a long tradition of relic worship in traditional China, especially the worship of Buddha's relics (*sarira*).[16] According to Buddhist legends, the historical Buddha attained enlightenment and transmitted his teachings to countless disciples. The cremation of the Buddha's body after his death

[14] On the prevalence of rumours and fantastical stories during the Maoist period, see Steve A. Smith, 'Local Cadres Confront the Supernatural: The Politics of Holy Water (Shenshui) in the PRC, 1949–1966', *The China Quarterly*, 188 (2006), 999–1022.

[15] Sherry B. Ortner, 'On Key Symbols', *American Anthropologist*, 75 (1973), 1338–46.

[16] On Buddhist relic worship practices in Asia in general and China in particular, see John S. Strong, *Relics of the Buddha* (Princeton, 2004); Eugene Y. Wang, *Shaping the Lotus Sutra: Buddhist Visual Culture in Medieval China* (Seattle, 2005); Eugene Y. Wang, 'Of the True Body: The Famen Monastery Relics and Corporeal Transformation in Tang Imperial Culture' in Wu Hung and Katherine R. Tsiang (eds), *Body and Face in Chinese Visual Culture* (Cambridge, Mass., 2005), 79–118; Chen Jinhua, 'Sarira and Scepter: Empress Wu's Political Use of Buddhist Relics', *Journal of the International Association of Buddhist Studies*, 25 (2002), 33–150; Bernard Faure, 'Relics and Flesh Bodies: The Creation of Ch'an Pilgrimage Sites', in Susan Naquin and Chün-fang Yü (eds), *Pilgrims and Sacred Sites in China* (Berkeley, 1992), 150–189; David Germano and Kevin Trainor (eds), *Embodying the Dharma: Buddhist Relic Veneration in Asia* (Albany, 2004); Kevin Trainor, *Relics, Ritual, and Representation in Buddhism: Rematerializing the Sri Lankan Theravada Tradition* (Cambridge, 1997); Justin Ritzinger and Marcus Bingenheimer, 'Whole-Body Relics in Chinese Buddhism—Previous Research and Historical Overview', *The Indian International Journal of Buddhist Studies* 7 (2006), 37–94; Alan Cole, *Text as Father: Paternal Seductions in Early Mahayana Buddhist Literature* (Berkeley, 2005).

(achieving *nirvana*) produced a large number of indestructible fragments called *sariras* (Buddha's relics). These were distributed to various kings and were enshrined and venerated by the royal families and Buddhist disciples. Over time these *sariras* became dispersed through gift-giving and other processes (most famously through King Asoka, who gathered all the Buddha's relics and redistributed them to 84,000 different locations in his empire, housed under 84,000 stupas)[17] and some were brought to China and other lands that came under Buddhism's influence. The ancient Buddhist monastery Famensi (Dharma Gate Monastery) in north-central China (near Xi'an) housed one of the Buddha's fingerbone relics, a prestigious relic in the Buddhist relic hierarchy.[18] In 1987, the underground reliquary was opened for the first time in more than one thousand years since the Tang Dynasty, and the Buddha's fingerbone relic, among countless other treasures, was rediscovered and retrieved.[19]

Similar to relics in the Christian tradition, relics in the Buddhist tradition traditionally also played legitimating and protective roles for rulers as well as ecclesiastical authorities. During the Tang Dynasty many emperors staged elaborate worship rituals for the Famensi Buddha's fingerbone relic. The emperor would open the Famensi crypt, take out the fingerbone relic, welcome it to the capital city, worship it for a designated period of time, and then send it back to be returned to the crypt. During the procession between the Famensi and the imperial palace the masses would also be able to pay homage to the relic, in a manner that might have looked similar to the mango worship. However, over time relic worship as a practice declined in China, never to achieve prominence again, until the exigencies of contemporary politics and international relations spurred the reform-era Chinese government to allow the Famensi Buddha's fingerbone relic to go on tour in Greater China (Hong Kong and Taiwan) as well as in Buddhist countries in Southeast Asia. As Buddhism's revitalization in China is gaining strength by the day, relic diplomacy will surely gain prominence as one of the ways China exerts soft power amongst its Asian neighbours.

Beside the political context and resonances with traditional Buddhist relic worship practices, the mango relic-making also needs to be examined in the context of Maoist revolutionary material culture (i.e. the ways in which Chinese people under Maoism conceived, made, and treated physical objects

[17] See Strong, *Relics of the Buddha*, chs. 4 and 5.

[18] On the Famensi Buddha relics, see Wang, 'Of the True Body'.

[19] It turned out there were four Buddha's fingerbone relics, one of which was authenticated as the real one ('true body', *zhenshen*) while the other three were so-called companion 'shadow bones' (*yinggu*), i.e. replicas.

and how in turn these objects impinged upon, framed, directed, and even transformed their lives).

The largest material-cultural context in which the Chinese lived during the Maoist period was the very scarcity of material goods. Under the Maoist centralized system of production and distribution, many things became resources to be mobilized for the advancement of the country. The needs of the people were satisfied minimally, as people were not supposed to consume wastefully. In urban areas people could only buy necessities through a system of rations and coupons (fabric coupons for fabrics and clothes, oil coupons for cooking oil, flour coupons for flour and flour products, special permits for buying bicycles or sewing machines, etc.). In rural areas most people were reduced to receiving and consuming food approportioned by their production teams in accordance with their earned work points. There were no markets in rural areas where people could sell and buy things. Cash was in short supply.

While there was a scarcity of most material goods, on the one hand, there was a profusion of certain kinds of material goods that came with the rising Mao personality cult on the other: Mao statues large and small (in marble, bronze, plaster, and plastic), Mao badges, The *Complete Works of Mao Zedong*, the *Mao Quotation Book* (also known as the 'red treasure book' or, in the West, *The Little Red Book*), propaganda posters, military uniforms (complete with the red star on the cap), Mao portraits (and portraits of Marx, Engels, Lenin, and Stalin as well as those of other top Chinese leaders such as Zhou Enlai and Zhu De and Communist heroes such as Lei Feng, a revolutionary soldier who was made into a model for emulation), processional floats laden with plastic sunflowers and giant portraits and painted wooden red flags, etc. This Maoist revolutionary material culture reached a zenith between 1966 and 1968, the height of the Cultural Revolution and the Red Guard Movement. It is estimated that a few billion Mao badges were made; different work units competed with one another to make badges with the best design and materials.[20] The production of mango replicas never reached the scale and immensity of the Mao badges, but the cultural practices in relation to the mango replicas were no less feverish or devout. Since these

[20] On Mao badges, see Melissa Schrift, *Biography of a Chairman Mao Badge: The Creation and Mass Consumption of a Personality Cult* (New Brunswick, 2001); Alice de Jong, 'The Strange Story of Chairman Mao's Wonderful Gift', *Reminiscences and Ruminations, China Information Anniversary Supplement*, 9 (1994), 48–54. For visual images of a wide variety of Mao badges (with captions in Chinese), see http://big5.chinanews .com.cn:89/gate/big5/bbs.chinanews.com.cn/viewthread.php?tid=90092 [accessed 26 March 2009].

practices were in direct relation to the mangoes as objects, these constitute material-cultural practices, or more specifically, for our purpose, relicking practices. These practices included receiving the mangoes (from Mao and from the intermediaries), preserving the mangoes, enshrining and arranging viewing of the mangoes, taking photographs with the mangoes, making mango replicas, sending the replicas out from the designated mango-receiving factories in Beijing to other workers' propaganda teams in other parts of the country, organizing mango-welcoming parties, parading the mangoes, hosting and ensuring the safety of the mangoes, and seeing the mangoes off. Below I will look at three of these mango-relicking practices in a little more depth: first, taking photographs of the mangoes and with the mangoes; secondly, making mango replicas; and thirdly, hosting the mangoes.

Taking photographs of the mangoes and with the mangoes

One of the first photographs of Mao's mango gift was one taken on the same day that the mango was received (in this case, a single mango). A photographic record of this act survives.[21] It is a black and white photograph of a single mango resting on a porcelain plate with floral decoration on the rim. Above the image of the mango are two text sections with words hand-written onto the photograph, as was common practice at the time. The top line reads: 'The great leader Chairman Mao forever heart connected to heart with us working class'. The section below reads: 'The precious gift given by a foreign friend to Chairman Mao—mangoes. Chairman Mao said: 'We don't want to eat them. Let Comrade Wang Dongxing bring them to the comrades of the eight regiments of Worker and Peasant Propaganda Team that are at Qinghua University.' Below the mango image is the 'signature' section: 'First General Machinery Factory, the first battalion of the third regiment of the Capital Worker and Peasant Mao Zedong Thought Propaganda Team; 19hr, Fifth of August, 1968'. At the right bottom corner is the photographic studio's name *Beijing xindabei zhaoxiang* (Beijing New Great North Photo). In other words, this is a *portrait* of the mango, one of the very first, since the time of taking the photograph was recorded: 7pm on 5 August (i.e. only a few hours after the workers received the mango). The meticulousness in recording the time of the mango portrait indicates how important this 'historic moment' was for the workers. This artefact seems to confirm Doctor Li Zhisui's account, that the mangoes were divided up by Wang Dongxing (Mao's chief of staff) and only one was brought to the propaganda teams of each one of the eight 'favoured' factories stationed in Qinghua (among dozens of

---

[21] The reader can view the photograph on Mowa's blog at blog.sina.com.cn/s/blog_541 cd2aa01000cg7.html [accessed 5 March 2010].

factories that sent propaganda teams to Qinghua, hence the reference to the specific battalion and regiment, referring to the way in which the propaganda teams were organized as they 'attacked' Qinghua). This photograph must have served as a prototype for future reproduction images such as posters and mango-brand cigarette packet covers (see section on replicas below).

People continued to take photographs with the mangoes and mango repli-cas long after the initial mangoes had presumably rotted or been consumed. For example, one photograph[22] shows a group portrait taken on 25 September 1968 (i.e. one month and twenty days after the mango-giving event). The photograph's caption reads: 'A group portrait of all the members of the Beijing City Machinery Construction Company who participated in the Capital Workers' Mao Zedong Thought Propaganda Team in Qinghua University.' The hundred-strong group of workers are neatly arranged into seven rows in front of a building. A large Mao portrait is displayed in the centre of the top row; a large red flag bearing the words 'Capital Workers' Mao Zedong Thought Propaganda Team' is behind the group; Mao's mango gift (most likely a replica) is encased and placed on a small table draped with red cloth in the lower centre position; Mao's 'little red book' is in everyone's hand and Mao badges on everyone's left chest. Group portraiture such as this one was a standard Maoist revolutionary practice. Whenever there were gatherings of model worker delegates to meet with Party leaders group por-traits would be taken, sometimes using a rotational camera to accommodate hundreds of people in one photograph. Each delegate would receive a copy of the photograph as a memento of the gathering and 'grace' from the Party leaders. In the case of the group portrait with Mao's mango gift, the partici-pating workers could bring the portrait back home (and presumably also to their work units) to relish for a long time afterwards. Indeed this was one of the ways the mango relic entered people's homes, as the centrepiece of a group portrait.

Making mango replicas

The initial motivation to make wax mango replicas was of course to counter and resolve the inevitable corruption of the fruit. It is not clear which one of the Beijing factories made the first mango replica, but the practice apparently spread and was copied by other factories (this imitation practice was already widespread in the making of Mao badges). But as the news of Mao's mango gift spread to all corners of the country, the pressure on the Beijing factories to share Mao's blessing mounted. In response to these requests from factories

---

[22] The reader can view the photograph on Zhao Qingwei's blog at http://zhaoqingwei.blshe .com/post/6424/172607 [accessed 18 Jan. 2010].

and revolutionary committees in other cities for Mao's mangoes, the Beijing factories made more mango replicas and started to send them out in all directions, thus inaugurating the phenomenon of Mao's travelling mangoes. Many cities or towns that received the mango replicas in turn made their own replicas in response to the demand from regions lower down in the hierarchy of 'central places'.

These mango replicas were one-to-one wax models of the original mangoes, complete with glass cases for proper display and protection. There were many different designs. Here we will look at one example (Fig. 1). The design of the glass container was quite innovative and ingenious. On the upper part of the front of the display glass dome is a portrait of Mao with red sun rays shooting outward from Mao's body. The inscription below the portrait reads:

> Respectfully wish Chairman Mao never-ending longevity / To commemorate the precious gift from the great leader Chairman Mao to the Capital Worker and Peasant Mao Zedong Thought Propaganda Team—mango / 1968 August 5 (Replica) / Given by Beijing Metal Smelting Equipment Parts Factory Revolutionary Committee.

These mango replica display glass containers resonate with the reliquaries containing the Famensi Buddha's fingerbone relics mentioned earlier. All four of the Famensi relics (one true and the other three so-called 'shadow' ones) are encased in elaborate yet different caskets. For example, one is encased in a nested series of multiple containers and another in a coffin-shaped container. All containers are made of gold or other precious metals and studded with precious stones.[23]

Lastly, a discussion of mango replica-making would not be complete without mentioning the mango posters, which can be understood as print replicas. One example is shown here (Fig. 2). It seems that the image was based on the photograph of the original mango gift mentioned above, with the mango resting on a porcelain plate with floral patterns. The poster includes a Mao portrait and a caption, which is a quote from Mao:

> Our country has 700 million people. The working class is the leading class. We should let the leading function of the working class in the Cultural Revolution and in all other tasks fully realize itself. The working class should also continuously raise their own political awareness through these struggles.

---

[23] More on the use of caskets in Chinese religious culture, see Julius N. Tsai, 'Opening Up the Ritual Casket: Patterns of Concealment and Disclosure in Chinese Religion', *Material Religion: The Journal of Objects, Art, and Belief*, 2 (2006), 38–66.

Fig. 1. A wax replica of Mao's mango gift in a glass container. The image is taken
from Dwight McWethy's website, The East is Red, devoted to selling Cultural
Revolution and other Maoist-era memorabilia (image used with permission).
See http://www.theeastisred.com/misc/misc10.htm

At the bottom of the poster is the line: 'The precious gift the great leader
Chairman Mao personally gave the Capital Workers' Mao Zedong Thought
Propaganda Team—mango'.[24]

---

[24] This poster is from Stefan R. Landsberger's collection of Chinese propaganda posters
(image used with permission). See http://chineseposters.net/themes/mao-mangoes.php.

Fig. 2. A poster of Mao's mango gift. The image is taken from Professor Stefan R. Landsberger's web collection of Chinese propaganda posters (image used with permission). See http://chineseposters.net/themes/mao-mangoes.php

Hosting Mao's mangoes

One is tempted to interpret the mango fever in terms of gift-giving cultural idioms because it is obvious that the mangoes were understood and presented as gifts by all concerned. First the Pakistani foreign minister visited Mao and gave him the basket of mangoes as a diplomatic gift,[25] then Mao gave the mangoes to the members of the propaganda work team as a gift, apparently to show his concern and support for them.[26] Then the original mango-receiving factories gave the mango replicas as gifts to members of the revolutionary masses in the rest of the country (the word used in these giving acts was always

[25] On diplomatic gifts see Nikolai Ssorin-Chaikov, 'On Heterochrony: Birthday Gifts to Stalin, 1949', *Journal of the Royal Anthropological Institute*, 12 (2006), 355–75; Nikolai Ssorin-Chaikov (ed.), *Dary Vozhdiam/Gifts to Soviet Leaders. Exh. Cat.* (Moscow, 2006); Nikolai Ssorin-Chaikov and Olga Sosnina, 'Archaeology of Power: Anatomy of Love', Introduction, in Ssorin-Chaikov (ed.), *Dary Vozhdiam*, 12–37.

[26] To Westerners who are not familiar with the practice of giving away someone else's gift to oneself this might come across as inappropriate if not rude, but the Chinese traditionally practise 'serial gift giving' or 'gift forwarding' (*zhuansong*, literally 'turn-around and give') quite often and quite matter-of-factly.

'to give as gift', in Chinese *zeng*). And the return gifts were usually also items in the revolutionary gift-barter economy. The mango replicas and other revolutionary gift items such as Mao badges were never sold in shops at that time (quite unlike today when they have become collectables and are sold in antique markets, on Chinese versions of eBay, and websites devoted to selling Cultural Revolution memorabilia such as The East is Red).

But I argue that in addition to the gift idiom another idiom was also in operation, that of hosting. Hosting refers to the act of inviting guests, treating them well (involving especially banqueting), and sending the guests off, all in accordance with prescribed protocols. The Chinese, from peasants to emperors, have traditionally treated hosting very seriously.[27] Hosting is at its core a moral and economic event production and a form of sociality. Hosting is a moral event production because a recognition and acknowledgement of social worth is communicated between, and co-produced by host and guest, and the hosting event always entails morally inflected judgements of all the details of the whole event (behaviour, utterances, gestures, levels of courtesy, politeness, and generosity). By being host, a social actor or a group of social actors are putting their status and reputation on the line. A well hosted event production maintains or augments the host's status and reputation, while a badly hosted event production can drastically drain the host's store of social-relational goodwill and affect his or her social standing.

When Mao gave the mangoes to the workers' propaganda team, he acted not simply as a gift-giver but also as a host, like an emperor sending his leftover dishes to his favourite ministers and princes after a meal. But the hosting idiom is even stronger on the side of the revolutionary masses. Even though they were guests at Mao's imaginary banquet table partaking of the bounty of the mango feast, they were at the same time hosts of the mangoes (we might want to call this the 'dialectic of hosting and being hosted'), as the mangoes were made to represent Mao's care for the workers and the revolutionary masses or even the very embodiment of Mao himself. Just as they 'invited' (*qing*) and hosted Mao portraits, Mao badges and *The Complete Works of Mao*, they also 'invited' and hosted Mao's mangoes (which is similar also to the ways in which various Buddhist communities hosted Buddhist relics).

To host the Mao mangoes successfully each factory or locale had to organize well the welcoming party, the display, and the sending off. Workers with the right class background and high political awareness were given the sacred task of actually holding the mango display containers during the transits and

---

[27] On hosting, see Adam Yuet Chau, *Miraculous Response: Doing Popular Religion in Contemporary China* (Stanford, 2006).

the parades. Enthusiasm and devotion was demonstrated by how large the crowd was that came out to welcome and view the mangoes. For example, when the mango came to Yulin City (a small prefectural city in Shaanxi Province), more than 5,000 city residents and soldiers came out into the streets to welcome the mango (replica) and the provincial workers' propaganda team delegation that brought the mango (replica) back from their trip to Beijing.[28]

I shall conclude my analysis of the mango relic-making in terms of what I call 'relic dialectics'.[29] The mango relic in Maoist revolutionary China, similar to relics in Christian and Buddhist religious cultures, exemplified the intriguing relationship (or dialectics) between uniqueness and sameness, authenticity and inauthenticity, convergence and dispersal, immobility and mobility, secrecy and display, proximity and distant yearning, corruptibility and incorruptibility.

The dialectic of uniqueness and sameness. Every relic is unique, yet it exists in a system or field of similar or similarly powerful relics. The Famensi Buddha's fingerbone relic exists in a world of a large number of Buddha relics dispersed all over the Buddhist world, each having its history of acquisition, worship, sometimes loss and retrieval, and store of miracles and legends. The mango received by one of the Beijing factories was isomorphic with the other mangoes given by Mao yet each could be treasured as a precious gift from Mao to that particular factory; after all, only eight of the dozens of factories were deemed worthy of the gift. But at the same time all the mangoes were perceived as collectively representing Mao's concern and care for the members of the propaganda team in particular and the entire working class and revolutionary masses in general. Therefore all the mangoes, including the countless replicas, possessed the same qualities, capable of inciting the same level of revolutionary fervour and devotion (at least in theory).

The dialectic of (possible) authenticity and (possible) inauthenticity. Fake relics were legion in the Christian and Buddhist relic traditions, or at least suspicions and accusations thereof. Because relics are endowed with power, the desire to acquire that power drove some to manufacture fake relics and parade them as authentic. And sometimes the fake (or copy) relics might acquire real power through being worshipped or because of having been close to the real one (e.g. the case of the 'shadow bones' of the Famensi Buddha's

---

[28] Yulin Prefecture Gazetteer Editorial Committee, *Yulin diqu zhi* or YLDQZ (Yulin District Gazetteer), (Xi'an, 1994).

[29] My formulation was partly inspired by Faure, 'Relics and Flesh Bodies'. Faure speaks of the dialectics of place and space, sacralization and humanization, fixity and mobility, and legitimization and delegitimization (180).

fingerbone relic). It is likely that many Chinese in 1968 'worshipped' the mango replicas as the original mangoes Mao gave to the Beijing worker and peasant propaganda team, even though there might not have been any intention to deceive. All the glass containers of the existent mango replicas indicate clearly that the mangoes inside were replicas (*fuzhipin*), but this fact might not have been emphasized. In any case, as mentioned above, the replicas were endowed with real potency.[30]

The dialectic of secrecy and display. In traditional Chinese Buddhist relic worship, very few people could actually see the actual relic. For example, only the emperor could invite the Famensi Buddha fingerbone relic out of the crypt, into the palace, and worship it in close proximity, presumably seeing or touching the relic directly after taking it out of the layers of reliquaries. The mango relic was treated very differently. It was displayed in full view of all the viewers who came to pay homage to it. But even so it was displayed in a glass container, so none of the viewers could touch it or smell it.

The dialectic of proximity and distant yearning. Relics are usually only effective in empowering someone when seen or touched or brought to close proximity (known as 'contact relic' versus the rarer 'body relic').[31] The Tang emperors worshipped the Buddha fingerbone relic by bringing it to the palace; more commonly, people make pilgrimages to sacred sites where relics are enshrined (common in both Christian, Islamic and Buddhist religious traditions). Worshippers sometimes have to travel very long distances in order to see or come close to the relics in question. Even though the mango relic was not enshrined in one place, most people who wanted to see it still had to travel a little bit and view it at designated venues such as factory auditoriums, city hall, or city square. People were arranged to form a long queue and file by the mango relic altar in an orderly and respectful fashion, as they could catch only 'an eyeful' of the mango before having to walk on and let the eager comrades behind them have their turn.

The dialectic of immobility and travelling/dispersal. Relics tend to stay immobile and be enshrined in one place (usually deemed as their final resting place in the case of Buddha's relics because they are considered remains of the Buddha's dead this-worldly body). But of course some relics got moved around quite a bit. In medieval Europe kings, queens, bishops, and cardinals

---

[30] Per Walter Benjamin's famous essay 'The Work of Art in the Age of Mechanical Reproduction', perhaps the replicas retained a high degree of potency because they were not reproduced by mechanical means? The mango posters certainly did not inspire as much devotion as the replicas.

[31] I thank Isabelle Charleux for alerting me to this distinction. See also Strong, *Relics of the Buddha*, 8–18.

gave one another all kinds of relics as political and diplomatic gifts.[32] As a result these relics travelled back and forth in Europe with the emissaries. The Buddha's relics were also dispersed and re-collected and re-dispersed, and just like Christian relics, some Buddhist relics were also subject to *furta sacra*.[33] However, compared with both Christian and Buddhist relics, the mango relics were unusually mobile. Most of the mango replicas travelled amazingly long distances, emanating from the national capital and ground zero of revolutionary wisdom, changing hands from one revolutionary committee to another, from one worker and peasant propaganda team to another, until they reached all corners of the country.

The dialectic of corruptibility and incorruptibility. This dialectic brings us back to the question of food items as relics. The real mangoes rotted, but the replicas could last forever. So strictly speaking the mango relic case does not demonstrate conclusively that food items can be made into relics because the wax mangoes were no longer real food items. But neither is the Famensi Buddha's fingerbone relic really the Buddha's fingerbone (it is much larger than any real human's fingerbone); it is supposed to be the post-cremation condensation of the essence of the Buddha's person and teaching. Real fingerbones are corruptible while the fingerbone relic will never be corrupted. It is always cognitively intriguing to see something that is supposed to rot that does not. Many past Buddhist masters' bodies became mummified (thanks to their high accomplishments), and were lacquered.[34] Mao's body lies preserved and waxed under the crystal display case in the Mao Zedong mausoleum in the centre of the Tian'anmen Square in Beijing.[35] Perhaps part of the mango relic's power was in its incorruptibility (the copy as real), just as Mao Zedong's thought was perceived to be incorruptible.

---

[32] See Julia Smith, 'Rulers and Relics c.750-c.950: Treasure on Earth, Treasure in Heaven', this volume, 73–96.

[33] See Faure, 'Relics and Flesh Bodies', 174–5.

[34] See Faure, 'Relics and Flesh Bodies'.

[35] On Mao's mausoleum, see Frederic Wakeman, Jr., 'Revolutionary Rites: The Remains of Chiang Kai-shek and Mao Tse-tung', *Representations*, 10 (1985), 146–93; Rudolf G. Wagner, 'Reading the Chairman Mao Memorial Hall in Peking: The Tribulations of the Implied Pilgrim', in Susan Naquin and Chün-fang Yü (eds), *Pilgrims and Sacred Sites in China* (Berkeley, 1992), 378–423. On embalming Communist leaders, see Ilya Zbarsky and Samuel Hutchinson, *Lenin's Embalmers* (London, 1998).

What Remains? Anti-Communism, Forensic Archaeology, and the Retelling of the National Past in Lithuania and Romania*

James Mark

From the 1970s, the application of forensic archaeology and anthropology to mass graves emerged as part of 'third wave' democratization in Latin America, Africa, and Europe.[1] Political organizations which represented victims of dictatorships, advocates for human rights, and, from the mid-1990s, the institutions of international criminal law, increasingly associated themselves with these emerging disciplines.[2] Initially, their methods were called

* I am grateful for funding and support from the Arts and Humanities Research Council and the University of Exeter. I would also like to thank participants at the 'Relics and Remains' conference, and John Czaplika, for their helpful comments.

[1] There is a large literature on the techniques of, and on the methodological and ethical issues associated with, forensic archaeology. For a comprehensive introduction, see Margaret Cox et al., *The Scientific Investigation of Mass Graves: Towards Protocols and Standard Operating Procedures* (Cambridge, 2008). For accounts which historicize the discipline and explore its linkages with the ideologies of late twentieth-century democratization: Laurent Olivier, 'The Archaeology of the Contemporary Past' in Victor Buchli and Gavin Lucas (eds), *Archaeologies of the Contemporary Past* (London and New York, 2001), 175–88; Francisco Ferrándiz and Alejandro Baer, 'Digital Memory: The Visual Recording of Mass Grave Exhumations in Contemporary Spain', *Forum: Qualitative Social Research*, 9 (2008): http://www.qualitative-research.net/index.php/fqs/article/view/1152/2578; Zoe Crossland, 'Buried Lives: Forensic Archaeology and the Disappeared in Argentina', *Archaeological Dialogues*, 7 (2000), 146–59; Alfredo González-Ruibal, 'Making Things Public: Archaeologies of the Spanish Civil War', *Public Archaeology*, 6 (2007), 203–26; Roxana Ferllini, 'The Development of Human Rights Investigations since 1945', *Science and Justice*, 43 (2003), 219–24; Pedro Funari, Andres Zarankin, and Melisa Salerno (eds), *Memories from Darkness: Archaeology of Repression and Resistance in Latin America* (New York, 2009). A 'mass grave' is usually thought to contain at least six bodies which were indiscriminately placed, were subject to clandestine burial, and whose unlawful deaths were intended to be concealed; see Cox, *The Scientific Investigation*, 12.

[2] The use of forensic archaeology to uncover war crimes started during World War Two, albeit on a small scale.

upon to provide evidence to try former elites.[3] However, legal cases built on grave excavations often proved difficult to bring to court: in some instances, representatives of past regimes had been amnestied, or crimes belonged to a past sufficiently distant to make prosecution unviable. In other situations, victims' families and their advocates objected to the instrumentalization of their relatives' remains in ignoble processes of 'judicial revenge', although they considered the recovery of these bodies as crucial in enabling the nation to 'turn a page' or for their own 'personal closure'.[4] Indeed, some advocated using human remains for educational purposes: to confront societies with the evils of dictatorship[5] or as a part of a broader civic engagement aimed at reconciliation.[6]

In the former Communist bloc in Europe too, excavations failed to lead to prosecutions of former elites.[7] Yet this science was attractive to those who founded new memorial institutions dedicated to constructing new

---

[3] In a few cases, such as Honduras, material was used.

[4] For a discussion of the contestations over the different uses to which bones should be put in the case of the Argentinian 'disappeared', see Ewa Domanska, 'The Material Presence of the Past', *History and Theory*, 45 (2006), 342–5.

[5] See Ferrándiz and Baer, 'Digital Memory'; Andrés Zarankin and Pedro Paulo A. Funari, ' "Eternal Sunshine of the Spotless Mind": Archaeology and Construction of Memory of Military Repression in South America', *Archaeologies: Journal of the World Archaeological Congress*, 4 (2008), 310–27.

[6] See, e.g., Chip Colwell-Chanthaphonh, 'History, Justice and Reconciliation', in Barbara J. Little and Paul A. Schackel (eds), *Archaeology as a Tool of Civic Engagement* (2007), 37. He notes that unearthing remains under the guise of humanitarianism can also be used by elites to avoid prosecutions, as they can ensure that the process of recovery is undertaken in such a way that it does not produce legally admissible evidence of criminality.

[7] Excavations of mass graves were carried out at Katyn (Poland), Vinnytsia (Ukraine), Vilnius (Lithuania), and Lasko (Slovenia) and at multiple locations in Romania. There were also attempts to unearth places of violence which former elites had attempted to hide; see, e.g., excavations at the House of Terror, Budapest; Vojna Camp, Příbram, Czech Republic; Museum of Genocide Victims, Vilnius; and the Yekaterinburg merchant's house where Tsar Nicholas II, his wife, and their children were thought to have been killed. On the Vinnytsia mass grave, see Irina Paperno, 'Exhuming the Bodies of Soviet Terror', *Representations*, 75 (2001), 89–118; for the excavation of the headquarters of the Budapest Party Committee, see István Rév, *Retroactive Justice. Prehistory of Post-Communism* (Stanford, 2005), 270–7; for an investigation of the meaning of bones of a 'national hero' in the late Communist and post-Communist eras in Bulgaria, see Maria Todorova, *Bones of Contention: The Living Archive of Vasil Levski and the Making of Bulgaria's National Hero* (Budapest, 2009); for a broader approach, see Katherine Verdery, *The Political Lives of Dead Bodies: Reburial and Postsocialist Change* (New York, 1999).

anti-Communist national identities. Immediately after 1989, spaces devoted to re-formulating the story of the Communist past were seldom established at national history museums, but rather by anti-Communist associations of former political prisoners, victims of Communism, or exiles, who renovated or rebuilt political prisons, sites of execution, former security service head-quarters, or internment camps. These were locations where stories of Communist-era violence, particularly that perpetrated by Stalinist elites and the Red Army in the immediate post-war era, could be powerfully evoked.[8] For some of these institutions, forensic archaeology promised to augment their attempts to retell the nation's history through the recovery of, and the scientific validation of, the bodily remains of terror.

This article will focus on two such institutions. Both were located at 'sites of terror': Lithuania's Museum of Genocide Victims was established in 1992 in the prison of the former republican headquarters of the KGB; Romania's Sighet Memorial to the Victims of Communism and the Resistance (Fig. 1) was founded in the same year in a rebuilt gaol which had, in the early Communist period, incarcerated some of the country's most prominent pol-itical prisoners. The character of their locations differed markedly: the former situated on the central boulevard in Vilnius, the latter in Sighetu Marmaţiei, a remote town on the Romanian-Ukrainian border. The Lithuanian project was initiated by former political prisoners, although the prison museum operated initially under the control of the Ministry of Culture before being transferred to the strongly anti-Communist, state-sponsored Genocide and Resistance Research Centre in 1997. The Romanian memorial was initiated by the Civic Academy Foundation, a liberal non-governmental organization which campaigned for the strengthening of civil society.

These institutions were part of broader attempts to inscribe a new national identity based on the experience of suffering onto the post-Communist land-scape. In Lithuania, for instance, reviving the memory of the violence and deportations of the Stalinist period—termed the 'Soviet genocide'—was viewed as an essential component of the anti-Soviet struggle by the nationalist

---

[8] Terror was put on display at political prisons (Sighet Memorial, Romania; Museum of Genocide Victims, Lithuania), former secret police headquarters (Stasi Museum, Berlin; House of Terror, Hungary), political camps (Vojna Camp, Czech Republic), and statue parks (Hungary, Lithuania). On why these sites were selected, see James Mark, *The Unfinished Revolution. Making Sense of the Communist Past in Central-Eastern Europe* (forthcoming, 2010), ch. 3. See also Péter Apor and Oksana Sarsikova (eds), *Past for the Eyes. East European Representations of Communism in Cinema and Museums After 1989* (Budapest, 2008).

Fig. 1. Main prison hall, The Memorial of the Victims of Communism and of the Resistance, Sighetu Marmaţiei, Romania. (Photograph courtesy of James Mark)

movement (*Sąjūdis*) in the late 1980s.[9] After 1991, these anti-Communist framings of the past took the place of Soviet histories, and new elites sought to embed them in Vilnius, a city which had become the capital of an independent Lithuania for the first time, and where nationalists felt their presence still

---

[9] Dovile Budryte, *Taming Nationalism?: Political Community Building in the Post-Soviet Baltic States* (Aldershot, 2005), ch. 6. The term 'genocide' had been used in this way by Baltic exile communities since the 1940s.

needed to be legitimized. Yet these new approaches were created in the context of other readings of the region's histories and landscapes. Both institutions operated within post-Communist cultures they considered to have insufficiently demonized the previous system. In Romania, this was attributed to the survival of significant numbers of Communist nomenklatura after 1989; in Lithuania, this was primarily linked to their neighbour Russia's failure to engage critically with the violence of dictatorship or the forced incorporation of Lithuania into the Soviet Union during the Second World War. Moreover, they aimed to establish these histories of Romanian and Lithuanian 'martyrdom' in regions which had witnessed the suffering of other groups, notably Jews and ethnic Poles. In the early 1990s, these alternative histories of victimization were often ignored by nationalists, and were taken up and championed only by small-scale local groups, and international organizations.[10]

Both institutions were to become aware of mass graves which they supposed contained the remains of inmates who had died or been executed in these prisons in the post-war period. Uncovering this evidence appeared to offer the possibility of irrefutably tying these locations to the two narratives they wished to establish: the criminality of Communism, and the suffering of the nation. Yet the bones refused to cooperate: in Vilnius, they found a range of bodies whose historical associations did not easily accommodate themselves to a simple anti-Communist message, whilst at the Sighet Memorial the remains of the so-called 'national heroes' could not be traced at all. Nevertheless, these institutions found ways to repackage these awkward and potentially threatening discoveries in their construction of new nationalist, anti-Communist spaces.

In the late twentieth century, newly democratizing systems across the world increasingly asserted their superiority to their dictatorial forebears not by the claim that they could better modernize the country or guarantee social equality or stability (as had often been the case earlier in the twentieth century) but by the fact that they would uphold the rule of law and protect the individual from the power of the state.[11] Thus after the 1970s, democracies

---

[10] On the exclusion of Holocaust histories in the early 1990s in Lithuania, see Dov Levin, 'Lithuanian Attitudes toward the Jewish Minority in the Aftermath of the Holocaust: The Lithuanian Press, 1991–1992', *Holocaust and Genocide Studies*, 7 (1993), 247–62. It should be noted that there were some initiatives: a small Jewish museum re-established in 1990 and a Holocaust Day in 1994.

[11] For this shift, see Greg Grandin, 'The Instruction of Great Catastrophe: Truth Commissions, National History, and State Formation in Argentina, Chile, and Guatemala', *The American Historical Review*, 105 (2005), 47–9.

increasingly demonized dictatorships on particular account of their violence and disrespect for legal process. The anti-Communist memorial institutions of the former eastern bloc were part of this phenomenon; spaces where these regimes perpetrated their greatest violence powerfully illustrated the conception of Communism as a system of horrific illegality. Yet these museums were also a response to the sentiment that Communism had not yet been sufficiently criminalized. The founders of the Sighet Memorial frequently argued that the revolution of 1989 had been betrayed and the destruction of Communism was incomplete: former elites had been allowed to survive, not faced trials, been able to block investigations into their crimes, and, as an insufficiently demonized group, continued to have an inappropriately large influence over society.[12] They conceived of their prison as a substitute courtroom where a 'cultural trial' of Communism could be held, and citizens given close encounters with irrefutable evidence of the previous system's criminality. According to one of its founders, Ana Blandiana, a poet and former dissident: 'When justice does not succeed in being a form of memory, memory itself can be a form of justice.'[13]

Yet it was only a particular form of suffering that these institutions emphasized: the martyrdom of the nation under Communism and Soviet imperialism.[14] Both prison museums picked out particular inmates whose experiences represented the wider victimization of the nation. The executions

---

[12] For a discussion of these attitudes, see Adrian Cioflâncă, 'Politics of Oblivion in Post-Communist Romania', *The Romanian Journal of Political Sciences*, 2 (2002), 85–93. It should also be noted that other non-Communists, or 'anti-anti-Communists', objected to these approaches, which they considered politically damaging processes that privileged taking revenge on the past over the needs of democratization; see, e.g., Vasile Ernu, Costi Rogozanu, Ciprian Siulea, Ovidiu Țichindeleanu (eds), *Iluzia Anticomunismului: Lecturi Critice ale Raportului Tismăneanu* (Chisinau, 2008).

[13] Ana Blandiana, 'Memoria ca formă de justiţie', *Dilema*, 518 (2003), 10.

[14] By contrast, mass graves from the Nazi period, such as the one in the Paneriei woods, where 70,000 Jews were exterminated between 1941 and 1943, were of much less interest to post-Communist elites. Known about in the 1960s, interest in excavation did not emerge until 2008. Interview with Prof. Dr Rimantas Jankauskas, forensic archaeologist at the Tuskulėnai excavation, September 2008. The site of Vilnius's historic Jewish graveyard in Šnipiškės also became a subject of part-Communist 'body politics'. The Soviets had cleared it of most of its remains as part of their post-war policies to erase Vilnius' multi-ethnic past and make it the capital of the Lithuanian Soviet Republic. Nevertheless, when in 2007 a plot adjoining the desolate site was earmarked for a large commercial development on its margins, concerned international voices, including the US Congress, spoke out. Once again, geologists and archaeologists were invited to 'reveal the truth' about the site: Laimonas Briedis, *Vilnius: City of Strangers* (Budapest and New York), 249.

of those who resisted Lithuania's absorption into the Soviet Union in the Vilnius prison were used to symbolize the so-called 'genocide of the Lithuanian nation' under Communism, whilst the Sighet Memorial employed the story of prominent politicians who had died in the prison as powerful icons for the wider suffering of Romanians. These accounts of 'national victimhood' were for the most part identified with the dominant ethnic group—Lithuanians and Romanians. The story of the persecution of others—such as Poles and Jews in Vilnius, or Hungarians and Jews in northern Transylvania—played a much smaller role. The loss of minorities in these regions through genocide, ethnic cleansing, and emigration was often viewed as a competing story of victimhood, and was not considered by institutions which saw themselves as representing the interests of a post-Communist nation now more closely congruent with its dominant ethnic group.[15]

However, these buildings could not always provide direct unmediated encounters with the evils of Communism or the suffering of the nation. These locations did not bear simple witness to Communist illegality; the crimes these buildings recorded were over forty years past, and nearly all direct evidence effectively removed. Sighet had not been used as a political prison since the 1950s, had fallen into ruins and had to be extensively reconstructed. Although the Vilnius prison had been used to incarcerate dissidents up until August 1991, half of it had been used to store KGB archive material since the 1960s, and the instruments and spaces of terror and killing which the museum wished to restore had been destroyed in the 1950s.[16] Thus visitors were shown reconstructed and re-imagined sites. The Sighet prison was extensively rebuilt (according to prisoners' reports) in the early 1990s, whilst in Vilnius the museum's centrepiece—the execution chamber used in the 1940s and 1950s—was uncovered and reconstructed with the help of archaeologists.

Moreover, the fact that these former prisons had witnessed multiple atrocities against different ethnic groups under various states meant that the sites' own histories had the potential to threaten the appearance of authenticity of their nationalist, anti-Communist approaches. The full histories of these locations made plain the contested and multilayered pasts of the regions in

[15] The Museum of Genocide Victims dealt neither with the Holocaust nor the ethnic cleansing of Poles. The Sighet Memorial attempted to reflect the ethnic diversity of their region, and provided rooms devoted to the suffering of ethnic Hungarians and Germans under Communism; however, its main focus remained the heroic Romanian martyrs and the loss of 'ethnic Romanian lands' to the Soviet Union after World War Two.

[16] Museum of Genocide Victims' visitors' leaflet.

which they were situated: the Vilnius museum's building had been used as a courthouse of the Russian Empire before 1914, the German state during World War One and then the Polish government between 1920 and 1940. It then became a Soviet political prison twice (1940–1 and 1944–91) and a Gestapo prison and barracks once (1941–4). The Sighet building had been used as a gaol by the Austro-Hungarian Empire from 1897, the Romanian state in the inter-war period, and the Hungarian state after 1941, before becoming a Romanian Communist political penitentiary after 1944. Moreover, until the Second World War, these prisons were located in two of the most ethnically diverse regions of Europe. Vilnius had been home to Polish and Jewish populations which had vastly outnumbered the ethnic Lithuanian community in the city (in the 1930s, there were only a few thousand Lithuanians out of a population of 200,000).[17] In the early twentieth century, the town of Sighetu Marmaţiei was dominated by Hungarians and had one of the largest Jewish communities in the region; indeed, it was the birthplace of Elie Wiesel, Holocaust survivor and Nobel Laureate. Crucially, these prisons were witnesses to the fates of these other ethnic groups; the Sighet penitentiary became a transportation centre for Transylvanian Jews being taken to Auschwitz,[18] whilst the Vilnius jail was run by the Gestapo between 1941 and 1944, hosted prisoners of multiple nationalities, and served as a barracks for the Vilnius Extraordinary Detachment, who were responsible for the annihilation of Jews in the district in 1942–43. Yet the Museum of Genocide Victims ignored these alternative histories: the remnants of the Gestapo prison, where Jewish, Polish, and Communist victims were interrogated and tortured, were almost entirely forgotten, whilst its historical displays, which began in 1940, omitted the period of German occupation between 1941 and 1944 altogether. In the context of early post-Communist nation building, the stories of other groups' suffering either seemed unimportant, or uncomfortably reminiscent of Soviet anti-fascist propaganda, or

---

[17] Theodore R. Weeks, 'Remembering and Forgetting: Creating a Soviet Lithuanian Capital. Vilnius', *Journal of Baltic Studies*, 39 (2008), 519–20.

[18] See Robert Fürtös, 'Sighet, preambul al Holocaustului, punct central al Gulagului', *Caietele Echinox*, 13 (2007), 226–41. Around 12,000 Jews were deported from Sighet to Nazi extermination camps. Some noted that Sighetu Marmaţiei would be an inappropriate location for the commemoration of the Holocaust in Romania as deportations were carried out there after its absorption into the Hungarian state in 1940; such an approach might suggest that the Romanian state was avoiding questions of its own complicity in the Holocaust by supporting commemoration in those regions where it had no responsibility for genocide.

were actively feared—in the case of the Holocaust for its capacity to drown out appeals to the suffering of the nation under Communism.[19]

It was in this context that archaeological excavation offered the possibility of reinforcing the historical messages which these anti-Communists wished to transmit through the physical recovery of Communist sites of terror, but which their buildings failed to make wholly authentic. At both prisons, political inmates had died or been executed and their bodies removed and disposed of at nearby sites, the locations of which were not publicly disclosed until after the collapse of Communism. At the end of 1993, Lithuania's national security service discovered documents relating to NKVD-KGB executions in the prison which pointed to the existence of a mass grave on the Tuskulėnai estate on the outskirts of Vilnius.[20] At the Sighet prison, former guards' testimony indicated that prominent national figures who had died whilst incarcerated had had their bones scattered in the town's 'Cemetery of the Poor', beside the Ukrainian border.

The searches for remains were neither initiated nor undertaken by the memorial institutions themselves. In January 1994, Lithuanian President Algirdas Brazauskas (an ex-Communist) established a national committee to oversee the investigation of the executions and the Tuskulėnai site: it appointed professionals from Vilnius University's Institute of Forensic Medicine, who carried out excavations on the mass grave between 1994 and 1996, and again in 2003.[21] At Sighetu Marmaţiei, the excavation was initiated by the Institute for the Investigation of the Crimes of Communism,[22] a body established in December 2005 by the Truth and Justice Alliance (*Alianţa Dreptate şi Adevăr*), a liberal coalition which had come to power in 2004 claiming to be the first post-Communist government to take justice for the victims of Communism seriously. The Institute aimed both to draw broader public attention to the previous system's crimes and, where possible, to bring perpetrators to trial.[23] Its director,

---

[19] For how Holocaust histories can seem to threaten attempts to tell the story of the 'victims of Communism', see James Mark, 'Containing Fascism: History in Post-Communist Baltic Occupation and Genocide Museums', in Apor and Sarsikova (eds), *Past for the Eyes*, 335–69.

[20] Audio-guide, Museum of Genocide Victims.

[21] Forensic archaeology emerged as a discipline in Lithuania in the 1960s; in Romania, it was a later post-Communist development.

[22] Interview with Marius Oprea, director of the Institute for the Investigation of the Crimes of Communism, May 2008.

[23] Its aims were, 'to investigate and to identify the crimes, the abuses and human rights violations... [and] notify the state's criminal investigation departments'; The Institute for the Investigation of Communist Crimes in Romania, *Investigations Department*

who had been trained as an archaeologist, established a department devoted to uncovering the remains of mass graves, in part to facilitate such prosecutions. It conducted excavations in the Cemetery of the Poor in July and November 2006.[24]

Forensic science was attractive to these memorial institutions in part because it had the potential to bolster their claims to provide bona fide 'cultural trials' of Communism. These disciplines treated historical mass graves as crime scenes, and conceptualized remains as evidence through which responsibility could be attributed for criminality.[25] Thus, even where prosecution was not possible, forensic investigation could provide a rhetorically powerful scientific account of the illegality of dictatorship. In Vilnius, archaeologists uncovered remains which had the potential to be turned into legally admissible evidence. Through the forensic identification of victims, the examination of both judicial accounts of the trials which had convicted them, and the NKVD records of their executions, they were able to isolate those who had given the orders for the executions, those who had carried them out, and the warders of the prison who had been responsible for transporting the bodies to the mass grave.[26] Moreover, they were able to demonstrate, through the examination of skulls of the victims, that the Soviet perpetrators could be tried for contravening their own criminal codes. According to the report:

> One hundred and twelve skulls were mutilated by daggers and five by hatchets. . . People were not only killed by gunshots, but also stabbed and knifed. . . we found the skulls, which had been deformed. . . with a special hoop. All these facts were evidence

---

Activity Report, May–December 2006 (Bucharest, 2006), 3. It mainly carried out excavations on the request of relatives of those killed for political reasons. It also produced films of these excavations such as 'Testimonies of Suffering' and 'The Dead'.

[24] Gheorghe Petrov and Cosmin Budeancă, *Raport privind cercetările arheologice desfăşurate în Cimitirul Săracilor din Sighetu Marmaţiei* (Bucharest, 2006).

[25] In Argentina, relatives of victims criticized forensic archaeologists for focusing too heavily on bones as objects of evidence, seeing their recovery as primarily providing comfort to the families of the dead. They also believed that excavations removed the symbolic power of the mass grave site which were 'no longer haunted by the uneasy ghosts of the disappeared'; see Zoe Crossland, 'The Reappearance of Argentina's Disappeared', in John Schofield et al. (eds), *Materiél Culture. The Archaeology of Twentieth Century Conflict* (London and New York, 2002), 130.

[26] Tuskulėnai Summary, Museum of Genocide Victims.

that some . . . were tortured . . . Thus, the henchmen had violated
Soviet criminal law, which allowed only fusillade [firing squad].[27]

Forensic archaeology was also appealing to these museums because, at least
initially, these projects focused on the recovery only of those 'national heroes'
who had perished in their prisons. The Vilnius excavation was framed as a
search for two Lithuanian participants in the struggle against Soviet occupation: the Catholic bishop of Telšiai, Vincentas Borisevičius, and a member of
the armed resistance in Vilnius whose relatives in North America wanted to
find his remains. Moreover, as the scale of the mass grave at Tuskulėnai was
revealed, so it was quickly constructed as a place of national martyrdom; the
General Procurator's Office, for instance, commenced a criminal lawsuit
against the perpetrators which framed the site as evidence of the 'genocide
of the Lithuanian people'. At Sighet, the excavation was originally conceived
of as a general site survey of the paupers' graveyard, although it was clear that
the archaeological team wanted to find the bones of the two most important
Romanian 'martyrs' who had died in the prison: Gheorghe Brătianu, interwar
leader of the right-wing National Liberals and Iuliu Maniu, interwar head of
the National Peasant Party.[28] Despite the fact they both, in all likelihood, died
of natural causes, the museum presented their deaths as symbols of the suppression of the nation. Brătianu, it was reported, was denied medicine aged
ninety following his refusal to renounce his belief in the union of Romania
and Bessarabia, a region which had become part of Romania in 1918 but was
incorporated into the Soviet Union in 1944. The recovery of the remains of
figures such as Borisevičius and Brătianu promised powerfully to tie these
museums' new historical accounts to seemingly irrefutable physical proof of
Communist-era suffering and thus aid their nationalization and simplifica-
tion of the history of the spaces they memorialized.

Dealing with the bones

Despite the work of archaeologists, these remains could not be used as objects
of evidence in criminal prosecutions; in Vilnius, for instance, it was concluded that as the crimes were chronologically distant, and the surviving
perpetrators had fled to Russia, a judicial process was impracticable.[29]
Rather, the importance of these bones lay in their capacity to aid new nationalist ways of memorializing the Communist past. These prison museums
and their associated grave sites became nationally and internationally

[27] Ibid.
[28] Interview with Oprea.
[29] Interview with Jankauskas.

important locations of anti-Communist commemoration: from 2004, the Tuskulėnai site was the focus for the annual national day of remembrance for Lithuanian victims of Communism; in 1998, the Sighet Memorial was declared by the Council of Europe, along with Auschwitz and the Peace Memorial in Normandy, as one of the most significant commemorative sites of the European continent. Yet the discoveries which forensic archaeology had enabled could not always easily be employed to support the narratives which these institutions wished to establish. The excavations revealed remains which had the potential to support different—and potentially threatening—histories.

Mass grave, Tuskulėnai estate, Vilnius

Often forensic scientists working at mass graves accepted the impossibility of individual identification, and settled for proving the existence of the atrocity, and on occasion the methods and identities of perpetrators.[30] Indeed, for the prosecution of crimes against humanity, and war crimes, personal identification was not necessarily the central issue. Forensic scientists needed only to establish that a set of bodies were killed because they belonged to a particular targeted group.[31] The process at the Tuskulėnai grave was an unusual one in that it included the distinguishing of specific victims. An excavation which had begun as a search for two individuals eventually led to the unearthing and forensic examination of the remains of seven hundred and twenty four bodies, from which around fifty individuals were identified.[32] This was done partly because they could: the Lithuanian secret service obtained a KGB register which listed the majority of those who were executed in Vilnius between 1944 and 1947, provided precise information about sex, age, and stature, and often included a photograph of the victim.[33] Families whose lost relatives appeared on the list often provided further photographic documentation and bodily samples which allowed the forensic scientists to use techniques such as skull-photo superimposition and DNA testing to

---

[30] Although uncommon, DNA testing has been used in some recent East European mass grave excavations; see Sarah E. Wagner, *To Know Where He Lies: DNA Technology and the Search for Srebrenica's Missing* (Berkeley and London, 2008), ch. 3.

[31] Kirsten Juhl, *The Contribution by (Forensic) Archaeologists to Human Rights Investigations of Mass Graves* (Stavanger, 2005), 23.

[32] Rimantas Jankauskas, Arūnas Barkus, Vytautas Urbanavièius, Antanas Garmus, 'Forensic Archaeology in Lithuania: The Tuskulėnai Mass Grave', *Acta Medica Lituanica*, 12 (2005), 71.

[33] Ibid., 72.

further identify particular victims.[34] Yet individual identification also reflected the values of late twentieth-century democratization which were not evident at earlier investigations of mass graves. Indeed, in the post-war period, sites of Nazi criminality were seldom excavated; where they were, the recovery of an indistinguishable mass of bones was often considered a sufficient illustration of the regime's inhumanity. For the Tuskulėnai project, however, the process of identification was valued in part because it allowed the bones of the executed to be returned to their relatives, and possible reburials. It was thus seen as a way of restoring dignity to the victim and their families which the Communists had refused them even in death.[35] The remains became an assertion of the superiority of a new political system based on legal protections: the return of bones illustrated powerfully the vital rights which only a democratic state could ensure.

Yet the discovery of detailed NKVD-KGB records proved double-edged. On one hand, they provided irrefutable proof of Soviet complicity, and enabled some families to recover their relatives' remains. On the other, this secret service documentation revealed that the grave contained the bones of individuals from a much wider range of national and ideological backgrounds than was initially supposed: alongside two hundred and six Lithuanian participants of the post-war anti-Soviet resistance, documents listed thirty-two soldiers and supporters of the Polish Home Army; eighty members of the Lithuanian police (under German control) who had collaborated with Nazis and their subordinate officers, or worked as supervisors of prisons and concentration camps; and two hundred and fifty-seven people of different national backgrounds who were sentenced for crimes against civilians and participation in crimes connected to the Holocaust.[36] It should be noted that there is good reason to doubt the validity of some of these accusations: Soviet authorities regularly categorized their enemies as Nazi collaborators or as being complicit in the killing of Jews, where the evidence was slim or non-existent.

---

[34] The Lithuanian Genocide and Resistance Research Centre, which managed the museum from 1997, was not heavily involved in the initial excavations. However, it subsequently played a major role in the memorialization at the site, and became responsible for administering families' requests for searches for relatives' remains amongst the exhumed material.

[35] Interview with Jankauskas.

[36] 'Tuskulėnai: Victims of Execution and their Henchmen (1944–1947)', Summary produced by the Genocide and Resistance Research Centre. The KGB archives lacked documentation on 157 people shot in the prison.

Nevertheless, this identification process polluted the category of the 'Lithuanian victim of Communism' that the site had initially been expected to support. The bodies of Polish, German, and Lithuanian Holocaust perpetrators proved the most problematic. First, their existence demonstrated that the site had not only witnessed Lithuanian suffering: the victims in the mass grave were multinational, and their biographies alluded to other tragedies whose scale might have the power to overshadow appeals to Lithuanian national martyrdom. Secondly, these remains did not straightforwardly document Communist criminality; they also demonstrated the role the Soviets had played in bringing an end to Fascism and the Holocaust in the region.[37] Thirdly, the category of 'victims of Communism' could no longer be equated simply with 'heroes' who had fought for an independent Lithuania: this grouping now included Holocaust perpetrators alongside anti-Communist resistance fighters, and, most problematically of all, those who had both fought for an independent Lithuania *and* undertaken the ethnic cleansing of Jews and Poles. It was therefore not surprising that some observers rejected the all-inclusive category of 'victims of Communism' and started to classify the bones according to those which belonged to either morally worthy or morally unworthy victims. They could not understand how the Soviets could have placed such an ethically confusing jumble of remains in one grave, and rebuked the Soviet security forces for not having anticipated the requirements of post-Communist Lithuanian nationalism in advance: 'It is as if the NKVD made this "cocktail" and jigsaw for our generation with the intention of puzzling us. Completely innocent people and fighters for an independent and democratic Lithuania are mixed up with those who participated in the Holocaust.'[38] The Genocide and Resistance Research Centre would have liked to separate them out; indeed, DNA technology made it theoretically possible to consider disentangling co-mingled skeletal remains.[39] However, at Tuskulėnai it was thought unfeasible: '[Our opinion] of the war criminals and Nazi collaborators [who were buried there] is

---

[37] For how the post-Communist Russian politicians criticized Baltic elites for undermining the liberation narrative, and why Balts saw this criticism as threatening, see James Mark, 'Containing Fascism'.

[38] Emmanuel Zingeris, quoted in Rokas M. Tracevskis, 'A Grave Fit for Whom?', *Transitions Online* (3 October 2003), 3.

[39] This is usually a very expensive procedure and is only carried out after 'politicized mass fatalities in wealthy countries' (such as 9/11 and the London Bombings of July 2005); Caroline Barker, Margaret Cox, Ambika Flavel, Joanna Laver, and Louise Loe, 'Mortuary Procedures II- Skeletal Analysis I: Basic Procedures and Demographic Assessment' in Cox et al. (eds), *The Scientific Investigation*, 306.

unfavourable, but there was no question of separating out the remains as the bodies had been disfigured by lime . . . and so the identification of them was impossible.'[40]

Whilst the morally problematic bones could not be separated out through forensic techniques, a process of memorialization served to erase the troubling and destabilizing associations of their co-mingling. This should be read in the context of a wider attempt to remould the Vilnius cityscape as a Lithuanian space in the post-Communist period. The city had been part of the Russian Empire between 1795 and the First World War, in Poland between 1922 and 1939, and then in the Soviet Union from 1944 to 1991. It had been dominated by Poles and Jews before 1939; only after the Holocaust, and deportations of Polish communities during and after the Second World War, did ethnic Lithuanians become a majority. It became the capital of an independent Lithuania for the first time in 1991, and nationalist elites sought to sponsor new memorial projects. One of the most important of these was the reconstruction of the Lower Palace of the Lithuanian Grand Dukes, a structure which was built before the Polish dominance of the city, and which had been torn down by the Tsarist state in 1801, sixteen years after Vilnius had been incorporated into the Russian empire.[41] The history of its construction, destruction and reconstruction was used to tell the story of a city once dominated by Lithuanian culture which had been destroyed under Russian (and then Soviet) rule, and which now could be restored in an independent Lithuanian state. Yet this narrative required the substantial marginalization of aspects of Vilnius' multi-ethnic past: Lithuanians had been only a small minority even when the palace was first erected under the Grand Duchy of Lithuania, a multi-ethnic empire the official languages of which were Old Ruthenian, Belarussian, Latin, and Polish (not Lithuanian), and the chief religion of which was eastern Orthodoxy.[42]

In this reshaping of the Vilnius cityscape, there was little room for the recognition of the sufferings of other groups. The wartime and post-war cleansing of the city's Polish communities was forgotten, in part because it drew attention to the fact that it was a Soviet policy which had in effect created the foundations for an ethnically Lithuanian Vilnius.[43] There was some

---

[40] Personal correspondence of the author with the museum, February 2007.

[41] For a discussion of this, see John Czaplicka, 'The Palace Ruins and Putting the Lithuanian Nation into Place. Historical Settings in Vilnius', in Daniel J. Walkowitz and Lisa Maya Knauer (eds), *Memory and the Impact of Political Transformation in Public Space* (Durham, 2004), 179.

[42] Ibid., 180–1.

[43] Weeks, 'Creating a Soviet Lithuanian Capital', 520–5. ·

attempt to recover aspects of Jewish culture,[44] although the Holocaust (in which 93% of Lithuanian Jews were killed) was not extensively commemorated in the immediate post-Communist period: a small museum devoted to the history of Vilnius' Jewish community was re-established in 1991,[45] but Nazi mass grave sites such as those in the Paneriai Woods were not excavated.[46] Some believed that Holocaust remembrance in Western Europe and North America drowned out an appropriate recognition of Lithuanian suffering, or still had the potential to exonerate the Soviets as 'liberators' of the Baltics from Fascism. Only in the late 1990s did it become common to accord weight to Nazi persecution alongside Soviet crimes. Even then, however, this new approach was often adopted only grudgingly and regarded as a foreign imposition associated with integration into European political and cultural norms, rather than as a domestic imperative.[47]

The form of memorialization chosen for the mass grave site stripped out the multi-ethnic character of the remains, and did not address their associations with the Holocaust. When the memorial site opened in 2004, the bones of all victims, regardless of their nationality or past political or religious affiliations, were placed within a columbarium sunk into an earth mound near the site of the mass grave. Here the remains were stored in hundreds of marked boxes placed in recesses in a circular wall that ran around a central chamber, where wreaths and other dedications could be left for the dead (Fig. 2). It additionally functioned as a storage facility, from where bones could be retrieved when families made requests to identify relatives. This choice of repository, which had been popular with Lithuanian Catholics prior to World War Two, effectively captured all the remains as representatives of Lithuanian suffering.[48] The entrance was framed by the double cross

---

[44] See, e.g., the rebuilding of the Great Synagogue.

[45] This was the 'Vilna Goan Jewish State Museum'.

[46] Interview with Jankauskas. By contrast, a mass grave made up of soldiers of Napoleon's army who died on the retreat from Moscow in 1812 received substantial attention: Didier Raoult et al., 'Evidence for Louse-Transmitted Diseases in Soldiers of Napoleon's Grand Army in Vilnius', *The Journal of Infectious Diseases*, 193 (2006), 112–20.

[47] Budryte, *Taming Nationalism?*, 184; James Mark, 'Containing Fascism', 333. A turning point in the collective memory of the Baltic states was signalled by the establishment of state-sponsored History Commissions in the late 1990s directed to investigate both Nazi and Soviet crimes. They were created in large part in order to prepare for integration into western historical and cultural norms as these countries joined the European Union.

[48] In 1991, a poll found that 69% of Lithuanians identified themselves as Catholics. The Catholic Church played a large role in developing and preserving Lithuanian culture, especially during those periods when Lithuanians had no state.

Fig. 2. Columbarium Interior. Repository for Bones from the Tuskulėnai Mass Grave, Vilnius, Lithuania. (Photograph courtesy of Prof. Dr Rimantas Jankauskas)

of St Vytis (Fig. 3), a symbol of both the destruction (and rebirth) of the Lithuanian nation. As part of the national revival in the nineteenth century, St Vytis on horseback came to represent the soon-to-be-liberated nation chasing the intruder out of the country; for this reason, his image was deemed

Fig. 3. Columbarium Exterior. Tuskulėnai Mass Grave, Vilnius, Lithuania. (Photograph courtesy of Prof. Dr. Rimantas Jankauskas)

subversive under Soviet rule and banned.[49] Moreover, the power of these remains was invoked annually on 14 June,[50] when this site was used for the official state-sponsored 'Day of Mourning of Hope', a commemoration of the Soviet repression of Lithuanians.[51] Yet some argued that these bones should not have been called upon in the name of post-Communist nationalism.[52] For them, the presence of Germans, Poles, and Lithuanians complicit in the Holocaust (whose co-mingled remains could not be separated out within the columbarium) meant that Fascists were being commemorated in the name of anti-Communism. Whilst the columbarium's supporters claimed that 'death

---

[49] Athena S. Leoussi, 'National Symbols: Ethnicity and Historical Continuity in Post-Communist "New Europe"', in Steven Elliot Grosby and Athena S. Leoussi (eds), *Nationalism and Ethnosymbolism: History, Culture and Ethnicity in the Formation of Nations* (Edinburgh, 2006), 179.

[50] On 14 June 1941, the NKVD started the mass arrests and deportations of Lithuanians during the first Soviet occupation.

[51] In addition, the buildings of the Tuskulėnai Manor, which were used both by the KGB and the Association of Water Sports as a sanatorium under Soviet rule, will be converted by the museum to house an exhibition on the 'spiritual genocide' of the communist period, focusing on the attempts to turn Lithuanians into the 'Homo Sovieticus'.

[52] See Briedis, *Vilnius: City of Strangers*, 247.

equalized the victims' and that they were being commemorated not for their lives but for the criminal nature of their demise,[53] others protested: Emmanuel Zingeris, director of the Vilna Gaon Jewish State Museum, declined to attend the opening ceremony, and the local Catholic Church refused to support the project.[54]

Cemetery of the Poor, Sighetu Marmaţiei

Two excavations were conducted at the Cemetery of the Poor by the Institute for the Investigation of the Crimes of Communism, overseen by the deputy chief military prosecutor of Romania. Its archaeologists hoped to unearth the bones of two prominent political figures who had died in the Sighet prison: Gheorghe Brătianu and Iuliu Maniu. The latter had had an iron support implanted in his leg as the result of surgery; thus, they hoped that his remains could be distinguished easily without DNA testing. Yet the process of excavation was challenging: the bones of political prisoners had supposedly been scattered amongst those of the town's poor, and the choice of locations for trenches reliant on the (often contradictory) witnessing of former prison guards. Moreover, the dig was terminated after disagreements between the Institute and the Sighet Memorial before DNA testing could be carried out.[55] The archaeologists discovered bones 'buried without respect': their bodies were facing west (which often denoted suicide) and had been placed outside the frontier of the formal Christian graveyard. They also uncovered the remains of children buried in the 1980s; some surmised that these were orphans, born as a result of Ceausescu's anti-abortion policies, who had perished living on the street.[56] Yet they did not find any bones that they could positively identify as belonging to political prisoners. Thus, unlike the Vilnius mass grave where the problems lay in the range of remains that were discovered, the concern at Sighet was the reverse: an absence of politically significant bones.

The failure to find the right sort of bones was not deemed problematic, however. After 1989, Romania's inability to recover the remains of its 'national martyrs', particularly those who were killed during the revolution of 1989, was used by anti-Communists to illustrate the incompleteness of the political transition and to inspire a continued anti-Communist struggle in the present.

---

[53] Interview with Jankauskas.
[54] Ellen Cassedy, 'A Controversy Exhumes Long-buried Memories', *Forward. The Jewish Daily* (12 November 2004).
[55] Interview with Oprea.
[56] Interview with Cosmin Budeancă, archaeologist on the Sighet excavation, May 2008.

Unlike elsewhere in central-eastern Europe, the fall of Communism in Romania was particularly violent: an estimated 1104 revolutionaries died. Moreover, hundreds of their bodies went missing and were probably destroyed by the Securitate. As in many other countries in the region, however, Communists survived in large numbers within the political system; more than a decade after the end of Communism, still 63% of the political elite had held positions in the Communist Party prior to 1989.[57] Former Communists often blocked investigations into the disappearances of those who had perished.[58] Thus for anti-Communists the absence of victims' bodies represented not merely the extreme inhumanity of the security services, but also the continuing power of ex-Communists to block a reckoning with this difficult past. Memorials were established in places where no evidence could possibly be retrieved, such as rubbish dumps and sewers, where the ashes of the bodies of the revolutionaries were supposed to have been deposited. Ceremonial processes were organized to accord victims whose bodies were lost proper funerary rites. In 1993, for example, citizens from Timişoara marched on Bucharest with urns to visit the site of the sewer where the bodies of their city's revolutionaries were thought to have been scattered; there they collected dust in the hope that a few 'molecules of the ashes of the heroes' would be amongst them.[59] Anti-Communist groups saw in their commemoration of lost bodies a respectful acknowledgement of the victims of Communism, which the post-1989 political elite had failed to engender.

The idea of absent remains became central to the memorialization established at Sighet. Rather than dismiss the Cemetery of the Poor because no bones had been found, the Memorial instead incorporated it into its visitor experience, by presenting it as a protected space in which the nation could shield its martyrs' lost bones from the continuing power of ex-Communists. Its memorial landscaping reflected the idea that the 'martyrs' remains' were present, but unrecoverable, due to the perfidy of the Communists (who tried to hide their bones amongst those of the poor), and the lack of post-Communist political will. Curators invoked the ideas of both presence and absence—that the bones were there, brutalized, yet undiscovered—creating a

---

[57] Figure from 2002, taken from Cioflâncă, 'Politics of Oblivion', 90.

[58] In June 2001, e.g., President Ion Iliescu, a member of the former nomenklatura, called for 'national reconciliation' based on 'erasing the problems of the past' and providing amnesty for those who had committed violent acts during the Romanian revolution.

[59] Sidonia Grama, 'In Between Places of Remembrance and Realms of Memory: The 15 Year Commemoration of the Romanian Revolution in Timişoara', *Philobiblon*, 10/11 (2005–6), 310–41.

Fig. 4. Cemetery of the Poor, The Memorial of the Victims of Communism and of the Resistance, Sighetu Marmației, Romania. Note the trees and bushes planted in the shape of Romania's borders. (Photograph courtesy of James Mark)

dramatic tension that enabled them to narrate new histories in a number of ways:

> According to local legend, it was here that the fifty-two dead from the political prison were secretly buried at night. Their graves could not be identified among the thousands of [other] graves . . . [so] to commemorate the sacrifice of these victims, a landscape project was developed in 1999. On 14,000 square metres of the cemetery, the outline of the country was drawn.[60]

Lines of trees and bushes were planted in order to outline the borders of Romania around those areas where the martyrs' remains were considered most likely to lie (Fig. 4).

The site articulated the idea that the bones still needed to be guarded, enveloped in an 'organic Romania' that represented the power of a newly risen anti-Communist nation to protect them from further violation. According to the guide, the vegetal map, 'through growth . . . will become an . . . amphitheatre, in the inside of which the country will remain like a

---

[60] Sighet Memorial guide.

"glade". The idea is that, in this way, the country keeps its martyrs in its arms and mourns them through the repeated generations of vegetation.'[61] The notion that these bones could also be called upon in the continued anti-Communist struggle was embedded in the cemetery's landscaping and iconography. In Orthodox beliefs in the region, the absence of a proper burial was not only calamitous for the soul of the deceased, but for the living too: the dead had the potential to return to punish those who had denied them the appropriate funerary rites. Indeed, in the county of Maramureş (where Sighetu Marmaţiei is located) peasant culture emphasized communication between the dead and the living; at funerals, 'lamenters attempt to convince the deceased not to depart'[62] and invite the return of the dead (but do not expect these pleas to be answered).[63] At an altar within the 'vegetal map', marking the location of the town of Sighet, masses were held annually to commemorate the martyrs and to call upon their spirit to aid the on-going anti-Communist struggle. Moreover, in an appeal to the supposed supernatural force of prominent victims such as Maniu, Brătianu and Daniel Ciugureanu, grave markers were installed and inscribed with exhortations to the dead.[64] A marker for Ciugureanu - who had been an advocate for the unification of Romania with the Bessarabian lands which were eventually absorbed into the Soviet Union after World War Two—read:

> This wooden cross is made to mark the symbolic place of the unidentified grave of the great national fighter killed in the Communist prison . . . In this earth the souls of the most powerful and famous are working for the country now . . . Dante's inferno [i.e. the Communist system] is going down to hell—the noble souls are going to paradise . . . the bones of the martyrs of Romania have melted away but the myths of the heroes rise from here, and prayers are rising from the servants of our people.[65]

Thus, even where bones could not be found they could still be invoked to support this new historical narrative; a dearth of remains did not mean an absence of evidence but rather illustrated the residual power of Communism

---

[61] Ibid.

[62] Gail Kligman, *The Wedding of the Dead. Ritual, Poetics and Popular Culture in Transylvania* (Berkeley, 1998), 177.

[63] Ibid., 156.

[64] These were not placed at the actual locations of graves, as they are unknown.

[65] Inscription on the Ciugureanu Cross, Cemetery of the Poor.

to block the truth about the past, and reinforced the necessity of calling upon the lost remains in the name of a resurrected anti-Communist nation.[66]

Conclusion

Forensic archaeology appealed to anti-Communists who wished to memorialize and condemn Communism at its places of imprisonment, execution, and violence, but were confronted with sites which had ambiguous pasts that threatened to undermine their telling of history. The archaeological excavation of the bodies of the victims of Communism, it was hoped, would provide incontrovertible evidence of the evils of that system and the suffering of the nation, and divert attention away from the other histories of genocide and ethnic cleansing that these places of imprisonment had often borne witness to. Yet the exhibition of archaeological finds was never a simple presentation of what was found; these institutions discovered that their display of victims' bones also required substantial artifice and re-arrangement. Far from providing clear anti-Communist messages about the past, the remains that were recovered had to be repackaged to exclude inconvenient truths.

The faith that these museums invested in archaeology to do their ideological work, and the subsequent artifice which was necessary to sustain the power of that project, was encapsulated by the process through which the Museum of Genocide Victims brought the iconography of the excavation into the body of the prison museum itself. Following the discovery of the mass burial at the Tuskulėnai estate, the museum employed archaeologists to search for the execution chamber where, it was thought, many of the grave's victims had initially been killed. Following the advice of former prison guards, it was discovered at a location marked as 'kitchen' on KGB maps, and was excavated in 1998. Situated below the political prisoners' cells, it became the centrepiece of the museum. Yet the execution chamber was not reconstructed to appear as it might have looked in the 1950s, in a fashion similar to the rest of the

[66] It should be noted that these were fundamentally political rather than religious sites, constructed to support a new national identity based around an anti-Communist story of national victimization. Religious imagery and ritual was used only in so far as it confirmed those basic political narratives: in Vilnius, a Catholic columbarium 'captured' all the grave's bones for the Lithuanian nation, erased the foreign origins of many of the remains, and thus confirmed the site as one of strictly local martyrdom; at Sighet, the Memorial fed off local Orthodox beliefs about the dead in order to invoke their memory in the name of an on-going anti-Communist struggle. In neither case were official religious bodies heavily involved; indeed, in Vilnius, the local Catholic Church and Jewish community refused to become associated with the site.

Fig. 5. Execution Chamber, The Museum of Genocide Victims, Vilnius, Lithuania.
(Photograph courtesy of James Mark)

building where prison cells were filled with narrow beds and the accoutrements of a Stalinist-era prison. Rather, it was displayed as a present-day archaeological dig in progress, with the credentials of forensic science laid out for the visitor to observe (Fig. 5). A glass floor was placed a foot above ground level. Visitors could stand on this and regard the dug earth below, on which objects such as a pair of glasses and a small piece of barbed wire were placed as if they had just been uncovered. Visitors were also directed towards a newly excavated drain where, it was claimed, the blood from executed victims flowed away, and to bullet holes in the wall. The display appeared to freeze the moment of revelation when the violence and brutality of the Communist system were finally revealed by archaeologists.

The chamber was in fact artifice masquerading as naturalism. The objects scattered on its floor had not been found there, but rather had been collected from the Tuskulėnai grave and had been then professionally arranged to mimic the popularly understood representation of an archaeological dig. The appeal to the moment of scientific discovery assured viewers that they were gaining an unmediated experience of terror. The visitor was simply being provided with the evidence of atrocity which the Communists had tried to hide and the museum simply uncovered and left untouched. Yet these devices were as much about concealment as they were about revelation: they distracted the audience from the notion that it had been an ideological decision to excavate, reconstruct, and display the Communist prison but not the Fascist era one. An awareness of the choice that had been made to reconstruct one apparatus of terror but not another would have had the capacity to erase the sense of authenticity that made the museum's stories of martyrdom so powerful. Thus forensic archaeology played a central role in the creation of new anti-Communist histories; it provided the powerful sense of an unmediated revelation of criminality and terror which could be utilized to tell the stories of national suffering that were at the heart of their new visions for national identity, whilst justifying the exclusion of those other stories which threatened the ascendancy of these accounts in post-Communist collective memory.

The Search for the Remains of Dedan Kimathi: The Politics of Death and Memorialization in Post-Colonial Kenya*

Daniel Branch

As long as Kimathi lies in Kamiti Prison, a colonial prison, we cannot be free.[1]

Modern Kenyan history is full of eloquent corpses.[2] Certain remains, through the debates and silences that surround them, articulate lucidly what it has meant to be a citizen or subject of colonial and post-colonial Kenya. It is unsurprising then that Kenyans and their historians have, like other Africanist historians, found discussions of the cultural practices surrounding death and dying fruitful for scholarly enquiry.[3] Few corpses, though, have attracted such prolonged attention as that of Dedan Kimathi, one of the Mau Mau rebellion's leaders executed by the British authorities in 1957. However, concern for Kimathi's remains did not arise for a long period after his death.

Not beginning until the early 1990s, the search for Kimathi's remains nevertheless lasted until reaching a fruitless conclusion on 15 January 2004. For a decade and a half, the family of the executed Mau Mau leader, veterans of that anti-colonial insurgency, and their sympathizers agitated for information pertaining to the exact location of Kimathi's grave inside the compound of the Kamiti maximum security prison. The cause of their confusion was understandable. Kimathi was buried in an unmarked mass grave after his

---

* This paper was first presented at the 'Relics and Remains' conference at the University of Exeter, September 2008 and subsequently at the 'Africa@Warwick' symposium in January 2010. I am grateful to the audiences at both events and the anonymous reviewers for their comments and suggestions.

[1] B. Kamau, programme officer for Release Political Prisoners, quoted in *Daily Nation*, 'Bringing Closure to a Dark Period in History', 21 Jan. 2004.

[2] 'Eloquent corpses' is a paraphrase of John Lonsdale in commentary on D. W. Cohen and E. S. Atieno Odhiambo, *Burying SM: The Politics of Knowledge and the Sociology of Power in Africa* (London, 1992), 110.

[3] R. Lee and M. Vaughan, 'Death and Dying in the History of Africa since 1800', *Journal of African History*, 49 (2008), 341–59. Yvan Droz and Herve Maupeu (eds), *Les Figures de la Mort à Nairobi: Une Capitale sans Cimetières* (Paris, 2003).

execution. After a series of false dawns from the early 1990s as one informant after another came forward with the supposedly precise details necessary to find the remains, a visit to Kamiti in January 2004 represented the last attempt at locating Kimathi's body with a view to a more fitting reburial. On that January day, Kimathi's family criss-crossed the prison's extensive grounds in the company of eight individuals who each claimed to know where the body had been buried nearly fifty years before. But none of these guides, who all either claimed to have been witnesses to the burial or in possession of reliable accounts of it, could agree on the location of Kimathi's remains. Furthermore, there was no agreement should a grave have been uncovered on what distinguishing features - such as clothing, position, or manacles— might identify Kimathi from those buried with him.[4] After leaving Kamiti that day, the Kimathi family's search became desperate and critical government support for their efforts was scaled back. In a nevertheless significant gesture that in all probability marks the official end of the search for the remains, the authorities erected a statue of Kimathi in downtown Nairobi in February 2007.

Kimathi was the best known of the Mau Mau rebels who fought against British rule in the 1950s. He hailed from the Nyeri district of the Central Highlands, the ideological and geographical centre of the Mau Mau rebellion. Kimathi's expertise in turning a bedraggled group of alienated Kikuyu in the Aberdare Mountains into a formidable guerrilla force earned him the fear of the colonial regime. At the war's beginning in October 1952, those forces and those based in the forest of nearby Mount Kenya held the upper hand. Able to escape capture by the British and well supported by local communities, the 25,000 or so forest fighters engaged the colonial state and its Kikuyu allies in a bitter guerrilla war. The tide only turned from late 1954, when a series of successful military operations on the part of the state's security forces caused the numbers of guerrillas to dwindle significantly.[5] At the same time, a bloody and repressive set of counter-insurgency measures targeted at the general population broke the ties between the guerrillas and their supporters. In all, up to 50,000 people lost their lives. All but a handful were Kikuyu insurgents and civilians.[6] Kimathi was finally captured in October 1956 and executed in February 1957.[7]

---

[4] 'Search for Hero's Body Fruitless', *Daily Nation* (16 Jan. 2004).

[5] D. Anderson, *Histories of the Hanged: Britain's Dirty War in Kenya and the End of Empire* (London, 2005), 230–88.

[6] J. Blacker, 'The Demography of Mau Mau: Fertility and Mortality in Kenya in the 1950s, a Demographer's Viewpoint', *African Affairs*, 106:423 (2007), 205–27.

[7] I. Henderson, *The Hunt for Kimathi* (London, 1958).

There was no inevitability that Kimathi's remains would become a matter of public interest. After all, for more than three decades from his death in 1957 to the early 1990s, the manner by which his body had been disposed of was largely irrelevant to the ways in which Kimathi was memorialized. Kimathi's remains were simply not a matter of public discussion.[8] Kimathi had not, though, been forgotten. Posthumously, he was a significant figure in the historical and political landscape of the post-colonial period. Moreover, he has been the subject of biographies,[9] plays[10] and novels.[11] Within certain narratives of Kenyan nationalism, Kimathi personified the struggle against British rule.[12] More than thirty years after his execution, however, Kimathi's body began to cause great public debate.

This paper sets out to answer why this interest in Kimathi's remains became a prominent public issue in the 1990s and 2000s. The paper begins with the significance of broader cultural and social processes that have impacted upon rituals surrounding funerals in modern Kenya. It then turns to consider what the new emphasis on the material remains of Kimathi tells us about the ways in which the substance of political debate has shifted in post-colonial Kenya. Although the paper comes to attach great significance to the importance of democratization as one of the triggers for this new engagement with the past, democratic it is not. Although the Free Kimathi committee occasionally called for the bodies of all those executed by the British during Mau Mau to be handed over to their families, little further attention has been paid to the question of mass graves that undoubtedly exist across the Central Highlands.[13]

Christianity and Land

There is both 'a deeper history of corpses' in Kenya and an established historiography of the dead.[14] David William Cohen and E. S. Atieno Odhiambo

---

[8] An exception being a question in parliament posed by G. G. Kariuki, MP for Laikipia. See G. G. Kariuki, *Illusion of Power: Reflections on Fifty Years in Kenya Politics* (Nairobi, 2001), 59, 61; A. Ngwiri, 'Freedom Day in a Nation that Shuns Real Heroes', *Daily Nation* (13 Dec.1998).

[9] T. Kanogo, *Dedan Kimathi: A Biography* (Nairobi, 1992).

[10] Ngugi wa Thiongo and M. G. Mugo, *The Trial of Dedan Kimathi* (London, 1976).

[11] S. Kahiga, *Dedan Kimathi: The Real Story* (Nairobi, 1980).

[12] For discussion of those often competing narratives, see E. S. Atieno Odhiambo, '*Matunda ya Uhuru* Fruits of Independence: Seven Theses on Nationalism in Kenya', in J. Lonsdale and E. S. Atieno Odhiambo (eds), *Mau Mau and Nationhood: Arms, Authority and Narration* (Oxford, 2003), 37–46.

[13] 'Group Launches Kimathi Petition', *Daily Nation* (12 April 2000).

[14] Cohen and Atieno Odhiambo, *Burying SM*, 18–19.

have made two seminal contributions to the study of post-colonial Kenyan politics and society through their analysis of the narratives surrounding the deaths of S. M. Otieno (1986) and Robert Ouko (1990).[15] That the subjects of these two accounts were members of the Luo community is not surprising. Burial has long been the established custom for the peoples of Western Kenya. Among the Kikuyu, of which Kimathi was one, and some of the other communities that settled around Mount Kenya in the heart of the country, burial had been reserved for the wealthy.[16] In other cases, burial was a taboo and corpses were instead left in the forests for the animals. Nevertheless, Kikuyu had eloquent corpses before Kimathi. Waiyaki wa Hinga, initially a key ally of the British forces during the conquest of the Central Highlands, died in 1892 while in transit to exile at the Indian Ocean coast. Waiyaki had fallen out with his erstwhile allies, and had been arrested. In Kikuyu oral tradition, Waiyaki was buried upside down in a deliberate transgression of custom. Waiyaki certainly died far from his ancestral home, a fate the first generations of Kikuyu urbanites sought to avoid by paying subscriptions to cooperative burial associations in the towns and cities that emerged in colonial Kenya.[17]

The concern of both Kikuyu migrants to the cities and Kenyanist historians with the subject of burial must partly be attributed to the growing importance attached to burial by Kikuyu in response to the spread of Christianity. The interest in Kimathi's remains should similarly in part be attributed to that same trend. Kimathi was, after all, a Christian too. But he was at the time of his death one of a small minority within both his Kikuyu community and Kenyans more generally who instead continued to practice local indigenous beliefs. Although the first missionaries arrived in the mid-nineteenth century, Christianity expanded most dramatically in the period after Kimathi's execution. Today, it is commonly thought that 80 per cent of the population are members of one Christian denomination or another.

The effects of Christianity should not be overstated. Within the memorialization of Kimathi there are non-Christian elements which, as Wale Adebanwi in a very different setting argues, relate to efforts to provide

[15] Cohen and Atieno Odhiambo, *Burying SM*; D.W. Cohen and E. S. Atieno Odhiambo, *The Risks of Knowledge: Investigations into the Death of the Hon. Minister John Robert Ouko in Kenya, 1990* (Athens, O., 2004).

[16] J. Lonsdale, 'The Moral Economy of Mau Mau: Wealth, Poverty and Civic Virtue in Kikuyu Political Thought', in B. Berman and J. Lonsdale, *Unhappy Valley: Conflict in Kenya and Africa* (Oxford, 1992), 344.

[17] J. Lonsdale, 'The Prayers of Waiyaki: Political Uses of the Kikuyu Past', in D. Anderson and D. Johnson (eds), *Revealing Prophets: Prophecy in Eastern African History* (London, 1995), 240–91.

contemporary African political movements with the power of the sacred through conveying a sense of ancestral approval.[18] Nevertheless, it is difficult to disagree with Ngugi wa Thiong'o who, in 1972, wrote that 'I cannot escape from the Church. Its influence is all around me.'[19] Christianity is ubiquitous in everyday political and social life, particularly by providing a common vocabulary which Kenyans of all regions, ethnicities, and classes can use in public political debate.[20] Christianity has also contributed to the creation of a cultural vernacular. While far from complete, a variety of customs related to social reproduction, including the handling of the dead, have become harmonized.

Disposal of the dead changed significantly over the course of the twentieth century. The custom of leaving corpses in the bush was abandoned under pressure from both Kikuyu converts to Christianity and local authorities during the colonial period and replaced with universal burial.[21] The practice of burial became commonplace, however, because of another introduction of colonial rule: private land tenure. With the issue of private land titles from the 1950s onwards the presence of the grave of an ancestor was incontrovertible proof of ownership and belonging.[22] The value of such proof of ownership has only increased since. Rapid population growth increased demand for land, making disputes over tenure more common. At the same time, the steady collapse of state legitimacy and the prevalence of land-related corruption meant that title deeds came to have little meaning.[23]

This use of burial as support for claims to land title has particular resonance among Kikuyu. In a precursor of the link between land, belonging, and death that would later become so prominent, the remains of Koinange wa Mbiyu's grandfather were exhumed from his grave in order to prove possession of land during the settlement of European farmers.[24] Disputes over land that have been part of Kikuyu public and private life since the 1930s have not since

---

[18] W. Adebanwi, 'The Cult of Awo: The Political Life of a Dead Leader', *Journal of Modern African Studies*, 46 (2008), 335–60.

[19] Ngugi wa Thiong'o, *Homecoming: Essays on African and Caribbean Literature, Culture and Politics* (London, 1972), 3; quoted in J. Lonsdale, 'African Pasts in Africa's Future', in B. Berman and J. Lonsdale, *Unhappy Valley*, 217.

[20] P. Gifford, *Christianity, Politics and Public Life in Kenya* (London, 2009); B. Knighton (ed.), *Religion and Politics in Kenya: Essays in Honor of a Meddlesome Priest* (Basingstoke, 2009); Lonsdale, 'African Pasts', 218.

[21] Lonsdale, 'Moral Economy', 377.

[22] J. Glazier, 'Mbeere Ancestors and the Domestication of Death', *Man*, 19 (1984), 133–47.

[23] J. Klopp, 'Pilfering the Public: The Problem of Land Grabbing in Contemporary Kenya', *Africa Today*, 47 (2000), 7–26.

[24] Lonsdale, 'Moral Economy', 378.

calmed. In attempts to alleviate tensions over land in the Mount Kenya region, thousands of Kikuyu were resettled across the country after independence. These Kikuyu settlers have, at times, met with considerable hostility from local communities who portray them as outsiders with no moral claim to land. This hostility manifested itself in violence around the 1992, 1997, and 2007 elections as Kikuyu settlers were targeted with theft, arson, and murder in the Rift Valley and Coast Provinces.[25] With the grip of Kikuyu settlers over their land tenuous and deeply contested, the graves of ancestors are powerful ripostes by migrant Kikuyu to those who claim the status of autochthons in contemporary struggles for resources.[26] As Joseph Githuku, at the funeral of his wife, child, and thirty-four other Kikuyu victims killed during the violence in early 2008 near Eldoret in the Rift Valley, told mourners during the requiem held in the town over a year later, 'We have nowhere else to go because this is our home'.[27]

Land and freedom

The concern with Kimathi's remains that arose decades after his death is then a reflection of the wider social significance attached by Kikuyu and other Kenyans to the matter of burial than had hitherto been the case. Cultural histories of Christianity and social histories of Kikuyu migration do not, however, explain all about Kimathi's remains. Political and economic explanations are also necessary.

At independence in 1963, Jomo Kenyatta's Kenya African National Union (KANU) government was reluctant to make any great public acknowledgement of the efforts of Mau Mau veterans. Kimathi and the Mau Mau rebellion did not lend themselves easily to benign appropriation by the post-colonial state. The rebels fought for *ithaka na wiathi* ('land and freedom' or 'land and self-mastery'). After the war concluded and negotiations for independence began, Mau Mau veterans and their supporters hoped that the departure

---

[25] D. Anderson and E. Lochery, 'Violence and Exodus in Kenya's Rift Valley, 2008: Predictable and Preventable?', *Journal of Eastern African Studies*, 2 (2008), 328–43; J. Klopp, '"Ethnic Clashes" and Winning Elections: The Case of Kenya's Electoral Despotism', *Canadian Journal of African Studies*, 35 (2001), 473–517; J. Oucho, *Undercurrents of Ethnic Conflict in Kenya* (Leiden, 2002).

[26] J. Lonsdale, 'Soil Work, Civilisation, and Citizenship in Kenya', *Journal of Eastern African Studies*, 2 (2008), 305–14.

[27] F. Nzwili, 'Church Election Violence Victims Buried with Plea for Healing', *Ecumenical News International* (15 May 2009), AllAfrica website http://allafrica.com/stories/200905150906.html [accessed 17 Jan. 2010].

of the British would be marked with a comprehensive programme of redistribution to the landless and land-poor that had joined the rebellion.[28] Moreover, the former insurgents expected that a programme of land reform undertaken by the colonial government during the war would be reversed. It was widely believed that the Kikuyu allies of the government, known as loyalists, had been able to manipulate that programme for personal gain and to punish Mau Mau sympathizers.[29] After independence, however, it became apparent to Mau Mau veterans and their supporters that no grants of land would be made. Instead, the government persevered with private land tenure as part of a broader capitalist development strategy centred upon the agrarian economy.[30] This policy commitment was driven in part by pragmatism and partly by ideology; Kenyatta and his closest advisers, including the future president Mwai Kibaki, were no socialists. Instead, their notions of development were those of the self-made man; namely the virtues of disciplined and productive labour.[31] Kenyatta berated those who after independence demanded his government pay greater attention to the redistribution of wealth as wanting 'free things' that had not been earned by labour.[32]

The 'free things' were the acres of land being reallocated following the departure of a large number of the European farmers. While significant resettlement schemes were established as the European farmers steadily drifted off the land, the acreage vacated had to be purchased. For the very poorest sections of Kikuyu society, therefore, independence did not alleviate the land hunger that had driven many of the Mau Mau rebels to the forests in the 1950s. Mau Mau veterans were outraged. One, A. N. Munyaua, wrote in a petition to Kenyatta that 'It is a remarkable shame for the nation to find the

---

[28] The best analysis of the motivations of Mau Mau's insurgents remains J. Lonsdale, 'Moral Economy'.

[29] M. P. Keith Sorrenson, *Land Reform in the Kikuyu Country: A Study in Government Policy* (Nairobi, 1967).

[30] R. Bates, *Beyond the Miracle of the Market: The Political Economy of Agrarian Development in Kenya* (Cambridge, 2005); G. Kitching, *Class and Economic Change in Kenya: The Making of an African Petite-Bourgeoisie* (New Haven, Conn., 1980); C. Leys, *Underdevelopment in Kenya: The Political Economy of Neo-Colonialism* (Nairobi, 1975); W. Ochieng', 'Structural and Political Changes', in B. Ogot and W. Ochieng' (eds), *Decolonization and Independence in Kenya 1940–93* (London, 1995), 83–109.

[31] J. Lonsdale, 'Jomo Kenyatta, God and the Modern World', in J-G. Deutsch, P. Probst, and H. Schmidt (eds), *African Modernities: Entangled Meanings in Current Debate* (Oxford, 2002), 48.

[32] G. Lamb, *Peasant Politics: Conflict and Development in Murang'a* (Lewes, 1974), 35.

people who fought for independence being the poorest in the country'.[33] Such sentiments were widely held and found expression in a variety of forms, ranging from subversive political groups through to independent churches.[34]

In the criticisms of Kenyatta's government by the opposition Kenya Peoples' Union (KPU), the memories of the Mau Mau rebellion were a valuable tool. Formed in 1966, the KPU sought to build support by drawing attention to the impoverishment of Mau Mau veterans as part of a much wider agenda of the distribution of wealth. But this was just one part of the KPU's platform. The new party took a position clearly to the left of Kenyatta's government on a wide array of economic and diplomatic issues.[35] The cause of landless Mau Mau veterans was then taken up by the KPU as the totem for a broader redistributive platform.

As a method of legitimization for the opposition, Mau Mau's memory was thus a source of discomfort for the government. Kenyatta and his government set out to avoid mention of the war and, without great success, tried to silence public debate on it.[36] Nevertheless, Dedan Kimathi could not be completely ignored. Indeed, the executed military leader dominated the limited attempts towards public memorialization of Mau Mau. Hardinge Street in central Nairobi was renamed in his honour in 1964. A similar accolade was paid to him in his home town of Nyeri. There and elsewhere in the Kikuyu-dominated areas of the Central Highlands, Kimathi's name was given to a variety of schools, community centres and other such local institutions.[37]

In an effort to placate critics, a limited programme of land grants for former Mau Mau rebels was attempted by the government in 1964. Some four hundred individuals received plots on the land of settler farmers who left following independence.[38] The recipients of these plots were the principal actors in the insurgency and their immediate families. Before the programme

---

[33] Kenya National Archives (KNA) KA/6/27, A. N. Munyua to President J. Kenyatta, 15 Nov. 1965.

[34] D. Branch, *Defeating Mau Mau, Creating Kenya: Counterinsurgency, Civil War and Decolonization* (Cambridge, 2009), 179–207.

[35] S. Mueller, 'Government and Opposition in Kenya, 1966–9', *Journal of Modern African Studies*, 22 (1984), 408.

[36] M. Clough, 'Mau Mau and the Contest for Memory', in E. S. Atieno Odhiambo and J. Lonsdale (eds), *Mau Mau and Nationhood: Arms, Authority and Narration* (Oxford, 2003), 251–67.

[37] Carl Dutto, *Nyeri Townsmen Kenya* (Nairobi, 1975), 54–5.

[38] Kariuki, *Illusion*, 43.

was wound down after becoming overwhelmed by demand, Kimathi's widow, Mukami, was similarly given a fifty-acre plot by the local authorities in Nyeri.[39] Land not bones were the matters that concerned the Kimathi family and the countless thousands of other Kikuyu households in a similar situation.

Following the crushing of the KPU and its eventual banning in 1969, certain individuals within KANU championed land redistribution and social justice. Most prominent among these was J. M. Kariuki, author of a widely read account of his time in detention during the 1950s and an MP for a constituency in which landlessness was particularly acute.[40] In one of many public critiques of Kenyatta's government, in 1974 Kariuki spoke of how

> ... in the hey-days of the cruel days that we fought for our *uhuru* ('independence'), the call for sharing the cake when won was unanimous; the cake would be eaten by all in equal or fair shares. There was not the slightest murmur that the cake would be shared by some while others languished in hardships. If my memory serves me right the word some never figured.[41]

In an effort to advance this wider critique of inequality in Kenyatta's Kenya, J. M. Kariuki drew attention to the fate of Mau Mau veterans. He was not concerned with token acknowledgements of past suffering. Speaking in 1974 of an unrelated namesake and one of the first generation of anti-colonial Kikuyu activists, Jesse Kariuki, J. M. Kariuki asked:

> Who is thinking about him today? All we are waiting for is to hear he is dead then go there with flowers and later on name a street in one of the main towns after him. He does not want flowers when he is dead. He wants the flowers now so that he can see the beauty of the flowers, and be able to touch and smell them. The important thing for him now is something to eat.[42]

---

[39] KNA VQ/10/12, L. K. Ngureti, President, Central Regional Assembly to E. Yates, Area Settlement Controller (East), 12 May 1964.

[40] J. M. Kariuki, '*Mau Mau' Detainee: The Account by a Kenya African of His Experiences in Detention Camps 1953–1960* (Nairobi, 1963).

[41] Library of Congress, Africa and Middle East Reading Room pamphlets collection, Kenya-Speeches, J. M. Kariuki, 'J. M. Kariuki Speaks His Mind', (Nairobi, 1974), 15.

[42] J. M. Kariuki to parliament, 21 March 1974, repr. as J. M. Kariuki, 'Assistance for Emergency Widows and Orphans', in Kareithi Munuhe (ed.), *J. M. Kariuki in Parliament* (Nairobi, 1975), 21.

J. M. Kariuki's depiction of the plight of figures such as Jesse Kariuki and the Mau Mau veterans and their families was not one of victimhood, but instead of their being denied what was rightfully theirs by virtue of their leading role in the struggle for independence. In his memoirs and other writings, J. M. Kariuki acknowledged the historical significance of Kimathi, noted his close relations with the Kimathi family, but was unconcerned with the subject of the Mau Mau leader's remains.[43]

To J. M. Kariuki and the KPU's leaders, speaking about Mau Mau was a fruitful way in which to participate in a debate about the merits of redistributive policies that were a critical part of debate in the 1960s and 1970s.[44] The memory of Mau Mau and of Kimathi continued to serve such a purpose through the 1980s following the succession of Daniel arap Moi after Kenyatta's death in 1978. Kimathi's importance, unsullied by the course of post-colonial politics, increased exponentially with Moi's reliance on repression in order to sustain his rule.[45] To those contemplating armed resistance to Moi's regime, Mau Mau and Kimathi were celebrated for establishing a militant tradition within Kenyan politics. Both the rebellion and its leader were appropriated to legitimize underground, Marxist-inspired political action that emerged to fill the vacuum created by the one-party state.[46] Kang'ethe Mungai, a member of the dissident Mwakenya group and political prisoner in the 1980s, later recalled how when he joined Mwakenya, 'I was made to raise one hand and face the portrait of Kimathi and swore to fight for a democratic Kenya and never betray my colleagues in Mwakenya.'[47] For the former political prisoner Maina wa Kinyatti, Kimathi 'lives on in the continuing struggle of our people for democracy and social justice', but even Kinyatti's writings scarcely make mention of Kimathi's remains.[48]

The search begins

As we have seen, Kinyatti's lack of concern for Kimathi's remains was typical of the political uses of Kimathi and Mau Mau between independence in 1963

[43] Kariuki, *'Mau Mau' Detainee*, 122.

[44] The best accounts of the politics of the immediate post-colonial period are C. Gertzel, *The Politics of Independent Kenya* (Nairobi, 1970); Henry Bienen, *Kenya: The Politics of Participation and Control* (Princeton, 1974).

[45] K. Adar and I. Munyae, 'Human Rights Abuse in Kenya under Daniel arap Moi', *African Studies Quarterly*, 5:1 (2001) [online] http://web.africa.ufl.edu/asq/v5/v5i1a1.htm [accessed 17 Jan. 2009].

[46] See anonymous contributions to 'Kenya: The Politics of Repression', special edn of *Race and Class*, 24 (1983).

[47] S. Mburu, 'How We Tried to Overthrow Moi', *Daily Nation* (12 March 2000).

[48] M. wa Kinyatti, *Mau Mau: A Revolution Betrayed* (New York, 1992), 93.

and the return to a multi-party political system in the early 1990s. It was that political change, part of the global fourth wave of democracy that began in Eastern Europe, which triggered the search for Kimathi's remains with which this paper began.[49] Indeed, the search for Kimathi's body was typical of global trends in the terms of political debate that have typified experiences of democratization across the world subsequently. Fittingly, it was one of the fourth wave's global figureheads that sparked the search for Kimathi's remains. Visiting Kenya following his release from imprisonment, Nelson Mandela addressed a large crowd in Nairobi on 13 July 1990. As part of his speech, Mandela acknowledged, 'our indebtedness to General Dedan Kimathi, the man who led the armed struggle in this country against the British very excellently'.[50] Inspired by Mandela's words, the first efforts aimed at finding the body and pressuring the state into organizing a more dignified reburial began soon after with the formation of the Dedan Kimathi Foundation.[51]

From the outset, this was an effort that ran alongside the pro-democracy movement that took hold in Kenya in the early 1990s. The efforts to find the remains were thus subject to the stresses the opposition more generally experienced. Political momentum for the search for Kimathi's grave was thereby slow to gather as its advocates were distracted by the fragmentation of the opposition movement prior to the 1992 elections and the associated violence that surrounded it.[52] The issue of Kimathi's remains returned to public debate only in 1995, when the Prisons Department made an effort to locate former employees who may have known where the body was to be found, but without success.[53] As the country moved towards the second election of the multiparty era in 1997, Kimathi's body had become established as a trope for critics of Moi's government. Presidential aspirants Raila Odinga and Koigi Wamwere promised voters they would exhume the remains.[54] However, the true driving force behind attempts to find the Field Marshal's body lay in an emergent civil society rather than parliament.

[49] M. McFaul, 'The Fourth Wave of Democracy and Dictatorship: Noncooperative Transitions in the Postcommunist World', *World Politics*, 52 (2002), 212–44.

[50] BBC Summary of World Broadcasts, 'Mandela Addresses Nairobi Rally', 16 July 1990. Also quoted in Clough, 'Mau Mau', 251.

[51] J. Kamau, 'Nation's Hero Continues to Lie Next to Rapists, Robbers', *The Monitor* (5 Dec. 2001).

[52] D. Throup and C. Hornsby, *Multi-Party Politics in Kenya: The Kenyatta and Moi States and the Triumph of the System in the 1992 Election* (Oxford, 1998).

[53] Kamau, 'Nation's Hero'.

[54] Clough, 'Mau Mau', 262; Muthui Mwai and Benedict Ng'etich, 'Let's Fight Together, Says Raila', *Daily Nation* (10 Nov. 1997).

The Free Kimathi committee of human rights activists, Mau Mau veterans, and the Kimathi family was formed in 2000. Initially the focus of the committee's activities was on the exhumation of Kimathi's remains and a subsequent state funeral. The campaign was launched with a range of cultural activities aimed at raising public awareness of Kimathi and his ignominious burial.[55] Despite the publicly stated primary interest in the fate of Kimathi's remains, the contemporary political concerns of the committee's activities were explicit. The committee was supported by Wanyiri Kihoro, a former political prisoner who by 2000 was an opposition MP for Nyeri town and fellow opposition figure, Peter Anyang' Nyongo.[56] Such connections enabled the Free Kimathi campaign to mobilize broad support from opponents of the Moi government.

At a demonstration held on the forty-third anniversary of Kimathi's execution, hundreds of protestors processed along Nairobi's main arterial roads. The protestors 'chanted anti-Moi slogans' and 'waved placards demanding the immediate release of Kimathi's body saying that the fact that his body was still buried in the grounds of Kamiti Prison showed that Kenya was still colonised'. The protest ended at Uhuru Park, where it was hoped Kimathi's body could be buried and which had itself become an important site within opposition politics as the location for protests against political detentions and by the Green Belt movement led by Wangari Maathai.[57] At the proposed site of the burial in the park, the Free Kimathi committee erected a billboard announcing their intentions, but this was torn down by police officers after just two days.[58] Protestors who attempted to reinstate the billboard on 2 March 2000 were arrested.[59]

Supporters of the campaign to exhume Kimathi's remains were convinced that the Moi government's reluctance to assist was a deliberate attempt to sabotage an otherwise simple task. 'The issue is not whether but when it will happen', one leading figure within the campaign asserted.[60] Hopes of finding Kimathi's body thus rose after the electoral victory in December 2002 of Mwai Kibaki and his National Rainbow Coalition over Moi's KANU party and the

[55] W. Thuku, 'Push for Kimathi Burial Launched', 17 February 2000.

[56] BBC Worldwide Monitoring, 'Kenya: Demo Planned to Petition State to Accord Mau Mau Leader "Decent" Burial', 17 February 2000.

[57] 'Release Kimathi's Body, Say Protestors', *Daily Nation* (19 Feb. 2000). For details of the Green Belt movement see W. Maathai, *The Green Belt Movement: Sharing the Approach and Experience* (New York, 2003).

[58] 'Kimathi Family to Sit-In', *Daily Nation* (2 March 2000).

[59] 'Group Launches Kimathi Petition', *Daily Nation* (12 April 2000).

[60] Kamau, 'Nation's Hero'.

retiring president's anointed successor, Uhuru Kenyatta. Incidentally, Uhuru Kenyatta is Jomo Kenyatta's son. Following Kibaki's victory, Kimathi's son, Meshack Wachiuri, told the *Daily Nation* newspaper that, 'All pro-reformists in the government including President Mwai Kibaki have made pledges that they would honour freedom fighters and respect our wishes should they assume power'.[61] Indeed, the new government moved swiftly. After less than two months in office, Kiraitu Murungi, the new Justice and Constitutional Affairs minister and himself a child of Mau Mau veterans, promised to locate, exhume, and rebury Kimathi's body.[62] The search proper finally began.

On 24 February 2003, prison warders at Kamiti spent the night fruitlessly combing the 1,200 acres of prison land for any indication of where Kimathi's remains were to be found.[63] A similarly hopeless search of the records of the Department of Prisons was undertaken.[64] Hopes that Kimathi's body could be found came to rest on former prisoners and guards from Kamiti who came forward to claim that they had either been eye-witnesses to the burial or had spoken to such witnesses who had since died. In early March 2003, Samuel Muchiri Njuguna, who was a prisoner during the Mau Mau war, claimed to have been part of a penal labour group responsible for burying Kimathi.[65] A further four such individuals had come forward by end of July of that same year.[66]

Any doubts about public enthusiasm for spending government money on finding Kimathi were dispelled by the overwhelming reception given to the 'discovery' of his fellow guerrilla leader, Stanley Mathenge. In truth a none too elaborate hoax involving an elderly Ethiopian, Ato Lemma Ayanu, a man claimed by two journalists to be Mathenge was flown to Nairobi in May 2003 and received a hero's welcome. As it became clear within hours of his arrival that Ayanu was simply an elderly Ethiopian farmer rather than a hero of Kenyan nationalism, the old man was hastily flown out of the country.[67] Although the government was a laughing stock for having paid for Ayanu's

---

[61] 'Kimathi Kin Urges State to Honour Burial Pledge', *Daily Nation* (7 Jan. 2003).

[62] 'The Battle for Reparations and Justice For All', *East African Standard* (16 Feb. 2003).

[63] 'Prison Warders Search for Grave of Hanged Freedom Fighter Kimathi', *East African Standard* (26 Feb. 2003).

[64] 'Prisons Department Unable to Trace Kimathi's Grave', *East African Standard* (12 June 2003).

[65] 'I Buried Kimathi, Claims Ex-Prisoner', *Daily Nation* (4 March 2003).

[66] 'Parliament: Four Offer to Identify Kimathi's Grave Site', *Daily Nation* (31 July 2003).

[67] BBC News, 'Doubt Cast on Mau Mau Hero', BBC News website, 31 May 2003 http://news.bbc.co.uk/1/hi/world/africa/2953048.stm [accessed 15 Feb. 2009].

visit, determination to find a real Mau Mau leader was only amplified by the Mathenge hoax. Less than a month later, it was announced that Kimathi would not just be found but also reburied in a section of the capital's Uhuru Gardens recently set aside for the burial of national heroes.[68] In November 2003, Kiraitu promised that the whole procedure would be completed in time for that year's national holiday held on 12 December to celebrate Kenya's independence. Yet another committee was formed, this time called the Exhuming Remains of Kimathi Committee, in order to find information relating to possible burial sites within the prison's boundaries.[69] That effort came to the forlorn denouement with which this paper began.

Markets and votes

Human rights activists commonly depicted the search for Kimathi's remains in the early 2000s in national terms. Yet when attempting to understand why it was that demands to find Kimathi's body began to be made in the 1990s and were supported by Kibaki's government after 2002, it is more important to examine Kikuyu politics and society. Support for the search for Kimathi's body formed a part of a wider re-engagement by Kibaki's government with the Mau Mau rebellion. A Heroes Committee was formed in July 2003 to adjudicate on the right of different historical figures, including Kimathi, to be termed a 'national hero' and buried in the new Heroes Acre.[70] The following month the ban on Mau Mau, which had remained in place since 1950, was lifted by the government.[71] Most importantly perhaps, the government supported a legal action announced in June 2003 against the British government for redress of alleged war crimes committed by colonial forces in the 1950s. At the time of writing (January 2010), that case was ongoing.[72]

Most obviously, those involved in the NARC victory over KANU were attempting to connect what was commonly known as Kenya's 'second liberation' with the first from colonial rule, of which Kimathi was the most potent symbol. But the particular interest in the official recovery of Mau Mau's history had much more to do with the complex political and social contests within the Kikuyu community from which Kibaki and many of his senior colleagues hailed. With the dual processes of economic liberalization of the key agricultural sector beginning in the 1980s and the return to

---

[68] D. Mugonyi, 'Mau Mau's Dedan Kimathi to be First in Heroes Acre', *Daily Nation* (1 July 2003).

[69] 'Kimathi Remains Search is Still On, Says Minister', *Daily Nation* (3 Dec. 2003).

[70] 'Awori Says Heroes Committee Formed', *East African Standard* (31 July 2003).

[71] 'Minister Lifts Ban on Mau Mau', *Daily Nation* (31 Aug. 2003).

[72] 'Mau Mau Case to be Filed Soon', *Daily Nation* (29 June 2003).

multiparty elections in the 1990s those intra-Kikuyu tensions were exacerbated. Celebrating Mau Mau's history, and particularly the role of Kimathi, offered to Kibaki and his government the possibility of, first, disarming attempts by dissident Kikuyus to mobilize broader support by appropriating Mau Mau themselves, and, secondly, ameliorating intra-Kikuyu social conflicts.

Throughout his two terms of office, Kibaki has faced a considerable political and security challenge from the group known as Mungiki ('masses' or 'multitude' in Kikuyu). Mungiki defies neat definition, operating variously since its foundation in the late 1980s as a Kikuyu cultural revival movement, a mafia-style criminal enterprise and political militia.[73] Mungiki emerged as a significant threat to public order prior to the 2002 elections and tensions between it and the state steadily intensified afterwards. Matters came to a head in 2007 when state security forces implemented a crackdown on Mungiki. A series of grisly murders attributed to Mungiki led to public outcry. In the subsequent security operations centred upon Kikuyu-dominated informal settlements in Nairobi, the state forces were accused of killing up to 500 people.[74] The violence in the wake of the 2007 elections did, however, force a rapprochement of sorts between the Kikuyu elite and Mungiki as Kibaki's faction used any means possible to retain control of the government.[75] Subsequently, however, the divisions between the two have re-emerged.[76]

While its motives and relations with the state may have been in a constant state of flux, Mungiki's core constituency remained largely unchanged; urban and rural Kikuyu youths disillusioned with both the Kenyan state and the actions of Kikuyu elites. In an effort to legitimize their struggle, Mungiki's members have appropriated the memory of Mau Mau and Dedan Kimathi specifically.[77] Njuguna Gitau Njuguna, one of the few public faces of the

---

[73] D. Anderson, 'Vigilantes, Violence and the Politics of Public Order in Kenya', *African Affairs*, 101:405 (2002), 531–55; M. Gecaga, 'Religious Movements and Democratisation in Kenya: Between Sacred and Profane', in G. Murunga and S. Nasong'o (eds), *Kenya: The Struggle for Democracy* (London, 2007), 67–84; P. Kagwanja, 'Facing Mount Kenya or Facing Mecca? The *Mungiki*, Ethnic Violence and the Politics of the Moi Succession in Kenya, 1987–2002', *African Affairs*, 102:406 (2003), 25–49.

[74] K. Allen, 'Questions Linger Over Kenya Killings', BBC News website, 10 Nov. 2007 http://news.bbc.co.uk/1/hi/world/africa/7088750.stm [accessed 13 Feb. 2009].

[75] BBC News, 'State "Sanctioned" Kenyan Clashes', 5 March 2008, BBC News website http://news.bbc.co.uk/1/hi/world/africa/7279149.stm [accessed 13 Feb. 2009].

[76] BBC News, 'Fresh Deaths in Kenya Sect Riots', 15 April 2008, BBC News website http://news.bbc.co.uk/1/hi/world/africa/7348173.stm [accessed 13 Feb. 2009].

[77] 'Journalist's Chilling Encounter with Mungiki, Police', *East African Standard* (24 June 2007).

group, told Nation Television in April 2008 that Mungiki was driven by Kimathi's creed that it is 'better to die standing than to live on your knees.[78] Co-ordinating the search for Kimathi's body alongside other symbolic measures promoting the agenda of Mau Mau veterans allowed Kibaki's government to contest Mungiki's claim to be the inheritor of Mau Mau's mantle.

Mungiki thrived in a climate of declining state authority within which insecurity became endemic within politics as the multiparty period developed.[79] While the violence of Mungiki was exceptional, the forms of politics that the group represented were not. Across Kenya, the effects of neoliberal market reform in the 1990s, particularly through reform of the agricultural sector, exacerbated pre-existing social inequality and produced intense class conflict. Mungiki and other such groups whose support is derived from class-based grievances but which assume the form of an ethnic movement perfectly represent what Bayart describes as the 'interweaving' of class and ethnicity typical of the politics of many post-colonial African states.[80]

Kibaki had never been able to count on the unquestioning support of Kikuyu voters. Many viewed him with suspicion as a result of his decision to run in 1992 against the champion of the pro-democracy cause, Kenneth Matiba. That split in the Kikuyu vote partly allowed Moi to retain power in 1992. While Matiba did not stand in 1997 due to ill-health, a divided opposition including Kibaki again contributed to Moi's survival. By 2002 Kibaki had to assert his political leadership of the Kikuyu community against the challenge of Uhuru Kenyatta. Uhuru Kenyatta was nominated as KANU's candidate by the outgoing Moi as a deliberate effort to divide the Kikuyu vote, partly along generational lines, and so weaken the opposition NARC coalition.[81] While Uhuru Kenyatta became an ally of Kibaki in the run-up to the

---

[78] BBC Worldwide Monitoring, 'Kenya: Outlawed Sect Declares War on Government', 14 April 2008.

[79] D. Branch and N. Cheeseman, 'Democratization, Sequencing, and State Failure in Africa: Lessons from Kenya', *African Affairs*, 108:430 (2009), 1–26; S. Mueller, 'The Political Economy of Kenya's Crisis', *Journal of Eastern African Studies*, 2:2 (2008), 185–210.

[80] J-F. Bayart, *The State in Africa: The Politics of the Belly*, trans. Mary Harper, Christopher Harrison, and Elizabeth Harrison (London, 1993), 58–9.

[81] J. Kariuki, 'Choosing the President: Electoral Campaigns in Northern Central Kenya', in H. Maupeu, M. Katumanga, and W. Mitullah (eds), *The Moi Succession: The 2002 Elections in Kenya* (Nairobi, 2005), 97–125; P. Kagwanja, ' "Power to *Uhuru*": Youth Identity and Generational Politics in Kenya's 2002 Elections', *African Affairs*, 105:418 (2006), 51–75.

2007 election, for most of the period after Kibaki's victory five years earlier he was one of the new president's most vocal critics.[82]

The official recognition of the search for Kimathi's remains needs to be understood within this particular social and political context. The appropriation of Mau Mau's history, in which the celebration of Kimathi was a central component, served three related political purposes. First, it allowed Kibaki to appeal to a populist Kikuyu and Kenyan nationalism which he had hitherto been unable to access as a political base due to his elitism. By celebrating Mau Mau and Kimathi specifically, Kibaki reached out to the poorest sections of society who identified most closely with the insurgency. Second, by celebrating Kimathi and Mau Mau Kibaki was able to dispute the claims of Uhuru Kenyatta to be the rightful heir to the nationalist generation of politicians. Whereas Uhuru Kenyatta's claim was inherited from his father, Kibaki attempted to prove his nationalist credentials through deeds. Third, and most significantly, the attention given to the history of Mau Mau by Kibaki and his government was aimed at unifying a politically and socially divided Kikuyu ethnic community. The efforts to find Kimathi's body and the public engagement with Mau Mau's history more generally formed part of an effort by elite Kikuyu politicians to rebuild the ties between rich and poor within Kikuyu society.

This attempted rebuilding of a Kikuyu political community was, though, very different from similar efforts earlier in the post-colonial period. In 1969, as Kikuyu control over the state seemed in peril, the president made a rare appeal to the legacy of Mau Mau. Kikuyu from across the Central and Rift Valley Provinces were corralled to attend oathing ceremonies at the president's home at Gatundu in Kiambu. There, thousands of Kikuyu promised to ensure that 'the flag of Kenya shall not leave the House of Mumbi'; Mumbi being the mythical mother of the Kikuyu people.[83] This was an appeal to an entitlement to power based on strength. In this reading of Kenyan nationalism, Kikuyu had fought the hardest for independence and thus deserved to retain power. The appeal to Kikuyu ethnicity made in the 1990s and 2000s was quite different. From assertions of rights based upon strength, political action and identity was reorientated towards the winning of recognition of historical

[82] D. Branch and N. Cheeseman, 'Briefing: Using Opinion Polls to Evaluate Kenyan Politics, March 2004-January 2005', *African Affairs*, 104:415 (2005), 325–36; G. Lynch, 'The Fruits of Perception: "Ethnic Politics" and the Case of Kenya's Constitutional Referendum', *African Studies*, 65 (2006), 233–70.

[83] Ochieng', 'Structural and Political Changes', 102.

grievances with a view to advancing claims to political office or state resources in the present. As with other such narratives of historical grievances in contemporary Kenya, those claims for recognition have most commonly been expressed in terms of ethnicity and locality.[84]

Among Kikuyu, past notions of working and developing the soil as a way of earning rights have increasingly given way to narratives of suffering, persecution, and loss.[85] Whereas the redistributive version of Mau Mau's history forwarded by the KPU and J. M. Kariuki was national in focus, the more recent demand for the recognition of the wrongs perpetrated against Kikuyu is concerned primarily only with that particular ethnic group. Designed to consolidate notions of Kikuyu ethnicity, or more specifically the Kikuyu voting bloc on which Kibaki's presidential bids were based, this version of history does so by repositioning Mau Mau into a more recent narrative of Kikuyu identity centred on notions of victimhood and bloodshed. This version of the past emphasizes the violence of the British counter-insurgency in the 1950s, Moi's removal of Kikuyu from positions of power following his accession to the presidency in 1978, the repression of the Kikuyu-led pro-democracy movement, state-organized violence against Kikuyu voters during the 1992 and 1997 election campaigns which resulted in the deaths and displacement of thousands, and finally the attacks on Kikuyu during the violence in the aftermath of the 2007 elections. Kimathi's relevance to contemporary Kikuyu politics is no longer based upon his strength and achievements, but instead upon his status as the ultimate victim of atrocity. From conveying no great meaning, Kimathi's significance came to be entirely represented by his bones.

Conclusion

The exact location of those bones will likely never be determined. It is, though, possible to identify precisely the reasons why Kimathi's remains became invested with so much significance in the 1990s and 2000s. Lying at the confluence of the streams of neoliberal political and market reform, migration, land tenure, and Christianity, Kimathi's remains embody much of what it has meant to be Kenyan over the past century. Those remains had been those of a guerrilla in the 1950s, a nationalist in the 1960s and 1970s, an

---

[84] See e.g., L. Hughes, 'Malice in Maasailand: The Historical Roots of Current Political Struggles', *African Affairs*, 104:415 (2005), 207–24; G. Lynch, 'Courting the Kalenjin: The Failure of Dynasticism and the Strength of the ODM Wave in Kenya's Rift Valley Province', *African Affairs*, 107:429 (2008), 541–68.

[85] Lonsdale, 'Soil, Work', 306–15.

underground subversive in the 1980s, a democract in the early 1990s, and a victim of anti-Kikuyu persecution in the 2000s.[86]

The position of Kimathi and Mau Mau within contemporary Kenyan political debate fits a broader, global pattern whereby political actors have increasingly exploited the powerful relationship between violence and identity[87] to solidify ethnic bonds or other forms of communal identity so as to contest elections.[88] To adopt Nancy Fraser's taxonomy of social justice, the changing nature of memorialization of Kimathi illustrates how the substance of Kenyan political debate followed a global trend and shifted over the post-colonial period from the realm of redistribution to recognition.[89] Put simply, Kimathi was used in the 1960s and 1970s as a vehicle for a broader discussion about the merits of a national redistribution of resources. By the 1990s the manner by which that history was being used was indicative of the emergence of newer forms of political identities and action as neoliberal politics and economics took effect. Underlying these shorter-term processes were the deeper trends of social and cultural change driven by Christianity, migration, and land tenure.

The interest in Kimathi's bones is then in part concerned with creation and preservation of a political community in a time of great stress. The parallel processes of economic reform, which resulted in considerable social tension, and political reform, which necessitated opening that tension up to electoral competition, profoundly altered public life in Kenya.[90] New languages and idioms were created or adapted by Kenyans in order to participate in this new era of markets and elections that were neither free nor fair.[91] Kimathi's grave

---

[86] W. Mutunga, *Constitution-Making from the Middle: Civil Society and Transition Politics in Kenya, 1992–1997* (Nairobi, 1999), 1–2; M-E. Pommerolle, 'Universal Claims and Selective Memory: A Comparative Perspective on the Culture of Opposition in Kenya', *Africa Today*, 52 (2006), 75–93.

[87] A. Sen, *Violence and Identity: The Illusion of Destiny* (London, 2006).

[88] See e.g., K. Chandra, *Why Ethnic Parties Succeed: Patronage and Ethnic Headcounts in India* (Cambridge, 2004); D. Posner, *Institutions and Ethnic Politics in Africa* (Cambridge, 2005).

[89] N. Fraser and A. Honneth, *Redistribution or Recognition?: A Political-Philosophical Exchange*, trans. J. Golb, J. Ingram, and C. Wilke (London, 2003).

[90] G. Murunga, 'Governance and the Politics of Structural Adjustment in Kenya', in G. Murunga and S. Nasong'o (eds), *Kenya: The Struggle for Democracy* (London, 2007), 263–300.

[91] R. Blunt, ' "Satan is an Imitator": Kenya's Recent Cosmology of Corruption', in B. Weiss (ed.), *Producing African Futures: Ritual and Reproduction in a Neoliberal Age* (Leiden: 2004); J. Smith, *Bewitching Development: Witchcraft and the Reinvention of Development in Neoliberal Kenya* (Chicago, 2008).

was just one part of this effort. The celebration of Kimathi and the search for his remains was one of several points that provided much needed cohesion to Kikuyu politics during this time. Cutting across these political and social divisions, Kimathi's remains became part of a new narrative of Kikuyu ethnicity in which 'violent deaths must be remembered/forgotten as "our own"'.[92]

[92] B. Anderson, *Imagined Communities: Reflections on the Origin and Spread of Nationalism* (London, 1991), 206.

Testimonies as Sacred Texts: The Sanctification of Holocaust Writing

Zoë Waxman

Auschwitz-Birkenau is now one of the most visited sites in the world. In 2009, 1.3 million people poured through its gates.[1] Governments across the world have particularly pledged to send schoolchildren to visit it—the British state, for example, has underwritten the cost of sending two pupils from every school in the country.[2] In that sense, at least, Auschwitz has become the focus for a strange sort of contemporary pilgrimage, and, indeed, it joined religious sites like cathedrals on the UNESCO world heritage list in 1979. Visitors to the camp are confronted with crematoria, bunk houses, and gas chambers, but also by the more personal effects of the thousands who died there. Like a grotesque parody of a healing shrine, prosthetic limbs are piled up; there are similar collections of toiletries, suitcases, shoes, and even human hair. These are now all that remain of the victims of the Holocaust, and in a collection of essays on relics, it would be easy to portray them as just that: the relics of a new, postmodern shrine. It would be easy to depict Auschwitz-Birkenau as a new Temple: the focus for a cult of the Holocaust, and the home of the relics that the cult venerates. Certainly, that is an argument that has been made.[3] Such a depiction of Auschwitz—and, indeed, of Jewish responses to the Holocaust as a whole—is mistaken, however. The camp may be the site of pilgrimage. Some visitors may view the displays in the museum as something rather like relics. Jack Kugelmass has argued that Holocaust tourism should indeed be seen as a 'secular ritual'.[4] Nonetheless, Jewish attitudes to the remains of Holocaust victims are both more complex

---

[1] http://en.auschwitz.org.pl/m/index.php?option=com_content&task=view&id=728&Itemid=7 [accessed 8 Jan. 2010].

[2] http://www.lfaproject.org.uk/home [accessed 8 Jan. 2010].

[3] Michael Goldberg, *Why Should Jews Survive? Looking past the Holocaust toward a Jewish Future* (Oxford, 1995). See also Gillian Rose, *Judaism and Modernity: Philosophical Essays* (Oxford, 1993).

[4] Jack Kugelmass, 'Why We Go to Poland: Holocaust Tourism as a Secular Ritual', in James Young (ed.), *The Art of Memory: Holocaust Memorials in History* (New York), 175–83.

and more definite than this suggests. They are more complex, because the display of these 'relics' provokes serious and often bitter debate. They are more definite because, in the final analysis, Judaism does not permit the creation or adoration of relics.

The displays of human hair in Auschwitz-Birkenau are a case in point. Shorn from the heads of women as they were processed on admission to the camp, the piles of hair form a striking and poignant memorial to the dead. Yet they are also highly controversial. Orthodox women are forbidden from displaying their hair. For many, to exhibit this hair is a double outrage: desecrating the memory of the murdered.[5] The other exhibits in the Auschwitz museum are, it is true, less troubling to Orthodox Jews. But they would be shocked to learn that they are regarded as anything like a relic, just as they would be appalled to discover that the site itself was regarded as a sacred space. Indeed, attempts by the Roman Catholic Church to establish a convent at Auschwitz were blocked by Jewish groups who argued that not only was this an improper attempt to expropriate a site of Jewish suffering, but also that the camps represented an unredeemable place where religion had died.[6] More than this, the strictly monotheistic and iconoclastic tendencies of Judaism—strongly influenced by the biblical imperative not to create graven images—leads mainstream Jewish theology to be highly suspicious about the notion of any relics, let alone those produced by the murder of six million Jews. In search of the sacred relics of the Holocaust, then, the historian is forced to abandon any notion of the relic as material fact—as an artefact or object—and look instead at the relic as immaterial remains, as text.

Strikingly, such an attitude even informed the behaviour of those who endured Nazi oppression, and who looked to the creation of texts rather than the preservation of material remains as a means of transcending the events of the Holocaust. '[O]ur existence as a people will not be destroyed', declared Chaim Kaplan in his diary of life in the Warsaw ghetto, 'Individuals will be destroyed, but the Jewish community will live on'.[7] Kaplan, an Orthodox Jew, Hebrew educator and Zionist intellectual, intended his diary to be 'a scroll of agony in order to remember the past in the future',[8]

---

[5] For details of the controversy see Timothy W. Ryback, 'Evidence of Evil', *The New Yorker* (11 Jan. 2010).

[6] See Emma Klein, *The Battle for Auschwitz: Catholic-Jewish Relations Under Strain* (London, 2001).

[7] Chaim A. Kaplan, *Scroll of Agony: The Warsaw Diary of Chaim A. Kaplan*, trans. Abraham I. Katsh (Bloomington, Ind., 1999), 30.

[8] Ibid.

and vowed 'I have made a rule for myself in these historic times not to let a single day go by without making an entry in my diary'.[9]

Although he risked his life to document his experiences, Kaplan was very much aware that the importance of his testimony lay not in its ability to deliver supposedly objective facts, but rather in revealing the immediacy of the Jewish suffering and the misery of lived experience:

> I am afraid that the impressions of this terrible era will be lost because they have not been adequately recorded. I risk my life with my writing, but my abilities are limited; I don't know all the facts; those that I do know many not be sufficiently clear; and many of them I write on the basis of rumours whose accuracy I cannot guarantee. But for the sake of truth, I do not require individual facts, but rather the manifestations of a great many facts that leave their impression on the people's opinions, on their mood and morale. And I can guarantee the factualness of these manifestations because I dwell among my people and behold their misery and their soul's torments.[10]

His diary, which fills six notebooks, not only contains descriptions of the suffering and deprivations of Warsaw Jewry, but also numerous Talmudic and scriptural references, emphasizing his continued commitment to the Jewish tradition of bearing witness. He writes:

> I am one of the fortunate ones whose pen does not run dry, even in this hour of madness. Anyone who keeps such a record endangers his life, but this does not frighten me. I sense within me the magnitude of this hour, and my responsibility toward it, and I have an inner awareness that I am fulfilling a national obligation, a historic obligation that I am not free to relinquish . . . I am sure that Providence sent me to fulfil this mission.[11]

More than this, Kaplan's appeal to the traditional Hebrew scriptures can be viewed as an implicit attempt to instil in his diary a sense of the sacred.

At the same time, however, this record was not just a holy relic. Kaplan, who came from a generation of inveterate diarists, had begun his own journal in 1933 and he was writing within a tradition that valued the preservation of the historical record and the collection of historical source material. There were numerous Jews writing in the ghettos of Eastern Europe. As Emmanuel

[9] Ibid., 25.
[10] Ibid.
[11] Kaplan, *Scroll of Agony*, 104.

Ringelblum, a historian, teacher, and social activist, who founded the secret *Oneg Shabbat* (Sabbath Delight—a codename for their covert Sabbath afternoon meetings), explained:

> Everyone wrote, journalists and writers, of course, but also teachers, public men, young people—even children. . . . A tremendous amount was written; but the vast majority of the writings were destroyed with the annihilation of Warsaw Jewry.[12]

Like Kaplan they wrote not only out of a specifically Jewish imperative to bear witness, but because they crucially recognized that what they were experiencing was an event of the utmost historical importance and therefore went to great lengths to gather material for future generations of historians. After the mass deportations of 1942 when 275,000 Jews were put in cattle trucks and sent to their deaths in Treblinka, the task took on even greater urgency. Ringelblum explains:

> The work of O.S. [*Oneg Shabbat*], along with the whole of our social and economic life, was disrupted. Only very few comrades kept pen in hand during those tragic days and continued to write about what was happening in Warsaw. But the work was too sacred and too deeply cherished in the hearts of the O.S. co-workers; the social function of O.S. too important for the project to be discontinued.[13]

Nor was Ringelblum alone. His sense that the work of *Oneg Shabbat* was a sacred duty was shared by others. Abraham Lewin, a staff member of *Oneg Shabbat*, describes their meetings:

> We gather every Sabbath, a group of activists in the Jewish community, to discuss our diaries and writings. We want our sufferings, these 'birth-pangs of the Messiah', to be impressed upon the memories of future generations and the memory of the whole world.[14]

As this suggests, the Jews writing in the ghettos were writing within a self-consciously Jewish tradition of remembrance.

It is worth considering what that Jewish tradition amounts to. Ringelblum, like others, saw the recording of Jewish life as an intrinsic part of Jewish culture. In more religious terms, for writers such as Kaplan, the cataclysm

---

[12] Cited in 'Introduction' in Jacob Sloan (ed.), Emmanuel Ringelblum, *Notes from the Warsaw Ghetto: The Journal of Emmanuel Ringelblum* (New York, 1958), xxi-xxii.

[13] Ringelblum, *Notes from the Warsaw Ghetto*, 389.

[14] Abraham Lewin, *A Cup of Tears: A Diary of the Warsaw Ghetto*, trans. Christopher Hutton, ed. Anthony Polonsky (Oxford, 1988), 120.

of the Holocaust irresistibly evoked comparisons with the destruction of the Second Temple in AD 70. This had brought biblical Judaism to a close: ending the sacred ceremonies held there and rendering the priesthood redundant. Worship moved to the synagogues. New rites were required and the rabbinate assumed a position of highest authority. As part of this effort, the Babylonian scholar Rav Ashi created the Talmud to record the rituals of the Temple service and create a substitute to allow Judaism to continue.

Within this context, it is not hard to see why some Jewish writers have seen Holocaust testimony as analogous to scripture. The Holocaust survivor and prolific author Elie Wiesel has declared that 'we have to write a new Talmud just as we did after the destruction of the Second Temple . . . in order to accentuate the new beginning'.[15] A similar point is made by the writer David Roskies, who argues that 'To understand the last collective response of a people in all its contradictions, one must look to the writers, who, because they shared the same fate and were intimately involved in all facets of the people's Armageddon, were able to transmute the screams into a new and terrible scripture'.[16] Indeed, he maintains that 'Ringelblum is to Oyneg Shabes [*Oneg Shabbat*] as Rav Ashi was to the Babylonian Talmud'.[17]

This is an extraordinary claim: one which raises testimony to the status of a sacred text. Just as Judaism continued after the destruction of the Temple through the creation of the Talmud, Roskies maintains, so it will continue after the destruction of the Jews through the creation of testimony. It is important, of course, to be careful about terms here. In the first place, the Talmud (which is a record of practices and commentary on the Law) is not the same—and does not receive the same veneration—as the Torah (which Judaism conceives of as literally the word of God). In synagogues, it is the scrolls of the Torah, and not the Talmud, that are venerated. But, in the second place, the Torah is never an object of worship in itself. Customarily, Jews talk of 'love of the Torah and the fear of Heaven'. As Louis Jacobs puts it, 'The term "fear", denoting worship, is never applied to the Torah'.[18] Thus Roskies' claim, whilst remarkable, cannot be seen as radically outside Jewish tradition. He does not blasphemously compare testimony to the Torah (which was given once for all on Mount Sinai), but to the Talmud. And he does not suggest that the material reality of testimony—the paper on which it

[15] Elie Wiesel, 'Jewish Values in the Post-Holocaust Future: A Symposium', *Judaism*, 16 (1967), 285.

[16] David G. Roskies, *Against the Apocalypse: Responses to Catastrophe in Modern Jewish Culture* (Cambridge, Mass., 1999), 202.

[17] David G. Roskies, *The Jewish Search for a Useable Past* (Bloomington, Ind., 1999), 25.

[18] Louis Jacobs, *The Jewish Religion: A Companion* (Oxford, 1995), 563.

was written, for example—is sacred in itself. There is no room within Judaism for the worship of objects. Even the Scrolls of the Torah are only ever venerated, never worshipped. Still, it is a questionable claim nonetheless.

To be sure, Ringelblum and his colleagues—regardless of whether they were religious or not—were very much aware that what they were experiencing was yet another chapter in the long history of Jewish suffering. Even though they shared the awareness that what they were experiencing was something unprecedented in history, they could not help but consider it in religious terms. This, coupled with the fact that they were writing in a state of extreme fear and hardship inevitably led them to conceive of their testimonies as 'sacred texts'. The members of *Oneg Shabbat* risked their lives to hold their clandestine meetings and gather their material and this, together with the urgency of their mission, fuelled their sense of a spiritual calling. This can be seen in Kaplan's choice to write in Hebrew, which was essentially a liturgical language at the time. His decision not only conveys his commitment to Zionism and the strength of his belief in a Jewish future, but also his sense of the Jewish past.[19] Almost all of those writing in the ghettos of Eastern Europe became painfully aware that they would not live to see the end of the war. Instead their writing would have to speak for them. Writing on whatever they could lay their hands on—children's copybooks, wine labels, used bits of paper—they did not see the texts in themselves as sacred, but rather their content.

Nonetheless, whilst some survivors such as Elie Wiesel and Emil Fackenheim, and some subsequent writers like David Roskies, want to retain the ineffable quality of any text produced under such horrific and unprecedented circumstances, the result of their project is that they overlook the other facts that mediate its writing—such as the need to provide historical record. Whilst they are right to take seriously the special claims made by the authors of these documents—and thereby not fall into the trap of many historians who simply mine this material for evidence, taking no account of the authors' intentions or the specific category of writing—their approach nonetheless threatens to dilute the significance of the testimony. Ringelblum and his colleagues—like the handful of witnesses writing in the concentration camps—might have conceived of their writing in sacred terms but they did not want it to become sacralized to such an extent that it would be left untouched by future historical research. The second part of this article will attempt to articulate an ethics of reading testimony and responding to the Holocaust that rescues the experiences of the witnesses from the self-contained canon of historical writing they have been placed in. However, the challenge is to do so

---

[19] A similar point is made by Alexandra Garbarini in *Numbered Days: Diaries and the Holocaust* (New Haven, 2006), 33.

in a way that does not normalize or universalize the experiences of both those who survived and those who did not survive the Holocaust.

Simply treating testimony as a literary text—exploring the mechanics of writing and representation—may be insightful, but such an approach often leaves little room to examine the social and historical climate of Holocaust testimony. In other words, testimony is not used to inform but provide illustration or simple evocation. As we shall see, critics such as George Steiner go so far as to argue that testimonies are so sacred all we can do is simply repeat them word for word. By ignoring the factors that mediate the writing of testimony—language, tradition, politics, identity—we might gain a vivid picture of the conditions witnesses were forced to endure but we will gain no greater understanding of the events of the Holocaust. Moreover we will not be treating testimony on its own terms. It was not just written as a religious record—a new Talmud—but also as a historical record. We will not be able to engage fruitfully, and authentically, with Holocaust testimony unless we account for these twin impulses. It is sacred text but also more than sacred text. It is historical record but also more than historical record. No account of Holocaust testimony can be deemed adequate unless it takes account of this.

The diaries and other writings that survived the war were discovered in the ruins of the ghettos, buried near bodily remains in the concentration camps, discarded in empty buildings, or were handed in by those entrusted with their care. Others were destroyed when the authors were deported to the death camps. Almost all of them come from those who did not survive and therefore in many ways they are indeed sacred texts for they come from beyond the grave. At the same time, however, they are invaluable historical documents which if read closely can provide us with a rich insight into the world that was lost and the suffering and destruction which befell the Jews of Europe. *Oneg Shabbat* was not a mystical institution but a carefully conceived research project. Before the war Ringelblum had worked for the ŻIH (*Żydowski Instytut Historyczny* (Jewish Historical Institute)) and was an affiliate of YIVO (Yidisher Vissenshaftlecher (Jewish Scientific Institute)). Ringelblum and his colleagues, drawing on years of historical training, went to great lengths to collect a wealth of information, particularly primary source materials.

As the choice of the Jewish name *Oneg Shabbat* suggests, the very act or process of bearing witness derived from long established Jewish traditions and was seen as an essential part of Jewish identity. The members of *Oneg Shabbat* were not writing as isolated individuals but as conscious members of the Jewish community. They were not seeking individual salvation but were writing to preserve their community. For Kaplan, too, the writing of his diary was a spiritual act that affirmed his Jewish faith. Indeed, for Jews throughout occupied Europe the act of bearing witness was one of *kiddush hashem* (sanctification of the Name of God) and an act of collective Jewish resistance. As the 81-year-old Jewish historian Simon Dubnow was led to his death in the Riga ghetto, he called '*Yidn, farshraibt* (Jews, write it down)'.[20] And in Auschwitz, Załman Gradowski, a prisoner forced to work in the crematoria at Auschwitz-Birkenau, buried his testimony 'to immortalize the dear, beloved names of those, for whom, at this moment, I cannot even expend a tear'.[21] Writing was a moral duty that overrode practical considerations. As we have already noted, Kaplan had explained: 'Anyone who keeps such a record [diary] endangers his life, but this does not frighten me. I sense within me the magnitude of this hour, and my responsibility toward it, and I have an inner awareness that I am fulfilling a national obligation, a historic obligation that I am not free to relinquish.'[22]

Survivors such as Elie Wiesel and the philosopher Emil Fackenheim go even further, arguing that the Holocaust is a sacred event, and that its significance is 'equal to the revelation at Sinai' in its religious importance.[23] This is an astounding claim—after all, it is at Mount Sinai that the Torah is given to Moses as a Covenant between God and the children of Israel. For Fackenheim, remembering the Holocaust thus becomes a quasi-religious act, revealed at Auschwitz through a 'commanding voice' spelt out in what he calls the 614th commandment—that is, the commandment which completes the 613 of scripture. The commandment is that:

> Jews are forbidden to hand Hitler posthumous victories. They are commanded to survive as Jews, lest the Jewish people perish. They are commanded to remember the victims of Auschwitz lest their memory perish. They are forbidden to despair of man and his world, and to escape into either cynicism or otherworldliness, lest they cooperate in delivering the world over to the forces of Auschwitz. Finally, they are forbidden to despair of the God of Israel, lest Judaism perish . . . A Jew many not respond to Hitler's attempt to destroy Judaism by himself cooperating in its

---

[20] As there are many different versions of this story it is impossible to know the precise words spoken by Dubnov.

[21] Cited in David Roskies (ed.), *The Literature of Destruction: Jewish Responses to Catastrophe* (Philadelphia, 1989), 548.

[22] Kaplan, *Scroll of Agony*, 104.

[23] Elie Wiesel, 'Words from a Witness', *Comparative Judaism*, 21 (1967), 43.

destruction. In ancient times, the unthinkable Jewish sin was idolatry. Today, it is to respond to Hitler by doing his work.[24]

This new scripture—which manages to incorporate the religious and the secular—commands Jews both to resist all attempts to eradicate their presence, and also to remember the dead. Fackenheim, a German-Jewish philosopher and Reform rabbi, who spent several months in the concentration camp at Sachenhausen before fleeing to Canada in 1939, identifies the Holocaust with revelation, believing, like Wiesel, that—as from Sinai—God addresses Israel from Auschwitz.[25] However, both Fackenheim and Wiesel believe it is impossible to fathom God's presence at Auschwitz—or absence of God at Auschwitz—because the Holocaust represents a crisis of understanding. To direct us in this abyss, survivors such as Elie Wiesel instruct us to turn to the testimonies of those who actually lived through the events of the Holocaust, because 'no one who has not experienced the event will ever be able to understand it'.[26] If the argument that the Holocaust defies comprehension is accepted, and—as Fackenheim believes—Wiesel is correct in his assertion that what happened at Auschwitz is 'a mystery begotten by the dead',[27] then it is not just the commitment to bear witness that is sacred, but testimonies also take on a sacred status.

For Fackenheim, it is the spiritual dimension of testimony that overrides everything. He argues that the commitment to bear witness is inextricably linked to the will to survive. Testimony therefore is born out of resistance—the attempt to thwart the Nazi oppressors. He writes that the '*recognition* of the Nazi logic of destruction helped *produce resistance to* a life-and-death struggle that went on day and night'.[28] Fackenheim goes on to claim that for the Jewish victims, it was their belief in God expressed through a commitment to Jewish continuity that commanded them to resist by bearing witness. In the Torah the command to bear witness is explicitly stated: 'And he is a witness whether he has seen or known of it; if he does not

---

[24] Emil Fackenheim, *God's Presence in History* (New York, 1970), 84.

[25] Ibid., 31.

[26] Elie Wiesel, 'Trivialising Memory', and 'Testimony at the Barbie Trial', in Elie Wiesel, *From the Kingdom of Memory: Reminiscences*, trans. Marion Wiesel (New York, 1999), 166, 187.

[27] Elie Wiesel, *One Generation After*, trans. Lily Edelman and Elie Wiesel (New York, 1970), 43.

[28] Emil Fackenheim, *To Mend the World: Foundations of Post-Holocaust Jewish Thought* (New York, 1989), 248.

utter it, then he shall bear his iniquity' (Lev. 5:1).[29] In the Jewish tradition bearing witness has a legal as well as religious obligation in that it seeks to establish truth and achieve justice. Not to bear witness is almost an act of betrayal.[30] The act of witnessing is part of the tradition by which one reaffirms oneself as a Jew: the Ten Commandments are referred to as 'the two tables of the testimony',[31] and the observance of the Sabbath bears witness to the fact that it was God, rather than man, who created the world in six days. The command for later generations to bear witness is also firmly rooted in Jewish history; for example, the Passover *Haggadah*[32] directs each Jew to view himself or herself as personally present at the Exodus from Egypt. Wiesel believes that the Holocaust 'was essentially a war against memory'[33] and in his Nobel Prize lecture of 1986, he went so far as to declare that 'if anything can, it is memory that will save humanity'.[34]

Fackenheim and Wiesel are right to stress the fact that the commitment to bear witness can be seen in many ways as being synonymous with survival. Countless testimonies support this. In the Warsaw ghetto Kaplan wrote that 'though it is now five days since any real food has passed my lips', 'My mind is still clear, my need to record unstilled'.[35] Even in the concentration and death camps the will to testify persisted. In Majdanek, Alexander Donat was instructed by the well known Jewish historian Ignacy (Yitshak) Schiper before he was killed that:

> History is usually written by the victor. What we know about murdered people is only what their murderers vaingloriously cared to say about them. Should our murderers be victorious, should *they*

[29] Cited in James Young, *Writing and Rewriting the Holocaust: Narrative and the Consequences of Interpretation* (Bloomington, Ind., 1988), 18. Young also points out that 'testimony' derives from the Latin for 'witness' (*testis*), which refers both to seeing something and also coming to know something (ibid., 19).

[30] See Emil Fackenheim, *Quest for the Past and Future: Essays in Jewish Theology* (Boston, 1970), 18.

[31] It is written: 'When He made an end of speaking with Moses upon Mount Sinai, He gave unto him the two tables of testimony, tables of stone, written with the finger of God.' (Exod. 31: 18, RSV).

[32] *Haggadah* means literally 'telling' and refers to the narration of Israel's Exodus from Egypt through blessings, psalms, songs, and midrashic commentary recited during the Passover Seder.

[33] Elie Wiesel, *Evil and Exile*, trans. Jon Rothschild (Notre Dame, 1990), 155.

[34] http://nobelprize.org/nobel_prizes/peace/laureates/1986/wiesel-lecture.html [accessed 12 Jan. 2010].

[35] Kaplan, *Scroll of Agony*, 383–4.

write the history of this war, our destruction will be presented as one of the most beautiful pages of world history, and future generations will pay tribute to them as dauntless crusaders. Their every word will be taken for gospel. Or they may wipe out our memory altogether, as if we had never existed, as if there had never been a Polish Jewry, a Ghetto in Warsaw, a Maidanek.[36]

While most prisoners lacked the physical and mental resources to write while in the camps, many survivors state that the urge to live to write their history never left them. For example, Samuel Drix writes of bearing witness as a 'sacred duty I owe to the martyrs of Janowska camp and Ghetto Lwów so that they should not be forgotten.[37] Like Kaplan in the Warsaw ghetto, Drix speaks of testimony as a categorical imperative. Moreover, the urge to testify is so strong that it almost becomes one with survival. David Wdowinski writes: 'In spite of hunger, illness and privation, there was a compulsion to record this period in all its details.'[38]

But whilst these testimonies reveal the spiritual importance of bearing witness, they also suggest that the will to bear witness performed a very important practical function. In the concentration camps prisoners constantly had to struggle against losing their mental capacities. The effects of starvation on the brain caused many to lose their memory—a precursor to death. Therefore the act of remembering was essential to survival. Ruth Elias, for example, writes that in Auschwitz, she and her friends 'knew intuitively that if we gave up spiritually and intellectually, we would be giving up all hope of survival'.[39] Testimony therefore cannot be seen in one-dimensional terms. It was neither purely spiritual nor purely practical. It was both.

Fackenheim and Wiesel each view the Holocaust as a unique event producing an unbridgeable gap between the world of the camps and the world of the interpreter. Indeed, Wiesel believes that the only way to preserve the essential inexplicability of the Holocaust is through silence, arguing that 'by its uniqueness the holocaust defies literature';[40] and 'Auschwitz cannot be explained, ... the Holocaust transcends history'.[41] Wiesel and Fackenheim share a

[36] Alexander Donat, *The Holocaust Kingdom: A Memoir* (London, 1967), 206.

[37] Samuel Drix, *Witness to Annihilation: Surviving the Holocaust* (London, 1964), xv.

[38] David Wolowinski, *And We Are Not Saved* (London, 1964), 83.

[39] Ruth Elias, *Triumph of Hope: From Theresienstadt and Auschwitz to Israel*, trans. Margot Bettauer Dembo (New York, 1988), 123.

[40] Cited in Alan L. Berger, 'Elie Wiesel', in Steven T. Katz (ed.), *Interpreters of Judaism in the Late Twentieth Century* (Washington, 1993), 377.

[41] Elie Wiesel, 'Trivialising the Holocaust: Semi-Fact and Semi-Fiction', *The New York Times*, 2/1 (16 April 1978), 29.

similar belief that testimony is sacred and more than sacred, that it uniquely expresses the inexpressible. They are also all aware of the double bind of the survivor. Although as survivors they are obliged to bear witness—to honour the dead—and they fought to survive to meet this aim, they are also aware that ultimately they are unable to represent the enormity of the Nazi crime. Therefore, while Wiesel as a witness believes that silence is the only true response to the Holocaust, he nevertheless cannot abandon what he has described as 'the obsession to tell tale'. Wiesel's memoir, *Night*, tells us that it was his strength of will that allowed him to survive and to testify. Nonetheless, he asks: 'how is one to say, how is one to communicate that which by its very nature defies language?'[42] Wiesel believes it is impossible to represent the Holocaust, because to do so is sacrilegious. Yet for Wiesel, it is testimony that is the only way of reaching this unreachable event because it is given by survivors, who, as the living dead, possess an ontological authority. They, he argues, have passed through the abyss and therefore are uniquely equipped to speak both for themselves and for those who perished. This ontological change almost turns survivors into a new priesthood replacing the priesthood lost at the destruction of the Second Temple in AD 70. This new priesthood is the source of a new set of religious texts. As Wiesel further argues: 'what happened at Auschwitz, should be conveyed in the same manner that the Talmud was taught, "transmitted from mouth to ear, from eye to eye".'[43]

The idea of testimony as a message from beyond the abyss is widely held—as is the notion that texts written by survivors possess an authority that transcends criticism. This position is also adopted by the literary critic George Steiner:

> These books and the documents that have survived are not for 'review'. Not unless 'review' signifies, as perhaps it should in these instances, a 'seeing-again', over and over. As in some Borges fable, the only complete decent 'review' of the Warsaw Diary or of Elie Wiesel's *Night* would be to re-copy the book, line by line, pausing at the names of the dead and the names of the children as the orthodox scribe pauses, when recopying the Bible, at the hallowed name of god. Until we know many of the words by *heart* (knowledge deeper than mind) and could repeat a few at the break of morning to remind ourselves that we live after, that the end of the

---

[42] Elie Wiesel, *A Jew Today*, 235.
[43] Elie Wiesel, *One Generation After*, 235.

day may bring 'inhuman trial or a remembrance stronger than death'.[44]

Strikingly, for Steiner, reading the sacred text of testimony thus implies not only a reverential attitude but also a reverential posture. Testimony has become the basis for a new liturgy.

David Roskies views the Jewish Warsaw ghetto chroniclers as 'comparable to that other great collective document of the Diaspora—the Talmud',[45] and states that the 'Warsaw ghetto chroniclers often moved beyond scientific objectivity' and 'were thrown back to the age-old models of commemoration—to the liturgy'.[46] For Roskies, the archives of *Oneg Shabbat*, the *Łódź Chronicle*, or the writings of the *Sonderkommando* at Auschwitz 'are finite and therefore (like the Talmud) constitute a closed canon'.[47] He argues that they are vastly different to the memoirs produced after 1945: '[a]s opposed to the writing *on* the Holocaust . . . Because of their insistence on the knowability of the destruction . . . they require a separate hermeneutics.'[48] Therefore, rather than viewing such material as mere narrative reports, sources of information, or eyewitness testimonies, they become *sheymes*— sacred relics bearing the *shem* or Name of God[49]—which instructed by the Talmud, Jews must remember and observe (Rosh Hashanah 27a).[50] David Patterson, also working in the field of Jewish studies, similarly seeks to interpret the literature of the Holocaust in spiritual or religious terms—he cites for example, the words of sixteen-year-old Moshe Flinker who wrote whilst in hiding with his family in Brussels, that: 'My diary has become a reflection of my spiritual life.'[51] He regards the transformation of these 'sacred' testimonies into historical documents as a process of regarding 'eyewitness accounts and sources of information, as data, and not as the outcries of Jewish souls that might implicate us in any way'.[52]

[44] George Steiner, *Language and Silence: Essays 1958–1966* (London, 1967), 193.

[45] Roskies, *The Jewish Search for a Useable Past*, 25.

[46] Ibid., 23.

[47] Ibid., 25.

[48] Roskies (ed.), *The Literature of Destruction*, 25.

[49] See David G. Roskies, 'The Library of Jewish Catastrophe', in Geoffrey H. Hartman (ed.), *Holocaust Remembrance: The Shapes of Memory* (Oxford, 1994), 32.

[50] On this subject see Isabel Wollaston, ' "Memory and Monument": Holocaust Testimony as Sacred Text', in Jon Davies and Isabel Wollaston (eds), *The Sociology of Sacred Texts* (Sheffield, 1993), 37–44.

[51] Cited in David Patterson, *Along the Edge of Annihilation: The Collapse and Recovery of Life in the Holocaust Diary* (Seattle, 1999), 43.

[52] Ibid., 7.

And yet, whilst these writers are no doubt sincere in their belief—and do undoubtedly speak for those many other writers of testimony who would argue that they alone can speak the truth about the Holocaust—this assumption that testimony is a new Talmud, requiring nothing more than repetition, inspiring nothing more than awe, is highly problematic. As we have already seen, those who wrote their accounts of life in the ghettos and the camps were motivated by a multiplicity of reasons. Some wrote to provide an accurate record; some wrote to survive; some wrote as a memorial to their families; others wrote as the last testament to the Jewish people. Still others wrote for reasons we will never know. Fackenheim's and Wiesel's contention that writing testimony was synonymous with survival is surely also accurate—but even in that case, the ways and means of survival were multiple. Any account of Holocaust testimony that does not recognize this fact risks distorting the very subject it seeks to describe, hermetically sealing Holocaust testimony into a very specific literary genre; its dynamics left largely untouched by historians.

Indeed, whilst theologians and other writers on the Holocaust—not to mention many of those who wrote testimony—make claims about the sacred quality of their texts, historians have been far less willing to take on these issues. In fact, they have traditionally been reluctant to engage with the testimonies of the victims at all. Even Martin Gilbert's innovative work *The Holocaust: the Jewish Tragedy*,[53] while structured by testimony, offers very little analysis of the sources on which it relies. And there is an even greater wariness when using the post-war testimony of survivors. Raul Hilberg, one of the foremost historians of the Holocaust (who fled from Vienna in 1939) has written: 'I have read countless accounts of survivors. I looked for the missing links in my jigsaw puzzle. I tried to glimpse the Jewish community. I searched for the dead. Most often, however, I had to remind myself that what I most wanted from them they could not give me, no matter how much they said.'[54]

Of course, there are some writers who are specifically concerned with the inner workings of testimony. But their conclusions are arguably unhelpful to the historian—or the student of sacred texts. For example, the work of the Italian philosopher, Giorgio Agamben, focuses on the limits of representation (to use Saul Friedländer's phrase)[55] and not the Holocaust per se. Agamben's

---

[53] Martin Gilbert, *The Holocaust: The Jewish Tragedy* (London, 1987).

[54] Raul Hilberg, *The Politics of Memory: The Journey of a Holocaust Historian* (Chicago, 1996), 133.

[55] See Saul Friedländer (ed.), *Probing the Limits of Representation: Nazism and the Final Solution* (Cambridge, Mass., 1992).

work looks at 'the difficulty we face whenever we try to communicate our most intimate experiences to others';[56] he argues that it is ultimately impossible to represent the Holocaust because: 'Testimony . . . contains a lacuna.'[57] By conflating testimony produced during the Holocaust with that written after the event—without exploring the relationship between the two—Agamben treats testimony ahistorically and fails to look at the socio-political economy of testimony: the factors that mediate its writing.

As this suggests, in many respects, arguments about testimony are reducible to a sort of dialogue of the deaf—with each side trapped within its own epistemology. For example, in the attack launched by David Patterson on James Young's account of testimony, the terms of the argument seem to obviate any sort of conclusion. Patterson is determined to defend the unique importance of testimony and refuses to accept any suggestion that the writers may have written without the benefit of all the facts. He accuses Young of 'assum[ing] a phenomenological stance that renders suspect the diary itself'.[58] This is because he is seemingly unable to concede the point made by Young that:

> [T]the reasons for which diarists wrote and the focus of their witness inescapably regulate, and at times restrict, the diarist's record . . . [and] In addition to time and place the diarists' very language, tradition and world view played crucial roles in the making of their literary witness.[59]

Thus we find ourselves in an impasse. Is testimony a new Talmud and the reading of testimony a new liturgy? Or is testimony merely a source of illustration or anecdote—compelling evidence, even heartbreaking witness—but ultimately no substitute for serious historical data? Or, is testimony, as Agamben seems to suggest, a highly specific genre of literature and one so complicated and problematic that it defies serious analysis?

In refusing to acknowledge anything that might detract from the privileged status of testimony Patterson, for one, situates what he terms 'the closed cannon of wartime writings'[60] outside of historical inquiry. He contextualizes testimony as a specifically Jewish phenomenon to be understood as part of the

---

[56] Giorgio Agamben, *Remnants of Auschwitz: The Witness and the Archive*, trans. Daniel Heller-Roazen (New York, 1999), 12.

[57] Ibid., 33.

[58] Patterson, *Along the Edge of Annihilation*, 7.

[59] Young, *Writing and Rewriting the Holocaust*, 25–6.

[60] Roskies (ed.), *The Literature of Destruction*, 26.

continuum of Jewish responses to persecution—as part of the 'library of Jewish Catastrophe'[61]—and as such places it beyond criticism. This overlooks the fact that witnesses did not intend their writings to be a 'closed canon'; in addition to wanting to leave a record of their own, and in particular, their families' existence, they also wanted to provide a basis for future historical research. Witnesses writing in the ghettos and concentration camps wanted future generations to do more than just remember them—they wanted to provide historical documentation of Jewish life during German occupation. For example, Ringelblum stressed the urge 'to capture every event in Jewish life in the heat of the moment, when it was still fresh and pulsating',[62] and went to great lengths to collect material for future historians. Furthermore, Ringelblum and other members of *Oneg Shabbat*, as a result of the constraints they were under, realized their diaries were fallible documents that would need to be interpreted and validated in the future. Still more importantly, and contra to the position of Steiner cited above they did not want people to become consumed by the poetics of suffering but instead wanted to provide as 'photographically true'[63] a picture as possible. As Ringelblum explained: 'Every superfluous word, every literary turn of language or embellishment grates on the ear and evokes resentment.'[64]

Remarkably, this was even true for those incarcerated in the concentration camps; even they were self-consciously writing texts which were more than purely personal, more than simply sacred, and which were intended to convey truths to future historians. Writing—in Wiesel's terms—within the abyss, they attempted to transmit a message to those that would follow them, a message which required interpretation and not just repetition. In Auschwitz-Birkenau, three men—Załman Gradowski, Załmen Lewental, and Leib Langfus, all ultra-Orthodox Jews—knew with complete certainty that they would never live to see liberation. Unlucky enough to become members of the *Sonderkommando* (special work/detachment) prisoners forced to work in the crematoria of Auschwitz-Birkenau, they knew that they had witnessed too much to be allowed to survive.[65] They united to document their experiences and between 1945 and 1962 fragments of notes and six diaries written by the

---

[61] Roskies (ed.), *The Literature of Destruction*, ch. 2.

[62] Ringelblum, 'O.S.', 10.

[63] Ibid., 8.

[64] Ibid., 7.

[65] However, some prisoners did survive to bear witness. These include Filip Müller, who together with Dov Paisikovic and Milto Buki, testified at the Auschwitz trial in Frankfurt in 1964. See his testimony, *Sonderbehandlung: Drei Jahre in den Krematorien und Gaskammern von Auschwitz* (Munich, 1979). For interviews with other survivors of

three men were found buried in aluminium cans, in jam jars, and in army mess tins in the pits of human ashes at the crematoria at Birkenau.[66] Gradowski urges the finder of his writings to continue digging the area to search for other manuscripts that might be buried there—we know of approximately thirty documents which have never been found:

> Dear finder, search everywhere, in every inch of soil. Tons of documents are buried under it, mine and those of other prisoners which will throw light on everything that was happening here. It was we, the Kommando workers, who expressly have strewn them all over the terrain, as many as we could, so that the world would find material traces of the millions of murdered people. We ourselves have lost hope of being able to live to see the moment of liberation.[67]

The writings in Yiddish and Polish, which have become known as the 'Auschwitz scrolls' (*Megilas Oyshvits* in Yiddish), were explicitly written to let the world know of their experiences.

Gradowski, who began writing notes soon after his deportation to Auschwitz in February 1943, was very much aware of his significance as a unique witness to the mass murder of European Jewry taking place in the gas chambers of Auschwitz-Birkenau. On the first page of his notebook, he wrote in Russian, Polish, German, and French: 'Show an interest in this document. It contains rich material for the historian.'[68] He goes on to describe how he was forced to lead the victims to the gas chambers; after the gassing, drag out the corpses; wash away the cyanotic acid; search the orifices of the bodies for hidden objects; extract gold teeth; cut the women's hair; place the bodies in the crematoria; oversee their incineration; and then remove the ash from the ovens.[69] But although the experience was unique—and uniquely

---

the *Sonderkommando*, see Gideon Grief, *Wir weinten tränenlos . . . Augenzeugenberichte der jüdischen 'Sonderkommandos' in Auschwitz* (Cologne, 1995).

[66] For a history of the manuscripts and their discovery, see Ber Mark, *The Scrolls of Auschwitz*, trans. Sharon Neemani (Tel Aviv, 1985). The last manuscript was discovered concealed in a thermos flask in 1980 when local schoolchildren were planting trees near the Birkenau crematorium.

[67] Załman Gradowksi, 'Manuscript of Sonderkommando Member', trans. Krystyna Michalik in Jadwiga Bezwinska and Danuta Czech (eds), *Amidst a Nightmare of a Crime: Manuscripts of Sonderkommando* (Kraków, 1973), 76.

[68] Cited in Nathan Cohen, 'Diaries of the Sonderkommando in Auschwitz: Coping with Fate and Reality', *Yad Vashem Studies*, 20 (1990), 524.

[69] Giorgio Agamben, *Remnants of Auschwitz: The Witness and the Archive*, trans. Daniel Heller-Roazen (New York, 1999), 25.

appalling—Gradowski's response shared similarities with the other Jews writing in response to the Holocaust. Like the members of *Oneg Shabbat*, the *Sonderkommando* prisoners—the ultimate witnesses to the destruction of the Jews—took pains to bury their writings to ensure they would not be forgotten by historians of the future. In the face of certain death they saw the writing and burying of their testimony as an important act of resistance— as well as proof of their existence. They clearly did not intend their writing to be sacralized but rather to inform the free world of the tragedy that had befallen the Jews.

Hence whilst Wiesel and Fackenheim have both stressed the essential incomprehensibility of the Holocaust, men such as Gradowski—who were as close to the destruction as it was possible to be—insisted that not only could what happened be told, it would be told. In burying his writing Gradowski was certainly aware that he was in many ways performing a sacred rite, but perhaps even more importantly, he was also conscious that such an act performed a very important practical function. As the theologian Isabel Wollaston observes, the writing of testimony can be understood as a symbolic 'tombstone' to the millions of Jews who were destined not to survive.[70] This is particularly important as the vast majority of the murdered Jews have no final resting place. For Wiesel, too, writing is 'a *matzeva* [Yiddish for memorial headstone], an invisible tombstone erected to the dead unburied'.[71] 'They did not even have a cemetery,' Wiesel explains: 'We are their cemeteries.'[72] However, the writings of the *Sonderkommmnado* do more than report on the destruction of the communities and memorialize the dead—they also ask to be remembered by future generations.

Thus, if we are to take seriously the writings of those who did not survive we must acknowledge that witnesses writing in the ghettos and concentration camps were rejecting the incomprehensible and risking their lives so that future generations might understand what had befallen them. The final line of Chaim Kaplan's diary written on 4 August 1942, before he was almost certainly transported to the gas chambers of Treblinka, asks: 'If my life ends— what will become of my diary?'[73] He entrusted his diary to a friend who smuggled it out of the ghetto. After the great wave of deportations from the ghetto in the summer of 1942 Ringelblum and the leaders of *Oneg*

---

[70] See Wollaston, ' "Memory and Monument": Holocaust Testimony as Sacred Text', 41. Cf. Elie Wiesel, *Legends of Our Time*, trans. S. Donadio (New York, 1982), 8–10.

[71] Wiesel, *Legends of Our Time*, 25.

[72] Irving Abrahamson (ed.), *Against Silence: The Voice and Vision of Elie Wiesel*, 1 (New York, 1985), 168.

[73] Kaplan, *Scroll of Agony*, 400.

Shabbat made plans to protect the archives. They sealed the materials in milk churns and ten metal boxes and buried them.

Nahum Grzywacz was 18 years old when he buried his own last testament along with the archives. He wrote:

> Of one thing I am proud: that in these grave and fateful days, I was one of those who buried the treasure . . . in order that you should know the tortures and murder of Nazi tyranny . . . We must hurry, because we are not sure of the next hour . . . I want the coming generations to remember our times . . . With what ardour we dug the holes for the boxes . . . with what joy we received every bit of material . . . How I would like to live to the moment when the treasure is dug out and the whole truth proclaimed . . . But we certainly will not live to see it.[74]

As he finished writing, he heard that the Germans had surrounded the building where his parents lived. He hurriedly wrote, 'I am going to run to my parents and see if they are all right. I don't know what's going to happen to me. *Remember, my name is Nahum Grzywacz*'.[75] The first part of the archives was discovered in September 1946, under the ruins of a house in the former Jewish quarter of Warsaw; the second part of the collection (including two of the milk churns)[76] was found there in December 1950. Without the guidance of Hersh Wasser—one of the only three survivors of *Oneg Shabbat*—it is unlikely that it would ever have been discovered. Unfortunately, the third part remains lost. Like the writings of the *Sonderkommando* buried in pits of human ashes, their writings have a tangible link to the places and events they describe.

The importance of these writings is undeniable. Without them we would have little sense of the internal history of Jewish life during the Holocaust. By risking their lives to document their experiences Jews writing in the ghettos and concentration camps consciously thwarted the Nazi aim to leave no trace of their existence. Ringelblum was very conscious of the fact that the Nazis intended to leave no trace of Jewish life in Poland. They were not content to

---

[74] Cited in Nora Levin, *The Holocaust: The Destruction of European Jewry 1933–1945* (New York, 1973), 324–5.

[75] Cited in Samuel D. Kassow, *Who Will Write Our History? Emanuel Ringelblum, the Warsaw Ghetto, and the Oyneg Shabes Archive* (Bloomington, Ind., 2007), 4.

[76] One of the two milk churns is on display at the Jewish Historical Institute in Warsaw; the other is now on permanent loan to the United States Holocaust Memorial Museum—preserved with the mud surrounding it.

leave no Jewish men, women, or children, but also set out to destroy synagogues, cemeteries, and libraries and burned letters, books, photographs, and
religious objects. Ringelblum wrote:

> History knows of no other example where the enemy has been so
> determined to wipe out every trace of the vanquished. After the
> Romans destroyed Jerusalem, they left the 'Wailing Wall.' After
> the barbarians invaded Rome, they left everywhere the [material
> traces] of Roman culture. The Moslem invaders, after they captured
> Christian Spain, turned churches into mosques. But what the
> Germans have done to Jewish cultural [antiquities] has no prece-
> dent in history.[77]

However, despite their best efforts, we are left with very little knowledge of
most of the dead. Wiped out with their entire families only few biographical
details remain—we do not know for example when it was that Kaplan and his
wife met their deaths in Treblinka. Hence we seize on what remains as material proof of the existence of the dead. Perhaps to salvage something from the
destruction of European Jewry we want to believe that whilst the victims may
not have been able to stop the process of extermination they were able to rebel
against the attempt to obliterate their humanity. What we are less willing to
accept is that this too was ultimately doomed. An overly reverential approach
to testimony not only overlooks the fact that Ringelblum and his colleagues
did not want their writings to be treated as untouchable sacred relics but as the
basis for profound historical research, but also skates over the fact that the
vast majority of victims of the Holocaust perished without ever writing down
their experiences.

Despite the enormity of the task, we need to commit ourselves to compre-
hensibility and not allow the elevated position of the witness to imbue testimony with a sacred status that prevents us from exploring it further. Buried
in milk churns or amongst the ashes of the dead, the sacred texts of the
Holocaust have an ambivalent existence; on the one hand they are sources
of important historical data and on the other they are outpourings of the
dead. Just as those writing about the Holocaust are engaged in a dual project—at once bearing witness to atrocity and seeking to understand it—so we,
as historians, are engaged in twofold endeavour. On the one hand we cannot
reject the empirical study of the Holocaust—the never-ending search to
uncover exactly what happened and why. This requires us to engage critically

---

[77] Cited in Kassow, *Who Will Write Our History?*, 367.

with the sources which will enable us to answer these questions. On the other hand we need to take seriously the cultural, even spiritual impulses, which led Jews like Ringelblum and Kaplan to record their suffering and to seek to transmit their testimonies to future readers. These were, from the first, sacred texts, but also from the first, they were more than sacred texts. Paradoxically perhaps, it is only by recognizing that these testimonies are a part of a particular genre, written within a particular tradition, and driven by a particular impulse that we can make sense of them both as historians and as humans.

List of Contributors

Daniel Branch is Assistant Professor of African History, University of Warwick.

Adam Chau is Lecturer in the Anthropology of Modern China, University of Cambridge, and a Fellow of Fitzwilliam College.

Paul J. Gillingham was Assistant Professor of History at the University of North Carolina, Wilmington. He is now at the University of Pennsylvania.

Alan Knight is Professor of the History of Latin America, University of Oxford.

Howard Louthan is Professor of History at the University of Florida.

James Mark is Senior Lecturer in History at the University of Exeter.

Josef Meri is Ariane de Rothschild Academic Director in Muslim–Jewish Relations at the University of Cambridge, and a Fellow of St Edmund's College.

Robert Morkot is Lecturer in Archaeology at the University of Exeter.

Robin Osborne is Professor of Ancient History at the University of Cambridge and Senior Tutor, King's College.

Ulinka Rublack is Senior Lecturer in Early Modern European History at the University of Cambridge and Fellow of St John's College.

Julia Smith is Edwards Professor of Medieval History at the University of Glasgow.

John S. Strong is Charles A. Dana Professor of Religious Studies at Bates College, Lewiston, Maine.

Alexandra Walsham is currently Professor of Reformation History at the University of Exeter. From 1 September 2010 she will be Professor of Modern History at the University of Cambridge and a Fellow of Trinity College.

Zoë Waxman is Fellow in Holocaust Studies, Royal Holloway, University of London.

Relics and Remains index